Advance Praise

"This book skillfully combines scientific depth, clinical tools, and warm-hearted support. It will be extremely useful for any clinician; others in the helping professions, such as coaches and human resources trainers, will also find much to value in its pages. Highly recommended."

—**Rick Hanson, PhD,** author of *Buddha's Brain,*
Hardwiring Happiness, and *Resilient*

"Karen Pando-Mars and Diana Fosha's *Tailoring Treatment to Attachment Patterns* offers a profound synthesis of attachment theory, brain science, and clinical practice. With a focus on AEDP (Accelerated Experiential Dynamic Psychotherapy), founded by coauthor Diana Fosha, this volume provides clinicians with specific tools to heal attachment wounds and transform insecure attachment patterns. Through an experiential, emotion-focused therapeutic approach, the authors illuminate how to create safety, foster secure attachment, and help clients process previously overwhelming relational experiences. This book is an essential guide for therapists dedicated to transforming relational trauma and fostering healing, love, and resilience in their clients' lives."

—**Stephen W. Porges, PhD,** creator of Polyvagal Theory

"I believe that a solid knowledge of attachment theory is crucial for therapists, and AEDP as presented in this book does a great job of explaining and applying it to therapy. Despite my differences with Diana in language ("parts" versus "defenses," etc) and in who becomes the primary attachment figure for the client (Self in IFS, therapist in AEDP), her process for deep healing is real and laid out clearly. Therapists of every stripe will also benefit from AEDP's emphasis on key qualities of therapists' presence and understanding of client attachment styles."

—**Richard C. Schwartz, PhD,** founder of Internal Family Systems

"This book is a delight! In mapping the fields of attachment and dynamic psychotherapies onto one another, it significantly advances Bowlby and Ainsworth's ultimate goal of a coherent framework for understanding and intervening in the complex patterns of emotion- and interaction-regulation that have their origins in early bonds. Whether ultimately resilient or precarious, these patterns are our durable life strategies. What delights me most is the kind and respectful framework Pando-Mars and Fosha maintain throughout."

—**Bob Marvin, PhD,** professor emeritus, University of Virginia School of Medicine, and founder and executive director, The Circle of Security Network

"*Tailoring Treatment to Attachment Patterns* is a beautifully crafted guide to creating attuned, attached, and safe nervous system experiences that lead to new patterns of connection. Drawing on their years of clinical practice and deep understanding of the science of attachment, Karen Pando-Mars and Diana Fosha highlight the importance of the parts both therapist and client play in the process of co-creating shared nervous system experiences and co-regulating moments. *Tailoring Treatment to Attachment Patterns* outlines the steps to building secure attachment and gives therapists a map to guide the process of accompanying clients on that transformational journey."

—**Deb Dana, LCSW,** author of *The Polyvagal Theory in Therapy: Engaging the Rhythm of Regulation* and *Polyvagal Practices: Anchoring the Self in Safety*

Tailoring Treatment to Attachment Patterns

Tailoring Treatment to Attachment Patterns

HEALING TRAUMA IN RELATIONSHIP

Karen Pando-Mars | Diana Fosha

Norton Professional Books

An Imprint of W. W. Norton & Company
Independent Publishers Since 1923

Note to Readers: This book is intended as a general information resource for professionals practicing in the field of psychotherapy and mental health. It is not a substitute for appropriate training or clinical supervision. Standards of clinical practice and protocol vary in different practice settings and change over time. No technique or recommendation is guaranteed to be safe or effective in all circumstances, and neither the publisher nor the author(s) can guarantee the complete accuracy, efficacy, or appropriateness of any particular recommendation in every respect or in all settings or circumstances.

Any URLs displayed in this book link or refer to websites that existed as of press time. The publisher is not responsible for, and should not be deemed to endorse or recommend, any website other than its own or any content that it did not create. The author(s), also, are not responsible for any third-party material.

For information about permission to reproduce selections from this book, write to Permissions, W. W. Norton & Company, Inc., 500 Fifth Avenue, New York, NY 10110

For information about special discounts for bulk purchases, please contact W. W. Norton Special Sales at specialsales@wwnorton.com or 800-233-4830

Manufacturing by Lake Book Manufacturing, Inc.
Production manager: Ramona Wilkes

ISBN: 978-0-393-71355-8

W. W. Norton & Company, Inc., 500 Fifth Avenue, New York, NY 10110
www.wwnorton.com
W. W. Norton & Company Ltd., 15 Carlisle Street, London W1D 3BS

1 2 3 4 5 6 7 8 9 0

To my husband, David and our daughter, Eva,
with deep love and gratitude for our affectional bonds
which nourish, anchor, and inspire me. —Karen Pando-Mars

To Scarlett Maya Pacheco Lubin-Fosha, to Connie Rhodes,
and to the 2023–2024 members of the AEDP
Vision Collective & Core Training Group:
You are the future! —Diana Fosha

Contents

Acknowledgments

Karen Pando-Mars

Writing this book about tailoring treatment to attachment patterns and healing trauma in relationships has been transformational. I learned a lot about asking for help and deepened my capacity to receive support, witnessing, and guidance. I have felt humbled while studying the body of attachment research and saturating in the insightful, gifted, courageous endeavors and accomplishments of John Bowlby and Mary Ainsworth. The continuity of contributions from their students and followers and those that contributed to the field through infant research and brain research provides an immense platform for psychotherapists. Many of these articles, chapters, and books about attachment and neuroscience call for more applications to the clinical practice of psychotherapy. It is my deepest hope, which I share with Diana Fosha, my coauthor extraordinaire, that this book bridges the outstanding wealth of attachment theory and research and brain science to complex, yet practical and specific clinical applications to help our patients heal attachment wounding and attachment trauma.

I could not write this book alone. From the first moments of meeting AEDP and its founder and developer Diana Fosha, I have experienced AEDP as my theoretical home, safe base, and secure haven. Diana has been figural, first as teacher, supervisor, and mentor, then colleague, friend, and cowriter. Thank you for seeing me and believing in me, for helping me to stretch and become. . . . It has been 20 years since we met, and of the many projects and endeavors we have worked on together, writing has been the place of my deepest learning and has provided me with the richest opportunities to grow.

Probably the best gift you could've given me was to feel safe while writing and sharing my writing to receiving your comments, edits, or suggestions. I experienced your rigor, yet spaciousness and honesty, about what needed clarifying, organizing, or elaborating. Our conversations and collaboration about this book have been an exciting and meaningful experience that is grounded with trust and confidence that our deep engagement serves a larger purpose to bring this book forward. Thank you, Diana, for how much this project was an experience of being *in it together.*

Early in my training, John Welwood was a most significant teacher and supervisor. He had studied with Eugene Gendlin (*Focusing*), and was known for integrating psychology and spirituality. With John I learned how to *be with* my patients with an experiential focus and to help them explore each unfolding step in their process. These intentions have been augmented and elaborated with AEDP, yet John's influence is with me to this day.

Janet Adler, teacher of the discipline of Authentic Movement has also been a significant influence in who I am as a therapist. Thank you for your presence and practice which helped to cultivate my capacity to see and be seen. To my Authentic Movement collective for profound experiences moving and witnessing each other over three decades and seasons of our lives: Rusa Chiu, Carol Fields, Cheri Forester, Harriet Glass, Lori Goldrich, Julia Gombos, Wendy Goulstein, Barbara Holifield, Kathee Milller, Shira Musicant, Noelle Poncelet, and Roz Parenti. Immense gratitude for your embodied voices, wisdom, and hearts.

Deborah Malmud followed the book's development from our proposal to the completed manuscript. Thank you for seeing and supporting this book to be the book it was meant to be. I appreciated your comments and feedback on early and mid-drafts of chapters; a light touch with important suggestions that helped to shape the book—while also allowing it emerge. I especially appreciated your patience when I asked for extensions to our due dates. Writing, while learning how to write such a book, was daunting at times. Somehow while holding the commitment to each due date, you accepted my process. And in the end, you said it was worth the wait. Thank you.

Bethany Saltman became my trusted writing coach and mentor. Thank you, Bethany, not only for helping me learn the craft of telling a story, but your particular dedication to the work of Mary Ainsworth through your book, *The Strange Situation*, made for deep companionship. You embodied the spirit of Mary Ainsworth in how you showed me delight throughout the writing—offering me a secure base for exploring while helping me learn how to create a secure base for the reader and consider them while writing the book. Your wisdom through the challenges steadied and helped me to recognize the predictable phases of my writing process. Each chapter needed time to gestate, before I could put words to the page. Sometimes my thinking about the therapeutic process needed to simmer or marinate. Often, I grappled with how to generate throughlines, which also involved wrangling. The latter was Diana's description, that I was wrangling themes while synthesizing the treatment and intervention chapters. Thank you, Bethany, for helping me to trust the process of writing a book.

Bob Marvin came to one of my presentations on Tailoring Treatment to Attachment Patterns in Charlottesville, where he was director of the Ainsworth Attachment Clinic. I will always cherish the first thing that Bob said to me when we met. He told me that Mary Ainsworth would be smiling at me from Heaven to see the work I was doing. When I was preparing an online course, I reached out to Bob for permission to use a photo of Mary Ainsworth. After that course, Bob and I started meeting weekly for over a year, maybe two. We spoke about attachment theory, his work as one of the home investigators in Ainsworth's Baltimore home observations, his graduate work in ethology, and many related topics that fueled my sense of connection to the early discoveries of Ainsworth and Bowlby. I felt his insistence that I get the connection between ethology and attachment. Bob's deep commitment to helping families change their attachment patterning is manifest in the Circle of Security work. I am very grateful for our relationship, which has evolved into a warm and caring friendship. When I ate lunch in his home, I was delighted to learn that the utensils for our meal had belonged to Mary Ainsworth. I am forever grateful to Bob for gracing me with the experience of time travel to the early days when attachment theory was in the making.

Thank you to the participants in an AEDP Essential Skills course module on attachment, who wanted to know what having different attachment styles meant in terms of treating patients. Your questions initiated my studying the configuration of each attachment pattern, creating the grids that are the centerpiece of this book, and developing intervention and treatment pathways that consider the origins of these patterns.

Thank you for the many conversations with course participants, experiential assistants, and faculty colleagues that have taken place throughout the formation of these grids. Your contributions, questions, and insights helped me organize and develop them. Thank you, Monica Bradley, Diana

Lightmoon, Anne Marshall, Trisha Rowe, Deb Lee Thornby, and faculty colleagues Mary Androff, Sigal Bahat, Anne Cooper, Jenn Edlin, Diana Fosha, Ron Frederick, Kari Gleiser, Richard Harrison, Karen Kranz, Jerry Lamagna, Ben Lipton, Annika Medbo, Ben Medley, Jeanne Newhouse, Jenna Osiason, Jacquie Perman, Natasha Prenn, Eileen Russell, Anna Christina Sungren, Barbara Suter, Gil Tunnell, and Danny Yeung. I learn so much from each of your brilliant minds and hearts and the particular angles through which you continue to enhance the model of AEDP. Thank you to my supervisees whose dedication to learning keeps me on my toes, where learning is an endless process of discovery.

To patients who have shared their innermost places and vulnerability with me, entrusted me to help them, and to those who allow their work to be shared for the benefit of therapist's learning, thank you from the bottom of my heart for your generosity and trust. I have learned so much throughout the course of each of your psychotherapy processes with me.

David Mars, my life partner, colleague, and primary attachment figure, thank you for being there every step of the way, and then some! You're the one I talked to when ideas were burgeoning or who I showed those "shitty first drafts." Thank you, Anne Lamott, for your phrase, aptly conveying that writing is not a seamless flow, but a work in progress that takes humility and a willingness to be with a mess. Thank you, David, for peering into those drafts with me and helping me to separate the grain from the chaff, for hearing new versions of the chapters freshly and encouraging me to trust what was coming before it was clear. Thank you for your love, support, and tolerance of another day or another evening when the book had all of my attention.

Eva Mars, my daughter, attending college from home during the pandemic, your presence and love uplifted my spirits. I bow to your deep kindness, understanding, and generous heart and to your perseverance when you wanted my attention when I was engrossed in writing—your grace in knowing when to let me be and your insistence when you had to reach me.

To my parents Betty Lynch and Alan Pando. Thank you for my life and your love. Thank you for holding the value of family through divorce and being inclusive with our new family constellations. To my brothers, Scott Pando and Mauro Pando, I have great love for each of you and our teamwork in caregiving our parents in their waning years, and especially appreciate when my book deadlines were near, how willingly you stepped up to support me. To my Uncle Mauro and Aunt Carrol, for your inspiration.

To my stepdaughter Heather Mars, my son-in-law Eric Weber, and my granddaughters, Gwen and Ellie, thank you for your tolerance and care when writing this book entered family and vacation time. I appreciate your support and understanding. And to my stepmom, Stacie Hunt, for your support and enthusiasm while I was writing this book and especially for helping me acquire key permissions for song lyrics.

To my friends, Suzi Hudson, LeeAnne Schlaf, Sigal Bahat, Elizabeth Greason, Jennifer Lowell, Bill Arigi, Bob Wynne, Tom Thurston, and Simone Rodin for checking in and asking me how the book was going and listening to what was on my mind. Thanks for your support, for being patient with my reclusiveness, and for celebrating the milestones with me.

And to the copyeditors at Norton: Mariah Eppes, Nina Hnatov, and Olivia Guarnieri, I very much appreciate your clarifying questions and making sure every citation matched its reference. Thank you for your attention to detail and your responsiveness to my questions. I appreciated having a sense of being on a team and receiving your support. Thank you to Jamie Vincent, McKenna Tanner, Natalie Argentina, and those at Norton who are still getting involved, for your help and work on this project.

To all who have shared your anticipating the arrival of this book with me, your interest and expressed excitement buoyed and gave me strength to persist. I hope you enjoy it.

Diana Fosha

Everything in my entire career has led to what it has taken to coauthor this book, and contribute to everything that is in it. Which would mean that I would have to acknowledge every significant relationship, personal and professional, with people deeply known through interpersonal interaction and people deeply known through their writing. Thus, in the service of succinctness, I have three acknowledgments to offer.

First of all, a deep thank you to my coauthor and the first author of this book, Karen Pando-Mars: In the 20 years (to date) that we've known each other, and the ten years that we've been working together on what has now become this book, it has been a privilege, an honor, and a delight to be in all the relationships (as you have also named them) that we have been in: as your mentor, colleague, supervisor, teacher, friend, coauthor, and then some others too (for example, co-leading the AEDP Vision Collective Core Training—see the second thank you, below). In addition to the monumental work that you have done to bring this book to fruition/completion. And one more thing I wish to acknowledge and express gratitude for: The countless moments of sheer joy at nerding out in resonant and expanding fashion. Those have been delightful and priceless.

My second acknowledgment is of Connie Rhodes and the 2023–2024 members of the AEDP Vision Collective & Vision Collective Core Training group: Kosu Boudreau, Gerald Brooks, Karla Amanda Brown, Nicky Cameron, Marsha Elliott, Jessica Guillory, Jennifer Jackson, Peter Muhwati, Sonya Parker, Lois (Heloise) Ridley, and James Santos. From the beginning, Connie Rhodes, who came on as DBEI consultant to the AEDP Institute in 2021, believed in the power of AEDP and its potential as a flagship model for healing racialized trauma. And as we have discovered, the effectiveness of the work on healing racialized trauma is only strengthened, enhanced, and made more real by connection, relatedness, attachment, laughter, joy, and friendship. Mary Main, one of the main (pun intended) figures in attachment theory and research, once said that "science is made by friends." Maybe we can say that "multiracial work seeking to heal racialized trauma is made by friends." My deep gratitude to Connie Rhodes, and to the AEDP Vision Collective & Vision Collective Core Training members for the embodied attachment relationships and friendships we have constructed. I look forward to seeing the contributions that will emerge from the work of this group, illuminating—among many other fundamental factors—the role of attachment in healing racialized trauma.

My third acknowledgment and thank you is to my little and growing nuclear family. I thank my amazingly beautiful, brilliant, and crazily high-EQ daughters, Molly and Zoe Lubin-Fosha for all you have taught me about attachment. Together, the three of us traversed many joys and many sorrows and many challenges and our own version of Kintsugi, the Japanese art of repairing with gold, the repaired version even more gorgeous than the original. Thank you for your belief in me and in my deep love for you no matter what. And, as we welcome the new members of our family, Molly's partner Wil Pacheco, and Molly and Wil's daughter, my granddaughter and Zoe's niece, Scarlett Maya Pacheco Lubin-Fosha, I thank Molly and Wil for finding each other and for bringing Scarlett into the world, and Zoe for being the best mischievously joyful aunt any kid could wish for. And to Scarlett, who at the time of this writing is five months and one day old, I thank you for coming into our lives and gracing them with toothless grins and endless possibility.

Preface: Using Attachment (Though Not Only) to Make Attachment Safe and Good Again

by Diana Fosha

Relationships hurt and relationships heal. Relationships traumatize and they save our lives. Our very first relationship, the attachment relationship, is necessary for our very survival: Mother Nature, aka evolution, placed a baby, wired to connect, together with a caregiver, wired to care, and made the bond between them the baby's path to survival, growth, and development. Yet, when the caregiving environment fails to support and nurture, and instead there is neglect and hurt, the attachment relationship needed to ensure our literal survival becomes the epicenter of deep emotional suffering: attachment trauma, or more generally, relational trauma, one of the most painful areas of human suffering, with far-reaching consequences. And when attachment relationships wound, the pain we feel is compounded by the pain of feeling alone.

In the face of such painful lapses by those supposed to care, protect, and love, the child is faced with "unwilled and unwanted aloneness in the face of emotions that are too painful or overwhelming to bear" (Fosha, 2021a, p. 38). Aloneness in the face of unbearable emotions, and/or aloneness in existential situations where we crave to feel seen, is at the root of psychopathology. Defenses arise in loco parentis—that is, they develop to compensate for caregiving and relational lapses. They protect against emotional and relational experiences that cannot be borne. Defenses develop not only to help the child somehow cope with overwhelming emotions and as best possible protect the integrity of the self; they also develop to help protect/maintain the crucial relationship with the caregiver, however flawed. In order to survive and function in untenable circumstances, the child brilliantly adapts, via "defensive exclusion" (Bowlby, 1980, p. 52). The child excludes from experience whatever aspects of their experience trigger their caregiver's anxieties, with costly consequences: Large swaths of human experience need to be excluded from the child's lived experience to ensure the survival of the bond, at the expense of growth and development. When defense mechanisms are thus habitually and chronically relied upon, the vitality-squelching consequences of defensive exclusion manifest in constriction and restriction of the personality. One result is that characteristic attachment patterns[1] develop: the two types of insecure attachment patterns, avoidant and ambivalent, as well as disorganized attachment.

Under stress, new relationships are responded to as though they were the old ones, and connection becomes synonymous with suffering. Thus, on one hand, we see how relationships are at the heart of emotional suffering and relational trauma. And yet, on the other hand, people and relatedness are the only medicine for relational ailing. Faced with this paradox, the question becomes "How do we use the relational medicine of attachment to make attachment and connection safe, and good, again?"[2]

The answer: This is what this book is about.

We want to show how we can engage with people whose core trauma is relational and how we can use a relationship, the therapeutic one, and interventions addressing relational experience, to heal relational wounds. Key to this is creating safety and security in the therapeutic relationship, so that, as per Bowlby (1988), it can function as a secure base for launching challenging and difficult explorations and a safe haven to return to. Those explorations must involve (a) a belief in the possibility of, despite prior history, co-creating safety, (b) therapeutic strategies to bypass the defenses that give attachment patterns their characteristic flavor, and also (c) ways to process the emotional and relational experiences that were previously defensively excluded from experience so that their adaptive riches can once again be used to live life fully. And furthermore, if a methodology exists to solidify and deepen these changes (see section on metatherapeutic processing below), so much the better. The goal of such a process would be nothing less than the rewiring of the internal working model—that is, the transformation of our patients' psychic organization, to restore security within oneself and trust in connection. Thus, attachment would become safe again.

What enables us to do that?

For our conceptual framework, we lean into attachment theory and research, including the neurobiology of attachment (Schore, 1994, 2019), as well as the work of the "baby watchers" (e.g., Beatrice Beebe, Daniel Stern, Colwyn Trevarthen, Ed Tronick) to inform a radically relational experiential treatment for adults with relational trauma. We use attachment- and development-based constructs to inform a granular and textured understanding of why—and how—attachment and connection come to be so fraught for our adult patients.

For our transformational therapeutics, we use AEDP, an attachment-informed transformational therapy, and its attachment-informed therapeutic stance, experiential interventions, and transformational phenomenology (Fosha, 2000b, 2021b; Hendel, 2018; Prenn & Levenson, 2025; Russell, 2015). An empirically supported therapy (Iwakabe et al., 2020, 2022; Notsu et al., 2022), AEDP is a healing-oriented model that eschews psychopathology, preferring to lean into what is adaptive and self-righting. In working to heal relational wounds to transform suffering and rewire the internal working model, AEDP weaves three equally important strands—attachment, emotion, and transformation—in its experiential methodology and interweaves them in a seamless fashion.

AEDP is the platform from which we launch this book. Over the last two decades, AEDP has articulated the theory and methodology by which the therapeutic relationship and its experiential interventions can transform insecure attachment patterns (Fosha, 2003, 2009b, 2017b; Frederick, 2021; Lamagna, 2011; Lipton & Fosha, 2011; Pando-Mars, 2011, 2016; Prenn, 2011). We have articulated how to go about healing from the get-go, and how to co-create safety and foster secure attachment even in people with complex posttraumatic stress disorder (PTSD; Gleiser, 2021). However, until this current volume, we have not articulated, in precise detail, the attachment pattern–specific "how" of how to go about transforming internal models of attachment, especially those of individuals for whom attachment beckonings intensify defenses rather than melt them.

The grids. In the pages that follow, using the conceptual framework of attachment theory and developmental work, as well as AEDP's transformational therapeutics, especially its understanding of attachment through the lens of affect (Fosha, 2000b), we introduce three grids developed by Karen Pando-Mars (2016). These grids are heuristics that offer (a) a granular, highly specific understanding of each attachment pattern; and (b) an equally detailed, textured highly specific therapeutics for how to work with each of them. The grid for each attachment pattern describes how that pattern is positioned across 10 different aspects or characteristics, such as characteristic defenses, characteristic fears, and characteristic responses to the arousal of attachment needs. The guide and inspiration for the therapeutic work is to be found in the first grid, which summarizes the 10 aspects of what secure attachment looks like, which is indeed what we hope to accomplish. The second grid describes the characteristics of the avoidant, ambivalent/resistant, and disorganized attachment patterns, tracking each of them along the 10 aspects. The healing orientation of our AEDP-informed approach is evident in that 1 of the 10 aspects examines the characteristic "seeds of resilience" contained within each pattern—however maladaptive for the person's current circumstances the pattern may be, we identify the potential for resilience contained therein. Based on this highly detailed understanding of each attachment pattern, the third grid organizes an attachment pattern–specific understanding of (a) our stance as therapists vis-à-vis people embodying that way of relating; (b) what we choose to focus on when we intervene; and (c) the precise nature of our intervention; as well as (d) what our aims are—that is, what we hope to accomplish in the context of each attachment pattern.

Attachment and transformation are core themes. At first glance, attachment and transformation may seem unlikely dyadic partners. However, in the context of therapeutic work that uses attachment to transform attachment, so as to "make attachment safe again" (Fosha, 2023), they are inextricably intertwined. Moreover, between a patient's historically informed attachment pattern and its transformation lie affectively laden, bodily rooted experiences of emotion and relatedness, and an experiential therapeutic method for effectively processing those emotional and relational experiences that could not be processed earlier by the patient alone.

These patterns, once brilliant strategies that emerged in the attempt to survive untenable situations and their unbearable emotional experiences, are exactly what structure current-day relational suffering. Reflecting a past long gone, reliance on those patterns no longer serves us. Strategies that were once instituted to keep us safe no longer do so. Without access to adaptive affective experiences, relationships end up being sources of hurt, frustration, and wounding. The key to rendering defense mechanisms and other aspects of each insecure or disorganized attachment pattern no longer necessary is to be found in *being able to experience the emotional and relational experiences heretofore defensively excluded.* Which leads us to the crucial role of experience, specifically *affectively laden, bodily rooted experiences within the therapeutic dyad.* With aloneness undone, together with the therapist, the patient can now start to tackle experiences that were previously too overwhelming to feel alone and required defense mechanisms to cope. Within the therapeutic dyad, with the therapist's help, those experiences can now be processed, so that their adaptive benefits can be reaped. It is a path we take to help our patients relinquish now-vestigial patterns and create the conditions for the eventual emergence of security, receptivity to love, and esteem of self.

Below, let's explore some aspects of attachment, transformation, and the experiential therapeutic methodology of AEDP for working with the affectively laden experiences that link them.

Attachment

A Developmental Clinical Framework

A developmental clinical framework informs our understanding of how insecurity and disorganization come about in the context of early attachment relationships. And how—unless there are changes in the relational environment—these patterns then get paid forward, manifesting in how people show up in their important relationships: intimate friendships, with their romantic partners, and as parents to their children. The roots of the patterns that we seek to transform and of the wounds we seek to heal originate in those early years. Accessing those early experiences, whether as an enacted pattern and/or as a memory, to illuminate how these currently problematic defense-based patterns were once actually brilliant adaptations is a crucial aspect of our therapeutic work.

The developmental framework has translational applications. Just as translational research takes scientific discoveries made in the lab and seeks to apply them in new treatments that benefit people, we seek to take the discoveries from attachment theory and developmental research on how children and their caregivers interact and translate them into treatment strategies that can help our adult patients. We work with adult patients and not babies or children, and we are therapists, and not parents. Yet we seek to embody the characteristics of security- and resilience-engendering attachment figures. We translate what we have learned from attachment theory and research and from the work of the baby watchers—Beatrice Beebe, Daniel Stern, Colwyn Trevarthen, Ed Tronick—and their studies of moment-to-moment caregiver–infant interaction to inform our therapeutic stance, moment-to-moment tracking of affective experience, and clinical practice to work therapeutically with adults.

Asymmetry and Symmetry: Ways of Being Together, Ways of Regulating Affect Together

The roots of connection and of our capacity to take risks, daring to explore and expand our horizons, are to be found in the asymmetry of our original attachment relationship—a deeply dyadic relationship involving two people, a deep bond connected through asymmetry—one more vulnerable and in need of care and affect regulation, the other, the attachment figure, "perceived" to be "older and wiser" (Bowlby, 1979),[3] and hopefully also "stronger and kind" (Marvin et al., 2002). This deeply dyadic yet asymmetric relationship with respect to care, protection, and moment-to-moment dyadic affect regulation—one needing, the other providing—describes the attachment relationship.

Whereas asymmetry is what defines the dyadic attachment relationship, symmetry, and the melding of mental and emotional states, is what defines the intersubjective aspects of dyadic relationships. In moments of intersubjective engagement, apparent differences of age, size, status, gender, social location, and other identity differentiators recede under the aegis of the engaged delight of shared interest. An adult and a little kid absorbed in building a sandcastle, a couple of strangers connected by witnessing an intense street scene, a patient and a therapist discussing with animation last night's World Series game. Through the intermingling of states of consciousness there is the delight of shared affect, of accompaniment, and of feeling understood through being joined in mutual interest. In those moments, differences in age, wisdom, and experience disappear. Joint attention is the equalizer.

Although the *asymmetric attachment relationship* is organized around care, protection, and affect regulation, and the *symmetric intersubjective relationship* is organized around shared attention, both relationships are ways of undoing aloneness and being deeply connected. The attachment aspect is forged through traversing whatever causes fear or distress, and the difficult emotions that arise, with the attachment figure supporting the more vulnerable partner's experiencing. The intersubjective connection "thickens," to use Ed Tronick's term, through sharing many different kinds of pleasurable moments of exploration and the positive emotions that accompany such moments.

What is crucial is that in both attachment and intersubjectivity, both members of the dyad matter. Be the dyad equal and symmetric, or linked through the asymmetry of need, these are mutually affecting relationships. Both members contribute to the relationship that is co-created. The emotional experiences of each member of the dyad matters, as both types of relationships are shaped through ongoing, moment-to-moment emotional exchanges. A dyad is about two people, each with their perceptions, feelings, and experiences, each important to what unfolds and to what is co-created through the coregulated interaction of their two selves. That both members of the dyad matter is something of profound importance to the type of therapeutic work put forth in this book.

The Therapeutic Stance:
Attachment Sprinkled With Intersubjective Delight

The stance of the AEDP therapist is rooted in attachment, sprinkled liberally with intersubjective delight in the patient. The therapeutic stance is thus conceived as having two strands. In the *asymmetric attachment-informed strand*, pain, suffering, fear, and shame are met with empathy and dyadic affect regulation, broadcasting the therapist's presence, active engagement, and willingness to help. Going "beyond mirroring," such a stance embodies not only a willingness to accompany the patient but also to bear and share in the patient's emotional pain. In the *symmetric intersubjective strand*, the therapist's focus is on the quintessential qualities of the self of the patient, and these are met with affirmation and delight. The therapist's delighting in and with the patient is one of the most powerful antidotes to the patient's shame (Kaufman, 1996).

It Takes Two to Tango and Two Means Two

In Bowlby's (1969/1982) work, it is not only the attachment behavioral system of the more vulnerable partner that is innate. The caregiver's caregiving is equally innate. The instinct to respond to the distress of a more vulnerable other with empathy and care, leaning in and wishing to help, is also wired: the caregiving behavioral system is the biological foundation for the therapist's actions in attachment therapeutic work (Fosha, 2000b). Furthermore, there is no attachment behavioral system without the caregiving system. As Winnicott (1960) also said, "There is no such thing as an infant, meaning, of course, that whenever one finds an infant, one finds maternal care, and without maternal care, there would be no infant" (p. 586). Attachment and caregiving are yoked. Along with the exploratory system, which comes to the fore when the attachment system has been soothed by the caregiving system, these three systems—attachment, caregiving, and exploratory—are inextricably linked and together constitute Bowlby's construct of attachment.

The therapist's genuine affective engagement and responsiveness is crucial in the work described in this book. As the phrase goes, "It takes two to tango." It also takes two to undo aloneness. It takes two to form an attachment bond. And it takes two to co-construct a *moment of meeting* (Buber, 1965, p. 104). It bears being explicit that, in fact two means two—which means that *you*, the therapist, and your affect, are part of the dyad too.

You Can't Do Attachment Therapy With a Still Face

The therapist's affect matters: It is an integral part of the work. Our emphasis on establishing a genuine relationship with the patient is rooted in the neuroscience of right-brain to right-brain coregulation, coordination, and communication to foster moment-to-moment psychobiological state attunement between the members of the dyad (Schore, 2019). Neither undoing aloneness nor dyadic affect regulation, nor expressing intersubjective delight, can be done with a neutral face or a flat gaze. Neutrality is actually contraindicated. The "still face" has no place in attachment-informed therapeutic work.

Emotional engagement and collaborative participation are key aspects of an attachment-informed therapeutic stance. Therapists are not only attuned to their patients' moment-to-moment state: Moment-to-moment, they are also attuned to their own shifting affective states. Therapists are "experientially involved in the relational matrix by reciprocating self-disclosing of [their] own immediate experiences, especially affective experiences in response to the client and/or process" (Iwakabe & Conceição, 2016, pp. 232–233).

The Internal Working Model Need Not Be a Life Sentence: The Power of Attachment to Transform & the Potential of Attachment to Be Transformed

Attachment transforms.

Attachment theory describes how the individual's regulatory strategies for negotiating emotion and relational experience result from the internalization of the regulatory strategies of the attachment dyad. There is often an unspoken assumption that once the attachment dyad's affect regulatory strategies are internalized in the individual's internal working model of attachment, they are immutable. However, that is not true.[4] We often fail to add the all-important qualifier that makes it true, which is that the stability of the individual's internal working model is contingent upon the stability and continuity of the relational environment over time. Change the relational environment and a different pattern of interrelated representations—of self, of other, of self–other relationship, of emotion regulation—emerges. This empirically validated fact is the fertile soil for a transformational attachment therapy.

Below, let's review research documenting both aspects of the internal working model: both its extraordinary stability in certain conditions and its remarkable flexibility in others.

Attachment Transforms the Psyche: Continuity of the Internal Working Model Over the Lifespan and Its Intergenerational Transmission

On the side of how attachment transforms and shapes development, we have powerful evidence that affect-regulating experiences with caregivers organize the psychic organization of the child (Cassidy, 1994; Fonagy et al., 1991a, 1991b; Hesse & Main, 1999, 2000; Main, 1995) and shape the landscape of the brain, particularly the right brain (e.g., Schore, 2009; Siegel, 1999). The characteristics of affect-regulating relationships are not only internalized but also immortalized through their transmission to future generations. The intergenerational transmission of attachment states of mind is a robust finding. Witness the continuity of the Adult Attachment Interview (AAI) ratings over time (Main, 1995, 1999a), and its uncanny capacity to predict the attachment status of babies yet unborn (Fonagy et al., 1991a). Attachment classifications also have been shown to predict academic and social functioning, predisposition to pathology, and vulnerability for trauma (see Main, 1995; Sroufe, 1996). Such evidence strongly supports the axiom that early experiences with caregivers shape lifelong patterns, which makes the possibility of affecting change seem quite daunting.

And yet—on the plasticity side of the paradox and on the side of how attachment can be transformed—we have equally powerful data that document the suppleness of the psyche and its attuned responsiveness to current conditions, especially those favoring self-righting tendencies (Emde, 1988; Lamb, 1987). Though less well-known, they are cause for therapeutic optimism.

Attachment Is Transformable:
The Plasticity of the Internal Working Model and Its Responsiveness to Changes in the Relational Environment

On the side of attachment being transformable, we look at three aspects of its plasticity: (a) the existence of relationship-specific attachment patterns in childhood, (b) a clinical vignette of an adult patient showing relation-specific patterns of attachment, and (c) evidence documenting the transformability of attachment patterns in response to changes in the relational environment.

Multiple internal working models, relationship specific. Attachment patterns are relationship dependent. In children, security or insecurity of attachment is *not* a characteristic of the *individual* but rather of the *relationship*: It is not uncommon for a child to be securely attached with one parent, and disorganized (or insecurely attached) with the other (Main, 1995). In the early years, a child's attachment pattern with a given caregiver reflects *that* caregiver's internal working model (Fonagy et al., 1991a). A child's attachment pattern with one parent can be drastically different from that same child's behavior and attachment pattern with the other parent. While over time these multiple working models become hierarchically organized, the wiring for different configurations remains, at the very least as wired-in dispositional tendencies, ready to be activated by the respective relational configurations.

And, as you will see in the following vignette, this doesn't only occur in childhood.

One person, two internal working models: a brief clinical vignette. Andrew, a single, cisgendered, heterosexual 43-year-old White man came into therapy, mortified by his way of being with his girlfriend: obsessively checking for texts and messages at all times of day and night, prone to fits of jealous despair, consumed by whether she loved him, and unable to concentrate on anything else. And Mara, the woman in question, was inattentive, rather careless with Andrew and his feelings, and not reluctant to fan the flames of jealousy. Andrew berated himself for his dependency. Enacting the ambivalent attachment pattern, to his detriment he neglected work and friends, fixated only on the rather indifferent Mara. Eventually that relationship broke up.

Sometime later, Andrew fell in love with another woman, Kelly, who loved him in return. From early on, Andrew's way of being and behaving with Kelly manifested as markedly different from his patterns with Mara. Now he was the one who delayed responding to Kelly's messages and relational gambits and was dismissive of her strivings for closeness. Andrew reengaged his work with singular drive. Despite a strong sexual attraction to Kelly, Andrew now embodied an avoidant attachment pattern: He de-emphasized the relationship, while extolling the virtues of work and autonomy.

Same person, two different internal working models in the context of two different relationships.

The transformability of attachment patterns: responsiveness of psychic organization to current relational conditions. Research documents that changes in the child's attachment status occur reliably and systematically as attachment-focused interventions produce changes in the caregiver (Marvin et al., 2002). In the work of the Circle of Security project, the attachment status of toddlers changed from disorganized to organized, and from insecure to secure as a result of changes in their caregivers. The caregivers' changes were the result of a 20-session group intervention protocol (Marvin et al., 2002). As a result of their therapy (only 20 sessions of group work to address strategies forged in lifelong histories of trauma!), the parents moved from trauma-based activation and defensive processes to increased empathy for their children. And, in response to these changes in their parents, the children's attachment patterns, demonstrating remarkable plasticity, subsequently transformed. Approaching this issue from a different angle—that is, children whose family constellation changed as a result of divorce—a parallel finding: New caregivers bring about changes in attachment status of the children (van den Boom, 1990). Finally, the research on earned security shows how after a lifetime of disorganization and trauma, finding that special someone can instantiate the transformation into security. And this is not Hollywood B movies, but rather research (Siegel, 1999/2020).

Without ignoring the powerful forces that perpetuate childhood patterns and their intergenerational transmission, the responsiveness of psychic organization to current conditions is a huge cause for celebration and data-informed therapeutic optimism.

Both aspects of the internal working model—its stability in the context of relational continuity and its responsiveness to relational environment changes—are immensely important. The stability over time of the internal working model and its intergenerational transmission tells us how people who are stuck in relational trauma got there. The more textured our understanding of how those patterns came to be, the better we can help our patients transform them. At the same time, the plasticity of the internal working model and its responsiveness to changes in the relational environment is a foundation for therapeutic change. This is where we come in. Creating conditions that are conducive to healing relational trauma, through how we are with our patients, through how we coregulate and coordinate with them aiming to co-create safety—we can construct the relational conditions our patients need for us to help them make attachment safe again. And sometimes make attachment safe for the very first time.

We now proceed from attachment theory and research to their translational applications in clinical work.

Pathways to Transformation: Experiential Therapeutic Work

Experiential Work

In addition to the orientation toward the healing and transformational potential residing within all human beings, equally fundamental in this work is the experiential focus of the therapy.

Working *experientially* refers to an intensive focus on moment-to-moment, present-tense, internal experience, especially the *felt sense* of an experience as it arises in the body in the moment in the here-and-now of the therapeutic encounter. It involves encouraging patients' attention to it, urging a staying away from "the head" and thinking, and instead urging a focus on noticing and sensing, and then proceeding to actively work on processing that experience. Working experientially also involves grounding the work in the tracking of moment-to-moment fluctuations in the affective experience of the patient–therapist dyad and process (see Hanakawa, 2021), and using those fluctuations to guide the choice of intervention.

This experiential focus is supported by a paradigm shift in our field, informed by the neuroscientific revolution of the last quarter century: From the previous privileging of top-down processing and attention focused on cognitions and behaviors, experiential work is part of "the shift to a bodily based [i.e., bottom up] emotional psychotherapy that integrates psychology and biology" (Schore, 2012, p. xii; see also Panksepp, 2009). AEDP innovations privilege the bottom-up processing of bodily based affective experience and center it as fundamental to transformational change. Its experiential techniques focus on embodied experiencing rooted in the moment-to-moment tracking of fluctuations in affective experience. This helps patients access somatically based aspects of their experience. In AEDP, healing, attachment, relatedness, and transformation are not only processes to be activated: They are also *vitally important bodily based* experiences to be explored and their therapeutic benefits reaped.

Dyadic Experiential Work: "Stay With It and Stay With Me"

Phrases such as "stay with it" or "be with that" are a mainstay of all the different therapy models that use the experiential method. Having bypassed defenses and now, with access to bodily rooted affective experience, therapists use this phrase to encourage the patient to focus on and "stay" or "be with" the emergent experience, so that the experience can deepen and continue to unfold.

This is used similarly in AEDP. We definitely want our patients to "stay with it." Yet we don't stop with "stay with it." Given the centrality we accord undoing patients' aloneness, we use an additional phrase: "Stay with me." We urge our patients on with the phrase "Stay with it and stay with me" (Fosha, 2017b). This compound phrase makes explicit the dyadic nature of our experiential work. It also reflects the importance we accord to patients' feeling safe in connection in order to be able to feel and process what they couldn't feel and process before when they felt alone.

An additional note: While the work is dyadic, experience belongs to the realm of the individual.

Much as the dyad, à la Winnicott, "holds" the work, and the patient's corrective experience of not being alone with overwhelming emotions is key to healing relational wounds, we want to make the implicit explicit: By definition, experience is personal, internal, and intrapsychic. Whether the *content* of the experience, or its object, so to speak, is grief or closeness or gratitude or the delight of intersubjective mind melding, the experience itself belongs to the individual and the individual alone. It is each individual's own experience that we are always working with, and it is what they will always have and be able to take with them. Our focus on the dyad is process and content. Experience remains the sacred realm of the individual's own private sensing, feeling, and knowing.

Dyadic Experiential Work With Emotional, Relational, & Transformational Experience

In AEDP, attachment and transformation are not only hoped-for outcomes of the therapy, nor are they only processes humming in the background. They are also rich experiences to be mined through experiential work. In addition to working experientially with emotions and sensations, AEDP methodology has pioneered experiential work with *relational experience*, with *self experience*, and with *transformational experience*. In the process, we have also expanded the phenomenological descriptions of the varieties of affective experiences that emerge in the course of experiential work with relational, self, and transformational experiences.

Centering therapeutic work with attachment and relational experience, I briefly review below dyadic experiential work in four realms—emotional, relational, self, and transformational—along with their respective affective experiences, and the specific corrective emotional experiences that constitute the completion of a round of processing in each realm.

Dyadic Experiential Work With the Emotions of Attachment Trauma and Wounding

Emotions have been evolutionarily wired into our brains and bodies because they help us survive. Jaak Panksepp (2009) called them "ancestral tools for living" (p. 1). They signal to us that something has changed in the environment and needs our attention (Damasio, 1999).

Emotions have a central role in attachment. As Bowlby (1980) wrote:

> Many of the most intense emotions arise during the formation, the maintenance, the disruption, and the renewal of attachment relationships. . . . Because such emotions are usually a reflection of the state of a person's

affectional bonds, the psychology and psychopathology of emotion is found to be in large part the psychology and psychopathology of affectional bonds. (p. 40)

When emotions can be processed to completion, they help us deal with the vicissitudes of attachment. We see this with securely attached children and individuals: Having full access to their emotions, they are able to process separations and loss, as well as connection and reunions, with the result that their functioning is enriched, and their resilience enhanced.

The story is different with those insecurely attached. The attachment figure is not able to support the more vulnerable partner to "feel and deal" with their emotions. Absent the caregiver's presence and help, unwilled and unwanted aloneness prevails, emotions overwhelm, defense mechanisms need to be instituted, and emotions are thus excluded. In therapy, the goal of the *dyadic experiential processing of the categorical emotions* is to help individuals first access these emotions; fully feel them; work through the associations and memories that were excluded along with the emotion; and then process the emotions to completion so that the benefits of their adaptive action tendencies can be reaped. When an emotion is felt and processed, its completion is marked by the release of the adaptive action tendencies intrinsic to it:

Emotion is the experiential arc between the problem and its solution: Between the danger and the escape lies fear. Between novelty and its exploration lies joyful curiosity. Between the loss and its eventual acceptance lies the grief and its completion. (Fosha, 2009a, p. 177)

This constitutes a corrective emotional experience because heretofore the individual was not able to have access to the emotion, nor to its adaptive benefits.

And if I may be so bold as to add to Bowlby's words to not only talk about psychopathology but also about healing, I offer the following additions to the passage from Bowlby quoted above:

Many of the most intense emotions arise during the formation, the maintenance, the disruption, and the renewal of attachment relationships. . . . Because such emotions are usually a reflection of the state of a person's affectional bonds, the psychology, psychopathology, *and psychotherapy* of emotion is found to be in large part the psychology, psychopathology, *and psychotherapy* of affectional bonds." (Bowlby, 1980, p. 40, with addition in italics by Fosha, 2024)

We seek to experientially process and work through both the affective experiences of the past that heretofore could not be processed, as well as the affective experiences of the here-and-now current therapeutic relationship.

Radically Relational Processing:
Dyadic Experiential Work With Relational Experience

There is a whole rich tapestry of here-and-now emotional, relational, and receptive affective experiences that constitute "the attachment-based relationship." Rather than letting attachment as a process just hum in the background and operate implicitly, in the work that we describe in this book and that you are about to witness, we don't just focus on the process of attachment: We therapeutically explore the *experiences* that constitute attachment. They are our focus, and we purposefully work with them, first explicitly and then experientially.

When our focus is emotional experience, the relationship "holds" the patient in their work with the emotions. In experiential work with relational experience, the relationship is *both* front and center, while still also holding the work. What do we mean by that?

Given what we have said about "stay with it and stay with me" and the importance of undoing aloneness and dyadic affect regulation in all aspects of the work we present here, "holding" (Winnicott, 1965) the relational work, and the patient within it, is just as important in the work with relational experience as it is in the work with the emotions of attachment trauma. The therapeutic/attachment relationship is the container that holds this work, the secure base from which the exploration launches and also its safe haven. However, in the experiential work with relational experience, *experiences* of relatedness are a primary focus of the experiential work. Both the "it" and the "me" of "stay with it and stay with me" apply to the relationship *and* its experiential exploration. This is especially so for the all-important work with the patient's moment-to-moment, here-and-now experience within and of the therapeutic relationship.

Two kinds of affective experiences are central in dyadic experiential work with attachment and relatedness: (a) dyadic experiential work with the experience of relatedness in the here-and-now of the therapeutic relationship, and (b) dyadic experiential work with receptive affective experience.

Dyadic experiential work with the patient's experience of relatedness in the here-and-now of the therapeutic relationship. Making the implicit explicit, we experientially explore the patient's moment-to-moment experience in and of the therapeutic relationship. We explore with our patients *their experience* of what it feels like to be connected (or not). Questions such as "What happens inside when I say that?"; "What is your experience of me?"; or "In this moment, what do you see in my eyes?" are trailheads for deepening further exploration. However the patient responds, it is then experientially explored, with follow-up questions and prompts such as "And what is that like in your body?" and "Stay with that . . . ," "Feel into that . . . ," "Be with it . . . ," and "Feel me with you."

Therapists' sharing and judiciously self-disclosing their own affective experiences is part and parcel of relational processing. It advances the work. As we said above, it takes two to tango. And as Prenn (2011) writes, "Self-disclosure is a secure attachment creating intervention. The quickest way to deepen an experience between two people is by one of them saying something personal or vulnerable. Therapist vulnerability is an invitation to patient vulnerability" (p. 310). Especially for patients who have had histories of not mattering to their attachment figures, or of having been regarded with anger or contempt, the felt sense of knowing they "exist in the heart and mind" of their therapist, and that their experience affects and touches their relational partner (i.e., the therapist), contributes immeasurably to their security.

This work requires therapeutic bravery, and it is indeed intimate and vulnerable. Not only for the patient but also for the therapist. In addition to therapist clarity about the purpose and intention of the disclosure and solid ethical grounding,[5] the experiential focus helps contain this all-important work and gives it intrinsic boundary-ness. The focus is always inward—on each person's own unique personal internal experience, the felt sense of which only one person, the individual themself, can access.

Dyadic experiential work with the patient's receptive affective experience. Attachment is transformative, not only as a foundational process but also an *experience to be harnessed in treatment.* Secure attachment is forged through the attachment figure's care, caregiving, attunement, empathy, love, and willingness to help.

Nonetheless, it is not sufficient for empathy, care, protection, and help to be offered. In order for them to be effective, they must be received. *Receptive affective experiences*—that is, experiences of feeling seen, loved, or understood—register that reception. Receptive affective experiences are key constituents of what it means to be attached: their exploration is a crucial aspect of attachment work in psychotherapy.

The emotional experience of receiving, or taking in, what is relationally offered is at the heart of attachment and of attachment work in therapy. If empathy, care, love, and/or protectiveness are given, but they are not "taken in," we encounter the barrier the patient has erected (most likely, for good historical reasons!) against the very experiences that they most yearn for. That barrier must be addressed in treatment. How to do that, in a fashion that is specific to each attachment pattern, is one of the central offerings of this book to the practicing clinician.

If the patient can "take in" what is being offered, we are in the realm of receptive affective experiences: feeling seen, feeling cared for, feeling felt, feeling "loved on," as one patient said. The experiential exploration of these receptive experiences is accomplished through questions such as "What is it like to take in this empathy you feel from me?"; "How does it land in your body?"; and "What does it feel like inside?" Positive receptive affective experiences, taking in the good stuff that the attachment figure has to offer, in contrasting juxtaposition with the relational traumas of the past, transform those experiences (Ecker et al., 2012), and lay the groundwork for security of attachment. They themselves constitute the corrective emotional experience.[6]

Dyadic Experiential Work With Self Experience

The experience of self and its representation is an important aspect of the internal model, and a positive valuation of the self as worthy and lovable is essential to secure attachment. Work with the self and the experience of the self is yet another valuable aspect of work aiming to transform insecure and disorganized internal working models.

Rooted in a neuroscientific understanding of the neurobiological core self (Damasio, 2010; Panksepp & Biven, 2012; Panksepp & Northoff, 2009), work with self experience is an emergent aspect of AEDP (Fosha, 2013a, 2021b; Medbo, 2023; Russell, 2021). One aspect of it involves dyadic experiential work supporting the emergence of the experience of self in those whose self is unformed, or experientially nonexistent (Medbo, 2023). Another aspect of work with self experience is Eileen Russell's work on the need to foster the emergence of experiences of agency, will, and desire in those whose attachment history resulted in developmental deficits in these areas. This can be at the level of identity in the context of historical antecedents of not mattering, not being seen, or not feeling that one can have an impact. Or it can be the result of the inhibition of and failure to develop the exploratory system, either through caregivers' selective inattention and neglect (errors of omission) or their downright discouragement of exploration through criticism, shaming, or punishment (errors of commission) for incipient moves in that direction.

The goal of dyadic experiential work here is the activation of self-adaptive action tendencies. These run the gamut from incipient manifestations of the very *experience* of having a self (Medbo, 2023) to emergent experiences of agency, will, and desire (Russell, 2021), and to experiences of authentic self-knowing and self-expression when authenticity needed to be defensively excluded (R. Harrison, personal communication, March 31, 2024). In the context of attachment, important and meaningful *self action tendencies* include awareness of one's own needs and learning how to trust and express them, and the willingness to stand up for oneself and one's beliefs. A felt sense of mattering and being able to affect what happens, the experiences of agency that Russell writes about is an essential component of healing ambivalent/resistant patterning. Finally, a felt sense of the core self, manifested in experiences of "this is me" and other experiences of the worthiness and goodness of the self, are a feature of core state, the integrated fourth phase of AEDP's transformational process (Fosha, 2013a, 2021c; Yeung, 2021).

Metatherapeutic Processing: Dyadic Experiential Work With Transformational Experience

AEDP's experiential methodology takes us from trauma and wounding to their healing:

- Being able to fully feel emotions and allow them to be processed to completion until their adaptive action tendencies and their riches are reaped is a corrective emotional experience. That this happens in connection with another "perceived as older and wiser"—that is, the therapist—is also a corrective relational experience engendering of attachment security.
- Being open and vulnerable and willing to explore the experience of self and other, while together, and neither withdrawing nor attacking nor falling apart, is a corrective emotional relational experience.

- Having receptive affective experiences of feeling cared for, feeling seen and/or understood, and being able to internally reap their benefits in feelings of self-worth and restored judicious trust in connection is a deep correction of prior experiences of being misunderstood, dismissed, or neglected.
- Being able to have an experience of one's self as existing is a corrective emotional experience for an individual who has felt they don't exist or matter. Similarly, being able to experience agency and will is a powerful experience for someone who heretofore felt hopeless to effect any changes in their environment.

All of these corrective emotional, relational, and self experiences that are invariably accompanied by positive affect represent the culmination or completion of a round of experiential processing.

Powerful as they are, the occurrence of these corrective experiences is not the end-all and be-all of AEDP therapeutic work, nor is it culmination of the transformational process in AEDP. What is often an end point in other treatment modalities is the starting point of a new round of exploration in AEDP: enter metatherapeutic processing. *Metatherapeutic processing*, or *metaprocessing*, is a systematic transformational methodology for working experientially with transformational experiences and their associated transformational affects. Extensively written about (Fosha, 2013b; Fosha & Thoma, 2020; Russell, 2015; Yeung, 2021), metaprocessing has also been the subject of empirical interest and investigation (DiCorcia et al., 2023; Iwakabe & Conceição, 2016). In AEDP, transformation is also not only a desired goal or process to be entrained, it is also an *experience* to be harnessed. And we have discovered something awesome: experientially processing the experience of transformation is itself transformational, begetting further transformations, each accompanied by characteristic, invariably positive, transformational affects (Fosha, 2000a, 2000b, 2021b, c; Fosha & Yeung, 2006; Russell & Fosha, 2008).

Here, transformational experiences are experientially processed as assiduously as traumatizing experiences, and the *transformational affects*, the positive affects that accompany transformational experiences, are attended to as carefully as the painful affects of trauma.[7] The practice of metatherapeutic processing involves experientially investigating what is healing *about* healing, in the context of a healing relationship.

In response to a corrective emotional/relational experience, the therapist explores the emergent positive experience, urges the client to focus inward on the experience of that moment of transformation and asks, "What's that like?"; "What's it like for you to start out with such shame about your weakness and to now be here, standing up tall and strong, full of compassion for your younger self?"; "What's it like for you not to feel alone, and to have had me accompany you through the thick and thin of your grieving?"; "What's it like for you to feel this lightness and unburdening?"; and "What's it like to witness my delight in you?" Then, upon the emergence and naming of each new positively charged experience that arises in response to that inquiry, the therapist follows that up by asking, "And what's *that* like?" It is a recursive process: Each round's reflection on an embodied experience of change for the better and its concomitant positive affects yields a new experience accompanied by new positive affects, which then in turn become the focus of the next round of alternating between experiential exploration and experience-near reflection, and so on. And on . . .

This Book

The AEDP theory and methodology summarized in this preface is the platform from which this book is launched. However, this book is not simply a natural application of AEDP to the subject of attachment trauma, it also signifies a broader advancement of AEDP theory and methodology. Moreover, it is a technical advancement in the treatment of attachment problems in general. We therefore offer this work as a practical guide to clinicians of all theoretical orientations.

This book introduces the next level of clinical and therapeutic specificity. By deeply going into the attachment patterns and their origins, it illuminates how to best work with each of them, thus forging paths of differentiated healing. The experiential work of therapy, as described in this preface, is delineated according to attachment pattern–specific considerations, including dyadic experiential work with emotion, attachment, and relational experience; receptive affective experience; self experience; and transformational experience.

In the chapters that follow, we offer a range of psychotherapeutic interventions and clinical decision points from an attachment pattern–specific vantage point: This applies to defense restructuring; to the specifics of the therapist's stance; and to specific interventions with emotion, relatedness, and self. Even countertransference matters are given attachment pattern–specific consideration. For each of the attachment patterns, common therapist reactivities are described and recommendations for specific metaskills are offered to help the therapist recenter more quickly in order to be able to work more effectively.

The versatility and range of the proffered attachment pattern–specific interventions are demonstrated with session transcripts. While the reader observes the patient's positive response to an intervention, what follows this beneficial response is where the work continues and AEDP begins its unique process of metaprocessing the emergent corrective emotional experience, allowing for the solidifying of gains and rewiring of attachment patterns.

Thus, attachment can become safe and good again, and for some, maybe for the very first time. And it can be manifested not only in the individual's internal sense of their self as worthy of being loved but also in their capacity to love and receive love. It can also be manifested solidly onward into other authentic adult relationships, and the secure child rearing of the next generations.

Trajectory of the Book, Chapter by Chapter

Diana Fosha

Part I. Foundations

"Foundations" is the title of Part I of this book, and it has three chapters that address the theoretical foundations of the grids and the granular approach of tailoring interventions to attachment patterns detailed in the rest of the book. Part I traces the movement in the field: first, "The Move to Attachment & Representation" (Chapter 1); then to "The Move to Regulation & Coordination" (Chapter 2); and finally, moving on to the theory of an attachment-informed transformational therapy, "The Move to Experience & Transformation" (Chapter 3).

Chapter 1. The Move to Attachment & Representation

In Chapter 1, to quote Mary Ainsworth (1967), "We are here concerned with nothing less than the nature of love and its origins in the attachment of a baby to its mother" (p. 429). The move to attachment in the field was ignited by John Bowlby's (1969/1982) bold assertion that reality matters. He maintained that the events in and experiences of the relationship between a child and a caregiver are critical to how children develop, and are formative of their attachment patterns, relational behavior, and personality development. Across the Atlantic, Ainsworth was developing similar ideas: In the earliest articulation of the idea of the "secure base," she maintained that independence and the courage and skills to leave home have their roots in children having a secure dependence on their parents.

While the immensity of Bowlby's contributions is widely recognized and he is given his due as the father of attachment theory and the giant he was, Ainsworth's seminal contributions are less well-known. Chapter 1 uplifts the work of Ainsworth by illuminating the importance of her contributions. They include the concept of secure base, that is, the attachment figure as a secure base for the child's launching into the world, the formulation of maternal sensitivity and responsiveness to infant signals as central to the development of attachment; and, based on her naturalistic observations of mothers in both Africa and the United States, descriptions of the attachment patterns. She also devised the Strange Situation Protocol (SSP), the central protocol for being able to study attachment patterns systematically, in the lab, which has shaped decades of attachment research.

Chapter 1 introduces key concepts in attachment theory and research through telling a story, the story of how attachment theory came to be and of its development. A historical frame is used to first track the move in the field to the centrality of attachment in shaping personality organization and relational patterns and the pivotal roles played by Bowlby and Ainsworth—initially parallel, subsequently deeply intertwined—in this paradigm shift. What the chapter tracks next is the move to representation. Bowlby's work on the internalization of attachment patterns in the individual's internal working model and concomitant representations of self, other, and self-other relationship is taken to the next level of representation by Mary Main's development of the AAI (George et al., 1985; Main et al., 1985, Main et al., 2008)

The building blocks of attachment theory and research, which will prove most useful to the therapist seeking to transform insecure and disorganized attachment patterns and help patients work toward achieving security, are introduced from the ground up through this historical frame. Important concepts that are presented (mostly) chronologically include the four constituent behavioral systems of attachment: the fear/wariness, attachment, caregiving, and exploratory behavioral systems. The fear/wariness and attachment systems help us understand the origins, both evolutionary and developmental, of our patients' experiences. The caregiving system is foundational for the therapist's role in therapy. The exploratory system provides the substrate for launching the experiential work, once safety has been co-constructed.

Another clinically useful contribution to what constitutes safety-engendering behavior that can be applied to the clinical situation are Ainsworth's Maternal Caregiving and Interaction Scales (Ainsworth et al., 1978/2015). The names of the subscales are evocative: Sensitivity vs. Insensitivity, Cooperation vs. Interference, Availability vs. Ignoring, and Acceptance vs. Rejection. Similarly, Bowlby's ideas of a *goal-corrected partnership* has a lot to offer attunement-valuing therapists.

Next was the move to representation. Bowlby introduced the *internal working model of attachment* as a mental representation of the attachment relationship within the internal reality of the individual, which continues to exert a powerful influence, even in the physical absence of the caregiver. As the internalization of the attachment relationship, it structures the person's sense of self—worthy and lovable, or not; of the other—available and trustworthy, or not; and of relational expectancies. It also reflects how emotion is regulated with this relationship. This is explicitly represented in AEDP's representational schema, *the Self–Other–Eemotion Triangle* (Fosha, 2000b; Frederick, 2021; Pando-Mars, 2021), which is first introduced in this chapter. Through the internal working model, the attachment dynamics between child and caregiver become part of the deep structure of the mind of the individual, structuring not only relational patterns, emotion regulation strategies, and relational expectations but, as Main subsequently demonstrated, also language, rhetoric, and communication.

By developing the AAI, Main made the same field-shifting contribution to attachment research with adults as Ainsworth's SSP did for attachment research into the behavior of children and their caregivers. The pattern of behavior and emotion with which kids deal with the emotions evoked by the Strange Situation reveal their already internalized attachment patterns that is, their internal working models. Same with the language behavior of adults in response to the challenge of the AAI, with its recognized ability to "surprise the unconscious" (George et al., 1985). The pattern of responses and the formal aspects of their language and communication patterns around emotionally laden explorations of their attachment experiences reveals the same about the internal models of adults.

The clinical implications of these constructs are explored and elaborated throughout Chapter 1 and come to clinical fruition in the later chapters of this book.

Chapter 2. The Move to Regulation & Coordination

Whereas Chapter 1 explores the building blocks of attachment, Chapter 2 goes micro. What are the moment-to-moment processes between baby and caregiver by which attachment patterns are first constituted and then internalized? Here we switch from the macro world of attachment theory and research to the moment-to-moment world of caregiver–infant patterns of interaction. While keeping emotions front and center, the naturalistic work of the baby watchers is supported and illuminated by the neurobiological and physiological mechanisms that are at play and the mechanisms that support them, while keeping emotions and their experience front and center. The key concepts that are deconstructed here are *regulation* and *coordination*: the regulation of psychobiological emotionally laden states, and the coordination between the two wildly different organisms of the young baby and the adult caregiver. The attachment dyad needs to find a common psychophysiological meeting ground. How that happens impacts both members of the dyad, not only the more vulnerable member. Through the mechanism of the expansion of dyadic states of consciousness, both dyadic partners are affected. And, when it goes well, it is enriching to both.

Looking at how attachment relationships become part of our neural circuitry informs psychotherapists about how to help our patients connect with themselves to process unresolved emotions and painful experiences from their past. Key to this chapter is the building of coordinated therapeutic relationships to help our patients access and regulate what was previously unbearable in the context of the individual's unwilled and unwanted aloneness.

This chapter chronicles how the brain develops in the context of attachment relationships. We look at emotions, how caregivers and infants develop coordinated relationships based on the moment-to-moment process of attunement, disruption, and repair, leading to the restoration of coordination. We discuss the role of right-brain to right-brain communication to establish attunement, the importance of the insula for the felt sense of the emotions, and look at what Porges's Polyvagal Theory teaches us about how the autonomic nervous system processes threat, stress and safety, and the neurophysiological circuitry that roots safety in social engagement. We end the chapter with a discussion of positive neuroplasticity and the conditions conducive to its activation. In addition to safety, which it shares with the social engagement circuitry of the autonomic nervous system, focused attention, novelty, and optimal arousal are other important factors that promote neuroplasticity. New experiences have the power to change the brain. In therapy, our aim to foster new corrective emotional and relational experiences is enhanced by focused attention. New corrective emotional and relational experiences that stimulate growth in neuronal connections also foster new perceptions to emerge in our patient.

In Chapter 3, we introduce AEDP, a healing-oriented model of experiential psychotherapy. AEDP puts the dynamic understanding of what happens between people into experiential therapeutic activities that are targeted specifically to both address the fallout of attachment wounding and to engage the forces of neuroplasticity to turbocharge positive change and transformation. In AEDP, accessing and experientially processing somatically rooted affective experience, including relational experience and transformational experience, is seen as key to the transformations it aims to effect in the healing of relational wounds and the rewiring of patients' internal working model of attachment (see also Frederick, 2021). Thus next, the move to experience and transformation.

Chapter 3. The Move to Experience & Transformation

Attachment theory is based on how human beings are wired to connect. AEDP is based on how human beings are wired to heal. Discovering the motivational forces that are innate to human beings can help to fuel patients' healing journeys. Treatment is based on the explicit and experiential use of the therapeutic relationship to help patients deal with the suffering in their lives that has prompted them to seek psychotherapy. Helping patients to process emotions to completion releases their adaptive action tendencies, which can mobilize self-righting, repair, and transformation.

Having done a deep dive into how attachment is constituted of its building blocks at the macro level (Chapter 1), and then explored, at the micro level, the moment-to-moment dyadic caregiver–infant interactions and the neurobiological and neuroplastic mechanisms supporting those processes (Chapter 2), we now engage *the move to experience and transformation*. We are ready to look at the healing mechanisms involved in what allows for transformational change in attachment patterns. To do so we use AEDP, a transformational experiential therapy, and an attachment-informed one at that. It is a therapeutic model that seeks to put positive neuroplasticity into clinical action. Its description completes Part I, the Foundations section of the book.

In its understanding of psychopathology, AEDP centers aloneness, specifically unwilled and unwanted aloneness in the face of overwhelming emotional experience. Consequently, AEDP privileges *undoing aloneness* as foundational to the experiential interventions that aim to heal relational wounds.

AEDP braids three equally important strands—attachment, emotion, and transformation—in its clinical theory. Its *four-state transformational phenomenology* is useful for guiding the moment-to-moment choice of interventions and evaluating their impact. So are its three representational schemas, the *triangle of experience* (TOE), the *Self–Other–Emotion* (SOE) *triangle*, and the *triangle of relational comparisons* (TORC). To draw special attention to one of these representational schemas: the SOE configuration, introduced briefly in Chapter 1 and elaborated here, is a schematic of the internal working model, with the regulation of emotional experience in the context of an attachment relationship specifically represented. Thus, in addition to the representation of the self, the representation of the other (i.e., the attachment figure), and the representation of their dynamic self–other relationship, we include emotion in this representational schema. Indeed, the internalization of the dyad's emotion regulatory strategies shows how the nature of the relationship between self and attachment figure becomes internalized in the individual's strategies with respect to regulating and processing emotion. In secure attachment, those strategies are adaptive, and the individual is also able to ask for help when their resources are not up to the task at hand. On the other hand, the emotion regulation strategies manifesting insecure attachment patterns reflect the individuals' histories of attachment trauma and require defense mechanisms to exclude emotional and relational experience in order to be able to function as best possible.

To present key concepts of AEDP, which will inform the clinical work showcased in the second half of the book, Karen Pando-Mars took a page from Mary Main who used Grice's maxims to inform her scoring of the AAI. Pando-Mars used the device of maxims to present 14 key aspects of AEDP, each identified by a pithy phrase. As a result, major aspects of AEDP healing-oriented attachment-informed theory and therapeutic stance, transformational phenomenology, and dyadic experiential interventions are presented in an accessible user-friendly way.

Part II. North Star

Chapter 4. Inspiration: A Portrait of Secure Attachment

(Spoiler alert: In this chapter, we tell you how the movie ends.)

The movie *Lion* (2016) tells the story of little Saroo, a 5-year-old boy who becomes hopelessly lost, wandering alone thousands of miles from his home. Yet the strength of his secure attachment is unmistakable as a guiding force that helps him not only to survive but also to lose neither hope nor resilience nor his capacity to love. When alone, he is able to soothe and self-regulate by calling on his memory (internal representation) of his mother. We see him on his journey, facing countless challenges along the way, his resilience constantly tested. Somehow, after 25 years, he is able to find his way home and be reunited with his family. On one level, the story is miraculous—on another it is a profound testimony to the power of secure attachment and how it instills resilience and the capacity to deal with adversity while nurturing the capacity to love.

We help our patients heal what has gone wrong by engaging the neural circuits in the brain that are active when things go right. The example of Saroo bringing his mother to mind when he was alone to soothe himself and self-regulate with his memory of his attachment figure brings to mind an AEDP practice: that is, how we use portrayals to invoke what is a natural mechanism of secure attachment.

In Chapter 4, we tell the story of Saroo in the movie *Lion* to paint a vivid portrait of secure attachment and its power. The goal of this work is to heal relational trauma and help work with the internal working models so that insecure and disorganized attachment can transform into organization and security. Saroo is our North Star, inspiring our work.

Part III. Translational Tools

Having laid the theoretical foundations of the work in Part I (Chapters 1–3) and having painted a clear picture of secure attachment, the North Star of our work in Part II (Chapter 4), we are now ready to engage the how-to of how we set about to heal relational trauma. We are ready to get into the specifics of what to do to transform insecurity and disorganization into security and organization, pattern by pattern, specifically and granularly.

We've come to the fulcrum of this work, the center of this book: the three grids developed by Karen Pando-Mars to tailor interventions to attachment patterns. In the next two chapters, we introduce the three grids and the wealth of information that is contained within them in clear and succinct form. They allow us to translate theory and research into pattern-specific understanding and interventions.

Chapter 5. The Three Grids for Tailoring Treatment to Attachment Patterns: Their Development

Chapter 5 begins with the origin story—that is, how the grids came to be. They developed in response to requests by trainees for more specific guidance on how to work with the different attachment patterns. The result of many years of clinical data gathering was the creation of three grids.

Ten aspects of the configuration of each attachment pattern. The configuration of each attachment pattern is broken down into 10 different aspects,[1] each a separate row on the grids. For each attachment pattern, the following 10 aspects, each in a row in Grids 1 and 2, are named and explored:

1. Caregiver characteristics: state of mind with respect to attachment
2. Caregiver characteristics: behavioral hallmarks
3. Response to the arousal of the attachment system
4. Seeds of resilience
5. Nervous system activation and affect regulation
6. Defense: characteristic defenses
7. Anxiety: characteristic fears
8. Patterns of affective competence
9. Self–other relational patterning
10. Internal experience and external reality (à la Fonagy)

Each of these 10 aspects is the vertical dimension of each grid.

The three grids. Grid 1, The Configuration of the Secure Attachment Pattern, tracks and describes secure attachment with respect to each of the 10 aspects. It represents, in grid form, what was presented artistically in the movie *Lion* and the story that was told in Chapter 4. Grid 2, The Configurations of Insecure Attachment Patterns: Avoidant, Ambivalent/Resistant, and Disorganized, has three columns, each column a specific attachment pattern. The avoidant, ambivalent/resistant, and disorganized patterns each occupy a column. Each pattern is characterized along the 10 rows of the different aspects.

The only row that's different between Grids 1 and 2 is Row 10: in Grid 1, it is "internal experience and external reality: in connection (à la Fonagy)." In Grid 2, Row 10 is "internal experience and external reality: disconnects (à la Fonagy)."

Grid 3, Clinical Markers & Interventions to Treat Avoidant, Ambivalent/Resistant, and Disorganized Attachment, is devoted to clinical interventions. Grid 3 also has three columns, each column devoted to one attachment pattern. However, the rows of Grid 3 are slightly but significantly different in that we are in the land of clinical interventions to address the issues thus identified in the rows. We discuss the 10 rows of Grid 3 in the summary of Chapter 6, the chapter in which clinical interventions are discussed. Here, suffice it to say, there are specific clinical interventions for each attachment pattern, specific to the issue identified in the each of the 10 rows.

Breaking down the configuration of each pattern of attachment gives therapists a way to identify what may be happening with our patients. By naming the distinct characteristics of each pattern, therapists can locate the specific aspects of a patient's way of being and what they might be pointing to in terms of an overall pattern.

After explaining how the grids came about, and introducing each of the three grids, this chapter explains what is important about each of the 10 rows. For each row, there is a discussion of its origins in terms of development, how it manifests in patients' behavior, and how it helps therapists understand that aspect of their patients' experience.

Chapter 6. Putting the Grids to Work

Chapter 6 moves to the columns of the three grids.

The chapter begins with secure attachment and Grid 1. Understanding the configuration of secure attachment helps us establish a secure base for treatment. It also helps us to identify, and thus enables us to affirm, secure functioning when it emerges in our patients.

Next is Grid 2. When we go on to deal with the insecure attachment patterns, we compare elements of these patterns by discussing the side-by-side cells of each configuration. We look at the whole configuration of each insecure pattern and discuss what manifests in patients who come to us with their relational suffering.

We have now arrived at clinical attachment pattern–specific markers and interventions and what is schematized in Grid 3. Here, markers and interventions are matched to the distinct elements of each pattern (each row corresponds to the same row in each of the grids).

1. Patient state of mind with respect to attachment
2. a. Therapist common reactivities
2. b. Therapist metaskills to counter caregiver behavioral hallmarks and therapist reactivities
3. Goals of interventions
4. Desirable adaptive action to encourage in the patient
5. Nervous system and affect regulation
6. Working with defenses
7. Working with anxiety
8. Building affective competence
9. Working with self–other relational patterning
10. Connecting internal experience and external reality

The row × column cells give a specific guide to interventions and therapeutic aspects to aim for.

There are two very distinctive aspects of this grid to highlight.

Therapist common reactivities. In this category are common therapist reactivities, yoked to the specifics of the attachment pattern. Rather than discussing these reactivities from the point of view of personal countertransference (i.e., as reflecting the therapist's own idiosyncratic response to the patient based on their own specific attachment histories), instead we focus on reactivities that are commonly encountered given the characteristics of the attachment pattern in question. For example, if the patient is rejecting, a common reactivity would be to feel rejected. It goes without saying, though we are saying it, that of course personal history has something to do with susceptibility to reactivity. However, here we focus on common reactions that are context specific to the pattern, rather than specific to therapist vulnerabilities.

Therapist metaskills to counter caregiver behavioral hallmarks and therapist reactivities. These metaskills are qualities of presence and being, qualities that are important to cultivate. Again, their heightened usefulness is attachment pattern specific. They include metaskills like courage and kindness when working with patients with an avoidant attachment pattern, or metaskills like calm strength and a collaborative stance when working with patients with a disorganized attachment pattern.

While therapeutic presence has to always be authentic to be effective, having a readily available understanding of our reactivities evoked by particular attachment patterns and readily available solutions to the quandaries those moments pose is highly reassuring therapist support. Even if one can't always muster these qualities on a dime, knowing that these specific metaskills and corresponding qualities are something to aim for and can be cultivated is a huge source of solace.

Chapters 5 and 6 describe the grids and what they hope to accomplish.

In the next section of the book, Part IV, the application of the grids comes to life, attachment pattern by attachment pattern.

Part IV.
How to Transform Insecure and Disorganized Patterns of Attachment With Specificity and Effectiveness

In this section, we bring the grids to life, and integrate them with the theory and research we reviewed in Part I, Foundations.

There are two chapters for each attachment pattern: Chapters 7 and 8 (avoidant attachment), 9 and 10 (ambivalent/resistant), and 11 and 12 (disorganized attachment).

The first in each pair of chapters, Chapters 7, 9, and 11, addresses the origins of and characteristics of the avoidant, ambivalent/resistant, and disorganized attachment patterns, respectively. These three chapters bring together the theory and research of Chapters 1 and 2, as well as additional studies specific to the topic. The goal of each of these chapters is to help therapists understand what we are seeing in the challenging and at times befuddling responses, behaviors, and patterns of our patients, and to help us understand the origins of these responses, behaviors, and patterns. This deepened understanding increases the coherence we feel with respect to the work before us. It can also nurture empathic mindful understanding, the most powerful antidote to reactivity.

The second in each pair of chapters, Chapters 8, 10, and 12, is where we see how to use everything explored to date—theory, research, and the specifics of the grids—to show how to tailor both therapeutic presence (i.e., therapist metaskills) and therapeutic interventions to each of the 10 aspects of each attachment pattern. We take all of that attachment-specific understanding and apply it specifically to how to work with each aspect of the attachment pattern so as to transform the pattern and aim toward security.

Each chapter is rich with transcripts of clinical examples from videotaped actual therapy sessions. The clinical material is analyzed moment to moment. Discussed in detail is the aim of interventions. Specific interventions are named, as are aspects of the therapeutic stance informed by the understanding of the attachment pattern, as well as common areas of personal struggle (areas of difficulty) for the therapist. We witness how it is possible to work with ourselves in those difficult situations to restore centeredness and the capacity to hold the work as it needs to be held.

One thing to highlight: While the generic aim of the work is to heal relational trauma and transform insecurity and disorganization into security, there are more granular goals for each attachment pattern. What we see here is that we hope to cultivate and enhance specifically those aspects of affective functioning that were defensively excluded. Thus, the nature of the adaptive action tendencies that we aim to release and the specific nature of the corrective emotional experience that the experiential work aims for will be different and will look different for each attachment pattern.

Chapter 7. The Formation of Avoidant Attachment (Grid 2)

This chapter identifies the formation of the avoidant pattern and characteristics of the pattern through the lens of the Strange Situation procedure; Mary Ainsworth's Baltimore, Maryland, home observations; and features of patients' language and communication in the context of the AAI. This gives a rich tapestry of understanding of how patients with the avoidant attachment pattern present for treatment.

The avoidant attachment pattern: A deactivating strategy with respect to attachment. The roots of the avoidant attachment pattern are to be found in a caregiver's state of mind that is dismissive of attachment strivings and needs. The behavioral hallmarks of these caregivers' ways of responding to attachment beckonings feel rejecting, intrusive, and humiliating to their recipient.

There is a kind of casualness with respect to abandonment out of lack of empathy for the child's needs and experience: "If you don't come here now, I am going to get in the car and leave without you." As Grossmann and Grossmann (1991) revealed, caregivers whose children develop an avoidant attachment pattern tend to have difficulty tolerating their child's crying. It is not uncommon to hear such caregivers say, "Stop crying! Stop being such a baby," to a crying baby.

The result of being on the receiving end of such attitudes and behaviors is the development of what is called a *deactivating strategy with respect to attachment* (Cassidy & Kobak, 1988). Because the child's attachment needs and strivings are met with rejection and even humiliation, and become inextricably associated with emotional pain, the child "deactivates" their attachment needs and yearnings, which become the object of defensive exclusion. The individual focuses on (defensive) self-reliance over reliance on help from others when needed, focuses on intellect over affect, and develops defenses against relatedness. Privileging auto-regulation and the preservation of self-integrity, the individual at all costs works to avoid any situation that might activate the dreaded emotional pain, shame, and or the humiliation of rejection. Relatedness itself becomes fraught and to be avoided. Over time, the avoidant individual comes to be dismissive of attachment, manifesting a tendency to withdraw when the relational temperature rises. Thus, the label of a deactivating strategy.

Dismissiveness and its consequences. The patient's dismissiveness, particularly of relational gambits, can be hurtful as well as off-putting to their dyadic partners. For both the individual's relational partner, but also at times very much so for the therapist whose relational gambits meet with indifference or disdain, dismissiveness can create a situation that can easily induce feelings of inadequacy and rejection. Similarly, the defense of privileging intellect over emotion can make for a sometimes intimidating presentation.

We hope that presenting the origins of the pattern will help therapists better navigate the challenges of dismissing and detaching behaviors, and will help cultivate the metaskills necessary to counteract such experiences. For example, understanding how acceptance is key to offset the aftermath of rejection offers the therapist a clear path of potential engagement based in empathy. More about this in Chapter 8.

Chapter 8. Working to Transform Patterns of Avoidant Attachment (Grids 1 and 3)

This chapter combines the use of all the grids to set the stage for transforming avoidant patterns of attachment. It has an attachment-specific grid, Grid 4, which combines the configuration of the avoidant attachment pattern (from Grid 2) with the clinical markers and interventions tailored to meet this pattern (from Grid 3). In addition, we use an avoidant pattern–specific version of two of AEDP representational schemas, the *avoidant pattern–specific Triangle of Experience,* and the *avoidant pattern–specific Self–Other–Emotion* configuration. The combination of the grids with these representational schemas allows for greater precision in the selection of interventions and in assessing the impact and effectiveness of interventions. The therapist can better orient to have a sense of where they are in the transformational process and where they wish to go.

The goal of dyadic experiential processing when working to transform the avoidant attachment pattern: The release of adaptive <u>relational</u> action tendencies. Because the avoidant attachment pattern is the result of a strategy that deactivates the importance of attachment yearnings and needs, the goal of defense work is to help the patient access relational experience, and then to have the dyadic experiential processing culminate in the release of *relational* adaptive action tendencies. For our patients with histories of strategies that deactivate attachment, focusing on relational adaptive action tendencies is one of the goals of treatment to help them build connection and relatedness with others, and come to a place of greater acceptance of their own needs and vulnerabilities. Case vignettes provide illustration and discussion of treatment and interventions.

Therapist metaskills for working with patients with avoidant attachment patterns: acceptance, respect, kindness, and courage. To counter the characteristics of the caregivers of individuals who develop avoidant attachment patterns that is, rejection of and humiliation for the expression of attachment needs and strivings, the therapist metaskills of acceptance, respect, kindness, and courage, when leaned into and cultivated, can have a great impact. Being met with respect and a fundamental appreciation of who they are can be moving to a person who is used to being dismissed or criticized. Validating their defenses as having been necessary for their survival in earlier times and affirmation of them as a person can greatly help the therapeutic alliance and the patient's investment in the therapeutic process.

The dismissive state of mind, therapist common reactivities, and the respective metaskills. The essence of the avoidant pattern constitutes a dismissive state of mind with respect to attachment and emotion, especially in the context of relatedness, and a distinct preference for linearity and logic over emotional engagement. It is not uncommon for an avoidant individual to respond dismissively to the therapist's relational invitations. Combine this dismissiveness with a privileging of intellect over emotion and of logic over empathy, and the patient can come across as arrogant or intimidating, which can lead the therapist to feel inadequate or foolish.

Knowing that the avoidant pattern–specific metaskills are kindness, courage, and acceptance can help the therapist be brave. Rather than letting the feelings of inadequacy drive an unwitting withdrawal from the patient, the therapist can seek to lean into those metaskills to recenter. Interventions that express acceptance of the patient and that focus on what the patient is doing well rather than on what they are missing or messing up can be powerful ways of disarming defenses and helping patients develop more comfort in the relational arena.

Corrective emotional experience: relational engagement with others and with self. Metaskills also demonstrate what constitutes a corrective emotional experience in the context of work to transform the avoidant attachment pattern. We want to restore that which was interfered with by the need for defensive exclusion. Given the deactivation strategy of the avoidant attachment pattern, the goal here is to help patients have good experiences of relational connection. We aim toward helping patients cultivate connections with important others, and also connection with their own self. As patients become able to feel empathy and compassion for themselves and their needs and yearnings, the capacity to feel empathy for and tolerate the pain of others without shutting down increases, and complex relational experience can be more readily engaged.

The case examples of Chapter 8 demonstrate the application of metaskills in different situations. The precision of the grids allows us to understand what interventions are best suited to the specific challenges of the avoidant attachment pattern and the corrective experiences we seek to foster.

Chapter 9. The Formation of Ambivalent/
Resistant Attachment (Grid 2)

The ambivalent/resistant attachment pattern: a hyperactivating strategy with respect to attachment. If the avoidant attachment pattern is the result of strategies that deactivate the attachment system, the ambivalent/resistant attachment pattern is the result of a *hyperactivating strategy with respect to attachment.* It is a way of managing the anxieties stirred up by caregivers who tend to be preoccupied and inattentive. The leading behavioral hallmark of their caregivers is preoccupation with self and inconsistency in their responses to the child's attachment needs. Responsiveness is hit or miss: the child doesn't know what to expect. Children with this attachment pattern heighten their attachment responses by crying, protesting, and/or being angry. Even when the caregiver is present and holding them, they are hard to soothe. In desperation, the heightening strategy is instituted to maximize the likelihood of getting a response. However, even when a response comes, the clamoring for attention continues. For those manifesting an ambivalent/resistant attachment pattern, the focus is almost exclusively on the other, at the expense of self and exploration.

Preoccupation (with the other) as a defense against genuine relatedness: emotionality as a defense against genuine emotion. Patients with the ambivalent/resistant attachment style present as highly emotional people with a relentless preoccupation with relationship. However, a closer look indicates that what we are witnessing is emotionality as a result of the hyperactivation strategy, and not the experience and expression of genuine emotion. The emotionality actually functions as a defense against emotional experience. The presentation is one of dysregulation, overwhelm, agitation, and failure to self-soothe or regulate. At the same time, there is a pressure and a heightened preoccupation with relationship. The focus is on the other and not on self experience. However the focus on the other, a sense that is never satisfied, functions as a defense against genuine relational experience.

Preoccupation, emotionality, and their consequences. The patient's preoccupation and high anxiety lead to a presentation marked by an often dysregulated, pressured, and frantic or desperate quality. There is a wall of words and a wall of emotionality. Much as connection is desperately desired, patients with ambivalent/resistant attachment often make it hard for the therapist to intervene. There is pressure to help, but no room to do so. The patient's preoccupation and desperation can be overwhelming to their dyadic partners: both for the individual's relational partner and at times very much so for the patient's therapist, who find it hard to intervene and feel effective.

This chapter explores the formation of ambivalent/resistant attachment and characteristics of the pattern through first looking at children's behavior in the Strange Situation procedure (corresponding with the Baltimore home observations and the AAI), and then how patients present in psychotherapy. We hope that showing the origins of the pattern will help therapists find ways to be of help when patients present with preoccupation and the kind of heightened anxiety and pressure for relief that develops when a person hasn't been able to rely on a contingent caregiving response.

Chapter 10. Working to Transform Patterns of Ambivalent/Resistant Attachment (Grids 1 & 3)

This chapter combines the use of all the grids to set the stage for transforming the ambivalent/resistant patterns of attachment. It too has an attachment-specific grid, Grid 5, which combines the configuration of the ambivalent/resistant attachment pattern (from Grid 2) with the clinical interventions tailored to meet this pattern (from Grid 3). In addition, we use an ambivalent/resistant pattern–specific version of two AEDP representational schemas: the ambivalent/resistant pattern–specific *Triangle of Experience* and the ambivalent/resistant pattern–specific *Self–Other–Emotion Triangle*.

The goal of dyadic experiential processing of the ambivalent/resistant attachment pattern: increase in self-regulation and the release of adaptive self action tendencies. Because the ambivalent/resistant attachment pattern is the result of a strategy that hyperactivates attachment yearnings and needs at the expense of self-regulation, self, self-development, and exploration, the goal of defense work with this attachment pattern is to cultivate access to self experience and to increase self-regulation, so as to eventually be able to access genuine emotion and genuine relatedness. One of the goals of treatment is the focus on adaptive *self* action tendencies, helping patients to develop their capacities to listen inside, to care and trust themselves, and to develop self-confidence and self-agency. We look at defensive strategies: how emotionality is a defense against emotion and how relational preoccupation is a defense against relatedness.

Therapist metaskills for working with patients with ambivalent/resistant attachment patterns: focus, firmness, directiveness, and care. To counter the preoccupied, self-involved, and inconsistent characteristics of the caregivers of individuals who develop ambivalent/resistant attachment patterns, the therapist metaskills of *focus, firmness, directiveness, and care,* when leaned into and cultivated, can have a great impact. In essence, with empathy, attunement, and care, therapists take the lead in co-constructing some structure and introducing some organization, thus stepping into their role as attachment figures. Here, the importance of attuned directiveness and firmness cannot be overstated.

The preoccupied state of mind, common reactivities, and the respective therapist metaskills. The patient's high anxiety, pressure, and preoccupation often leads therapists to become overwhelmed and feel ineffective. Also, because emotionality is not emotion, another common reactivity is that therapists might feel unaffected and then guilty for not feeling more empathic toward the patient's distress. The metaskills of directness and kind firmness allow the therapist to lead and structure, but do so with care and attunement. This experience is, in essence, having a responsible attachment figure who does not abdicate the focus on the patient and on what the patient needs. It can greatly help these patients' anxiety regulation.

Corrective emotional experience: the emergence of self experience on behalf of the self— agency, initiative, and genuine self-reliance. Having sacrificed exploring for being afraid to miss an opportunity for connection, the goal of the dyadic experiential work is to help patients access their own internal experience of emotions and relational experiences. The result of these interventions is a greater capacity for self-regulation, and with time, the corrective experience of attuning to self and enjoying the fruits of greater self-reliance, initiative, and agency on behalf of the self. With these capacities on board, relationships have the potential to stabilize and relational work can be fruitful.

The case vignettes in this chapter illustrate treatment and interventions, include discussions of therapist common reactivities, and therapist metaskills we can call upon to rebalance ourselves when working with patients with an ambivalent/resistant attachment pattern. They demonstrate how to take the lead and yet be available to help the patient in a bottom-up exploration to gain access to and process core affective experiences, including self and genuine relational experiences.

Chapter 11. The History of the Disorganization Category (Grid 2)

Strategies with respect to attachment needs and yearnings shaped the avoid-ant and ambivalent/resistant patterns: deactivation and hyperactivation, respectively (Chapters 7 and 9). However, here, when we are in the realm of disorganized attachment and parental unresolved trauma, *failure of strategy* is the operative descriptor. The term "fright without solution" (Hesse & Main, 1999, p. 484), and our recently coined term "attachment without solution" (Fosha, this volume), capture that essence. In response to their children's adaptive attachment strivings, caregivers who are unresolved for trauma respond in ways that are either frightening or frightened (both of which are scary for the child, the latter because it's confusing). When the person who is supposed to protect you from danger is one and the same person who is scaring you, there is no solution: There is no solution to either your fear or to your attachment needs. That is the quandary of the children for whom this category was created, a quandary that continues to operate for the adults with this history when they come to us seeking treatment.

The concept of *disorganized attachment* arose by default. Initially these were the children in Ainsworth's samples in the United States who could not fit into any of the three existing classifications of secure, avoidant, or ambiva-lent/resistant. These "uncategorizable" children became the focus of Mary Main's studies.

This chapter traces the development of the concept of *disorganized attach-ment*. It also describes the profoundly evocative behavioral characteristics of the children and summarizes studies with both older children and adults who present with disorganized attachment patterns. As the children man-ifesting the initially paralyzing clash of contradictory action tendencies grow up, they eventually develop some strategies to deal with the early failure of strategy. Thus, the subtitle of both chapters on disorganization: "The Collapse of Strategy and the Strategy of Collapse."

To broaden our understanding of disorganized attachment, we present the face-to-face interaction studies of Beebe et al. (2014, 2016) and also bring in Karlen Lyons-Ruth's (2006) invaluable longitudinal research illu-minating the nature of disrupted parental communications of the caregivers of children demonstrating disorganized attachment.

The disorganized attachment pattern: the collapse of strategy and the strategy of col-lapse. Whether the disorganized pattern is pervasive, or whether it surfaces under stress, we are in the realm of the patient's trauma and dissociation:

fragmentation, freeze, fear, disorientation/confusion, fragments of intense affect, uncollaborative parts, disordered thinking, and incomplete expressions. We also witness defensive experiences of disconnection: spacing out, numbing out, and the light going out of the eyes. This is the phenomenology of disorganization.

The strategy of collapse: anger, caregiving, and controlling as defenses against emotion and relatedness. As we've learned from the longitudinal studies of Main et al. (2005), Lyons-Ruth, and others, by the time children of parents with unresolved trauma reach the age of 6, we encounter two main types of defensive strategies: in addition to collapse as a strategy, we encounter controlling strategies either through being angry/threatening or through role reversal and caregiving. Clearly these are challenging clinical situations for the clinician, requiring skillful intervention and metaskills galore. We review these strategies in the next chapter.

Chapter 12. Working to Transform Patterns of Disorganized Attachment (Grids 1 & 3)

Again, we bring in three grids to help us organize what's happening with patients who manifest disorganized attachment. And we introduce a disorganized attachment–specific grid, Grid 6, that combines patterns of disorganized attachment (from Grid 2) and interventions tailored accordingly (from Grid 3).

The unresolved/fearful/frightening state of mind and common therapist reactivities. The patient's disorganization and inconsistent presentation, be it from moment-to-moment or from session to session, presents challenges for the therapist. So can the strategy of angry/threatening means of trying to exert relational control. And in a different way, the exertion of control through role reversal and caregiving can also be quite disorienting. While different presentations of the unresolved, fearful, and/or frightening state of mind can evoke different common therapist reactivities, these reactivities usually involve confusion, worry, a loss of one's footing, and in a parallel process to the patient's formative developmental experiences, a paralysis due to contradictory feelings, intensions, and incompatible action tendencies.

Therapist metaskills for working with patients with disorganized attachment: reliable/ constant, boundaried, calm strength, and collaborative. Whether the caregivers of patients now presenting with the disorganized attachment pattern were frightened and/or frightening, these patients had little experience of competent consistent caregiving by an attachment figure. Most lacking were experiences of kind, respectful, boundaried, role-appropriate communication and collaboration. The therapist's embodying of affective competence with respect to the patient's disorganization and working to hold the therapeutic frame with coherence and kindness counteracts the chaos of earlier life. The metaskills of being *reliable, boundaried, constant, collaborative, and having calm strength* can contribute to the patient's experience of safety, and over time, of being in good steady hands.

The cultivation of these metaskills, grounded in the understanding of the origins of the patient's phenomenology and dynamics, can also go a long way toward helping therapists deal with these common reactivities. Cultivating these metaskills will make more likely the operation of an adaptive feedback loop, rather than a nonproductive one. A feedback loop where the patient's fearful and/or frightening presentation destabilizes the therapist who in turn, becomes momentarily, or for even longer duration, confused or frozen, which of course only contributes to escalate the patient's anxiety and sense of unsafety, is one we wish to counter. Through the cultivation of the metaskills of being reliable/boundaried, constant, collaborative, and having calm strength we hope to bring a different, more productive feedback loop online. Without needing to know more than we know, the therapist's embodying a calm, reliable presence, with coherence and honesty and bids for collaboration can, in turn, help steady the patient, signaling to them that the relational environment being co-created is different, and safer, than the one(s) encountered earlier in their lives.

The goal of dyadic experiential processing of the disorganized attachment pattern: increase in internal security and collaboration (between parts), increase in relational security and collaboration, and the release of adaptive action tendencies of emotion, relatedness, and self experience. As any and all areas of function and experience can be at risk in the disorganized attachment pattern, for any given patient, the experience processed to completion of any and all core affective experiences and their intrinsic adaptive action tendencies can constitute a corrective experience. However, given the invariable fragmentation and/or dissociation between parts that is common with disorganized attachment patterns, the experience of kind, mutually respectful collaboration, both relationally and intrarelationally, as well as the development of internal security, are corrective experiences of major import.

To summarize: In this chapter, we identify all of the categories of adaptive action, self, relational, and categorical emotion action tendencies for the goals of interventions to help patients build trust in self and other as part of the process of healing disorganized attachment. We look at how what once was a collapse of strategy in children has often grown into defensive strategies by adulthood. Defenses against emotion through the use of dissociation, fragmentation, and numbness. Defenses against relatedness through caregiving and controlling, threatening, or collapsing. We use case vignettes to illustrate treatment and interventions designed to counteract the impacts of disrupted and disordered attachment. We identify common therapist reactivities that get triggered. We also detail therapist metaskills we can draw on to help.

Epilogue

The book ends with a few brief riffs on why we love our patients.

One Last Thing: Who Did What

Karen Pando-Mars & Diana Fosha

Detailing the specifics of each attachment pattern (in terms of affect regulation, caregiver state of mind, characteristic defenses, and characteristic fears) and then tailoring interventions to the specifics of each attachment pattern has been the focus of the work of Karen Pando-Mars for the last decade. Karen gave birth to the grids, nurtured their development, and explored the implication for their application to therapeutic interventions aimed at change and rewiring. All the case examples in the book are hers. In addition, uplifting the importance of Mary Ainsworth's contributions to attachment theory and research is also the result of Karen's deep dive into Ainsworth's work. Pando-Mars's contribution of the grids and the tailoring of clinical interventions to attachment patterns is a major contribution to AEPD theory and practice.

Diana Fosha gave birth to AEDP in 2000 (Fosha, 2000b). Ever since, along with her brilliant and soulful AEDP colleagues, Fosha has been nurturing the growth, expansion, and ever-evolving development of AEDP as a living emergent transformational theory, experiential practice, and detailed phenomenology of transformation (2021b).

This book is a labor of love and collaboration, as well as separation–individuation.

The main chapters of this book were written by Karen Pando-Mars, with substantive input and contributions from Diana Fosha over their many drafts and rewritings. Chapter 3, on AEDP, is the writing of Pando-Mars. The preface, and this trajectory, were written by Fosha, with input from Pando-Mars.

Tailoring Treatment to Attachment Patterns

PART I

FOUNDATIONS

1

The Move to Attachment & Representation

The young child's hunger for his mother's love and presence is as great as his hunger for food, and that in consequence her absence inevitably generates a powerful sense of loss and anger.
—(BOWLBY, 1969/1982, P. XXIX)

Preamble to Chapter 1

Read what follows in this chapter knowing that here are the foundations for what this book is about. Get a granular understanding of how basic attachment theory and research have an enormous amount to contribute to helping us be better therapists to our patients. Concepts like "secure base," "safe haven," "maternal sensitivity and responsiveness to infant signals," and "defenses arising to compensate for insecure caregiving" are central to the development of attachment patterns and their eventual (if needed) rewiring. Key concepts of what we develop in later chapters have their origins in what is presented historically in this chapter.

What we now take for granted were revolutionary discoveries that took some time to be accepted, much less become part of the mainstream.

Read what follows in this chapter with an eye toward your own work with your patients.

Introduction to Chapter 1

Psychotherapists must be natural observers of our patients, much like Mary Ainsworth and John Bowlby began their study of attachment as natural observers through a relational lens of genuine dyadic engagement. We come to know our patients on a relational level through our connection to them as we pick up their nonverbal signals of communication and notice how they appear. We notice what does and does not happen in our patients, and within ourselves, in the present moment. We attend to what goes on between us and how this conditions our relational environment for psychotherapy. We recognize how collective forces outside of the room affect all of us and show up in how our patients, as well as ourselves, perceive safety and danger. And we do so with care. In order to identify and respond to our patients with the most attuned and insightful care, deep understanding and attentive presence is required.

The arrival of attachment theory and its wise recognition of the importance of the interactive connection between infants and caregivers throughout development (i.e., "from the cradle to the grave", Bowlby, 1979, p. 153) provides insight into not only how human beings grow and develop but has brought profound understandings about our first relationships that have changed the field of psychotherapy. While John Bowlby is clearly recognized as the father of attachment theory, Mary D. Salter Ainsworth's role is less well-known. Ainsworth was a partner and true other[1] to Bowlby. Her pioneering research was just what was needed at that moment in time for attachment theory to become fully recognized. In addition, in her own right, Ainsworth's contributions were groundbreaking and phenomenal. "Phenomenal" not only as an adjective, though that too, but phenomenal because of the cascade of observation and research on development that elaborated and provided empirical evidence for Bowlby's groundbreaking, integrative theory that continues to this day, and also because of her rigorous dedication to phenomena itself through her original, naturalistic observational studies.

This chapter features highlights from the trajectory of each of their lives and work, at first parallel and then deeply intertwined. Psychotherapists benefit from their research and all that their work sets in motion—and we will get to the substantial contributions from each of them—but first a short homage to trace the origins of attachment theory. John Bowlby's and Mary Ainsworth's dedication to understanding the nature of love and attachment evolved into a revolutionary field of study, still captivating followers and expanding research, now spanning over eight decades. How Bowlby and Ainsworth came to know what they know through deep observation and inquiry, far-reaching collaborations, persistence, and commitment, is inspiring.

Attachment theory provides a foundation for the work of psychotherapy. In addition to what it has to offer about raising secure and insecure children and key features of development, and how it came into a field of its own, it sheds light on the ways of discovery and meaning making, which are also instrumental for psychotherapists on the front lines of helping people to heal and transform.

Part 1: Bowlby & Ainsworth and the Growth of Attachment Theory

Bowlby's Beginnings: Early Life Experiences Are Key to a Child's Development

From his early days, Bowlby was dedicated to understanding how early life experiences and actual events were key to a child's development. He recognized the profound impact of maternal separation, deprivation, and loss on children's adjustment and mental health. He looked at how the child developed affectional ties with their mother/caregiver. His search to understand the origins of this relationship led to the development of attachment theory.

After completing his undergraduate degree at the University of Cambridge in 1928, where he studied what is now known as developmental psychology, Bowlby worked as a volunteer in a residential school for maladjusted children. He was struck by two children in particular. We include this history because it demonstrates Bowlby's attention to the significant characteristics of two boys, and how he was moved to understand what would motivate their behaviors. One, a teenager, was quite isolated, remote, and affectionless. He was expelled from a previous school for theft, and the major note about him was that he had never experienced a stable relationship with a mother figure.

The other younger boy was about 7 or 8, quite anxious and followed Bowlby like a shadow (Ainsworth & Bowlby, 1991). These boys influenced Bowlby's decision to specialize in child psychiatry and psychotherapy. Bowlby was drawn to investigate how the actual events of a child's life differentially impacted the child's personality development. He recognized that the parents were influenced by their early experiences with their own parents.

Right here, we see the seeds of attachment theory.

At the London Child Guidance Clinic, Bowlby began systematic research comparing a group of 44 juvenile thieves and a control group to study his hunch about the impact of prolonged maternal separation and/or deprivation. In 1944, this landmark research was published as "Forty-Four Juvenile Thieves." He found that prolonged experiences of mother–child separation or deprivation of maternal care were much more common among the thieves than in the control group, and that such experiences were especially linked to children diagnosed as affectionless (Ainsworth & Bowlby, 1991; Bowlby, 1944). With this publication he launched what would evolve over decades to become the deep roots of attachment theory.

Bowlby's view departed from the prevailing attitudes of the psychoanalytic community at that time. Overall, Freud and other psychoanalysts recognized the importance of a child's first relationships as formative of their personality. However, their way of understanding these relationships was based on the adult's current behavior and mental life, and from there they looked retrospectively through memory and fantasy to gather theories about the nature of their problems (Bowlby, 1969/1982). Bowlby's insistence to look at the child's actual experience in the present, while the child was still a child, was revolutionary. Even more radical was his turn toward ethology, the study of animal behavior. He sought to identify signals and behavioral repertoires of animals to understand the evolutionary foundations of the social aspects of attachment bonding, which influenced the development of attachment theory.

Ainsworth's Beginnings: A Secure Base Is Key to Developing Independence and Confidence

While "secure base" has become a common term in the attachment-informed parlance of psychotherapists, few know that its originator is Ainsworth, and not Bowlby, as commonly assumed. Bowlby adopted the term, but Ainsworth originated it.

In 1940, 10 years before she met John Bowlby, Mary Ainsworth wrote her dissertation on William Blatz's (1966) security theory. The basis of Blatz's security theory was that first, in infancy and early childhood, individuals need to have a secure dependency with their parents in order to develop the courage and skills necessary to leave their familiar home. Ainsworth's (Salter, 1940) dissertation explored that theme and concluded that when children have a secure base with their parents, they have more ease in developing the independence and confidence to venture out into the greater world.

Patterns. Mary Salter Ainsworth's dissertation was entitled "An Evaluation of Adjustment Based on the Concept of Security" (Salter, 1940). Given that there were no approved quantitative techniques she could apply to this study for her dissertation research, Ainsworth developed two self-report scales to assess an individual's security or insecurity. The first scale related to the parents; the second related to the friends. Although she and her mentor, Professor Chant, were unable to quantify her results, she nevertheless did see the same pattern of scores per person across both of her two scales. The scales discerned how much of a person's security rested on immature or mature patterning and whether there was a "pseudo security based on defense mechanisms." Most important were her findings, "that where familial security is lacking, the individual is handicapped by the lack of what might be called a *secure base* [emphasis added] from which to work" (p. 45).

When she was conceptualizing adult adjustment in terms of security, Ainsworth identified the immature or mature pattern. She documented that "the *pattern* [emphasis added] of adjustment (over domain) is more significant for the understanding of the individual than any single measurement or any total score" (Salter, 1940, p. 13). In Ainsworth's (1983) autobiographical essay she says this "blew her mind." As she herself reflected, she had been "searching for and finding patterns in my research ever since!" (p. 4).

When Ainsworth joined Bowlby's research team at the Tavistock clinic in London in 1950, she was intrigued by Bowlby's quest to understand the adverse effects on development and the child's distress that resulted from prolonged separations from their parents. While initially Ainsworth expressed concern and unease with Bowlby's turn toward evolutionary theory and ethology, nonetheless she was riveted by naturalistic observation and data collection.

Once she began her research into infant care and observed mothers with their babies in Uganda, Ainsworth saw with her own eyes how much ethology had to offer as a framework. Through her observations, she saw human babies and children use their mothers as a secure base to explore their surroundings, much as other mammals did.

The Beginnings of Attachment Theory: Bowlby and Ainsworth Converge

Signals. In his pivotal article introducing attachment theory, the first of three, "The Nature of the Child's Tie to His Mother," Bowlby (1958) drew from his studies in ethology to posit that five instinctual signal behaviors were formative of a child's attachment. He saw crying, sucking, following, smiling, and clinging as *instinctual responses* whose function helped to promote proximity to a parent and to evoke responses that required caregiving activity. He identified that these instinctual responses both activate and terminate: The baby's state activates their crying, which initially draws the mother and the mother's caregiving response terminates it. The completion of this unit of interaction results in an emotional state that is particular to each behavior. For instance, when the cry of distress brings soothing, the resulting emotional state is contentment. Or, as Bowlby notes, "a baby's smile is a social releaser of maternal behavior," which he furthers by describing "a baby's smile beguiles and enslaves their mothers!" (p. 368). Smiling evokes connection, encouragement, and care. Crying calls for comfort, for safety. This response system demonstrates how the growth of love between the caregiver and the child developed—to meet an emotional need brings a feeling of calm and gives rise to ties of affection. He argued against the *cupboard theory of love*, the prevailing views of learning theory, which based the child's bond to their mother on her gratification of the child's basic physical needs, like hunger. In contrast, Bowlby proposed that these instinctual responses extended beyond feeding the child into a more expanded provision of care for their emotional well-being and survival.

After its publication, Bowlby sent this article to Ainsworth. One can imagine her eyes lingering over the places in the article where Bowlby was woeful about the inadequacy of studies of human infants, and the fact that some of his hypotheses remained untested. In my mind's eye I envision that Ainsworth was eagerly surmising his questions as he began to examine these instinctual behaviors of infants in their first year of life. He defined sucking, clinging, following, smiling, and crying as five of these specific attachment-inducing behaviors. Picture Mary Ainsworth remembering the infants and mothers she was observing in Uganda, and remembering the interview questions she asked the mothers specifically about these behaviors: "Why do you think the baby cries?" and "What do you do when the baby cries?" She was interested not only in what was occurring with the baby but in how the mother understood and responded to the baby. And I can feel my own heart beating with excitement for the interactive potential of the conversation that was about to take place between Bowlby and Ainsworth in 1959, after he sent this article to her.

Now this is history!

A meeting did occur between Bowlby and Ainsworth around this time, which sparked a renewed dialogue and furthered their development into collaborators and colleagues. They held ongoing conversations and communications by letter over decades, supporting each other and providing each other with a safe haven and a secure base, as they established their evolutionary ethological orientation to attachment theory (Ainsworth & Bowlby, 1991). Ainsworth's mother–infant observational studies, first in Uganda and then in Baltimore, Maryland, led her to develop empirical methods for testing some of Bowlby's theories about attachment. Through her detailed observations and methodological research, she recognized individual differences in attachment behavior and expanded the theory itself by developing a way to classify these behaviors. Her contributions to attachment theory also included the concept of the *attachment figure as secure base for the child's exploratory behavior* and the formulation of *maternal sensitivity and responsiveness to infant signals as central to the development of attachment patterns* (Bretherton, 1992, 2003).

Patterns, Impressions, and Conjectures From the Uganda Study: The Early Recognition of Individual Differences

Attachment does not develop willy-nilly according to some inner, genetic, regulating mechanism, but rather is influenced by conditions in the baby's environment. (Ainsworth, 1967, p. 387)

How does attachment develop? Bowlby named five instinctual attachment-evoking response behaviors. How did these five instinctual response behaviors come into view in what Ainsworth observed between the babies and their mothers? What happened when the baby was separated from the mother became one of the events through which to observe the difference between a lack of discrimination and the development of the differential response, when babies started to prefer their own mothers. In their earliest weeks of life, the baby could be taken from their mother's arms and given to someone else without showing signs of distress nor disturbance. And yet over the course of the first year, the baby started showing an increased preference for their mother. After which, the baby showed distress when separated from their mother. When the babies were differential in their crying, they soothed when given to their mother or they protested when separated from her. Questions about the meaning of distress arose. At what age and stage is the occurrence of crying more pronounced when the child is separated from the mother? Is distress upon separation a signal of attachment behavior? Ainsworth searched to understand what factors facilitate, delay, or prevent the development of attachment.

Throughout the course of the Ganda[2] study, Ainsworth saw how mothering goes beyond the giving of routine care to ensure the baby is fed, clean, warm, dry, and safe. Optimally, mothering involves more, especially in the emotional realm. How the mother handles the baby, the way she holds and carries them, the quantity of physical contact, the sharing of mothering duties, and the mother's response to the baby's emotional states—these all set the conditions that influence the interaction between the mother and child. Studying these interactions led Ainsworth (1967) to hypothesize "that it is through these responses that the infant develops his attachment and that the responses serve to mediate his attachment once it is formed" (p. 332).

Here is the basis for her comment, "Attachment does not develop willy-nilly according to some inner, genetic, regulating mechanism, but rather is influenced by conditions in the baby's environment" (Ainsworth, 1967, p. 387). Noticing individual differences between infants led her to study the variable conditions at play during their interactions with their mothers. She saw firsthand how the mother's way of being with her baby influenced the baby's internal sense of security or insecurity. She recognized that the development of attachment is the result of an interactional process between constitutional elements of each baby and their mother's infant-care practices. She classified the infants into three categories: the securely attached group (16 children), the insecurely attached group (7 children), and the "nonattached" group (5 children). She referred to this latter group in quotations with a caveat that this group was "not yet" attached. This will eventually become an approximation of the avoidant category. Ultimately, this beginning of Ainsworth's classification system was systematically validated in the Strange Situation Protocol (SSP: see below for a description of the SSP).

Ainsworth (1967) made the following impressions and conjectures from this study:

1. *Instinctual behaviors, not drives, are what constitute attachment behaviors.* Here, we see the results of Ainsworth's "volte-face," her turnabout, as she herself changed her view. Through the Uganda study, she was convinced that interaction and feedback leads to the growth of attachment and not primarily the satisfaction of the drives for food, warmth, and comfort.

2. *From mother—infant interdependence, independence emerges.* This development has a dual basis that is composed of the competence of the infant and encouragement on the part of the mother. She noted again and

again how the secure child moves out and away from the mother to explore, comes back to the mother for comfort or safety, and keeps track of the mother's whereabouts. Here, the interactive nature between the child's capacity to make use of the mother as a secure base from which to explore, and a safe haven to return to for comfort and care, is crystal clear.

3. *Individual differences in the methods of infant care are related to differences in the babies' development of attachment.* Three main variables in infant care stood out to be statistically significant in the study. The first was the amount of care provided by the mother. This had to do with the mother's availability, providing both accessibility through which to be sensitive to the child's signals and opportunities for interaction. When the mother is attuned to the baby's state and mood, and her response is well-timed, their interactions are marked by mutual delight. Second was the mother's excellence as an informant. This in essence is the mother's reflective self-function (Fonagy et al., 1991b) or capacity for mentalization (Fonagy et al., 2002): It refers to how interested the mother is in the baby, whether she is free enough of her own insecure preoccupations to be perceptive about how the child expresses their needs, wishes, and preferences, and how she takes pleasure in sharing about the baby and wants to volunteer information about them. Third was the mother's attitude toward breastfeeding. This bears on the importance of positively toned mother–baby interactions. Fourteen out of the 16 mothers of securely attached babies reported without qualification to enjoy breastfeeding, and 12 of the babies showed signs of positive interactions around feeding with their mothers. There was a sense that while this had to do with the pleasure of breastfeeding itself, this also indicated the mother's and baby's overall enjoyment with each other.

Is Attachment Behavior an Active or a Passive Process?

Questions about development and attachment, and notions of gratification and childhood dependency were brewing during these early days. Bowlby (1979) took the stance that attachment is an active and lifelong process and contrasted it with the theoretical conception that childhood dependency is passive, and in later years is regressive and undesirable. He saw attachment behavior as a necessary part of the biological equipment to ensure survival, not only in childhood but throughout life. hence, the much-quoted phrase "from the cradle to the grave" (p. 153). In direct contrast to Freud's notion of the infant as a passive recipient, and aligned with the views of Bowlby, Ainsworth also saw the baby as an *active participant* in the attachment relationship:

> She was impressed by the babies' active search for contact with the mother when they were alarmed or hurt, when she moved away or left even briefly, and when they were hungry—and even then, she was struck by their initiative in seeking the breast and managing the feeding. (Ainsworth & Bowlby, 1991, p. 339)

Further evolving the ideas proposed in her dissertation about security theory and continuing to develop her ideas after the Ganda study, Ainsworth gathered evidence about the interrelationship between dependency and interdependence and the significance of the *secure base*, which turns out to be one of the most salient features of the attachment relationship, and crucial to the work that is the topic of this book.

Attachment Theory Is Launched, 1958–1963

After the publication of "The Nature of the Child's Tie to His Mother," Bowlby (1958) visited Ainsworth in Baltimore in 1959, and they discussed his emergent attachment theory and her discoveries from the Ganda study. He invited her to participate in the Tavistock Mother–Infant Interaction Study Group that met biannually. There, she presented her findings of the Ganda study to this interdisciplinary, international study group. Renewed with enthusiasm for developmental research, and now with the support of her department at Johns Hopkins, she began the second longitudinal study with middle-class American mothers and their infants in Baltimore in 1962–1963.

Based on her empirical observational studies in Uganda, in this second endeavor, Ainsworth was prepared to target the research with more-focused questions. She established guidelines for observers to notate specific infant attachment behaviors, the situations in which they might appear, and the mother's response to them. Ainsworth's preliminary field research from the Ganda study, ongoing conversations with Bowlby as he was involved in writing his first book about attachment, and students who were participating in her research helped her to refine the scope of the Baltimore study. While the Baltimore study was underway, she continued to examine the material from her Ganda findings. She published the results of this first empirical research in attachment in *Infancy in Uganda* in 1967. Unfortunately, this amazingly impressive book is out of print, and it is woefully hard to find.

Ainsworth also encouraged many of her students at Johns Hopkins to begin their own dissertation research in the field of attachment. "She was generous and demanding . . . a combination that produced an exceptionally productive group of students: Mary Blehar, Inge Bretherton, Jude Cassidy, Virginia Colin, Roger Kobak, Mary Main, Robert Marvin, Everett Waters, Sally Wall, and Patricia Crittenden. . . . " (Crittenden, 2017, p. 7), to name a few.

Ainsworth's Baltimore Study: Observations in the United States

The Baltimore study is unsurpassed for the thoroughness and specificity it captured about mother and infant interactions. Again, this study was built around naturalistic observation. There was less emphasis on verbal interview and instead the focus was on direct observation, through regularly scheduled home visits that were consistent across the sample of 26 participating families. Taking place in a Western industrialized society, with the referrals from pediatricians, Ainsworth was able to build the sample and standardize the protocol. Families were recruited before birth and were observed beginning in the first month and ending at 54 weeks. Each visit lasted 4 hours and continued every 2 weeks throughout the course of the study.

Data of the mother–infant pairs were compiled during each quarter of the first year of life. Detailed notes about the mother–infant interactions were collected and examined to explore what happened in the earlier quarters that may have influenced infant behaviors in the later quarters. For instance, the babies who were picked up when they were crying and soothed in the first quarter showed fewer bouts of crying in the fourth quarter. Ainsworth noticed it was not the *amount of time* the mother held the baby but the *way she held* the baby that settled them. She soothed them enough that when they were put down, they rather automatically crawled off to explore. Babies who were picked up with care and tenderness tended to soothe readily, while babies who were handled gruffly and with impatience were more inclined to be fussy and cling when put down. Rather than studying the growth of attachment per se, Ainsworth was observing specific components of the child's attachment behavior in the fourth quarter: their frequency of crying and whether they used their mother as a secure base. She was looking at what these interactive behaviors indicated about the mother's caregiving and how this affected the outcome of a child's security or insecurity. We address the specifics of Ainsworth's findings as relates to the development of the insecure patterns in Chapter 7, "The Formation of Avoidant Attachment," and Chapter 9, "The Formation of Ambivalent/Resistant Attachment."

Meanwhile, Bowlby was in the process of incorporating control systems theory into his development of attachment theory. Control systems theory was based on principles of regulation and uses terms like "fixed action patterns," "predictable outcomes," and "set goals" to identify adaptive, goal-directed behavioral interactions between humans and their environment. A systemic view was useful to conceptualize attachment. Bowlby realized the biological existence of an attachment behavioral system, having one of its set goals to be proximity to the attachment figure. He saw how this began with the early instinctual behavioral patterns he described in his first publication (1958) but recognized that these patterns and goals become increasingly more complex as the child grows and develops. He also identified the reciprocal, innate process in the mother, which he called the caregiving behavioral system. During the Baltimore study, Ainsworth was examining characteristics of the mother's responsiveness to her child, which we can now identify as vivid displays of the caregiving behavioral system in action.

The Maternal Caregiving and Interaction Scales

Ainsworth (1978/2015) developed the Maternal Caregiving and Interaction Scales to define and measure observable behaviors and interactive sequences between mothers and their infants during the home visits in the Baltimore study. These scales were originally passed around as mimeographed (paper copies) worksheets, and it wasn't until the book *Patterns of Attachment* (Ainsworth et al., 1978) was reissued in 2015 that these highly significant scales were included in the addendum. While many attachment-informed psychotherapists recognize that sensitivity and responsiveness are caregiver qualities associated with secure attachment, few may actually know that they were originally part of the scales used during the Baltimore home observations. Therefore, we are excited to introduce them.

Through the Ganda study, Ainsworth observed how the mother's excellence as an informant revealed her attitudes about caregiving, which were reflected in her behaviors toward and with her children. Here, in the

Baltimore study, the caregiving behaviors echoed what was seen in Ganda, but the scales captured what was observed at a more granular level. They capture what specifically takes place and how it plays out. Given that the study was conducted with mothers and infants, to be true to the historical reference, the caregiver is referred to as the mother. However, in the 21st century with an increased awareness of gender fluidity and same-gendered parents, as well as adoptive and foster parents, we say caregiver and infant dyads. We hope you'll accept the usage of the term "mother" here as an attempt to be true to reporting the results of Ainsworth's study. In later sections of the book, when we explore the broader applications of these findings, we shift to the term "caregiver."[3]

The Maternal Caregiving and Interaction Scales comprise four scales. Each scale defines how the mother interacts with her child with insightful detail, which is rated numerically between 0 and 10. Observers look for signals of the child's instinctive behavior and the manner and perceptiveness of the mother's response. The first scale measures the mother's sensitivity vs. insensitivity to the baby's signals. The second scale measures the mother's cooperation vs. interference with the baby's ongoing behavior. The third scale measures the mother's physical and psychological availability vs. ignoring and neglecting. The fourth scale measures the mother's acceptance vs. rejection of the baby's needs.

While Ainsworth's scales were originally developed to provide quantitative measures to characterize what builds secure and insecure attachment, they are meaningful for psychotherapists. Specifically, they highlight explicit attachment and caregiving behaviors that occur on a regular basis. Such vivid descriptions of mother–infant interactions can help psychotherapists to identify behaviors and patterns that show up relationally with our patients and how they are with their intimate partners, family members, and children. The scales are referenced in the intervention chapters (Chapters 8, 10, and 12) for potential applications to psychotherapy.

The following sections summarize the main themes of each of the scales: Sensitivity vs. Insensitivity, Cooperation vs. Interference, Availability vs. Ignoring, and Acceptance vs. Rejection. These themes may represent dynamics that appear between psychotherapists and patients. With that said, it is important to acknowledge that the patients we work with are not children and that we as psychotherapists are not their caregivers. While our patients have unresolved trauma that happened to them at very young ages, in this book we address psychotherapy with an adult population. As such, our interactions are sometimes based upon the *stronger, wiser other* (Bowlby, 1979) position of an attachment figure who provides care and enough safety to promote exploration and healing.

The following explanations of the Maternal Caregiving and Interaction Scales stay close to Ainsworth's descriptions of behavior and remain shy of quoting her verbatim, while attempting to convey the essential components of her observations.

Scale 1: Sensitivity vs. Insensitivity to the Baby's Signals

This variable deals with the mother's ability to perceive and to interpret accurately the signals and communications implicit in her infant's behavior, and given this understanding, to respond to them appropriately and promptly. (Ainsworth et al., 1978/2015, p. 357)

There are four essential components:

A. *Awareness of her baby's signals.* Ainsworth et al. (1978/2015) has identified two conditions of the mother's awareness. The first is the mother's *accessibility* and the second is described as her *threshold of sensitivity.* She must be accessible to the baby's communications to be sensitive to them. However, Ainsworth recognized that accessibility itself is not the only criterion that determines sensitive awareness. A mother's sensitivity can be measured in thresholds. The most sensitive mother has the lowest threshold; she is alert to the baby's more subtle, minimal cues. Mothers with higher thresholds perceive only the more blatant and obvious cues. Ainsworth perceived mothers with the highest thresholds to be "oblivious," even inaccessible. While it would seem that having access to the baby's signals would make it more likely that the mother would be able to interpret what the baby needs more accurately, it turns out that this is not always the case. Sometimes the mother picks up one signal of distress and misinterprets it for another. She may be alert to the baby's subtle mouth movement and misinterpret it as hunger, rather than a signal of dismay needing attention.

B. *An accurate interpretation of the signals.* Here, Ainsworth et al. (1978/2015) has looked deeply into the mother's accuracy in interpreting the baby's signals. She names three components: *awareness, freedom from distortion,* and *empathy.* Once the mother has picked up the baby's signal, is her awareness free from distortion? Is she able to empathize with what the baby is feeling? When the mother's perception is distorted, she is more inaccessible or prone to misperceiving the baby's signals. Ainsworth realized how the mother might misread the baby's signals according to her own biases, wishes, or needs. If she becomes impatient, she may misread the baby's slowing down while eating as a sign of satiation or she may read the "baby's fussy bid for attention" as a sign of fatigue and put them to bed. Mothers need to understand the baby's feelings to be able to respond with sensitivity, but they also need to be aware of themselves and how their mood might affect their perception of what is going on with the baby.

C. *An appropriate response to the baby.* In this definition, Ainsworth is both categorizing what happens, while also providing some definition for attunement and empathy. She notes that a sensitive response must be appropriate to the situation and to the baby's communications. During the first year, giving the baby attention when they make eye contact or reach out is a direct response to their behavior. This helps them feel understood. She also notes that during the second year, more compromise might be needed to provide limit setting versus giving in to what the baby ostensibly wants. Ainsworth et al. (1978/2015) identified that the most important element of the appropriate response is that the interaction is *well resolved, well rounded,* and *complete.* For example, if the baby wants to be held, they are held in a way that is felt as long enough and in such a way as to be satisfying. This is one of the characteristics of mother–infant interactions that was observed in the Baltimore study and found to be of particular significance. When the baby is put down, and they are not immediately seeking to be picked up again, they demonstrate the experience of being settled.

D. *A prompt response to the baby's signals.* Promptness to the baby's communication is what makes the mother's response contingent on the baby's own signal. Ainsworth saw repeatedly that when the mother's response matches the baby's signaling, the baby has a feeling of efficacy. The baby experiences that their signals make sense to the mother. Her timely and appropriate response provides the baby with a feeling of well-being: a feeling of competence for managing their social environment.

The Sensitivity vs. Insensitivity scale provides exquisite detail about the building blocks of responsiveness. As psychotherapists, it behooves us to develop an awareness of our accessibility to our patients' verbal and nonverbal signals, and what contributes to our being able to perceive them accurately. These are the building blocks of responsiveness in therapy, too.

The next scale, Cooperation vs. Interference, explores mother–infant interactions with respect to the mother's attitude toward the baby as a separate, autonomous being. This scale is applicable to how therapeutic dyads come to work together and how communication contributes to flow and coordination versus disharmony and disruption.

Scale 2: Cooperation vs. Interference With Baby's Ongoing Behavior

> The central issue of this scale is the extent to which the mother's interventions are initiations of interaction which break into, interrupt or cut cross the baby's ongoing activity rather than being geared in both timing and quality of the baby's state, mood and current interests. (Ainsworth et al., 1978/ 2015, p. 363)

There are two essential components:

A. *The extent of actual physical interference with the baby's activities.* This scale looks at how the mother interacts with the baby around routine behaviors like feeding, changing the baby's diaper, and moving from room to room. Ainsworth et al. (1978/2015) explores whether the mother can see the baby as a separate, active person with a mind of their own whose actions and wishes are valid. The mother's behavior may range from *conspicuously cooperative* to *highly interfering.* The most cooperative mother avoids imposing her will on the baby. She engages in such a way that integrates her wishes, moods, and responsibilities with the baby's wishes, moods, and activity. She picks up cues from the baby—rather than interrupting the baby, she looks for a natural break in the baby's activity where she can divert or invite their attention toward what she may wish for them to do. For instance, at bedtime she may join in and then gradually slow down their interactions, helping the baby shift to a more relaxed state, more conducive to bedtime. Thus, the mother sets a mood that helps them both to coordinate in a mutual direction.

B. *The sheer frequency of interruptions.* Interruptive behavior refers to how the mother is interacting when she picks up and puts the baby down. The key factor is how much the interaction is handled according to the mother's timing or preferences and/or whether she considers the baby's state or wishes. A mother shows a low range of interruptive behavior when she is mildly inconsiderate of the baby's wishes and mood, without much regard to what would make for smooth transitions for the baby between activities. A mother shows highly interfering behavior when she appears to assume the baby is hers with no rights of their own and she imposes her will, standards, and whim on the baby. The most conspicuous interfering mother may be physically forceful by interruption or restraint, whereas others may be conspicuous for the sheer number of interruptions, seeming to be "at" the baby with instruction, control, or direction.

Questions for psychotherapists regarding this scale have to do with alliance building. How might therapists consider how factors of cooperation and interference influence the development of coordination and collaboration in the therapeutic relationship? How do we gain our patient's cooperation and willingness to enter terrain that has been avoided? And how do we intervene in places where bringing attention to a stuck pattern could feel like unwanted interference, especially when the strategy related to this pattern might be the patient's very best way of adapting to difficulties early in life? It is not hard to speculate how the most interfering experiences would impact an individual's sense of self and confidence to explore in their own right.

Scale 3: Physical and Psychological Availability vs. Ignoring and Neglecting

The central issue of this scale is the mother's accessibility to the baby, with emphasis upon her responsiveness to him. Although the essential component of psychological accessibility is that the mother be aware of the baby, she is not truly available unless she also actively acknowledges and responds to him. (Ainsworth et al., 1978/ 2015, p. 369)

There are three essential components:

A. *The mother's accessibility is that the mother is aware of the baby and actively acknowledges and responds to the baby.* Ainsworth describes that the highly accessible mother is able to keep her baby in her perceptual awareness, within reach, so that she can have her receptors aware of them, even when out of sight. She can divide her attention between the activities of her own life and persons and things without losing awareness of the baby. Even if the baby is in another room, she can register a sound or a signal and shift her attention to readily respond to the baby. When she enters the room, she naturally acknowledges to the baby that she is aware of them.

B. *Ainsworth perceives the mother to be inaccessible if for prolonged periods or frequently she does not acknowledge or respond to her baby.* The mother may be aware of the baby's communication, and she may even be in the same room, yet she may still be nonresponsive. The inaccessible mother may ignore the baby's behavior for reasons of her own mental health. She may be blocked by her defenses and distort the baby's signal in such a way that she loses the incentive (her innate caregiving instinct) to respond. It seems that for these mothers the babies exist more in their minds, and their caregiving is in response to a thought about the baby and what they *should* need, rather than in response to the baby's *actual* signals. This was found to be a characteristic of mothers of avoidant babies.

C. *The other kind of inaccessibility Ainsworth noticed is the mother, who might be frequently imperceptive, yet when the baby is persistent enough, can sometimes shift out of her own preoccupation and notice the baby.* While she may be defensively unaware, she is not completely impervious. This scale accounts for the mother's bare acknowledgment of the baby's presence and not the quality of care given. The inaccessibility is most obvious when the baby is signaling, and the mother is or is not responding—though sometimes the baby's efforts pay off.

Some of the more active babies who are persistent and keep expressing their needs are different from the babies who give up. This may be a manifestation of their own resilience or confidence that the child knows their mother will respond even if it takes some effort. This contrasts with other babies, some of whom have ceased signaling because they have become accustomed to being ignored. So, when rating the mother's accessibility, observers needed to distinguish between this giving-up response from the quiet of a baby who trusts their mother will respond to their signal.

Scale 4: Acceptance vs. Rejection of the Baby's Needs

This scale deals with the balance between the mother's positive and negative feelings about her baby—about having a baby and about this

particular one—and with the extent to which she has been able to integrate these conflicting feelings or to resolve the conflict. . . . It is assumed
that the arrival of a baby poses a potentially ambivalent situation, and
that for all mothers there are positive and negative aspects. (Ainsworth
et al., 1978/2015, p. 374)

In this scale, Ainsworth looks at the balance between the positive and negative poles of the mother's feelings about her baby. While having positive
and negative feelings with a baby is natural, Ainsworth is concerned with
how the mother expresses them and how she is able to balance them, given
her life's situation. At the positive pole, can love and acceptance encom-
pass frustration, impatience, or limitations? Can positive feelings defuse
the negative elements? Are the negative feelings able to be subsumed
under the positive ones? On the negative pole, is there anger, resentment,
hurt, or irritation? Ainsworth looks at how these feelings may limit or conflict with positive ones. Are they leading to more or less overt rejection
of the baby? Are positive feelings able to be integrated with the negative
components?

This scale covers the degrees to which a mother is accepting and can
understand and empathize with her baby or how she may be pseudo accepting, which may lead to building resentments, underlying hostility, and/or an
occasional outburst of irritation. This pseudo acceptance can interfere with
satisfying responsive exchanges with the baby and can add up to rejection.
Some forms of rejection are subtle, and more covert. Others are unmistakable and overt, as obvious as "I wish this baby was never born." Ainsworth
noted how overt rejection is expressed when the mother calls her baby by
demeaning names, or disparages the baby, conveying hostility. The most
integrated accepting mother has positive feelings toward the baby and even
when momentary anger or frustration arises, she can deal with it in such
a way that she does not take it out on the baby. There is a sense that she
can overall hold the baby in positive regard with caring understanding of
herself and the baby.

As a psychotherapist, I welcome the opportunity to consider how deep
acceptance is the corollary to rejection and how to intervene with parts of
our patients that are problematic or challenging, within an overall frame of
acceptance of the person. This scale identifies the most intense rejecting
behaviors from a parent, and degrees of how a child's early needs and/or
existence as a separate person can be rebuffed and disregarded. There is

complexity in the balance between positive and negative feelings, which gives pause to consider how to address negative feelings when they arise with patients and within ourselves as psychotherapists. Such feelings may provide clues about what might be indicated for exploration.

Next, we present Ainsworth's Strange Situation Protocol, how it first came to be developed, and a description of it that serves us in the chapters where we refer to the findings of the Strange Situation to describe the formation of insecure patterns of attachment.

The Strange Situation Protocol (SSP): Complement to the Maternal Caregiving Interaction Scales

The Strange Situation Protocol (SSP) was first developed to accompany the Baltimore study. Ainsworth and her assistant Barbara Wittig designed a standardized laboratory procedure, the SSP, to evoke attachment behaviors that did not appear in the familiarity and routine of the Baltimore home environments. The SSP was given to infants at about a year old, at the end of the year of home observation. The infant was introduced to a stranger and a playroom full of toys. The mother was initially present, and then left for brief separations, followed by her return, for eight episodes of increasing stress, most of 3-minutes duration. If the baby became unduly distressed, the episode was curtailed. If the baby needed more time to engage in play, the episode might be prolonged. The SSP was designed to study the balance between exploratory and attachment behavior and individual differences in the child's ability to make use of the mother as a secure base for exploration and a safe haven for comfort.

Episodes of the Strange Situation:

1. Mother and baby enter the room, which is stocked with toys.
2. Mother and baby are alone in the room, playing.
3. A stranger comes into the room and joins mother and baby.
4. Mother gets up and leaves.
5. First reunion: Mother knocks and calls from outside the door, carefully opens the door and steps inside. She was instructed to pause for a moment to see what the baby does, then to go ahead and respond. Unobtrusively, the stranger slips out.
6. Mother gets up, makes a point of saying, "Bye-bye. I'm leaving. I'll be back."

7. The stranger comes into the room and tries to comfort and soothe the baby and get them to play.
8. Second reunion: Mother comes in. She was instructed to pause and see what the baby does, then to go and pick the baby up.

Each of the episodes were designed to replicate the various kinds of situations that occur on a regular basis in real life. For instance, the mother brings the baby to a friend's house, and the baby is left with the "stranger" while the mother uses the bathroom or when the mother leaves the room and returns in a few minutes (Ainsworth et al., 1978/2015). The episodes are designed to study the activation and termination of the attachment and exploratory systems. Generally, when the stranger enters the room, this tends to activate fear/wariness in the baby, which terminates the exploratory system. The baby stops playing and looks wide-eyed at the stranger, then looks at their mother, and crawls to her. This reaching for their mother, for a safe haven, is activation of the attachment system. The children's separation and reunion behaviors turned out to be the most useful to demonstrate the individual patterns in attachment behaviors.

The infant's attachment relationship was classified into one of three major groups: the secure (B) group, the insecure/avoidant (A) group, and the resistant/ambivalent (C) group. As Ainsworth was dedicated to fine-tuning the variations within each category, there were eight final subgroups in all. For the purposes of this book, we stay with these three main categories. The addition of the classification and disorganization (D) group is discussed in Chapters 11 and 12.

In the secure (B) group the children used the mother as a stable base, and showed signs of missing her during separation and moving toward her either by smiles or greeting behavior or by proximity-seeking behavior during the reunions. In the avoidant (A) group, the children were more inclined to avoid contact and proximity with the mother, showed little distress when she left, turning away rather than toward her when she returned, often turning toward the toys. When picked up they tend to lean away from her and stiffen or squirm to get down. The children in the resistant/ambivalent (C) group appeared distressed when their mothers left the room, and had difficulty engaging with the toys/exploring. They showed a mixture of seeking and resisting contact throughout the separation and reunion episodes, thus appearing ambivalent toward their mothers. They may have been clingy, passively avoiding exploration, and were unable to find comfort in their mother when she returned (Ainsworth et al., 1978/2015; Solomon & George, 2008).

What a powerful tool!

Offering a way to capture "the effects of the first year of life in 21 minutes," the SSP has become the gold standard of attachment research (Crittenden, 2017, p. 4). In succeeding decades, this protocol has been enthusiastically adopted by other researchers, replicated often, and used in numerous ways. Instead of using the SSP at the end of research, Alan Sroufe and Byron Egeland, in Minnesota, conducted studies that began with the SSP to establish a baseline. They developed the Minnesota longitudinal study, which follows children into adulthood across a 30-year lifespan (Sroufe et al., 2005). Robert Marvin and colleagues (Powell et al., 2014) have incorporated it into their Circle of Security work, helping mothers learn how to read their children's signals, how to respond to what is cued up and needed, and how to appropriately respond to what is miscued and needs repair, helping to build the resources of a secure base and haven.

Part 2: Attachment Theory—Patterns, Systems, Phases, & Internal Working Models

Recognition of Patterns of Attachment Brings Recognition to Attachment Theory

> We are here concerned with nothing less than the nature of love and its origins in the attachment of a baby to its mother. (Ainsworth, 1967, p. 429)

Ainsworth's explorations through naturalistic observation, first in Uganda and then in Baltimore, led her to discover a few ageless truths about the nature of love and attachment. Even though she and Bowlby were developing attachment theory with empirical studies to back it up, the idea that children need more than food to build ties of affection with their caregivers was still considered revolutionary and for another decade would be at odds with the prevailing views of both the psychoanalytic and social learning theory communities.

From the Ganda study, Ainsworth recognized that individual differences in methods of infant care are related to differences in the babies' development of attachment. In the Baltimore study, she looked closely at the growth of attachment through the home observations of mothers and infants. She observed different characteristics of the mother's caregiving behaviors and how they influenced the individual differences between children, which progressed into distinct patterns of attachment behavior. Through the SSP, she developed empirical research that led to the classifications of secure and insecure attachment patterns.

Recognition of the profound nature of the individual differences in children and their caregivers, and the interrelationship between them, has rocked the field of psychology since Ainsworth et al.'s (1978/2015) book *Patterns of Attachment*, which finally brought greater acceptance and acknowledgment to the field of attachment. How patterns of security and insecurity appeared in patients in clinical settings motivated our quest to develop understanding and guidance for psychotherapists to help our patients heal. Looking at how attachment develops when things go "right" provides direction when we are helping our patients who developed insecure patterns in relationships when things go "wrong."

Through the 1960s, while Ainsworth was absorbed in teaching at Johns Hopkins, researching through the Baltimore study and writing up the results of her Ganda study, she was in close collaboration with Bowlby. They provided each other with immense support, being each other's safe haven and secure base, communicating through written correspondence for many years, discussing their ongoing formulations about attachment theory before the field of psychology caught up with them. Bowlby continued to speak with researchers and theorists around the globe, furthering his investigations about the affectional ties between caregiver and child, conceptualizing the growth of attachment and how deprivation and the loss of a parent figure could be so profoundly devastating for the child. He was actively engaged in conversations not only with his fellow clinical psychoanalysts but also with leading researchers from different theoretical backgrounds, including, but not limited to, learning theory, ethology, anthropology, cognitive and systems theory, and with people of such renown as Margaret Mead, Jean Piaget, Konrad Lorenz, Robert Hinde, and Ludwig von Bertalanffy.

Interweaving Bowlby and Ainsworth and the Growth of Attachment Theory

In his first book about attachment, Bowlby (1969/1982) explained his formulations of four innate biological systems of attachment behavior: the fear/wariness behavioral system, the attachment behavioral system, the caregiving behavioral system, and the exploratory behavioral system. He identified that from the first few days and weeks of life, an infant has *instinctual responses*, which he asserted are attachment behaviors designed to attract the caregiver's attention. As such, these signals are part of the child's attachment behavioral system. They inform the caregiver about what the infant needs. The caregiver has a complementary, instinctual caregiving behavioral system. When the caregiver responds accurately to the child with loving attention, this brings a synchronized feeling of well-being. Being met and cared for becomes a pleasurable, reinforcing experience for both infant and caregiver, developing secure attachment. And when the caregiver is compromised in their ability to respond and unable to meet and attend to their child's needs, difficulties increase for the pair, leading to the kinds of differences and development of insecure patterns that Ainsworth noticed and investigated.

Bowlby elaborated how the attachment behavioral system (in the child) and the caregiving behavioral system (in the caregiver) are reciprocal and interactive. For example, when the fear/wariness behavioral system is activated in the child from internal or external conditions, children express alarm, instigating the attachment behavioral system. In turn, this activates the caregiving behavioral system in the caregiver, which mobilizes them to notice the signal, make an accurate inference about what the baby needs in this moment, and then meet that need. The caregiver is biologically wired to protect and attend to the child, except in cases when the caregiver's caregiving behavioral system is encumbered in such a way that activates their own fear and insecure patterns. Their reactivity interferes with their ability to pick up and/or respond to the baby's signal accurately. When the appropriate and necessary care is given and received, the signaling of the attachment behavioral system comes to rest. The child is wired to then experience the urge to explore, engaging their exploratory behavioral system to learn about their surroundings. We explore their implications and applications to psychotherapy throughout this book.

The infant and caregiver interactions (motivated by each of the attachment and caregiving behavioral systems) become internalized in the child and form sets of expectations about future interactions. In the case of the caregiver who is unable to meet their child in the moment, it is likely their own attachment behaviors were not met sufficiently when they were a child. And the corollary, when the child's needs are met, a corresponding internalization occurs. Bowlby saw these internalized experiences as forming mental representations, which predict how future relationships will fare. He called these representations *internal working models*, which is now a widely known construct due to attachment theory, although the term came to Bowlby through studies in ethology. "Bowlby had discovered the notion of internal working models from an eminent zoologist who studied the behavior of octopi" (Young, 1964) but its origin was an influential book by philosopher and psychologist Kenneth Craik (1943) titled *The Nature of Explanation* (Bretherton, 2005, p. 16).

John Bowlby: From Ethology to Control Systems to the Phases of Attachment

Bowlby's development of attachment theory was also informed by control systems theory. Control systems[4] is a general theory about how things work in a purposeful way—whether organisms, animals, humans, or machines. A most familiar example of this functioning is homing missiles. The heat-seeking missile is guided by midcourse corrections to reach its target. Bowlby (1969/1982) describes that the special feature that allows a machine to achieve this predetermined goal is feedback:

> This is simply a process whereby the actual effects of performance are continuously reported back to a central regulating apparatus where they are compared with whatever initial instruction the machine was given; the machine's further action is then determined by the results of this comparison and the effects of its performance are thus brought ever closer to the initial instruction. (pp. 41–42)

The instrumental feature of control system theory was the idea of purposeful action. Bowlby applied the concept to the attachment behavioral system: how internal settings are necessary to provide the feedback that guides the organism to achieve its aim. Initially the caregiver regulates the baby's needs by responding to the baby's signals. Yet once the baby is regulated, their condition will change and therefore the caregiver will need to notice a varying sequence of signals and responses to register the baby's changing needs and then to meet those needs.

For example, a baby cries, the mother hears the cry (feedback) and discerns (by way of her internal process/setting) what is needed. When she responds by picking the baby up and the baby roots, she offers her breast, the baby suckles (more feedback), and they both settle into what optimally is mutually satisfying breastfeeding. In Phases 1 and 2 (birth–6 months) of the development of attachment, this kind of caregiving response to the baby is the *predictable outcome* of the child's signaling behavior.

Bowlby chose the term "set goal" to identify how the target of what is being regulated may be a time-limited event or an ongoing condition. There is a back-and-forth in the process of achieving a set goal. The caregiver's response to the baby's cry includes their perception of the signal (feedback) and an organized plan to respond. According to Bowlby, the set goal is a specific relationship, in this case between the baby and mother. It contains an internal representation in the baby (or in the caregiver) of a relation between the baby and mother.

In control theory, the movement toward achieving a set goal was referred to as goal-directed behavior. However, Bowlby preferred the term *goal-corrected behavior* as it better describes the way attachment behavior is "corrected" to navigate the discrepancy (and reality) between what is happening and the set goal. Interactive behaviors between caregivers and children shift according to the call-and-response patterns of the baby and the caregiver. In Phase 1: preattachment (birth to 8–12 weeks) and Phase 2: attachment in the making (baby is 3- to 6-months old), the caregiver responds to the baby's signals, which have the predictable outcome of regulation. The caregiver has a set goal in mind when they recognize and meet what the child's signals indicate they might need.

Bowlby identified that Phase 3: the consolidation of attachment (between 3–6 and 18–36 months) is reached when the child is capable of purposeful action and can now motivate goal-corrected attachment behavior. When the child can move purposefully toward proximity or seeking and maintaining contact with their primary attachment figure, the child's aim becomes the set goal that the child and their caregiver now coordinate. This is the phase where the growth of attachment is seen as taking hold between the infant and the caregiver; the child's capacity to actively engage attachment behavior with a primary attachment figure is underway.

Next, we elaborate the goal-corrected partnership.

Phase 4: The Goal-Corrected Partnership

Goal-corrected partnership (Phase 4) is possible when the child and their attachment figure understand each other's minds as distinct and develop the capacity to coordinate their set goals through collaboration, conflict, and negotiation (Bowlby, 1969/1982). The fourth phase, "goal-corrected partnership," takes place somewhere after the third year and at about age 4, when children can understand that their mother/attachment figure has a mind of her own, full of her own internal experiences—feelings, thoughts, and goals—and that those internal experiences can be and often are different from the child's own. For instance, a 3-year-old child who wants to give their mother a birthday present might give her a truck that they have loved. On the other hand, when a child reaches the age of 4, give or take, they may choose to give their mother a bracelet, because they now know that she really likes bracelets.

Children are developing their abilities to understand what motivates their mother's movements toward and away from them and are beginning to really think about how they can interact with her to alter her behavior. Based on observations, the child becomes able to infer something of the mother's own "set goals" and something of her plans to achieve them. They can understand what she may be holding as expectations, wishes, and feelings and compare this with what they have in their own mind about a set goal. Do they match? Can they communicate what they each have in mind, holding what is similar and different simultaneously, and communicate together to reach an agreement? With this increased understanding, Bowlby (1969/1982) "sees the groundwork is laid for the pair to develop a much more complex relationship with each other, one which I would term partnership" (p. 268).

This phase of *partnership* enhances relating in a secure manner. Take the example of a child who communicates a desired outcome with their mother/caregiver. When both mother and child can express what they want, while also holding and understanding what is important to the other, they are most likely to achieve a satisfying result. There is increased differentiation. As the child recognizes that the caregiver is an "other" who has their own ideas, this supports their ability to predict what will happen with some accuracy. With this differentiation comes the capacity for seeing through another's eyes. While this may not be accomplished by all children at this age, a clear demarcation begins as the child becomes more capable to observe, infer, and communicate with greater understanding of self and other.

Achievement of this kind of partnership is visible with older preschoolers who share goals, plans, and feelings with their parents. They can organize their attachment behavior at a higher level with the ability to recognize that their relationship with their attachment figure is continuous, even when separated from their attachment figure for hours—or even days—at a time. There is trust that the attachment figure will be available to respond if called upon to help (Bowlby, 1973). Greenburg and Marvin (1982) describe that a set goal for older children should no longer be seen as mere physical proximity or contact but rather as a way to develop a *shared plan* for that proximity. At this level of partnership, when this capacity comes online, attachment behavior and the need for predictability and responsiveness can happen by exchanging thoughts and feelings, and hopes and plans. And then both can share their reactions, agreeing and disagreeing, and knowing whether they agree or disagree while negotiating a shared plan together.

Goal-corrected partnership is an important element of attachment relationships for psychotherapists to recognize as we establish conditions to build a secure base for treatment. We must work together as we support the patient's exploration, noticing what kind of accompaniment and encouragement is necessary to help them face and process unresolved experiences. Such a process calls for mutual trust, understanding, and collaboration to be successful. The platform of a goal-corrected partnership is pertinent to describe what happens in a secure functioning psychotherapy relationship.

Psychotherapy and the Exploratory Behavioral System of Attachment

In this section we look at the four interactive behavioral systems of attachment relationships: the fear/wariness behavioral system, the attachment behavioral system, the caregiving behavioral system, and the exploratory behavioral system. When the child's attachment behavior is met with a suitable caregiving response, and settles them, this quiets their attachment behavior, which then naturally gives rise to the exploratory behavioral system. Here we examine how this applies to psychotherapy.

In young children, when the child is animated with excitement, the novelty of newness can bring the child to shrink away. The way their attachment figure meets them, providing a safe haven to reassure them, makes a world of difference. In psychotherapy, when a patient is exploring unresolved issues, they too might encounter something novel and feel an urge to pull back. Often, entering the uncharted territory of an emotional and/or relational nature means approaching what has previously been avoided, which can provoke anxiety. Even when patients are deeply committed to their healing, facing next steps along the way can be daunting. The more insecure their attachment relationships have been, the higher the Richter scale for exploration. How psychotherapists stay in contact and engage with them is of utmost importance.

We address emotional regulation in depth in Chapter 2 and in our chapters on treatment, yet for this section it seems important to link how the interplay of the three behavioral systems related to attachment is most applicable to psychotherapy. When our patients' attachment behavioral systems are activated, we can engage with our reciprocal caregiving behavioral system to provide care and comfort. We can meet our patients with a regulating presence and encouragement in places that seem dark and scary. Perhaps when they were children, *these* were the places where they were alone and afraid, without an attachment figure available with whom they felt safe. And perhaps *these* were the unresolved and painful places, which gave rise to insecure patterns and didn't resolve because of the prevalence of defensive tactics and strategies. We aim to be with them so they *can* feel safe enough to explore what may be painful or frightening, to bring whatever attention is needed to tend to what is difficult.

While for the purposes of this book we have been clear that we are not the parents and our patients are not our children, it is also true that our biological wiring serves our profession. We aim to use ourselves relationally to bring healing to our patient's wounds that have relational voids. An attachment figure is sometimes perceived as a stronger, wiser other (Bowlby, 1979): one who has walked this path before and knows the lay of the land. Bowlby (1988) identifies attributes of this role when he describes the "clearly identified individual who is conceived as better able to cope with the world . . . when the person is frightened, fatigued, or sick and is assuaged by comforting and caregiving" (p. 27).

How Internal Working Models Develop

What happens when the child's signals attract what they need from the caregiver and what happens when they don't? How about when the response is minimal, infrequent, or inconsistent? These are the questions that arose out of Mary Ainsworth's research in Ganda. The answers to these questions became clearer through the Baltimore studies and the SSP.

Ainsworth began to see the internal working model at work when she examined the behavior of infants during the SSP. She noticed attachment behavior in how some children's crying intensified as their mothers departed, but others didn't seem so distressed. She contemplated the differences between children who calmed down more easily, and those who were so difficult to soothe. She wondered about the children who seemed not to display attachment behavior at all. Was it their age and the fact that they were "not yet attached," as she originally supposed? Or were those babies already anticipating rejection from their caregivers? Here she was ahead of John Bowlby: She began to infer that those children, at 1 year old, had an internal representation of their parents as nonresponsive, and were defending against an expectation of nonresponse with avoidance.

When a child can rely on knowing their attachment figure is available for them when they desire, they grow in confidence and trust of being met by the world and the people in it. They learn that they can ask for help when needed and that they can lean on others for support (Bowlby, 1973; Bretherton, 2005). When unable to rely on their attachment figure, a child is much more prone to anxiety and may come to see the world and its people as unresponsive or unpredictable. If the mismatch between what is needed and what is given happens often, the child may rely on *defensive exclusion* rather than their caregivers. They may block awareness of an external stimulus that might scare or reject them. They might block awareness of an internal stimulus that threatens to overwhelm or fracture them. Or they may become angry at the caregiver who is inconsistently available or accessible (Bowlby, 1980). Most children will do what is needed to maintain the relationship with their caregivers, even if it means excluding awareness of emotional or relational factors that interfere with these relationships.

As we look at how caregivers and infants interact during each phase of the growth of attachment, we can see how the behavioral systems of fear, attachment, caregiving, and exploration are completely intertwined. Bowlby construed how each system has an activation point and a termination point, beginning and ending with the corresponding behavioral responses between the infant and their caregivers, between a particular stimulus, its need, and its satiation. He determined that in Phases 1 and 2 of the growth of attachment, the infant's signaling draws the predictable outcome from caregivers. At consolidation of attachment in Phase 3, the child engages actively with purposeful, goal-corrected attachment behaviors directed toward an attachment figure. These attachment behaviors become more complex as children become older and exchanges between the caregiver and child grow to include what the other holds in mind. By the time the child is around the age of 4 the attachment relationship can grow into a goal-corrected partnership with each having increased awareness of and capacity to communicate with each other's state of mind. At this phase, the dyad can develop ways to collaborate and negotiate what is needed to achieve shared plans for their set goals.

Woven through this complexity is what happens during caregiver/child interactions when things flow and synchronize versus when they go awry. These experiences become internalized as expectations. They can be positive and well functioning, or they can be negative and fraught, forming the child's secure and insecure representations about the environment and their place in it.

How Experiences Become Internalized Representations

How does this happen? How do children develop in such a way that how they are treated becomes how they expect to be treated? Bowlby gathered inspiration from many sources. Piaget (1952) theorized that a child builds a primitive cognitive map that becomes an internal representation, which comes very close to Bowlby's construct of the internal working model. Yet according to Bretherton (1985), Bowlby's inspiration derives from Craik (1943), whose work was focused on how individuals form mental models of reality to predict future events. Craik stated,

> If the organism carries a small-scale model of external reality and of its own possible actions within its head, it is able to try out various alternatives, conclude which is the best of them, react to future situations before they arise, utilize the knowledge of past events in dealing with the present and future, and in every way to react in a much fuller, safer and more competent manner to the emergencies which face it. (p. 61)

Craik was known as one of the earliest cognitive theorists. His views that the mind tries to choose the safest future outcomes of potential actions based on knowledge of past events seems to address more than cognition. In describing how the mind perceives present realities and uses this knowledge to forecast future realities, he is addressing how experiences are held and various alternatives are tried out. This seems like an experiential process that is happening internally. Essentially, different mental scenarios are practiced and from there future action is chosen. No wonder Bowlby incorporated Craik's term, the "internal working model," to name how attachment experiences become internalized as guideposts upon which future predictions are based.

Bowlby was intrigued by how the inner workings of the brain function to construct these models, and he continued to collect understandings from ethology. The zoologist/biologist John Young studied how animals and organisms need to have some sort of cognitive map of their environment to adapt and survive. Through studies of octopi, Young gleaned that the brain builds working models out of "unit parts" that can be constructed and assembled to become working models of the environment. Digging deeper, Young located the cells of their component parts by forms of their dendritic branches. The dendrites are the parts of cells that communicate with other cells. Bretherton and Munholland (2008) pointed out that "Bowlby maintained the human capacity for foresightful and insightful behavior was difficult to understand *without* [emphasis added] making the assumption that the brain builds up mentally manipulable models of their environment and the self within it" (p. 16; Bowlby, 1969/1982).

This was a key development between Craik's assertions and Young's findings. Organisms, animals, and children must be building models of their environments based on events that have occurred, and their brains are assembling and reassembling this information to forecast what will happen next time. In response to their caregivers, children make predictions that inform how they behave, and as the child matures, their predictions become more complex.

Building Blocks of Internal Working Models

The essence of working models is that they store information to be able to make predictions. It goes something like this: A child takes in experiences that become data points. Through their imagination they try out potential scenarios to make predictions about the future. There must be a measure for internal consistency. Bowlby (1969/1982) states that "The more adequate the model, the more accurate its predictions; the more comprehensive the model, the greater the number of situations in which its predictions apply" (p. 81). To achieve a set goal, a person makes plans, which involves their mental processes of reflection to build, revise, extend, and check for consistency. The child needs not only a model of their environment, but a sense of how they belong, their own skills, and potentialities. Ultimately, Bowlby asserts that two working models develop: one of the environment and one of the organism.

Here are the origins of the internal working models of self (i.e., the organism) and other (i.e., the environment).

Bowlby posits that children build up their inner worlds to develop their models. Children continually gather experiences of the world around them and how the people in that world, including themselves, are expected to behave. These experiences can be seen as the component parts that Young suggested, which are assembled while the child is making their working models. A new experience is taken inside and becomes one of the component parts that can be reassembled into a new working model. Following Craik's description, the child considers what has occurred in the past and chooses from various alternatives to make plans to deal with what is anticipated about the future. The experiences the child has with their attachment figures become the data that are represented internally and influence the development of these models. Thus, *internal working models* are referred to as *internal representations*. The degree to which the attachment figure's caregiving interactions meet and coordinate with the child's needs contributes to how the children develop internal working models of self and other as secure or insecure attachment.

The Self–Other–Emotion Triangle: A Representational Schema of the Internal Working Model

For those of us visual learners, having a representational schema provides a way to see our patient's unfolding moment-to-moment experience. The Self–Other–Emotion (SOE) Triangle (Fosha, 2000b) is a representation of the internal working model and depicts the relational matrix between what originally becomes internalized representing the self, the other, and representing emotion (see Figure 1.1). In Figure 1.1, the individual's internalized representation of the other (the attachment figure) is represented at the upper right corner of the triangle. The individual's internalized representation of the Self (their child self) is represented at the upper left corner of the triangle. The individual's internalized representation of emotion and how it is processed is represented at the bottom corner of the triangle

The relationship between the other (the past caregiver/the current therapist), the self (the past child/the current patient), and emotion is interrelated.

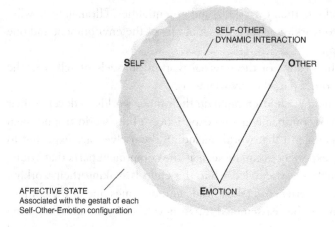

Figure 1.1 The Self–Other–Emotion Triangle
Fosha, 2020

The way the other treats the self, who is having an emotional experience, becomes internalized and represented as the way the self subsequently relates to their own emotion, to their self, and to the other. When emotion is acknowledged and accompanied it can unfold in a genuine progression, facilitating the self's connection to their emotional experience and developing a secure manner of being and relating with their self and with an other. When the other's response to emotion is rejecting, shaming, or mistreating, the self becomes compromised in their capacity to relate to their own emotion, developing an insecure strategy that inhibits their capacity to connect to and be with their emotional and relational experiences. Thus, see how the SOE triangle is a visual representation of our internal working models, showing how the emotion regulatory strategies of the dyad become internalized in the individual's emotion regulatory strategies.

Foreshadowing here, psychotherapists have a specific and pointed opportunity to inhabit the position of a healing other. One who is sensitive and responsive helps to bring about corrective emotional and relational experiences. What if each new, corrective experience is factored in as a component part to the building of a new working model? When we welcome and have the capacity to be with the patient's emotion, we can help them connect to and express their emotional experience. We aim to provide a new configuration of the SOE relational matrix that can help our patients heal past ruptures with their natural emotional expression and the impact from past relational ruptures, thus forging the possibilities of new internal working models.

Expectation and Anticipation: When Things Go "Right" and Things Go "Wrong"

The urge to keep proximity or accessibility to someone seen as stronger or wiser and who *if responsive is deeply loved* [emphasis added], comes to be recognized as an integral part of human nature and as having a vital role to play in life. (Bowlby, 1991, p. 293)

Bowlby on Internal Working Models

In the second volume of his trilogy on attachment, Bowlby (1973) describes these working models of attachment figures and of the self with such clarity, we quote him directly. He identifies that an individual builds working models of their world and their place in it, for the purpose of perceiving events, forecasting the future, and constructing their plans. Essential features highlighted in italic are discussed following the quote:

> In the working model of the world that anyone builds, a key feature is their notion of *who his attachment figures are, where they may be found, and how they may be expected to respond.* Similarly, in the working model of the self that anyone builds a key feature is their notion of how *acceptable or unacceptable he himself is in the eyes of his attachment figures.* On the structure of these complementary models are based that person's forecasts of *how accessible and responsive his attachment figures are likely to be should he turn to them for support.* And, in terms of the theory now advanced, it is on the structure of these models that depends, also, *whether he feels confident that his attachment figures are in general readily available or whether he is more or less afraid that they will not be available—occasionally, frequently or most of the time* [emphasis added]. (p. 203)

Biology has designed many ways to ensure our adaptation and survival. Having an internal working model based on experiences with our attachment figures gives us the ability to forecast how personal relationships will fare. Each working model establishes a set of rules, through which we appraise actions, thoughts, and feelings. They are learned from the first year of life though childhood and adolescence. These models and the rules they contain inform a person's expectations about the world and the people in it, informing our predictions based on past experiences and present circumstances (Bowlby, 1973).

The following features describe how the internal working models of self and other are established, and as such are themes to notice with patients in psychotherapy.

The first feature, "who his attachment figures are, where they may be found, and how they may be expected to respond," points to the internal working model of the other: what the self has inferred about the other. "What does the self imagine about their attachment figure (the other)?" In simple terms, "Is there someone who is there for me? Will they be available? Will they get what I need?" Each of us has internalized the experiences we had, and usually we anticipate what will happen based on what did happen.

The second feature Bowlby highlighted speaks to the internal working model of self, "how acceptable or unacceptable he himself is in the eyes of their attachment figures." Through what the self has experienced in the reflection of the other, a person (self) feels whether they are acceptable, or not. Questions of self-worth arise. Based on how we have been received, beginning with our attachment figure(s), we develop expectations about how we will be received throughout life. How the self has been viewed is often internalized as "how I feel about myself" and "what I think about me." Many patients who come into psychotherapy struggle with how they feel about themselves. Some patients report implicit or explicit negative messages they have felt or heard from their parents, which reveal painful sources of what they have come to believe: deep-seated expectations of being unacceptable, unlovable, and undesirable.

Compounding the experience of whether a person finds self-acceptance in the eyes of an attachment figure is the way the attachment figure conveys the message about whether they are available for help when needed. The third feature Bowlby names is the self's perception of the other in these kinds of interactions: "How accessible and responsive are their attachment figures likely to be should he turn to them for support?" The answer to this question becomes the internalized experience from which the self bases the forecast whether his attachment figure will be available if they reach to them for help. "If I need them, will they be there? Will they respond?" The individual's ease and trust of being able to reach out for help depends on their early experiences and how their caregivers showed up for them.

The resulting appraisal, "whether he feels confident that his attachment figures are in general readily available or whether he is more or less afraid that they will not be available—occasionally, frequently or most of the time," shows the takeaway of these interactions. The confidence with which a person can rely on an attachment figure is a direct reflection of how available their attachment figure usually was. And here we have a clear example of the complementary nature of the self and other internal working models. When the attachment figure is generally available a person develops confidence about asking for help. On the other hand, when the attachment figure is generally not available, a person often becomes anxious, predicting the other will likely not be present, and that most likely, there is no help to be had. The perception of caregiver availability influences how much fear or confidence a person has when facing a potentially alarming situation, based on their prediction of whether they will be alone or accompanied (Bowlby, 1973).

For psychotherapists, recognizing the power of the way our patients predict and interpret what happens in their current-day interactions between self and other is crucial to the healing process. Bowlby describes that a person's confidence in an attachment figure is based on two variables. One aspect is based on whether the attachment figure is the sort of person who is judged as likely to be responsive to calls for protection and support. The second aspect is about the self. Is the self the sort of person who the attachment figure (or other) is likely to respond to in a helpful way? Is the self worthy? For a young child the models of self and other often become internally represented in a complementary manner. How one is regarded by their caregiver confirms how the person comes to regard themselves and others. A child who is unwanted, and treated so, grows up to believe not only that they are unwanted by their parents but believes, and fears, that they are essentially unwanted by anyone. On the other hand, a child who is well loved grows up confident in the affection of their parents and believes that anyone else would find them lovable (Bowlby, 1973).

These models of self and other do not have to remain so intertwined that the other's (primary attachment figure's) behavior is forever engraved as a defining measure of the self. When a child understands the other's frame of mind, the child can get that the parent might not always be available when the child wants their attention. They can understand when the parent might be otherwise occupied and unavailable. In a secure internal working model, the child's self-worth is distinct and separate from the parent's momentary unavailability.

At the heart of healing lies differentiating the insecure internal working models of self and other. When psychotherapists take the place of an other who provides a positive experience—one that values, understands, and responds to our patient—we help them to value their self and thus, we disrupt their harmful anticipations. When an individual has new experiences of the other, this can counter their negative expectations about both self and other.

Understanding the formation of internal working models is paramount for psychotherapists. Internal working models result when a person internalizes the way they have been treated and how they come to establish rules and expectations that are carried into future relationships.

Even when the old tracks are well-worn, there is the possibility of disentangling the model of the other from the model of the self. In an attachment-oriented psychotherapy—and this is crucial to what this book is about and its foundations in modern positive neuroplasticity, interpersonal neurobiology, and affective neuroscience—we can set the relational conditions for new experiences to disconfirm the old representations and move toward transforming the internal working model. By studying what happens when things go "right," we can adopt principles of security to treat the problems that occur when things have gone "wrong."

Part 3: Flexibility & Inflexibility, Defensive Exclusion, and the Adult Attachment Interview

Attachment is manifested through these patterns of behavior, but the patterns themselves do not constitute the attachment. Attachment is internal . . . built into the nervous system, in the course of and as a result of the infant's experience of his transactions with his mother and other people. This internalized something that we call attachment has aspects of feelings, memories, wishes, expectancies, and intentions, all of which constitute an inner program . . . , which serves as a kind of filter for the reception and interpretation of interpersonal experience and as a kind of template shaping the nature of outwardly observable response. (Ainsworth 1967, p. 429)

One of the markers of secure attachment in adults is valuing attachment relationships. Open communication within attachment relationships is another marker of secure attachment. When individuals can talk about how they get along, the expectations they have of one another, and the implicit or explicit rules that have been established, there is potential for checking and revising what is needed for these relationships to flow. This is even more enhanced when one can understand and hold another's thoughts, feelings, wishes, and realities in mind. When this happens in the family, pathways are established for collaborative communication in relationships. Growing up valuing relationships and having a flexible orientation that includes understanding self and other are attachment experiences that become internalized as secure working models.

So, what does it mean to be flexible in attachment relationships? I find this to be one of the most important, though infrequently discussed features of Mary Main's (2000) work. She initially identified flexibility versus inflexibility in attention when she was describing children in the SSP. The children who were classified as secure were able to shift their attention under conditions of attachment stress. They were able to alter the focus of their attention in keeping with changes in circumstances, such as using the attachment figure for comfort after a period of separation, and once settled, they shifted their attention to play with toys in the room. In contrast, children who were classified as insecure showed an inflexible attention by focusing on only one aspect of their surroundings. The children classified as avoidant disengaged from the stress of separation by turning away from their attachment figure and focusing on toys in the room. The children classified as ambivalent/resistant maintained focus on their attachment figure to the exclusion of exploring their surroundings.

Studying how attachment patterns develop and become internalized informs many facets of relationship that arise during psychotherapy. We can notice degrees of flexibility and inflexibility in how patients engage with us and in how we engage with patients. Problems that developed from moment-to-moment interactions that were less than optimal in childhood can be treated through a more optimal moment-to-moment intentional process between patient and therapist. How we meet our patients in a relationship is essential to helping them heal their wounding that stems from past relationships. Setting positive conditions to foster secure attachment, and to enhance collaborative communication and flexibility, is vital to the healing process. In the following section, we look at inflexibility in how children grew to rely on defensive exclusion when they couldn't rely on their caregivers.

Bowlby's Defensive Exclusion

From the beginning of Bowlby's investigations and research, in conjunction with his colleague James Robertson, Bowlby was keenly interested in understanding the phenomena of children who were suffering from loss. He recognized how they went through reactions of protest, despair, and detachment, and how detachment is ultimately a defensive process. In her research, Ainsworth recognized that even young children were responding defensively to their attachment figures, especially during the separation and reunion episodes of the Strange Situation. It became clear to her that the children's defenses were specifically correlated to their caregiver's attachment patterns, especially when the caregivers were outright rejecting or inconsistent in their caregiving behavior.

When attachment figures fail in their capacity to be available and responsive, children turn to rely on *defensive exclusion*. When they cannot rely on their caregivers for help or protection, they use secondary measures to exclude awareness of that which they cannot manage alone. Bowlby outlined in detail how the use of defensive exclusion establishes patterns that lead to the construction of insecure working models.

In *Loss* (1980), the third volume of his trilogy, Bowlby describes how he came to the term "defensive exclusion." He begins with a general discussion about information processing in humans. Selective exclusion is a mechanism in the brain that manages the inflow of information and is a necessary, adaptive process. It is designed to maintain a balance between the amount of incoming information and a person's capacity to make use of it. Selective exclusion protects an individual from being overwhelmed by too much sensory input or distracted by too many attention-grabbing diversions. In the case of adverse conditions and circumstances in childhood, we can see how selectively excluding many kinds of information is adaptive. A child living in an unruly household with chaotic outbursts may sit quietly absorbed with their toy cars, appearing oblivious to the sounds of clashing pots and pans. However, by the time a person reaches adolescence or adulthood, the self-protective measure of continuing to exclude certain types of information can be maladaptive (Bowlby, 1980).

Bowlby (1980) recognized that defensive processes posited by psychoanalysts operate in a similar manner, and thereby he came up with the term "defensive exclusion" (p. 45) to specifically name what humans do to cope with hardship and distress. While the process of selective exclusion indeed provides adaptive functions, defensive exclusion might be helpful short term to help the child cope, but becomes maladaptive when individuals become habituated to and identified with their patterns; thus, inflexible.

Understanding how defensive exclusion operates helps psychotherapists orient to what may be occurring with our patients. As humans grow and develop, defensive exclusion comes into play when individuals need to protect themselves from what might be otherwise overwhelming. Excluding certain forms of information becomes a self-preserving defensive mechanism to help them cope. However, such exclusion may impact how these life experiences become stored in long-term memory.

When experiences are too difficult, overwhelming, or painful to manage, excluding aspects of these experiences from further processing makes the whole of the experience unobtainable to integrate. Thereby, a lack of accessibility to one's own history becomes "a form of amnesia" (Bowlby, 1980, p. 45). Having an amnesic barrier prohibits a person from having access to their memories. As an adult, an individual might recall certain events in their early life and yet be disconnected from their emotional valence and thereby unable to grasp the impact or significance of the memory. Or a person might have upwelling emotions that are out of proportion to their current life circumstances, without recognizing that the emotion is intensified because it touches on something related to their early life history.

Bowlby (1980) identifies "perceptual blocking" (p. 45) as another form of defensive exclusion, which results when information from the sense organs does not arrive to a person's awareness. One of my patients did not see her father in the room when she went to say goodnight to her mother. Her mother inquired, "Why are you not addressing your father?" She literally did not see him there. And the truth was that she was afraid of him. Perceptual blocking is a naturally occurring form of defensive exclusion. Preventing awareness of signals that bring fear or distress is another adaptive shield that interferes with the processing of underlying emotions. Amnesia and perceptual blocking are common defensive strategies that limit our human capacities for navigating the stresses of life. Many of our patients arrive for psychotherapy feeling compromised or caught in repetitive cycles, without understanding what is happening or what could be different.

Helping patients to become aware of defensive exclusion is often a crucial step in treatment to unravel stuck places in relationships. Patients benefit when they register how they are impacted by events in their life that are held in their nervous systems and emotional memory. They need to remember enough to understand how certain aspects of their current lives are connected to their prior history. When our patients can process their unresolved feelings, especially with a psychotherapist to accompany them in places where they were alone and unaided, and then reflect on their experiences to make sense of them, they can decipher what is truly adaptive from what is maladaptive.

Our next exploration unpacks the research of Mary Main and her colleagues about how individuals speak about their early attachment experiences. It is not only what individuals say or don't say, but how they speak that is so illustrative. These studies can inform psychotherapists of what to look for in our patient's discourse, and to recognize markers of security and insecurity in how they communicate about their attachment relationships. As well, it is helpful for psychotherapists to recognize patterns of defensive exclusion that are revealed by how patients speak. This research demonstrates not only how children's patterns emerge in direct correlation to their parents' patterns but also highlights the cyclical nature of development: how children grow into adults who influence the next generation of children. And on it goes.

Mary Main: Language and Attachment and the Adult Attachment Interview

Mary Main (1999b) read the Nobel Prize–winning linguist Noam Chomsky and was riveted by his study of "the human capacity for creating sentences which have never before been heard or spoken, and the generation of grammatically correct sentences by rule-bound processes, using rules we are unable to recite" (p. 685). She was inspired to study psycholinguistics at Johns Hopkins. However, the selection process for the doctoral program was based on apprenticeship, and Mary Ainsworth was the professor who accepted her.

Only Ainsworth's program was about mother–infant research. Her book *Infancy in Uganda* was recently published, and she was collecting and studying data from the home observations of the Baltimore study and from the Strange Situation laboratory procedure. Main's acceptance was with the condition that she would do her dissertation on attachment, specifically Strange Situation behavior.

This was troubling for Main. She was not interested in infants. She describes that from the age of 2 she was drawn to language in the form of natural speech. She was keen on words, though sometimes they confused her. For example, one memory she cites is that her parents called her a "pill" (a common description of an impetuous child from the 1950s). She retorted back to her parents "I am a *little girl*! I know what pills are, and a little girl *cannot also be a pill*!" [emphasis added] (Main et al., 2005, p. 249). She describes how her parents soothed her by explaining how some expressions were metaphors and they were using language in ways that she did not yet understand, but that she need not be worried about (Main et al., 2005).

Main was dismayed about entering Ainsworth's program because she did not see how she could find, much less follow, her most compelling interest. She did not see how babies and individual differences in patterns of mother–infant interactions had any connection to language. Her philosopher husband encouraged her that any field can be approached from many angles, "and that, learning to recognize variations in emotional relationships in children too young to speak could still eventually bring me back to language—perhaps enriched by this seemingly unpromising vantage point" (Main et al., 2005, p. 249).

I find this heartening to see how Main, with her fascination with the acquisition of language, was reluctantly guided toward her life's work in the moment she said yes. Little did she know that what intrigued her about Chomsky's universal rules about grammar is as intrinsic to human beings as attachment. One of her major contributions to the field would indeed combine both language and attachment through discoveries of individual differences in patterns of language discourse.

The Adult Attachment Interview

The discoveries of the Adult Attachment Interview (AAI) and elaborations of these findings provide yet another attachment tool very relevant to the practice of psychotherapy. This semistructured interview protocol, designed to "surprise the unconscious" (George et al., 1985), consists of about 20 questions about an individual's early relationships with their caregivers. The scoring of the AAI is determined by an incredibly intricate analysis of the verbatim transcripts of the interview and the patterns of discourse that emerge through the individual's responses. The results, based on the relationship between the subject's experience of their childhood, and their state of mind in describing their experience, expresses their overall attitude toward attachment.

These studies demonstrate how attachment patterns and internal representations maintain across time. The AAI's focus on the individual's state of mind provides a way to further understand what makes Bowlby's goal-corrected partnership such an important development of secure attachment. In a goal-corrected partnership, each person is capable of understanding the mind of another, while also holding what is in their own mind at the same time. They can collaborate; coordinate; share ideas, thoughts, and feelings; broker conflicts; and make plans. Through the AAI, we study components of the state of mind of an individual and can see how it functions independently and autonomously in secure relating, or how in insecure relating the mind remains in reaction to another, producing states of mind that are dismissing, become entangled, or confused/disoriented. These patterns illustrate what is working and what is not working that contribute to a person's capacity to know their own mind and to know the mind of another. The AAI depicts how attachment has become internalized, and through a speaker's patterns of discourse we can recognize areas that warrant exploration in psychotherapy.

How the AAI Works

Hesse (1996) stated that "the most central tasks of the AAI are to (1) produce and reflect upon relationships and experiences related to attachment history, *while simultaneously* [emphasis added] (2) maintaining coherent conversation with the interviewer" (Main et al., 2008, p. 35). It is this dual focus of the AAI that makes it such a generative instrument. Like in the work of psychotherapy, what a person knows (i.e., the content), and how the person discloses what they know and don't know (i.e., the process), can be quite revelatory.

The substantive structure of the AAI begins when the interviewee is asked to describe their relationship with each of their parents or the primary caregivers in their early life. Five adjectives or phrases are asked for to best represent each of the parent figures. Examples given might be "loving," "kind," "difficult," "fair," and "mean," which are followed by a request for a specific episodic memory to illustrate each description. This part of the interview is striking since each individual's elaboration of the adjectives may or may not support their chosen word or description.

This question, and many of the others, are unusual for how the material that unfolds takes the interviewee in directions most likely to "surprise the unconscious" (George et al., 1984; Main, 1995). Often these questions rouse emotionally charged events in childhood, which the interviewee may or may not have previously reflected upon or disclosed to anyone. Each presentation of their experiences varies according to what the individuals share, what they say, and how they remember their early experiences. Some individuals report little memory, responding with "I don't know" or "I don't remember." Others match their chosen words with a corresponding memory. Some meander and go off track, while others contradict themselves. Some show the capacity to tolerate shifting points of view in a search to be most accurate (Main, 1991, 1995).

Some questions in the AAI are geared to reveal how the individual regulated emotion during their childhood, what they would do when they were upset, injured emotionally or physically, and then what kind of help or care they received from caregivers (Main, 2000; Main et al., 2008). The interviewer probes to learn about the nature of the attachment experiences the person had as a child. How the person talks about these events and issues is the revealing factor, which is the hallmark of Main's interest in how language discourse and attachment experiences are correlated.

At the foundation of the AAI is the person's reflective functioning. Pondering how these experiences with their parents has affected their personality provides an opportunity to reflect on factors that have influenced their development. Other questions gather insight about how the person remembers feeling about each of their parents, whether they felt close to them and how they feel about their parents now. A most significant question assessing for the person's reflective functioning is what they understand about *why* their parents behaved as they did during their childhoods. How well the interviewee understands what motivates their parents' actions is key to the AAI and the kind of question that can be fertile ground for psychotherapists to explore with our patients. How readily can they reflect not only about their own attachment experiences but what they believe has motivated the actions of others close to them (Fonagy et al., 1995)?

Steele and Steele (2008) describe the AAI . . .

questions serve to activate the attachment system in the adolescent or adult respondent by taking the adult back in his or her mind to childhood or earlier life circumstances, when the attachment system was *previously* activated. Thus, the AAI can be seen in this light as a test of the extent to which one can remain balanced and coherent when thinking about

previously occurring attachment-related events or circumstances that
were emotionally upsetting, while showing understanding and/or valuing
of the persons and relationships concerned. (2008, p. 8; see also Dozier
& Kobak, 1992)

What is most salient for predicting security is *not* what level of trauma a
person has experienced in their life but *how they have processed and metabolized*
their experiences to be able to speak about them in a coherent and cohesive manner.

Bowlby (1973) tells us that a person's state of mind can be described by
their internal representations or working models. The SSP was designed
to activate an infant's attachment system to study and measure how the
infant behaves with respect to a particular person. The AAI protocol studies a person's attachment system by asking interviewees to think about
experiences in which their attachment system was activated. This uses the
reflective process and engages how attachment has been internalized and
represented. Thus, the AAI measures the person's state of mind toward
their overall attachment history, rather than to a particular relationship.
The results are assigned to one of the four or five classifications. When
administered to parents, each state of mind as determined from this interview predicts a corresponding pattern of infant response to the parent in
the Ainsworth Strange Situation (Main, 1995). The AAI research furthers
Ainsworth's research into the impact of maternal caregiving. She looked
at how mothers behaved toward their children, finding the qualities of
sensitivity and responsiveness to be instrumental in secure attachment.
The AAI takes the next step by identifying *how* the parent's state of mind
about attachment directly correlates to their child's pattern of attachment. In essence, the caregiver's state of mind governs how they interact
with their child, which in turn impacts how the child develops secure or
insecure attachment.

It's remarkable to see how each step of attachment research elegantly
builds onto the next, allowing us to see into what is happening behaviorally
and then what contributes to that behavior. These are the layers we can
address with our patients in psychotherapy. As we discover more about the
internal working models of our patients, we can help them to notice how
these models operate, where defensive exclusion might be happening, and
what issues need addressing.

Grice's Maxims

Discovering the work of the linguistic philosopher Paul Grice was the perfect accompaniment to Main and Goldwyn, who were interested in detailing specifications for identifying and rating coherence in the transcripts of discourses attained by the AAI. In addition to their 9-point scales, Grice's maxims were extraordinarily well suited as a means for analyzing the narratives. Grice had formulated what he considered to be a general overriding principle for achieving cooperative, coherent, rational discourse, called the cooperative principle (Grice, 1975). The four underlying maxims are:

1. *Quality*: Be truthful and have evidence for what you say.
2. *Quantity*: Be succinct, and yet complete.
3. *Relation*: Be relevant to the topic as presented.
4. *Manner*: Be clear and orderly.

The transcripts of speakers who could adhere to each of Grice's conversational maxims were classified as secure autonomous, whose babies were likely to be classified as securely attached. The transcripts of speakers who violated one or more of Grice's maxims were classified as insecure: either organized dismissing, whose babies' attachment would likely be classified as avoidant, or organized preoccupied (also referred to as entangled in the AAI classification system), whose babies' attachment was likely to be classified as ambivalent/resistant. Much later, after the classification and scoring systems for the AAI were developed, two more categories were named: one is unresolved/disorganized, in which the parent's state of mind is unresolved for trauma and their baby tended to be classified as disorganized/disoriented. The last category was seen as unclassifiable—since the speakers vacillated between dismissing and preoccupied strategies, enlisting two incompatible organized strategies.

The characteristics of those classified as secure autonomous showed their valuing of attachment figures and attachment-related experiences. There was apparent objectivity in how they described and evaluated their attachment relationships. They were found to be coherent by way of having access and the ability to evaluate memories while remaining truthful and collaborative (Main, 1995). The speech in these individuals had qualities of freshness, speaking with words and phrases that sounded original and unrehearsed. Main (1991) also noticed a quality of *metacognitive monitoring*.

This was reflected by the speaker's search for accuracy and consistency, often changing their descriptions to get closer to the truth that they were realizing (Main, 2000). In terms of Grice's maxims, they met the maxims for quality, quantity, relevance, and manner—and engaged in a way that was collaborative with the interviewers (Main, 2000; Main et al., 2008).

The discourse of the organized dismissing speakers reveals a devaluing of attachment relationships, minimizing their importance, giving descriptions of a caregiver without a supporting memory to corroborate. While on the surface dismissing speakers may appear collaborative, these kinds of internal contradictions render their responses untruthful. Thereby, the dismissing interviewee was likely to break the first maxim of Grice's, quality, for lacking truth and evidence, and the second, quantity, for being overly succinct or insisting on lack of memory for childhood (Main, 1995; Main et al., 2008).

Speakers whose discourse was deemed as organized preoccupied met the maxim of quality for how they identified the challenges of childhood experiences. However, the speaker's interviews revealed an excessive, confused preoccupation with their attachment figures that tended toward passivity or anger, seeming unconscious in how it was shown rather than stated. The discourse contained lengthy descriptions, which were often associative, entangled, and confusing for the interviewer—which was seen as noncollaborative. In terms of Grice's maxims, they violated the maxim of quantity by going on at excessive length, the maxim of relevance by straying from the topic, and the maxim of manner by confusing or peculiar phrasing: using psychological jargon, childlike speech, and nebulous phrases (Main, 1995, 2000; Main et al., 2008).

Move to the Level of Representation

Mary Main, Nancy Kaplan, and Jude Cassidy wrote a seminal article in 1985 in which they used the findings of the AAI to reconceptualize how individual differences appear in attachment behavior and in the formation of internal working models. They referred to this as the "move to the level of representation" (p. 66). They expanded the construct of looking at attachment at the behavioral level—as measured and studied by home observation and the SSP—to looking at how attachment is represented in the mind, studied, and measured through the AAI. They discovered how the internal working models of attachment correspond between parents and their children. They found . . .

where the parent's own experiences and feelings are not integrated, restrictions of varying types are placed on attention and the flow of information with respect to attachment. These restrictions appear in speech in the form of incoherencies and in behavior as insensitivities. (p. 100)

Thus, internal working models reflect not only individual differences in nonverbal behavioral patterns but individual differences in language and structures of the mind.

This extremely influential article presented the findings of the AAI, how the *state of mind* of the individuals who were interviewed show varying responses, and like the children studied through the SSP, they are different, but not that different. The first organized patterns they identified were secure, insecure dismissing, and insecure preoccupied.

Main recognized that the secure and insecure attachment patterns delineate into organized versus disorganized. In this section, and the preceding one, we discuss the organized patterns of attachment and refer the reader to both Chapter 11, "The History of the Disorganization Category," and Chapter 12, "Working to Transform Patterns of Disorganized Attachment," for discussion about disorganized attachment. The organized pattern is one that has a singular attentional focus, whether it be flexible or inflexible. The *secure* pattern shows attentional flexibility; the children move responsively between separation and reunion, showing and expressing feelings, allowing themselves to be soothed by their attachment figure when upset and able to direct and redirect attention to exploration. In the AAI, the corresponding pattern of *secure autonomous* also shows attentional flexibility. The speaker shows the capacity to recognize the importance of attachment relationships, and indicates flexibility among various aspects of missing, needing, and depending on others (Main, 1995). Other significant characteristics of the secure autonomous were "an ease in discussing attachment that suggested much reflection prior to the interview and a lack of idealization of parents or of past experiences" (Main et al., 1985, p. 91).

In the organized insecure avoidant patterns, the children's attentional strategies show degrees of inflexibility; their attention orients to the toys in the room, diverting away from the attachment figure, inhibiting their attachment needs. They tend to show minimal expression of affect, neither joy in play nor sadness in response to the attachment figure's comings and goings. The *dismissive* pattern in the AAI corresponds to the *avoidant* infant, and similarly, the individual's attention in a relative sense is oriented away from the importance of attachment, away from attachment needs, and toward an insulated self-reliance. If something negative was named regarding the caregiver, it was often reported in such a way as to be "good for me—I got stronger, and so on." Related to these descriptions, in Grid 2, The Configurations of Insecure Attachment Patterns (see Chapter 5), under avoidant, *wall of silence* is listed as a defense. Less for the number of words spoken, but more for what occurs when patients are asked about or confronted by issues related to attachment or emotions. Their responses can be hard to access.

The pattern of *ambivalence/resistance* in children showed degrees of inflexibility by their difficulty shifting attention away from the parent/caregivers toward the toys and the environment, to the point that even sometimes the separation segments of the SSP needed to be curtailed. Even when the parents returned, the children were still difficult to soothe and often remained angry, and/or passive, thus the term "resistant." In the AAI, the corresponding *preoccupied* strategy reveals the individual's challenge in shifting attention away from caregivers, still fixing to please them. They were inflexible in how they were caught in expressions of anger at past relationships with caregivers, to the exclusion of self-expression/exploratory behavior. Sometimes these adults attempted to draw the interviewer into agreement about how awful their caregivers were. In clinical practice, the term "wall of words" came to describe the discourse of patients with ambivalent/resistant patterning (Pando-Mars, 2016). In Grid 2, wall of words describes one of the verbal defensive strategies of this patterning, for the way words can be used to block relational contact and conceal more than reveal relevant emotion(s).

Flexibility occurs much more frequently in secure patterning and is something psychotherapists will want to cultivate in our patients through the course of treatment. We may also notice our own tendencies toward being flexible and inflexible, especially when treatment may not be flowing. Bowlby said people's attachment security can differ across relationships. Main et al. (1985) state with respect to the AAI that language and the structures of mind change according to the person's state of mind. They write,

Internal working models of relationships also will provide rules for the direction and organization of attention and memory, rules that permit or limit the individual's access to certain forms of knowledge regarding the self, the attachment figure, and the relationship between the self and the attachment figure. (p. 77)

This suggests how important it is to help our patients to establish a secure state of mind with us to make the most out of psychotherapy.

How is it that internal working models provide not only rules for what to expect in relationships but also strategies that influence how attention and memory are organized? This relates to what Bowlby identified in defensive exclusion: how children will exclude awareness of that which they cannot manage alone. Main (1995) provides an excellent description of how defensive exclusion develops when she describes what happens with the organized insecure attachment patterns of infants that are understood as behavioral strategies. She writes,

> In the service of maintaining these behavioral strategies, children avoidant or resistant with the primary caregiver in infancy may actively attempt to maintain a particular attentional/representational state. These states—eventually experienced as a kind of *"felt-security"* [emphasis added] and held in place by anxiety—may in adulthood be maintained through discourse violations and transmitted to the infant through insensitivity to infant signals. (p. 409)

The (now-adult) caregiver's defensive exclusion of their own needs makes them insensitive to their infant's signals, which prompts the infant's/child's turning to rely on defensive exclusion.

Attachment experiences are represented internally and extend beyond nonverbal patterns of behavior into how the mind holds, perceives, and remembers attachment experiences. To consider what this means in terms of psychotherapy treatment, Paul Wachtel (2014) has written about how hard it can be for some people to know what to talk about in psychotherapy: what matters to bring in and what issues are significant. The factor of fixed attentional states would seem to be at play here. When the primary caregiver is rejecting or unreliable in their availability, finding ways of coping that bring some degree of felt security would appear to be the next best thing. And to relinquish such strategies would be all the more difficult because they make up for something that was missing. Letting go of defenses would naturally raise anxiety and perhaps reveal painful experiences of unmet needs, longing, heartbreak, or despair. Therefore, as we continue to explore how psychotherapists can set conditions for helping patients to heal, Chapter 2, "The Move to Regulation & Coordination," looks at affect regulation from an attachment perspective, addressing brain development, mother–infant interaction studies, and neuroscience. All contribute to how psychotherapists can establish dyadic coordination and dyadic regulation in our work with patients to help them to feel support and thereby gain flexibility and access to matters of importance.

2

The Move to Regulation and Coordination

*Regulated and synchronized affective interactions with a familiar,
predictable primary caregiver creates not only a sense of safety, but
also a positively charged curiosity, wonder and surprise that fuels the
burgeoning self's explorations of novel, socioemotional and physical
environments. This ability is a marker of adaptive infant mental health.*
—(SCHORE, 2003, 2019A, P. 10)

*Research on mother–infant communication might seem very far from
the clinician's day-to-day concerns in the practice of adult treatment.
But in fact, the moment-to-moment self and interactive processes of
relatedness documented in infant research are the bedrock of adult
face-to-face communication as well. They provide the background
fabric for the verbal narrative that is in the foreground.*
—(BEEBE, 2019)

REGULATION IN HUMAN BEINGS INCLUDES THE PROCESS OF NAVIGATING
distress or alarm, and the emotions associated with it, with the purpose
of restoring balance. Between caregivers and children, there is a dynamic
equilibrium that is constantly changing due to circumstances in the child's
internal and external life and the caregiver's capacity to respond effectively. Children need their attachment figures and caregivers for protection,
survival, emotional and physical well-being, and also for help regulating
their emotions: All of these are needed for optimal functioning. Emotions
and affect are at the core of human experience. Whether we are alone or
accompanied in the face of overwhelming emotions—be they negative or

positive—influences how we relate to emotions—our own and those of others—and our range of expression.

Bowlby's conceptualization that working models of self and other are complementary is pertinent to the issue of affect regulation (i.e., the regulation of emotions associated with the vicissitudes of attachment). A child who has been responded to with appropriate comfort and care in times of distress gains confidence in their capacity to express themselves. According to Ainsworth and Bell (1972), "Maternal responsiveness provides the conditions for a normally functioning infant to influence what happens to him by influencing the behavior of his mother" (p. 3) and "The responsiveness of a mother figure to the infant's signals promotes the development of infant communication—and hence the development of social competence" (p. 4). When the child's affective signals bring the necessary attention and aid for regulatory assistance, they build trust in the caregiver, and confidence in their capacity to draw the help that is needed. Over time being understood leads to self-understanding; being listened to leads to listening to oneself. Bowlby allegedly said, "What cannot be communicated to the mother (caregiver) cannot be communicated to the self." Being contingently connected to one's attachment figure leads to one's being connected to oneself: Dyadic regulation is at the heart of self-regulation and brings heart to communication with others.

Experiences that evolve into patterns between caregivers and children become represented internally, as we discussed in Chapter 1. So do the emotions associated with the patterns that are discussed in greater detail in Chapter 3, when we review the SOE configuration. In the current chapter, in order to dive more deeply into the interactive, dyadic processes that underlie regulatory functions, we look at the studies of the "baby watchers" of mother–infant interactions (Beebe & Lachman, 1998, 2014; Stern, 1985; Trevarthen, 1979; Tronick, 1989, 1998). Then we focus more specifically on how the emotions associated with attachment behaviors are processed by the dyad, and become wired into our nervous systems (LeDoux, 1996; Schore, 1994, 2019).

Perhaps the best news from the so-called decade of the brain, which began in the mid-1990s, is the science of positive neuroplasticity, and how under conducive conditions, our brains have the capacity to heal and repair impeded growth (Doidge, 2007, 2016; Hanson, 2013; Hansen & Hansen, 2020), and continue to do so throughout our lives. As psychotherapists, we can maximize the effectiveness of psychotherapy by understanding mechanisms in the brain and the nervous system that allow the processing of our emotions and by implementing practices that harness positive neuro-plasticity to galvanize change and transformation in our patients.

Our adult patients enter treatment with varying pathways and obsta-cles for self-regulation and the regulation of their emotions, and often need our help. When a therapist chooses a stance as an attachment figure, we embody the role of one who is available to provide dyadic regulation. Psychotherapists can make use of our own nervous systems to foster the growth of emotional regulation in our patients. Thus, we aim to attend to their nervous system arousal and what may be needed to help them to up regulate or down regulate to facilitate exploration and healing. Regulation in our adult patients optimally includes being in touch with somatically rooted emotional experience, characterized by (a) a balance between think-ing (reflection) and feeling (emotion), (b) awareness of self and other, and (c) having enough activation to be able to connect with emotions yet not so much activation that it leads to being overwhelmed by them.

Implicit Memory Is Elemental
in Patterns of Attachment

In the following section, we introduce some of the caregiver–infant inter-action studies and look at the intricate interplay of face-to-face communi-cations in the formation of attachment and affect regulation. Microanalysis of these interactive patterns reveals minute details of how on a moment-to-moment basis infants and caregivers engage with each other, falling in and out of sync. The way each caregiver and child navigates the process of attunement, disruption, and repair points to areas that lie at the root of regulatory aspects of our patient's internal working models. We do this because in these studies are the foundations that explain our approach to psychotherapy and the attuned tailoring of interventions to the different attachment patterns. These studies are foundational.

Many of our early affective experiences with caregivers become coded into implicit memory—that is, they are wired into the early formation of our nervous systems. For psychotherapists, keen awareness and obser-vation of what shows up nonverbally in our patients helps us to register what is being expressed implicitly and may lie outside of our patients' self-awareness. Seeds of our patients' nonverbal interactive behaviors lie in their earliest attachment relationships. When we help our patients to slow down and become curious about what may be stirring as they begin sharing with us, we may discover what significant terrain we are in.

Attachment From the Beginning

The umbilical cord is literally our original lifeline to growth and development. Following birth, this lifeline is replaced by the relationship between caregiver and child. In the time when Bowlby was developing attachment theory, the logic of the day was that babies form attachments with their caregivers because the mothers feed the babies and provide for their basic needs, such as warmth and comfort, proximity, food, rest, stimulation, and cleanliness. The prevailing attitude that the caregiver is meeting the baby's physiological needs is the basis for attachment.

Yet, Bowlby and then Ainsworth were developing a very different understanding of how a child develops secure ties to their attachment figures, and what truly nourishes well-being. Attachment is essential to survival. Attachment brings so much more than satisfaction of needs. How these needs are met is infused by an emotional interplay that fosters connection, trust, and well-being: a call-and-response between child and caregiver.

A video produced by Beatrice Beebe shows a 10-minute-old baby held face-to-face with his father who sticks his tongue out at the baby. The baby responds by sticking out its own tongue, immediately imitating the father's action. This sweet moment illustrates our human predisposition to relate and connect from the get-go. It's wondrous to see the way a 10-minute-old baby and their father express delight in each other's presence. Their dynamic interaction exemplifies the *vitality affects* identified by Daniel Stern (1985) that rise between parent and child. The baby responds to the father, who is looking for a response from the baby. Call-and-response are part of rapport building. Hormonally, it is driven by dopamine and laden with oxytocin, fomenting the tracks toward social engagement, positive reinforcement, developing recognition, and mattering from the start. The father's deliberate gesture to the baby, and the baby's response to the father demonstrates how delight and orientation take place between parent and child.

Along with Beebe and Lachman (2014), Beebe et al. (2016), Stern (1985, 2010), Ed Tronick (1989, 1998, 2009), and Colwyn Trevarthen (2001, 2009) elaborate the bidirectional aspect of caregiver–infant communications and emphasize how the signals and cues conveyed by an infant are significant affective communications springing from a sentient being, which must be sensitively received and actively engaged by the caregiver. The infant's subjective experience becomes capable of intersubjectivity with their caregiver, which Trevarthen (2001) recognized, saying that "the infant can be involved, even at six weeks, in a comprehensive mutual and reciprocal engagement of motive states colored by subtle emotional expressions" (p. 102). This back-and-forth exchange between infant and caregiver is a form of instinctive communication, which Mary Catherine Bateson named "protoconversations," seeing how they set the stage for the learning of language (Trevarthen, 2001).

Each member of the dyad is biologically wired to connect, and this begins at the beginning. When caregivers engage with the baby emotionally, respond in such a way that meets their baby's needs, help them to reach their goals, and restore equilibrium, they are establishing bidirectional trust and understanding, which uplifts the baby's system with vitality and connection (Stern, 1985). Mutual call-and-response lays the tracks for attachment bonding and affect regulation, and gives rise to establishing secure and/or insecure attachment.

In the following section, we discuss some of the caregiver–infant interaction studies. What happens in the first weeks and months of life sheds light on how early experiences with their caregiver influences the child's capacity for relatedness. Relatedness with their caregiver is internalized into the child's nervous system and impacts how they develop their patterns of regulating emotion. Through these interactive studies we see how the capacity for self-regulation grows from the baby's experience of dyadic affect regulation and what happens to set this development on or off course.

The Origins of Relatedness in Mother–Infant Interaction Studies

Mother–infant interaction studies echo and further elaborate and deepen Ainsworth's observational work. They examine how the communications between caregiver and child affect the growing infant's sense of self and foster healthy development. Beebe and her research collaborators studied face-to-face interactions between mothers and infants at 4 months old and have found their results to corroborate the Strange Situation studies. While the Strange Situation is designed to study separation and reconnection, and attachment and exploration, Beebe's interaction studies focused on moment-to-moment "facial mirroring" and "disruption and repair" during 3-minute intervals of "play." Microanalysis of videotapes that show mother–infant

social patterns and regulatory behaviors, usually below conscious awareness, reveal what becomes procedural learning or implicit memory (Beebe
& Lachman, 2014).

Coders of these films are looking at face-to-face communication
exchanges, such as attention and gaze; facial and vocal affective expressions;
physical orientation: how the mother is sitting up, leaning in, or looming,
while also observing the orientation of the infant's head and whether the
infant is leaning in or arching away; and other's affectionate versus intrusive
touch of the infant. The infant's touching self, mother, object, or reaching
toward mother reveals how touch brings soothing or is interfering (Beebe
& Lachman, 2014).

Schore describes the attunement that takes place during mother–infant
interactions as the process of affect synchrony, which is crucial to regulating infants and important to establishing psychotherapeutic relationships.
Schore (2012) states,

> The more the mother contingently tunes her activity to the infant during
> periods of social engagement, the more she allows him to recover quietly
> in periods of disengagement, and the more she attends to his reinstating
> cues for reengagement, the more synchronized their interaction. In play
> episodes of affect synchrony, the pair are in affective resonance, and in
> such, an amplification of vitality affects and a positive state occurs. (p. 32)

Schore (2012) relates affect synchrony to psychotherapy when he says:

> At the most essential level, the intersubjective work of psychotherapy is
> not defined by what the therapist does for the patient or says to the patient
> (left brain focus). The key mechanism is how to be with the patient, espe-
> cially during affectively stressful moments (right brain focus). (p. 44)

While we value interventions much more than Schore suggests in the latter
part of the above quote, nevertheless, we very much agree that "being with"
our patients and how we are with them at moments of intense interaction is
crucial. To imagine being with our patients in a way that meets them at this
most essential level, mother–infant interaction studies reveal key aspects of
what takes place during mutual affective coordination.

To illustrate how regulation operates through mutual affective coordination we turn to Beebe's work. Beebe et al. (2016) examined the

mother–infant interactions frame by frame, in 20-second intervals, to see the subtle and rapid details of changes that occur between each member of the dyad. These films show how babies and their mothers have a remarkable range of engagement and disengagement behaviors, and that both are active participants in exchanges of pleasure and distress, dysregulation, and coregulation. Throughout repeated sequences of interactions, babies develop *expectancies*. As these sequences repeat, babies begin to anticipate how the interactions will proceed, which become represented as their internal working models of attachment (see Beebe et al., 2016, Chapter 1). When the child has reached 12–24 months of age and can move toward and away from their mothers on their own, what took place during the interactions at 4 months old predicts how they will classify through the SSP.

Understanding how expectancies develop, and how they appear, is an asset for the psychotherapeutic work of setting conditions for security with our patients, to help them develop new expectancies and consequently help transform their insecure or disorganized internal working models. When babies and mothers are tracking with each other and enjoying moments of connection, there is a synchrony of pleasure, shared and expanded, which can be stoked and calmed in such a way that amplifies and regulates positive affect, building secure dyadic coordination.[1] When babies show distress and their mothers respond to their cues in such a way that mirrors their distress, babies often settle, allowing recoordination to take place. If the baby turns away, and the mother is patiently present when they look back, they develop expectancies that when they need a moment to self-regulate, mother is okay and will be there when they return. She neither abandons nor intrudes.

These aspects of engagement don't need to be perfectly matched and attuned. The child may need space, and it may take the mother a moment to realize this. If the baby frowns and shows upset, and their mother's expression matches theirs with a downturned lip or look of concern, babies can experience being reflected accurately and met in a moment of distress. The mother may look away as the child is turning back, but the child may then whimper or become fussy. When the mother hears the protest or cry and matches and mirrors the infant's sound, this communication can bring the pair back into contact. Trust builds when a momentary disruption leads to reconnection and repair, especially when the mother's empathic joining successfully regulates the baby's distress and helps both members of the dyad shift into a pleasurable state.

These sensitive and attuned responses build the infant's expectancies that they can be met and understood. As described above, affective engagement does not mean perfect attunement. Rather it is made of momentary adjustments of falling in and out of sync, forming interaction sequences that develop into meaning-making skills that Karlen Lyons-Ruth (2006) describes as necessary for "sharing affective evaluations and shared intentional states with others . . ." (p. 597). Through such moments of verbal and nonverbal interactive communications, infants engage actively with their caregivers. When their caregivers are reading their affective cues and responding contingently, this bidirectional communication provides pathways that help both members of the dyad to "feel felt," to use Dan Siegel's (2010) apt phrase (i.e., to feel effective, sensed, and known; Beebe et al., 2016), building trust in self and other, and building their capacity to understand and be understood (Fonagy & Target, 1997, 2002).

It is not hard to imagine such interactive moments with our psychotherapy patients. For example, in the process of seeking to understand and attune to our patients, we may find ourselves engaging with our patients though eye contact. The patient might look away and then back to reconnect. We might wonder what is going on in the way our patients make and break this connection, as they look toward and away. When does eye contact with our patients increase connection and togetherness and when does it seem to bring discomfort? And what might this reveal about our patients' expectancies?

Sometimes eye contact stretches into a mutual gaze. There can be a quality of absorption, a deep experience of receptivity. Contact at this nonverbal level has the power to enhance the experience of resonance and feeling felt (Siegel, 2010) to undo aloneness, to promote "existing in the mind and heart of another" (Fosha, 2000b, p. 57; Fosha, 2021a, p. 34).

During her psychotherapy session, one of my patients was looking down and away from me while experiencing strong emotion. When she looked up, she was surprised to see my eyes focused on her. Our interaction revealed her expectation that she would not be seen, which directly related to her experience of not seeing her reflection in her mother's eyes. Even worse was what she had seen in her mother's eyes and internalized: blankness and the absence of delight. Her implicit memory and its subsequent expectancy were disrupted by the new experience of our interaction.[2] When my gaze stayed with her, even when she turned away, and was there to greet her when she returned, a new experience was available to be had. It was possible for her not to be alone in a time of distress. A couple of months later, after an explicit exchange about our growing relationship, we both found ourselves lingering in a mutual gaze, quietly savoring the experience of seeing and being seen. Deep nourishment happens in seeing oneself being seen and can bring about repair at an essential place of meeting and being understood.

Sometimes mothers and infants are out of sync, and psychotherapists can benefit from considering some of the ways Beebe et al. (2016) identified patterns of mismatch in mothers and infants. Mismatches in affective signals occur when an infant's expression is met by a discordant reaction in the mother. For instance, discomfort expressed by the infant is met by a wide smile on the mother's face. Or when the baby averts their gaze, the mother anxiously pulls for their attention to come back. The mother may loom over the infant, feeling worried that the baby's turning away is a sign of dislike for her. She might engage in sequences of chase and dodge. When the infant leans back and squirms, and instead of backing away a bit, or giving the baby space, the mother moves forward, intently trying to capture the infant's attention; she is probably unaware or unable to register what her baby actually needs.

It is human nature to be imperfect in attuning to each face-to-face expression when mother and infant are playing and engaging. In fact, studies have shown that mismatched states, sometimes referred to as *interactive errors*, occur in approximately two thirds of the time in face-to-face interactions (Tronick, 1989). The significant element is how the mother responds when the baby indicates something is amiss, and how quickly the dyad returns to a coordinated state. When the pair can readjust within a couple of seconds, these studies, when the babies are 4 months old, have predicted their secure attachment at 1 year (Beebe et al., 2016).

Beebe highlights that when the mother does not recognize nor shift her response to ease the baby's distress, the distress is likely to escalate.[3] Such mismatches are disturbing. Beebe is clear in her communications to the observers of these painful encounters that this mother is most likely unresolved for trauma herself. Her infant's distress triggers the mother's own abuse or loss from early life, activating her own historical wiring. She may be dysregulated and confused by her baby's upset or see the baby as unsoothable. The baby may turn away, grimace, wiggle their arms and legs to show displeasure and a desire to change the input somehow, to signal to the mother that something else is needed. Yet, such upset often increases the mother's stress and distress, leading her to feel helpless and incompetent. Her reaction may even show fear, rage, or disgust.

The baby's averted gaze can be a signal of the baby's self-regulation in an attempt to manage arousal (Beebe et al., 2016). However, when the mother is unable to adjust her behavior to meet and respond contingently to her infant's distress, disturbance grows and confusion sets in. The baby develops expectancies that they cannot be understood. This painful cycle generates dismay for both mother and child. Both members of the pair are miserable, in what is developing to be an insecure/disorganized dyad. We explore aspects of how this dynamic may appear in our adult patients in Chapter 11 and how specifically we can intervene in Chapter 12.

We emphasize that not all mismatch and disruption leads to disorganization. During caregiver–infant interactions the movement between coordination and miscoordination is ongoing and a natural part of a relationship, which is happening two thirds of the time in face-to-face communications (Tronick, 1989, 1998). Through his research of coordinated states between mothers and infants, Tronick describes the infant as an active participant, who regulates their internal states with behaviors like looking away and self-touch, and seeks to initiate interactive exchanges with behaviors like looking toward and smiling. Both the mother and the infant play an active role in reading each other's implicit communications, and this bidirectional engagement informs what Tronick refers to as *mutual regulation* (Tronick, 1989, 1998). Infant and caregiver make meaning of each other's displays of emotion and adjust their responses accordingly to coordinate their interactions.

For instance, the baby is looking toward an object at a bit of a distance, and reaches toward it, but cannot take hold. If the caregiver sees the direction of the baby's attention, they might bring the object closer to the baby, who can then grasp it. By sensing the baby's goal, and scaffolding their attempt, caregivers attune to their child's intentions. This may bring a surge of positive affect and synchronous pleasure to both members of the dyad, feeling the success of their collaboration. These are also the beginnings of what Bowlby was referring to as goal-corrected behavior. When the caregiver demonstrates understanding of the baby's wishes and helps the baby to reach the object they are seeking, the baby, through coordination with their caregiver, gets a sense of being effective to navigate the discrepancy between what they want and achieving it (see Chapter 1, p. 30, for goal-corrected behavior).

If the caregiver is not available to assist the child, the child might become frustrated. Yet the child is equipped with "self-directed regulatory behaviors" (Tronick, 1989, p. 113). The child can cope by redirecting their attention away from what is upsetting; they can self-soothe by sucking their thumb, thus shifting a negative state into a positive one. This might provide a respite after which they might reengage with their goal or their caregiver. Such moments of recalibrations are part of the infant's early development of self-regulation, which goes hand in hand with the dyadic regulation that occurs with their caregiver. When there is a misunderstanding or a misreading of the other, this generates a miscoordination that needs repair.

How Dyadic States Expand Consciousness

Tronick's caregiver–infant studies look at the meaning-making function of dyadic communication and regulation. When the caregiver understands signals from the infant, they provide an appropriate response. The appropriate response can also be to repair a miscoordination. They can apply their understanding to scaffold their infant's interests and goals, which helps their infants to develop more capacity to operate with more complexity. Thus, both members are part of a dyadic system that expands each of their own consciousness to develop more coherence. Tronick (1998) says, "At this moment of forming a dyadic state of consciousness, and for the duration of its existence, there must be something akin to a powerful experience of fulfillment as one paradoxically becomes larger than oneself" (p. 296). When the caregiver responds to the attachment behavior of their infant, and when the infant is met by the capable response of the caregiver, they each take on aspects of the other's consciousness. As a process of mutual regulation occurs, something beyond each individual emerges as synchronization takes place and each one's consciousness is expanded. Through this enhanced connection, new potentials can appear, growing new awareness, new abilities, and new realizations, giving rise to mutual delight and vitality (Stern, 1985; Tronick, 1998). What a perfect description and aspiration for psychotherapists as we help our patients to reach their goals and transform their patterning through the relational experiences of psychotherapy!

What This Means for Psychotherapists

When we are working with patients, there are key dyadic moments to look out for; something new and different is happening in our meeting as patient and therapist. Perhaps a spontaneous unfolding begins to flow, as one interaction lands and unexpected emotion comes forth. There might be halting or hesitation that warrants attention and exploration. When disruption occurs, the important step is to notice the disconnection with an intention to understand what happened and what is needed to move to repair, so recoordination can follow. Such moments fuel the potential to enhance and restore our patient's trust in the capacity for relational connection. The research of caregiver–infant interaction studies reveals how influential our interactive communications are. What originally happens in the formation of secure and insecure patterning recurs during the change process in psychotherapy. Beebe and Lachman, and Tronick's research into attunement, disruption, and repair, normalizes the place miscoordination plays in everyday life. It illustrates mechanisms for enlarging our capacity for dyadic engagement and consciousness and enhancing our patient's capacity for making meaning about experiences that may have originally been bewildering and disturbing.

This is crucial for psychotherapists. While we do not need to be continually attuned to our patients, we do need to register their signals and help them to face and express what may be happening within themselves and/or between us. Disruption and even rupture is not the problem, as if it were a fait accompli. The moment of rupture can be expanded. Disruption needs recognition, rupture needs repair, and miscoordination needs recoordination. When psychotherapists have a disruption with a patient and we can help both ourselves and the patient through it, something can move beyond the breakdown as we find our way to regain equilibrium and connection. We both can discover that we are bigger than what happened. We don't have to be perfect; we only must want to know what we need to know to correct the miscoordination, and stay engaged to help the other feel seen, understood, and significant enough. Sometimes this happens during an exchange that goes back and forth a few times. Sometimes repair takes repeated efforts over many sessions.

I want to share a relevant experience. When I was a patient, over 15 years ago, I experienced a disturbing miscoordination with my psychotherapist during a session. I remember the moment vividly. I was struggling with a repellent feeling when seeing my therapist's face and was unable to find words for my experience that felt acceptable to speak aloud. I looked down and away from her. And then, sitting across from me, she ducked her head underneath my gaze, and peered up into my face. I felt ashamed, like I was caught doing something wrong. I didn't understand why she peered in so closely, which intensified my feeling of discomfort and dislike.

We never spoke about this interaction. She didn't give her action any words, nor did she help me to explore what caused me to avert my gaze. In hindsight, this exchange factored into the end of our therapy relationship, which I want to emphasize was not because of what happened but because we didn't talk about it, nor did we ever find a way to repair the initial lack of attunement, which then became a rupture that was never tended.

Considering Tronick's description, an expansion of consciousness was greatly needed—I needed a larger vessel than fear and inhibition to explore my unpleasant reaction—and I needed her help. I imagine she needed more perspective to deal with whatever was evoked in her, to help her engage in other than a chase and dodge, and then an upside-down loom interaction with me. I share this because the importance of this interaction is more evident the more I learn about caregiver–infant interactions and the meaningful occurrences that appear nonverbally. To register that the patient could be looking away to self-regulate at a difficult moment, the therapist might consider how the attachment system is at play and notice whether any disruption might have occurred. Even more simply, we don't need to know exactly what happened and why. We need to register, though, that something happened. We can simply notice the looking away and check in with the patient. And it might take being courageous to meet such moments with engagement and curiosity.

In AEDP, psychotherapists are trained to make the implicit explicit. We work explicitly with the relationship. In the case above, ideally an AEDP therapist could notice "Oh, I see you are looking down now, did something just happen?" or "Would it be okay to explore if something is coming up between us or something difficult is arising?" Depending on how established the relationship is makes a difference in how the therapist might pose such an inquiry. The point is that during our interactions, our patients give us broad or subtle cues about what they are feeling. Being attentive and respectful to these affective signals from our patients is essential to generating safety to be present together with whatever arises. Our sensitive response can offer acceptance and willingness to hold and engage with material that might reveal our patient's historical wounds from miscoordination and disconnection.

Parent/child and adult/adult relationships work in this same way. The willingness to explore and communicate about missteps and disruptions can lead to repair and an expanded consciousness as each member of the dyad grows through greater understanding of self and other.

Mother–infant interaction studies provide behavioral examples that converge with findings from applied neuroscience and interpersonal neurobiology: our earliest experiences shape how our brains develop and what we come to expect in ourselves and from others. Before the age of 2 years, blueprints of early experiences are stored in implicit memory and form the neural circuitry of our internal working models. These models, and how they are wired, govern how we perceive self and other, and how we regulate and express ourselves in our attachment relationships throughout our lives.

When children have been raised with loving care, are helped to regulate intense affective states, and are guided with understanding, they develop a sense of themselves as capable and lovable. Their self-representation is one in which the self feels worthy of protection and responsiveness. The other comes to be represented as responsible and reliable (Fosha, 2000b, 2021b), someone who will show up when help is needed. On the other hand, when children are not met adequately, and instead the response or lack of response is misattuned or frightening, children grow with a sense of unworthiness, a lack of feeling known and understood, and untrusting that others are available and capable to respond. The self-representation is one in which the self is unworthy and/or incapable and others are represented as untrustworthy and unreliable (Fosha, 2000b, 2021b), and as such, emotions cannot be processed by the dyad, and thus not by the self. Internal representations of self and other are set down in our neural circuitry. In the following section we look at the neural underpinnings involved in different parts of the brain and their somatic markers and what this contributes to affect regulation with our adult patients.

Linkages in the Brain

Neuroscience Underpinnings of Secure and Insecure Attachment

The most significant consequence of early relational trauma is the loss of the ability to regulate the intensity and duration of affects. (Schore, 2003, p. 141)

Looking at how caregiver–infant interactions affect how infants develop expectancies about their caregivers directly relates to what Ainsworth and Bowlby recognized as the internalization of attachment. From her earliest studies Ainsworth (1967) realized that not only do experiences between infants and their caregivers become internalized and form patterns but that this process involves an "inner mechanism which we identify with central nervous system functions" (p. 436). Bowlby recognized that at first, an infant's capacity to cope with emotional stress is coregulated by interactions with their mother/caregiver. As the child develops and becomes purposeful in their aim to achieve goals, they show the beginnings of self-regulation as they seek interactions with another or find internal mechanisms to auto-regulate. Both Ainsworth and Bowlby were attempting to identify how mechanisms in the infant's brain were influencing and being influenced by their attachment experiences. Early on, Bowlby suggested that the limbic system was a part of the brain associated with attachment behaviors (Bowlby, 1969/1982; Schore, 2000b).

Bowlby (1969/1982) explored how attachment behavioral systems were a way to understand more specifically the concept of "evolutionary adaptedness" (p. 64), that is, how young beings survive and learn to cope with stress. Sroufe (2005) elaborated that confidence in one's capacity to remain organized, even in the face of high arousal, begins with entraining regulatory capacities through dyadic attachment relationships. He defined attachment as the dyadic regulation of emotion (Sroufe, 1996), and Schore (2000a, 2000b, 2000c, 2001) asserted that attachment theory is in essence a regulatory theory. According to Schore, Bowlby's early ideas about attachment and the brain hold up at the end of the decade of the brain—and were "prescient" (Schore, 2000b, p. 29).

At the time research about how the brain processes emotions was entering the picture (Damasio, 1994; LeDoux,1996), contributions from affective neuroscience and interpersonal neurobiology began to describe how our attachment experiences become etched into our nervous systems. Experiences that occur in the first 2–3 years of life, during the growth of attachment, are happening while the infant's brain is developing. They shape the infant's maturing brain and thereby directly influence the brain's neural circuitry, which is forming lifelong patterns of its stress response, and social/emotional capacities (Bowlby, 1969/1982; Schore, 2001). Cozolino (2006) describes, "In relationships, like mother and child, we are constructing neural networks in the brain, transposing maternal behavior into biological structure" (p. 87).

Research data show that the infant brain's right hemisphere develops before the left hemisphere (Schore, 1994, 2003, 2012, 2019b). Simply put, the right brain has been considered the emotional brain while the left is described as the thinking brain. The right brain processes nonverbal signals and is more holistic and imagistic. Early on, the infant's maturing right brain processes are impacted by their caregiving experiences, as they process information through the brain stem and the limbic system. The right brain is also what gives rise to the infant's developing stress response and their capacity to regulate emotions (Schore, 2019a, 2019b; Siegel, 2012). The right brain records implicit memory and is primarily involved during the formation of the child's early expectancies and internal working models.

The left hemisphere of the brain begins to come online in the second year of life. It is verbal and linguistic, linear, analytical, and logical. It is the domain of cognitive strategies. Interestingly, while the right brain is known to process intense emotions—negative ones like rage, fear, disgust, and shame—the left brain processes the "highly verbal emotions," like guilt and worry (Schore, 2019b), but also positive ones, like love and joy (Davidson & Schuyler, 2015).

Since the mid-1990s, there has been an increased use of brain imaging, such as functional magnetic resonance imaging (fMRI) and single-photon emission computed tomography (SPECT) scans to determine what regions of the brain are at play in a particular way and time. Early on, Schore (2001) drew upon the brain imaging research to provide evidence for the initial growth of the right hemisphere of the brain. He wrote,

> This developmental principle is now supported in a recent photon emission computed tomographic (SPECT) study by Chiron et al. (1997), which demonstrates that the right brain is dominant in preverbal human infants, and indeed for the first 3 years of life. (p. 32)

In the next section, we identify what regions of the brain and the nervous system are involved in attachment experiences and how related emotions are activated and terminated, forming implicit memory and internal working models of self and other. How the child learns to regulate and express affective and relational experiences directly relates to the adults who they become; understanding more about how the brain functions can help us attend to the adults who arrive for psychotherapy.

Neural Circuits of Attachment and Innate Human Potential

The attachment relationship . . . directly shapes the maturation of the infant's right brain, which comes to perform adaptive functions in both the assessment of visual and auditory socio-economic communication signals and the human stress response. (Schore, 1996, p. 63)

Infants are forming expectation sets of safety and threat in the way they experience and share emotional states with their caregivers, which include moments of attunement, disruption, and repair (Beebe & Lachman, 2016; Tronick, 1998). This depends on how long the dyads are in or out of coordination, and how well they resolve these experiences influences what they come to anticipate, and the meaning they associate with these events (Tronick & Gold, 2019).

Attachment communications take place right brain to right brain between the infant and the mother/caregiver. Bowlby proposed that in attachment relationships, the infant detects human feelings through "facial expressions, posture, tone of voice, physiological changes, tempo of movement and incipient action" (Schore, 2012, quoting Bowlby, 1969, p. 120). The right brain is picking up, processing, and recording these experiences, which Mary Ainsworth was observing as the mother's/caregiver's way of being with the child: how she delights in her child (Ainsworth, 1967) and how sensitively she responds and is available to care for her child (see the Maternal Caregiving and Interaction Scales; Ainsworth et al., 1978/2015; Chapter 1).

Schore (2012) suggests that the caregiver's complementary right-brain response involves "attending to, perceiving, recognizing, monitoring, appraising and regulating non-verbal expressions of the infant's more and more intense states of positive and negative affective arousal" (p. 8). This is the interactive process between caregiver and child, and just as significant as regulating negative arousal is encouraging exploration and the stimulation of positive states, like curiosity and wonder.

There is also growing recognition of the existence of a neurobiological core self: a core mammalian neural subcortical organization, cross-species (Damasio, 1999, 2010; Northoff & Panksepp, 2008; Panksepp & Northoff, 2009). Each one has a unique capacity for self-organization that integrates body, brain, and environment to orient the organism in its support of life goals according to "Self-Related Processing . . . the process that transforms stimuli from simple signals to a meaningful (i.e. valuative) part of the organism's functioning" (Panksepp & Northoff, 2009, p. 199). Northoff & Panksepp (2008) assert that "Neuroscience can now pursue what ethology has surmised . . . which is the idea that all mammals share foundational brain substrates"—of subcortical and cortical midline structures—"for a core self that allows them to be active creatures in the world as opposed to simply passive recipients of information" (p. 259). To us, this supports how infants come to be active participants in their development of attachment and speaks to our adaptive nature that is innate to human beings and other creatures. And it speaks to how, in conditions that are conducive for healing, self-righting comes online. More about this in the sections ahead on neuroplasticity.

Recognition that infants come into the world as self-directed beings gave further distinction to Bowlby's ideas, which countered the "cupboard theory of love." Trevarthen (2009) wrote that human babies are born with an innate predisposition to relate to another human being: From the get-go "they are equipped with intentions and feelings" (p. 59). They are subjectively capable of expression and intersubjectively capable of relating. As per Stern (1985), babies are born with "a sense of a core self" (p. 27; Damasio, 1994). Contrary to earlier prevailing views, infants are wired to communicate in relationships as themselves from the earliest moments of their existence.

Since the right brain is so figural in terms of the child's development, it is fitting for psychotherapists to recognize our right-brain to right-brain engagement with patients as an essential aspect of treatment. Wounding that happened through failures in early attachment is recorded in implicit memory. When we look into our patients' eyes, when we greet them with warmth and the prosody of our voice conveys delight and welcome, we are signaling a right-brain to right-brain positive affective response—how we feel as we invite patients into our mutual space. So much of our communication takes place nonverbally and implicitly. Providing attention and care involves the very attributes Schore describes about the infant's caregiver's response. As attachment-oriented psychotherapists, we lean into our innate wired-in caregiving behavioral system (Bowlby, 1969/1982) to receive and engage our patients. We open our perception to recognize how they arrive, and to attune to them we might make subtle adjustments to meet them where they are. We notice their nonverbal signals and appraise their well-being, their emotional state, their nervous system activation or calm, and their facial expressions, and offer coregulation to their positive or negative arousal. This is all largely happening implicitly while greeting each other and getting started in our session may be in the foreground.

Beginning at Birth

The child's brain encodes such caregiving moments in implicit memory in the young preverbal brain that is growing through right-hemispheric interactions. It is important to grasp how the attachment behavioral system and the caregiving behavioral system are innate biological predispositions. The earliest signal-and-response behaviors are evidence of the equally innate neurobiological core self. As Trevarthen (2009) said, each human being is equipped with sentience, intentions, and emotions, and this enables their attachment behavioral system (Bowlby 1969/1982) to attract and draw the attention of their caregivers. Caregivers who are also equipped with the complementary neurobiological tendencies, their caregiving behavioral system (Bowlby, 1969/1982), can respond with tenderness and sensitive care, to protect and delight in a mutually rewarding communicative system that promotes survival and well-being. When all goes well, our early relationships give rise to the security of attachment and the development of an optimally functioning brain, a healthy capacity to respond to stress and to engage socially. Dan Siegel describes well how this caregiving behavior eventually shapes a brain that is capable of regulation:

> We create non-reactivity by developing circuits in our brain that enable the lower affect-generating circuits to be regulated by the higher modulating ones. This balance between emotion arousal and its regulation is often conceptualized as the relationship between the sub-cortical limbic amygdala and the pre-frontal cortex. (2007, p. 211; 2017)

The miracle is that even when things do not go so well, each human being produces their best adaptations and strategies so that the organism can survive and get along as well as possible. This is the miracle of what we call *defenses*, which are protective mechanisms. The neurobiological self is still there, yet access to its organizing integrative capacity may be hindered. As Schore (2001) describes, the development of the brain suffers in less-than-optimal circumstances. He writes that "early relational traumatic assaults of the developing attachment system inhibit right brain development, impair affect regulating capacities, and negatively impact infant and adult mental health" (p. 11). When relational environments are compromised, rather than enhancing the development of cortico-limbic structures, growth is inhibited, stress-coping deficits occur and are expressed by dysregulation of social, behavioral, and biological functions (Schore, 2000b, 2000c, 2019).

We see this in our adult patients; often those with insecure patterns of attachment have difficulty managing their arousal. When they become activated, they over- or underregulate their emotions, which impacts their expressive capacity for communication. They do not have the higher-governing cortical circuits, such as the prefrontal cortex, connected to provide stabilizing information to offset what has led to imbalance. Siegel (2017) describes that an optimally functioning brain is one that manages "the flow of energy and information" (p. 26). We might consider that to heal insecure patterns, our patients need help to bridge the missing links between regions of the brain. Such healing is enhanced by providing new and corrective experiences that can engage the forces of positive neuroplasticity to forge new neural pathways to strengthen and build new neural connections (Doidge, 2007, 2016). Psychotherapists are in a special position to foster the restoration of our patients' innate potential to manage arousal and to regulate emotional experience. To support this, we take a closer look at what is happening in different regions of the brain.

As we discussed in Chapter 1, certain environmental conditions trigger the fear/wariness system, which activates the attachment behavioral system. What regions of the brain are involved when these conditions arise, and what influences are forming the infant's internal working models? As stated above, the right hemisphere is processing information from the brain stem and the limbic system. The *brain stem* is in the lower part of the brain and regulates some of the infant's internal physiological conditions, such as respiration, heart rate, temperature, and arousal. The *limbic system*, which processes experiences related to emotion, attachment, and stress, is composed of the autonomic nervous system (ANS), the sympathetic and the parasympathetic branches, the hypothalamic–pituitary–adrenal (HPA axis) cortices, and the amygdala. In times of real or perceived danger the sympathetic branch of the ANS gives rise to the body's fight/flight response, and to responsive action in times of safety and regulation (Graham, 2013). The parasympathetic branch responds to real or perceived danger with shutdown and numbing out, and in times of safety and connection responds with healing and repair.

The *amygdala* goes through a critical period of growth in the third trimester of pregnancy and is essentially functional at birth (Schore, 2019b). It is involved in the appraisal of meaning and in the activation of emotion. It reads cues from facial expressions and voice tone, as well as sounds and signals from both the internal and external environment, and is known for its ability to "hijack the higher brain." When the unconscious alarm that there is threat or danger goes off, the HPA axis releases adrenalin and cortisol into the sympathetic nervous system (SNS), triggering heart rate increases and respiration increases, as the body prepares for fight-or-flight activity. Here is where a caregiver's timely and attuned response has the capacity to comfort the child and regulate their nervous system.

The *anterior cingulate*, developing in the cortical regions of the brain, begins to come online around 2 months after birth (Schore, 2019b), during the preattachment phase as attachment is growing between infant and caregiver. The anterior cingulate is involved in resonating, caregiving, developing attachment behavior, and focusing attention, and is also connected to movement. Many gestures reflect caregiving activities: holding tenderly, hugging, comforting touch, and the contrary; reactive pushing away and pulling back from contact.

Sensitive and appropriate responses lead to the healthy wiring of interconnected circuits in the brain when the alarm of the child's wariness system is met by the soothing of the caregiver's caregiving system. The experience of soothing and calm is not only received by the upset infant but registers in their developing brain as the fact that upset can be relieved. When the child's need is met by the caregiver and internalized, this alleviates pressure and soothes their nervous system activation. As Cozolino (2006) described, the mother's caregiving behavior becomes biological structure, which influences the growth of the child's nervous system and is part of what regulates the child and helps them to feel seen and understood. Developing the ability to process emotional experience is enhanced when the caregiver helps the child by giving them the needed biologically regulating presence.

Also involved in this early developing brain are the *insular cortex* and the *prefrontal cortex*. The *insula* is our connection to the felt senses, and in the next section we bring in some of the pioneering contributions of Bud Craig about the processing of energy-draining and energy-enriching emotions by the right and left insula, respectively. The *right orbitofrontal cortex*, which is part of the prefrontal cortex, begins to come online at 10 months of age and continues to develop over the next 20 years, and throughout life (Schore,

2019b; Siegel, 2012). It is one of the higher-modulating parts of the brain, capable of connecting to and regulating what stirs from the subcortical areas of the amygdala and the limbic system. As it develops, the prefrontal cortex is the area of the brain that can reflect on experience, bringing meaning and understanding to what is happening as it is happening.

Consider how a parent sees a child stamping their feet and leans in and says, "Wow, it looks to me like you're really mad!" The parent's naming the child's feeling is a way to join the child and possibly bring understanding and relief. At the very least, it gives attention to a feeling that can be talked about. In the same way, as adults, when our reflective mind can identify what we may be feeling, we can choose how to manage the feeling and how to handle the moment.

A few nights ago, I was beginning to make dinner and my adult daughter approached me and asked if she could help. I found myself feeling agitated and snappy, wanting space. However, I also had an awareness that I was feeling tight and stressed from feeling pulled in too many directions at once. I knew that the tension I felt had nothing to do with her. Saying this to myself helped me to recognize what was going on inside me, which helped me to contain my agitation enough to be available to appreciate her offer and shift into a collaborative dinner-making experience. This occurred when I was in the process of writing this chapter, and it stood out to me how this was an example of my prefrontal cortex serving to help me regulate the potential reactivity from my limbic system, naming what I felt, recognizing its source, and setting my intentions on having a positive evening with my daughter.

Initially, the caregiver provides the child with reflective awareness and the responsive action. As the child's prefrontal cortex develops, this sets the stage for their own self-awareness. As the higher regions of the brain become capable of monitoring and managing the lower regions of the brain, the child, and the adult they become, have more capacity for self-regulation and more confidence in their ability to manage stress.

Schore noted that after the age of 3, there is a shift in the child's right-brained dominance as the left brain and language centers of the brain come online. He was particularly interested in the shift that Bowlby noted as the goal-corrected partnership emerged and the child begins to be able to perceive the intention of the other's state of mind (Schore, 2000b). Schore proposes that it is this quality of brain development that allows for the perceptual shift that Bowlby described. He sees the left brain as more capable of processing thoughts and thinking through what is happening with another. This works optimally when the developing brain has been nourished by positive relational conditions that help the brain to grow its interconnectedness and sturdy connectivity, allowing for activation, regulation, reflection, and understanding of self and other to form and to flow. The social and emotional learning that happen in attachment relationships operate and extend across the human lifespan are supported by optimal brain development (Bowlby, 1979; Ainsworth, 1991). As Ainsworth (1990) says, "The organization of attachments to parent figures in infancy influences the way in which the individual responds to the central tasks of each major later phase of development" (p. 465).

In insecure attachment, when a person suffers hurt, deprivation, or loss, and their needs for care and help are untended, rejected, and/or met unreliably, there is a greater likelihood of the brain not developing to its full capacity for interconnected circuitry. Lapses of attentive and suitable care become internalized, with missing linkages, forming templates that give rise to negatively valanced expectation sets—internal working models—which play out in current life relationships. Certain patterns and behaviors compose distinct categories of insecure attachment. Truly understanding this progression will make it easier for us clinicians to step aside from taking personally patients' resistant, avoidant, and/or hostile reactions and from getting activated or triggered ourselves by the very patients we wish to help.

Emotions and Communication

Many of the most intense *emotions* [emphasis added] arise during the formation, the maintenance, the disruption and renewal of attachment relationships. The formation of a bond is described as falling in love, maintaining a bond as loving someone and losing a partner as grieving over someone. Similarly, the threat of loss arouses anxiety and actual loss gives rise to sorrow; while each of these situations is likely to arouse anger. The unchallenged maintenance of a bond is experienced as a source of security and the renewal of a bond as a source of joy. (Bowlby, 1980, p. 40)

Human beings are wired to express emotion. From their first moments, when an infant is distressed, they cry. When frustrated, they get angry. When they are threatened, they become fearful. When they experience relational connection, they express joyful exuberance. Emotions are part of the earliest communication system between children and caregivers, and when met with loving attention, they become woven into the fabric of a relationship. And when these emotions are not shared or responded to sufficiently by caregivers, and the relational threads fall short, are frayed, or become tattered, the children learn to exclude their awareness and expression of emotion.

In his studies, Bowlby was inspired by Charles Darwin (1872/1965), who recognized how emotions are universal, part of evolution, and crucial to the survival of the species. Emotions are experienced as body sensations (James, 1902) and have facial expressions that appear cross culturally in humans, making them universally identifiable (Darwin, 1872/1965; Tomkins, 1962, 1963). Emotions have a trajectory that concludes with an adaptive action on behalf of the self (Frijda, 1986). Antonio Damasio (1998) described

> emotion and the experience of emotion, are *the highest-order direct expressions of bioregulation in complex organisms* [emphasis added]. Leave out emotion and you leave out the prospect of understanding bioregulation comprehensively, especially as it regards the relation between an organism and the most complex aspects of an environment: society and culture. (p. 84)

Jaak Panksepp (2009) calls emotions "ancestral tools for living" (p. 4).

Emotions are part of how we appraise what happens in our environment and they inform our values about who and what is important to us. They provide motivation and direction. The infant's brain development is experience dependent on the emotional communication between mother/caregiver and child (Schore, 2001; Tronick, 1989, 2009). Emotions are elemental to communication and when a person grows up secure, they often have a secure relationship with their emotional life, the capacity to be with their affective experiences, to express them, to navigate them even when they are intense, and to share them with others, both in times of joy and sorrow.

And the corollary is true with insecure attachment. To experience emotions can feel dangerous, and be unsettling and disturbing. Here, understanding the constellation of different patterns of insecure attachment provides psychotherapists with valuable assets, and is introduced in Chapter 5's presentation of the grids: a comparison of the configurations of secure and insecure patterns of attachment. The grids provide a side-by-side look at how the ways we cope with emotion and relatedness depends on what happened and didn't happen early on with our caregivers and the neural circuitry that formed in terms of arousal (limbic system activation), hypoarousal, and hyperarousal, and its impact on affect regulation. We address these features comparatively in Chapters 5 and 6, and specifically to each pattern of insecure attachment in Chapters 7–12.

There are a few more aspects of brain development that can help to light our way and next we call attention to how we experience emotions, which begins with the way one feels: from the "feeling of being alive" to having a sense of self that is constructed through a collection of global emotional moments (GEMs; Craig, 2010, 2015). We define and examine GEMs in the following section, after discussing a bit about interoception. This capacity for registering what happens to us (i.e., the process by which we internalize what we experience in our attachment relationships, how we attune and coordinate—or not—and how what happens moment-to-moment in those dyads) becomes internalized as our own self-regulatory capacities.

Emotions and Interoception

How do we feel what we feel? Interoceptive awareness connects us to physiological changes throughout the body, and to the felt experience of body sensations, from sensations of coolness and itching to the more complex felt experiences of emotions and their corresponding feelings. According to Craig (2002, 2015), interoception involves the bidirectional communication between bodily sensation and multiple levels of cortical oversight. Interoception provides the substrate for the experience of sentience, of having a feeling and knowing one is having a feeling. All of this is possible due to the insula cortex. In functional imaging (fMRI) studies, each of the six primary emotions—anger, fear, disgust, happiness, sadness, and surprise—show up as activation in the anterior insula, whereas affective bodily feelings emerge in the midinsula (Craig, 2009, 2015).

The right and left sides of the anterior insula have different roles in the processing of emotion and energy. The right insula is connected to sympathetic activity and withdrawal behavior: warnings to not take risks based on historical precedents. It is more aroused by survival emotions, the negative emotions that Craig (2015) labels as "energy draining." The left insula on the other hand is connected to ventrally mediated parasympathetic activity. It is the seat for affiliative emotions and positive affect and calm, and is associated with approach behaviors: the willingness to explore, joy, and what Craig calls the "energy-enriching" emotions (pp. 258–259).

When so many of our patients have difficulties with emotional awareness, regulation, and expression, to recognize the role the insula plays in interoception and picking up the felt sense of what is happening in the body can be illuminating and inspiring. As well, we must consider how this awareness develops in combination with the role that caregivers play in affecting the brain's involvement in the recognition and processing of emotion, and how we as psychotherapists step in.

Feeling emotions is both a highly individual and a relational process. Emotional communication between infants and caregivers has been discussed and illustrated throughout this chapter. Here, we are looking at the role interoception plays as foundational to the individual's experience and also how a person builds a relationship to their own emotional life. As psychotherapists, an important aspect of attunement is resonating and feeling with our patients to accompany them and help them to explore their own experience of emotion. Sometimes our focus is helping patients to become aware when they are not aware, and to identify what they are not aware of. In essence, we are helping our patients develop their capacity for interoception. We help them orient to what is happening on a bodily level, by helping them to notice that what they are speaking about through memory and association has an impact on how they feel in the present moment. By encouraging our patients to tune into the immediacy of the here-and-now we have an opportunity to pick up the shifts and permutations of how their beingness is unfolding through data that emerge from their somatosensory experience on a moment-to-moment basis. To make use of the insula, we must be in touch with the information that the insula provides.

The insula has an integrative capacity for processing what arises throughout the body and captures what Craig (2015) calls the GEM: an overall felt sense that represents the current conditions of the body, emotion, energy, and nervous system. He says, "The global emotional moment comprises all vivid feelings in the immediate present. It represents the phenomenological emotional presence, the current feeling state, the material me, or the *sentient* [emphasis added] self" (p. 222). And through this collection of GEMs one can moment-to-moment track and attune, as well as moment-to-moment track what happens and how one is changing over time. And the interesting thing is that these GEMs are recorded in memory and the combination of them can give rise to a sense of self.

Here's an example: A patient, Sally, comes in after an intense blowup with her partner. They have what can be classified as a volatile relationship, one where issues related to trauma and trust repeatedly surface in their interactions. When we began working together, Sally would become extremely dysregulated by conflict with her partner, to the point of panic. She became flooded with worry and unable to identify her own boundaries. We have been identifying and processing Sally's early trauma and the complexity she experienced growing up with a mother who was clearly unresolved on her own violent trauma. Our work has been stabilizing for Sally and has helped her to access her core sense of self, steadiness, and firmness.

Not surprisingly, Sally is married to someone who is challenged by their own unresolved traumatic past. In a recent session, Sally described what occurred the prior night. As she told me what happened, I realized she was coherently naming GEM followed by GEM experiences. Although disturbed by the repetition, she also appeared somewhat regulated as she told me how she felt. She identified feeling hurt (GEM), and then felt distant (GEM), so she took space. As the night progressed, a loving feeling emerged and she wanted to reach out to leave her partner a message: "Good night, I love you" (GEM). However, when she left the message, she saw that her partner's notifications were turned off. She felt agitated (GEM). But then she realized that she felt much better than the kind of devastation she would have felt 2 months ago (GEM).

We can almost trace Sally's process of alternating between her right and left insula. While her awareness may not have entirely shifted an energy-draining experience to one that was all enriching, it certainly helped her to recognize her progress. When Sally's approach to her partner was unmet, and the current situation remained unresolved, she was able to tolerate the distance from her partner with enough differentiation and calm to hold her agitation.

Polyvagal Theory & the Neural Circuitry That Promotes Safety

Polyvagal Theory, developed by Stephen Porges (2009), describes the nervous system in terms that elucidate specific pathways of the human stress response and relational engagement. More and more, clinicians are leaning into Polyvagal Theory for how it highlights specific neural networks to describe what happens because of how attachment and caregiving experiences become internalized.

Polyvagal Theory describes how humans have evolved and developed three distinct neural circuits that are hierarchical in how we respond to perceived safety, danger, and life threat. The newest circuit is the branch of the vagus nerve in the ventral vagal complex (VVC), which is part of the parasympathetic nervous system and mediates the behaviors of social communication, referred to as the "social engagement system." This is experienced in conditions of safety. The middle circuit is the SNS and mediates the defensive strategy of mobilization in the face of danger. The oldest circuit is the branch of the vagus nerve in the dorsal vagal complex (DVC), which is part of the parasympathetic nervous system and mediates defensive immobilization, which comes to the fore when we feel our very survival is at stake (Porges, 1994, 2003a, 2003b, 2004, 2009, 2010, 2017).

The hierarchy refers to how a being will organize during conditions of stress. According to Polyvagal Theory, first they will recruit from the social communication system (VVC). When this fails to elicit a necessary response, the system will shift to the defensive strategy of mobilization (SNS), and last will resort to defensive immobilization (DVC). One system can override the other, usually from the newest to the oldest, and a change of state will provide access to different structures of the brain. Understanding each of these circuits will enrich the clinician's understanding of what happens in the body–mind, how to recognize telltale markers, and how to recognize what we can actively utilize to encourage the neurobiological experience of safety.

There are a few terms that need introduction to orient how we can best make use of Polyvagal Theory. The first is neuroception. *Neuroception* is an evaluation of safety or danger that happens below conscious awareness. Porges (2004) introduced the term to indicate that a neural process is taking place distinct from and more primal than perception. Neuroception is proposed to instantaneously shift one's physiological state based on the capacity to decode safety or threat in the environment based on interpreting the intentions of biological movements, such as voices, faces, and hand movements. Not surprisingly, neuroception is conceived to be triggered by brain areas, such as the temporal cortex, in communication with the amygdala (Porges, 2017). While neuroception may give rise to activation, interoception is the mechanism by which we become aware of what we feel.

Another term referred to in Polyvagal Theory is myelination. *Myelination* is a term in anatomy that is defined as the process of forming a myelin sheath over neural fiber. Myelin is a fatty coating that affects how nerve impulses are transmitted. The ventral vagus nerve is myelinated, which enables faster and more tightly controlled neural circuits. The dorsal vagal nerve is unmyelinated, which creates more static in the system (Porges, 2010, 2017).

We see the significance of myelination as we continue to describe each of the three neurological circuits and how the growth of myelin is impacted during neuroplasticity.

The newest circuit, the VVC, is myelinated, links to both the face and the heart and lungs (regulating organs above the diaphragm), and originates in a brain stem area called the *nucleus ambiguous* (Porges, 2017). It connects to cranial nerves that affect facial expressions and vocalizations and instantiates a feeling of safety. The ventral vagus circuit brings the *social engagement system* online, which is accessed with eye contact, gaze, voice tone and pace, and prosody of speech. These are reminiscent of the nonverbal behaviors Bowlby described about how the infant detects human feelings in attachment relationships, the right-brain to right-brain communication Schore talks about, and what mothers and babies use to attune to each other in the dyadic interactions tracked by the "baby watchers" (i.e., Beebe, Stern, Trevarthen, and Tronick). The social engagement system is a description of security in action, as the myelinated ventral vagal circuit transmits a feeling of soothing and calm to promote the safety feeling. For psychotherapists, the social engagement system may well describe the neurophysiological platform we are aiming to establish as part of setting conditions for a secure base with our patients, the platform from which we hope to launch our trauma-processing work.

The oldest vagal circuit is unmyelinated, travels to the gut (affecting organs below the diaphragm), and originates in a brain stem area called the *dorsal motor nucleus of the vagus* (Porges, 2017). The DVC is activated in times of life threat and mediates immobilizing defensive strategies. With fear, the unmyelinated dorsal vagal results in motoric immobilization and behavioral shutdown, such as the freeze response, feigning death, and collapse, as well as dissociation. There is also the nonproblematic aspect of immobilization, that being when a state of immobilization without fear occurs: It is the complete letting go, the kind of release that happens in intimacy, postorgasmic sexual experiences, sleeping together, and also, emotional catharsis.

The dorsal vagal system is very important to recognize in our patients who have traumatic backgrounds; the exploration of attachment and relatedness can be triggering in unforeseen ways. According to Polyvagal Theory, the static of the unmyelinated dorsal vagal nerve contributes to confusion and misreading of cues. We see this when engagement with a psychotherapist who is offering responsive attention in the here-and-now activates a fear response in the patient. When someone has experienced "fright without solution" (Hesse & Main, 1999), and is subsequently unresolved for trauma, difficulty in reading cues accurately is a part of their disorganized attachment. When the person who is supposed to be your protector turns out to be the one you fear—the impossibility of handling attachment experiences can bring about a collapse of defensive strategies. The collapse can appear like *sleepy torpor*, identified in a case example in Chapter 11 as the defensive shutting down/dissociation resulting from the dorsal vagal response stimulated by the activation of the patient's attachment system. Other signs of dorsal vagal response that arise clinically can be yawning, spacing out, staring off, a clouding over or blurriness in the eyes, and feeling disconnected; in other words, a sensing that the patient has gone offline.

The middle, or the second oldest circuit is a mobilized state of defense that activates the sympathetic part of the ANS. In states of fear, or perceived danger, there is a withdrawal from the ventral vagal circuit, and the mobilization of fight-or-flight defensive strategies (Porges, 2017). Patients are often seen to respond with hostility or defensive anger. On the positive side, when this circuit is activated without fear, play can also initiate mobilization, which has positive implications for use in a therapeutic situation (i.e., when a client is slipping into an area of sleepy torpor). Engaging a patient with playfulness, or reaching out with an unexpected humorous light twist, might bring laughter or lightness, dispel tension, and energize the intersubjective space between us.

In treatment, to help our patients regulate their sympathetic arousal, psychotherapists can invite the social engagement system to come online, to build avenues of connectivity with the patient to accompany them and help them find their window of tolerance. The *window of tolerance* refers to a range of optimal arousal in which there is not too much stimulation to be overwhelming, nor too little to be numb or disconnected to experience (Siegel, 1999/2020). When sympathetic activation rises, patients may need help to down regulate their arousal. When the DVC is triggered and its unmyelinated nerve is sending and receiving signals full of static, we may want to focus our intention on up regulating our patient, and nudging the social engagement system to foster a sense of relational connection. The aim would be toward building a neurophysiological state of resonance and capacity to experience safety. This can be complicated with patients with unresolved attachment trauma and is addressed in more depth and complexity in Chapter 11, "The History of the Disorganization Category," and Chapter 12, "Working to Transform Patterns of Disorganized Attachment."

It turns out that one aspect of neuroplasticity is "the laying down of myelin by the supportive glial cells, enabling action potentials of ions flowing in and out of the neuron's membranes to stream . . . [leading to] more coordinat[ion] in timing and distribution" (Siegel 2017, p. 177), which strengthens ventral vagal functioning. Here, the science of neuroplasticity tells us how growth is possible. Even in the case of too much static in the system, there is a mechanism that can grow and repair neurological deficits. So, when we do discover how to reach our patients despite the activation of their dorsal vagal circuit, the science of neuroplasticity reinforces our efforts.

By understanding the effects of the dorsal vagal response, trauma survivors often find relief and validation for the times they were frozen and unable to escape abuse. To understand that their physiology was in a state of immobilization can reduce shame. And then, good news! By engaging in new experiences of relatedness and exploring their feelings, neuroplasticity informs us that it is possible for the brain to lay down more myelin and affect how signals are transmitted at a neuronal level. Literally engaging new experiences summons the missing elements that help our brains to heal.

Neuroplasticity: Hope From Brain Science to Psychotherapists

The word *heal* [emphasis added] comes from the Old English *haelan* and means not simply "to cure" but "to make whole." (Doidge, 2015, p. xx)

Neuroplasticity is the property of the brain that enables it to change its own structure and functioning in response to activity and experiences (Doidge, 2007, 2015). As we've been discussing, our brains form neural circuitry through experience, and how we perceive experience has to do with how our brains have formed. Our brain can be altered for the worse by the trauma of a brain injury, a stroke, by damages inflicted over time, and by the deficits of growing up in stressful conditions that lack the necessary stimulation for optimal brain development. And yet, incredibly, our brains are never static, but continue to develop and respond to our experiences over our lifetimes (Cozolino, 2006; Schore, 2019; Siegel, 2017).

The science of positive neuroplasticity informs us that we are wired with the potential for self-righting and healing, and also for connection. We are wired to connect and to grow, to correct what has gone wrong and to make up for the environmental stresses and failures that have become developmental lapses (Doidge, 2007, 2015; Hanson & Hanson, 2020; Siegel, 2017). Herein lie the jewels for psychotherapists. Not only are we wired to heal but the more we know about the specific ways to stimulate positive neuroplasticity, the more hope and potential we can hold for our patients.

The brain's capacity to change for the better happens in the optimal conditions we set for psychotherapy. By now, safety comes to mind as a primary target for such conditions. And more, conditions of safety, mediated by the social engagement system being online, enhances the potential for exploration and accompaniment with a trusted other. To engage new experiences requires support to take the necessary new steps, and sometimes it takes many supported steps, and even more supported steps. To venture into new terrains one may need coaxing across what is feared to be a perilous passage. The willingness to experience a previously dreaded emotion requires a patient to shift patterns of defensive exclusion and expectations about relatedness. Before presenting the chapters dedicated to intervention strategies across patterns of attachment, we continue to open the gifts from neuroscience about how to make use of change moments with our patients, and what we can do to enhance the potential of positive neuroplasticity.

In addition to safety, focused attention, novelty, optimal arousal, and repetition promote positive neuroplasticity (Hansen & Hansen, 2020). New experiences have the power to change the brain. In psychotherapy, our aim to foster new corrective emotional and relational experiences is enhanced by focused attention. Leaning in, we help our patients face what they have avoided and to regulate what they feared to be overwhelming. In this way, we are both helping them to engage with novelty, and to navigate toward an optimal state of arousal to explore and bring about a corrective experience. Corrective emotional experiences (Alexander & French, 1946) have the potential to release stuck and stored emotions, and to free the adaptive action that is their innate inheritance.

Having new experiences generates neural firing and strengthens and grows synaptic connections (Cozolino, 2006; Doidge, 2007, 2016; Siegel, 2017). The stimulation of such growth builds new neural pathways and delivers neural impulses more specifically and deliberately throughout the brain. Recall from Chapter 1 our discussion following Young's ideas about how the octopi brain builds working models of its environment through the construction and assembling of unit parts. Now, studies in neuroplasticity show that new experiences foster the growth of new neural pathways, which may well be what is necessary for rewiring internal working models.

Each time psychotherapists engage in helping our patients to face what they have avoided and to regulate what they feared to be overwhelming, we are helping our patients to be with what they previously expected was unmanageable. Furthermore, in doing so, and then being able to process what was previously unprocessable, leads to the positive affects associated with the completion of emotional experiences. What was previously feared as overwhelming becomes associated with a sense of accomplishment or a feeling of hope and confidence. We repeat these activities often in a psycho-therapeutic process, as we proceed step-by-step to help our patients reduce their reliance on old reactive patterns. By connecting with their genuine emotional experiences, allowing a responsive connection to form, often accompanied by positive affect, they are encoding new neural pathways. These new relational and emotional experiences have the power to harness positive neuroplasticity. Consider that when a patient has new experience, we are supporting new dendrites to sprout in their brain—and what grows from these dendritic branches can continue long after sessions have ended!

Neural integration is another feature of neuroplasticity. New synaptic connections grow through the experiences we foster with focused atten-tion, novelty, arousal, and repetition. An integrated brain is one that allows the flow of energy and information in the brain, where these new connec-tions are forming, which allow the higher regions of the brain to know about, regulate, and reflect what stirs from the lower regions of the brain (Siegel, 2017). When we help our patients to have an experience, then pro-cess that experience, and then reflect on their experience, we bridge the gaps to increase neural integration and self-understanding, which is pre-cisely what we do in AEDP when we metaprocess (see Chapter 3, pp. 129).

AEDP's metatherapeutic processing, or metaprocessing for short, is ideally suited to harness the growth of neuroplasticity (Fosha & Thoma, 2020). By alternating between experience and reflection, metaprocessing helps patients to not only have new experiences but to know they have had the experience. By initiating a period of such focused attention and reflect-ing upon emergent experiences, metaprocessing helps neural pathways that were previously dissociated and lacking stimulation to connect. Through a recursive exploration, new neural pathways are stimulated and grow, thus increasing interconnectivity and increasing the patient's capacity for sus-taining and building an integrated brain.

New possibilities arise and now our patients may realize that they are more willing and capable of feeling their emotions or allowing themselves to lean in with another person. New corrective emotional and relational experiences that stimulate growth in neuronal connections also foster new perceptions to emerge in our patients. Perhaps less static in the nervous system allows for them to read other people's cues more clearly. As new neural circuitry forms, our patients have a greater capacity to feel and attune to their neurobiological core self and to those relationships near and dear that inhabit their worlds.

In Summary

In this chapter we've seen how the original studies of Bowlby and Ainsworth, and of the baby watchers, Beebe, Stern, Trevarthen, and Tronick, establish the origins of affect regulation and were validated and elaborated on by neuroscientists to show just how specifically the experiences that happened between child and caregiver develop the neural circuitry of the brain. Polyvagal theory provides another way to identify the neurophysiological states of safety, danger, and threat and how these are recognized as distinct neural platforms. They are reminiscent of patterns exemplified by security and insecurity and the self-organizations AEDP refers to as self-at-best and self-at-worst. Very much like Main et al. (1985) said, when experiences of emotion and feelings are not integrated, restrictions are placed on the flow of information with respect to attachment. In different states of mind, different access to cognition, memory, and affect are available. Polyvagal theory attributes this accessibility to the physiological states. The convergence of all of the above is that in states where safety prevails, a person has the most access to emotional and relational security.

In the next chapter, we discuss AEDP, which is a model of psychotherapy that puts the dynamic understanding of what happens between people into experiential therapeutic activities that are targeted specifically to address the fallout of attachment wounding and engage the forces of neuroplasticity to turbocharge change and transformation. Above all, AEDP attributes its strength to the innate potential of healing and self-righting that comes to the fore when the relational conditions are right, then the transforming powers of emotions can be engaged and fully processed, and then amplified through metaprocessing. In the following sections of the book, we focus first on the configurations of each pattern of attachment, and subsequently on clinical applications and specific intervention strategies to help our patients heal.

3

The Move to Experience & Transformation (and the Rewiring of the Internal Working Model in Therapy)

Lodged deeply in our brains and bodies lie dispositions for
healing and self-righting that surface under conditions of safety,
they are there for the awakening from the first moments of the
first session onward, for the duration of the treatment.
—(FOSHA, 2021A, P. 28)

All of these lines across my face, tell you the story of who I am.
So many stories of where I've been, and how I got to where I am.
But these stories don't mean anything, when you got no one to tell them to.
It's true, I was made for you.
—BRANDI CARLILE, THE STORY, 2007

MUCH LIKE MARY AINSWORTH AND JOHN BOWLBY WERE INTENT ON understanding the nature of love and attachment, Diana Fosha was drawn to understand the process of transformation and how people heal. With clinical acumen, dedication to phenomenology, and a deeply engaged heart, she developed AEDP®.

Rooted in attachment theory, mother–infant developmental studies, interpersonal neurobiology, emotion theory, body-based approaches, and transformational studies, AEDP is a relational, experiential, transformational model that helps people heal attachment trauma (Fosha, 2000b, 2021a, 2021b; Russell, 2015; Tunnell & Osiason, 2021). As scientific insights from the "decade of the brain" were exploding, Fosha (2003) was in conversation with researchers and neuroscientists, advocating for a truly bidirectional dialogue not only for neuroscientific research to inform clinical practice but also for clinical practice to inform research. This dialectic has evolved and what we have is a state-of-the-art model of psychotherapy that has now completed its second round of follow-up research for a 16-session time-limited version of AEDP treatment (Iwakabe et al., 2022). Findings show that AEDP treatment is a highly effective, transdiagnostic model (DiCorcia et al., 2023; Iwakabe et al., 2020). The 6- and 12-month results confirm that people maintain their treatment gains (Iwakabe et al., 2022). These results provide empirical support for the long-term effectiveness of AEDP for alleviating a variety of psychological problems, such as depression, subjective distress, automatic negative self-statements, experiential avoidance, and difficulties in emotional regulation, as well as enhancing positive functioning, such as self-compassion, self-esteem, and flourishing (Iwakabe et al., 2020, 2022).

Now we know that what inspires so many AEDP psychotherapists worldwide is empirically supported. AEDP works: Indeed, many of our patients not only get better but they also continue to improve after treatment has ended. Not only do patients find relief from suffering but they feel enriched by having deepened capacities for living life fully. They show increased flourishing, which is characterized by calm and acceptance, positivity, connectedness, vitality, and energy (Fosha et al., 2024; Fosha & Thoma, 2020).

Before delving deeply into the specificity of tailoring treatment to different patterns of attachment, in this chapter we present the overarching model of AEDP. Understanding AEDP is crucial, as AEDP is the ground that gave rise to this project to design treatment and interventions with attachment patterning in mind, and it is the model that is the therapeutic home of the work shown here. This chapter is about the AEDP approach and provides some glimpses into the fundamental aspects of AEDP. We begin with how Diana Fosha came to be oriented to transformation.

AEDP defines *psychopathology* as the result of the individual's unwilled and unwanted aloneness in the face of overwhelming emotion (Fosha, 2000b, 2021a, 2021b). The implications of that understanding for clinical work are clear: undo aloneness, so that together, patient and therapist are able to process the emotions that were too overwhelming for the patient to deal with alone.

Traditional psychoanalytic and psychodynamic psychotherapy viewed the forces of resistance as a principal mechanism of psychopathology and as a hindrance to psychotherapeutic process. Fosha moved away from psychopathology as an organizing principle of treatment (Tunnell & Osiason, 2021). Instead, Fosha centered the innate drive in all human beings toward healing, self-righting, and repair. Recognizing this motivational drive as a counterpart to constrictive resistance, she coined the term *transformance* to convey the essence of these constructive, expansive forces (Fosha, 2008, 2009a). Emphasizing the importance of safety for the potential of transformance to be actualized, Fosha (2003) turned to attachment theory and research for a deepening of how security and safety are dyadically created.

While leaning into the power of transformance and drives toward healing and growth, AEDP respects the constrictive forces of resistance as arising out of strategies representing the best solutions for protection under the circumstances (Russell, 2015). Transformance and resistance each have specific psychic organizations they fuel. The work of AEDP strives to set conditions of safety to engage transformance and bring a hope-driven organization online, in order to facilitate working with the patient's threat or dread-driven organizations (Fosha, 2021a, 2021b). We begin by introducing how AEDP leans into transformance and facilitates the undoing of aloneness. We call on these essential factors when we address the patterns of insecure attachment, in which more of the constrictive forces are at play.

How AEDP Came to Be

Fosha (and later joined by AEDP faculty, AEDP supervisors, AEDP certified therapists, and other clinicians) traced interactions with patients in the natural setting of the psychotherapy relationship, noticing with incisive awareness what happens *between* and *within* therapist and patient. Based on observation, AEDP articulates the phenomenology of the transformational process. Through study of this phenomenology AEDP identifies prime affective change mechanisms and their markers.

From the beginnings of attachment theory, we've seen how Bowlby, Ainsworth, and Main, through naturalistic and empirical observation and ongoing collaborations, came to understand how attachment develops as a force of nature, full of interlacing, interconnected systems of behavior that are biologically driven and impacted by what happens in present-moment experience. How to engage the forces of transformance, while relieving the aftermath of wounding, AEDP focuses on bringing about change in the present moment. Markers of change are universal and have a bodily rooted component. To enter a healing process, patients need to have a new experience, which should be corrective (2002). Fosha's classic introduction to AEDP is

> From the beginning, the patient needs to have an experience, a new experience, and that experience should be good, that is it should feel right and true. From the moment of the first contact and throughout treatment thereafter, the aim and method of AEDP is the provision, facilitation, and then experiential processing of such experiences. (2021a, p. 28)

From the first moments of contact, the AEDP therapist is aiming to co-construct safety with the patient, and to provide and facilitate new relational and emotional experiences, with specific attention to the undoing of aloneness characteristic of attachment trauma. We are actively tending to what arises each moment while being with the patient. Like a nesting doll, patients hold inside them many representations of all that has come before, smaller versions that represent significant ages and stages that have formed who they are and how they function. Residing at the deepest center is the neurobiological core self (Fosha, 2013a; Panksepp & Northoff, 2009), whose organizing, integrative capacity is inherent to the core of all human beings. When a person arrives to psychotherapy, three aspects of self are mingling in the balance: the motivational drive of transformance toward healing and self-righting, survival-based patterning from the fallout of trauma, and manifestations of the unbreakable neurobiological core self. This balance is impacted by the extent of trauma and insecure parenting to which a person has been exposed as well as by the power of their resilience potential (Russell, 2015).

For an AEDP therapist, how we tend moment by moment and what we attend to is informed by the ethos and methodology of AEDP (Hanakawa, 2021). The ethos of AEDP is captured by its conviction that just as people are wired to connect and wired for attachment, people are wired to heal and to grow, which is what is subsumed under the construct of *transformance*. Having an explicit experiential focus harnesses the forces of positive neuroplasticity. AEDP's strength is how it moves to transform a person's suffering into flourishing and a connection with their core sense of self, innate to all human beings (Fosha, 2021b; Fosha & Thoma, 2020).

How to set this in motion informs the AEDP therapist stance, therapeutic activities, and clinical methodology.

AEDP's Three-Factor Theory of Change:
Attachment, Emotion, and Transformation

According to Fosha (2002), "A model of therapy needs at its essence to be a model of change" (p. 2). AEDP is focused on change rather than pathology, on harnessing the mechanisms of what goes right, rather than seeking to reverse the mechanisms of what goes wrong (Fosha, 2021a; Yeung, 2021). AEDP's theory of change has three factors: attachment/relatedness, emotion, and transformation. We begin by introducing them distinctly, yet this is a bit of a false separation as you will see how they build upon one another, and are truly inseparable strands, stronger for how they are woven together. The way the therapist engages with and creates a deep holding environment for the patient invites unresolved material and affective experiences to surface so they can be explored and processed. Through this processing and in-depth metatherapeutic processing of the experience of change, transformation unfurls.

This transformation can be straightforward when our patients arrive ripe and ready, and also when AEDP's methodology and the chemistry between therapist and patient flows. Yet there are times that treatment doesn't gain traction so easily. By slowing down and looking closely at how psychotherapists bring ourselves to the work, studying the complexity of the patients we are attempting to help, and delving into the ways we can tailor our treatment methods and interventions, we add implements to our tool kit, and fortify our clinical expertise and our human resourcefulness.

After we address the three factors of AEDP, we introduce the maps and schemas that guide AEDP. Having a way to identify markers of a patient's presentation moment-to-moment and in the overall process of change helps us to orient to what is happening and then choosing how we intervene.

In the final section of this chapter, we introduce AEDP's maxims, inspired by Grice's maxims,[1] which are specific phrases used in teaching AEDP and supervision. Through each of the maxims we continue to present how the factors of attachment, emotion, and transformation incorporate important interventions and methodologies to bring about change.

The Relationship Factor: Attachment

AEDP understands psychopathology as the result of an individual being alone during unbearable suffering, experiencing physical, emotional, sexual abuse, or neglect (Fosha, 2000b, 2021a, 2021b). In addition to enduring overwhelming emotion from such traumatic events, many sustained injuries also come from what AEDP identifies as *caregiver errors of omission and/or commission* (Fosha, 2000b) in which the parental responses to their child's efforts to express needs or seek help with their emotions was met with rejection, inconsistency, or humiliation. In such circumstances, defensive strategies are adopted as an alternative to responsive caregiving. Many of our patients have warded off their affective communications as an adaptive move to protect themselves and their attachment relationships.

To treat the broken connection and betrayals of trust that underlie insecure attachment and attachment trauma, it is paradoxical and yet necessary that healing should take place in relationship (Frederick, 2009, 2021; Pando-Mars, 2016, 2021). AEDP therapists pay exquisite attention to building a therapeutic relationship that establishes secure attachment between therapist and patient. It is not enough that the attachment between us operates implicitly in the background as a container for the work of psychotherapy. No. We help patients to engage explicitly with our care, our help, and our understanding. We want to know that our presence is felt and makes a difference in easing anxiety and easing the feeling of being alone with dreadful suffering. And when this isn't happening, we want to know. Being in connection takes precedence, for our work requires a co-constructed connection to establish safety. Thus, the patient's experience of the relationship needs to be an explicit and experiential focus of the therapeutic work (Fosha, 2006; Lipton & Fosha, 2011; Prenn, 2011).

The AEDP therapist stance utilizes the *safe haven* and the *secure base* (Ainsworth, 1967; Ainsworth et al., 1978/2015; Bowlby, 1988). The safe haven is established by the therapist's way of being with the patient, to welcome and delight in them, to affirm their transformance strivings, and to help them regulate their emotions dyadically. The secure base offers a platform that provides stability to help patients to feel safe enough to explore their interior worlds and their psychological issues, to access and follow their emotions and new relational possibilities to new levels of completion. By providing a safe haven and a secure base, we aim to undo the aloneness that has plagued our patients. This presents a therapeutic contrast to the expectancies they may have developed from bearing too much unwanted aloneness during past experiences of anguish and distress.

Another strong orientation that fuels the AEDP therapist stance is affirming the patient at key moments. The AEDP therapist is on the lookout for what is going right, for aspects, qualities, or behaviors of the patient that are markers of their transformance strivings (Prenn & Fosha, 2016). We notice and focus on our patient's strengths and capacities that stand out as remarkably clear or sometimes lie just beneath the surface, like a shy child peeking around the edge of a door. We want to help our patients to recognize when they are on track, and to lean into a new emergence that supports their growth (Prenn & Levenson, 2025). Many of our patients with insecure attachments blossom when such recognition lands and is met with an internal awareness and they realize "Yes, this is true." By reflecting and experiencing these connections with intention, AEDP is harnessing neuroplasticity. Savoring and digesting the nectar of new, positive experiences allows a natural process of neuronal growth and integration to occur.

The Emotion Factor

Motivation is intrinsic to emotion. Each emotion contains within it *the pulse towards its own completion. . . . Emotion is the experiential arc between the problem and its solution:* [emphasis added] Between danger and the escape lies fear. Between novelty and its exploration lies joyful curiosity. Between loss and its eventual acceptance lies the grief and its completion. (Fosha, 2009a, p. 177)

Many of our patients who come to psychotherapy have difficulties with emotional regulation. Their relationship to emotion, and thus themselves, has been compromised. AEDP centers the processing of core affective experience in the context of an emotionally engaged therapeutic relationship. Core emotions, such as sadness, anger, fear, disgust, surprise, and joy, are universal (Darwin, 1872/1965; Tomkins, 1962, 1963) and have adaptive action tendencies (Frijda, 1986). When we allow our emotions to run their course, they can inform and prepare us to act with respect to the circumstance we are facing. Fosha's (2009a) statement, "Emotion is the experiential arc between the problem and its solution" (p. 177) describes the beauty of how emotions serve up adaptive action. The following sentence, "Between danger and escape lies fear," vividly depicts the motivating factor of fear in conjuring pictures of either running away from peril or running to protection.

AEDP facilitates the exploration of patients' somatic and affective experiences to harness the adaptive forces of emotions in the service of healing. To do so, AEDP's methodology recruits affective change processes, which are "naturally occurring adaptive mechanisms of quantum change, that are discontinuous" (Fosha, 2002, 2005, 2021a, p. 29). To help our patients shift from using their survival-based strategies, AEDP focuses on specific affective change processes. The AEDP research team refers to them as AEDP's Magnificent 9. Broadly speaking, a few of the adaptive change mechanisms that instigate changes are: disarming defenses, undoing aloneness, being explicit with relational experiences, processing categorical emotions, intrarelational work with parts of self, and metaprocessing transformational experience, which can lead to transforming our patient's emotional patterning.

Helping our patients heal their wounds from being alone and untended requires helping them to let go of protections against their emotional memories and internal disconnection. For some, developing the willingness to experience and feel emotions can be fraught, which makes the attuned and responsive accompaniment of a therapist such an important part of overcoming barriers against emotion and against feeling alone. With moment-to-moment tracking, we can sense how and when to offer direction or encouragement, affirmation, or regulation. We can help them to unpack the "felt sense" of their affective experiences (Gendlin, 1982, 1996). Patients often want to know *what they feel*, before fully experiencing what is arising. We need to help them to *feel into the feeling*, as knowing and understanding usually follow emotion rather than precede it. We can lend our confidence that making room to process emotions through their waves to completion yields not only release but the benefits of their adaptive action potential on behalf of the self.

AEDP engages a specific technique called *portrayals* to help patients access, heighten, and deepen their core affective experience to bring emotions to completion (Fosha, 2000b; Medley, 2021). Literally, portrayals use the imagination to create real or imagined scenes from the past, present, or future to bring about a reparative, wished for or feared experience to facilitate the processing of unresolved material (Prenn, 2010). These are one of the most powerful affective change processes we can employ toward repairing the ruptures and fallout of insecure attachment. Portrayal work is illustrated and discussed in Chapter 8, "Working to Transform Patterns of Avoidant Attachment"; Chapter 10, "Working to Transform Patterns of Ambivalent/Resistant Attachment"; and Chapter 12, "Working to Transform Patterns of Disorganized Attachment."

The power of the change process in AEDP is related to two phases. The combination of first processing core affective experience to completion, and second, metaprocessing the transformation of the self that results from doing so, in the presence of an available and attuned therapist, is the central agent of change in AEDP (Fosha, 2017b; Fosha & Thoma, 2020; Iwakabe et al., 2020, 2022). Metaprocessing the experience of transformational change is discussed in the next section. What is essential here is that both phases happen in the holding environment co-created by the partnership between therapist and patient.

The Transformation Factor

At its core, AEDP is a theory of transformation: change that transforms the self. AEDP is guided by a four-state map that articulates the phenomenology of transformation, which is described in the next section. The transformation here is not something that happens by sleight of hand, like turning a stone into a dove. Nor is it an ancient, mysterious alchemy that turns lead into gold. Perhaps the art of *kintsugi* comes close, where broken pottery is repaired with gold to become something more beautiful through the repair. One of the most powerful transformational tools in AEDP is *following transformance*. By detecting and affirming markers of each individual's motivational drives for self-righting, healing, and growth, AEDP therapists harness the gold of this innate healing force that exists within each individual (Fosha, 2008, 2009a). Thereby, healing and transformation are intrinsic to being human.

Another transformational tool is the light AEDP shines on what arises from the individual's core self (Damasio, 2010). At a neurobiological level, Panksepp and Northoff (2009) recognize that "all mammals have foundational brain substrates—in sub-cortical and midline structures—for a core self that allows them to be active creatures on the world rather than passive recipients of information" (p. 259). Damasio (1999, 2010, 2018) and Panksepp and Northoff identify a felt-core self that develops through self-related processing, having an integrative capacity for self-organization. This core self is informed by body, brain, and environment and guided by self-related values to orient the creature toward their life goals. These neurobiologically based aspects of self inform what Fosha (2013a) refers to as the felt *core self*, which is affirmed through recognition processes (Fosha, 2009a, 2021a, 2021b) and is harnessed in core state, which is State 4 of the transformational journey, and is described below. The core self is our innate biological inheritance, the neurobiological potential that guides our becoming and integrates it into being.

In the process of setting aside adaptive strategies that were substitutes for authentic relating, our patients often discover that what was broken was not the self but trust in the connection of a bond. Placing relational ruptures in the right relationship to self allows the reparative gold of the core self to restore connection to both self and other. This connection sets the stage for another transformational tool in AEDP: processing emotion to completion, where once-warded-off affective experiences are processed and their adaptive action is released. Then, processing continues through the exploration and release of transformational affects, the State 3 affects of change, and State 4, core state (Yeung, 2021).

The transformation factor is about how therapists apply AEDP to set the stage for transformation from the beginning and throughout treatment. We help our patients to transform negative emotions into positive emotions, shifting the valence from energy-draining experiences to energy-enriching ones (Craig, 2015). Then we ask them to notice and to process the experience of change with metatherapeutic processing (Fosha et al., 2019), which helps our patients to turn around and see themselves with new perspectives that deepen and expand the experience of self. Metatherapeutic processing—or metaprocessing for short—is a quintessential AEDP intervention, which is the methodical and intentional way AEDP therapists help patients to process an experience of change. Whether the change is a felt shift in the moment-to-moment unfolding of experience, or a patient processing a wave of emotion, or is related to the overall arc of the session, metaprocessing provides patients with an opportunity not only to have a new experience but to know they have had it and to explore its new effect (Fosha, 2000b, 2017a, 2021a, 2021b). Later in this chapter, in the section on transformational affects, we present the palate of transformational affects that metaprocessing yields, which in 2008 was recognized as State 3 among the four states in AEDP (Fosha, 2008).

When we invite our patients to inhabit the visceral and somatic experiences that accompany change for the better, transformation is a natural, unfolding, spiraling process. Through metaprocessing, we engage the visible and sensory evidence of what broadens and builds the self (Frederickson,

2013, Frederickson & Joiner, 2018). By taking time to soak in new experiences, we relish and integrate what is evolving, so that as Rick Hanson (2013) says, we can "help these mental states become good neural traits" (p.16). Having new experiences stimulates neural firing and lingering in those experiences and encodes new neural pathways, engaging positive neuroplasticity.

Last but not least in the transformation factor is the work that takes place with patients in State 4 in AEDP, which is core state. Core state is a place of arrival, where the patient integrates transformational experiences into the self, which gives rise to the core self. Herein lies the capacity to put together one's autobiographical narrative, having a sense of where the individual has come from, with a fuller and fresher perspective regarding the potential of where the individual is going.

Ultimately AEDP aims to transform suffering into flourishing, which is marked by qualities of calm and acceptance, positivity, connectedness, vitality, and energy—to help our patients not only move through what has limited them and made them feel stuck but to mobilize and actualize new potentials and unleash new capacities that open doors to unlimited possibilities. AEDP's conviction about the possibilities of change for the better, earned secure attachment (Roisman et al., 2002; Main et al., 2003, 2005; Saunders et al., 2011), and the rewiring of internal working models has much to do with the maps that have been created that point out markers in behavior that both guide the way and reveal what changes occur in the phenomenology of transformation.

Knowing Where We Are & Where We Want to Go: The Phenomenology of the Four-State Transformational Process in AEDP

AEDP has mapped out the phenomenology of the transformational process (Fosha, 2000b, 2008, 2021b) to describe markers of the four states and the three state transformations that patients undergo in the process of healing and change. This map serves as an orientation and a guide. Below, the four states are identified and followed by the therapist's specific aims and activities, which is the help we provide in AEDP.

The AEDP therapist follows the moment-to-moment unfolding of the patient's experience, noticing markers and signals to guide our choice of interventions. The defensive strategies that make up each insecure pattern of attachment show up for the most part in State 1. That's because, in essence, the insecure patterns of attachment develop when the care-giver is unable to support the child in experiencing the emotions asso-ciated with attachment events (separations, losses) and/or with their lives. Thereby, anxiety and the use of defenses become the child's way to cope with lapses in the caregiver–child interactions (Frederick, 2021; Pando-Mars, 2021).

State 1: Stress, Distress, Symptoms, & Transformance

Therapeutic Activity: Co-Construct Safety, Undo Aloneness, Detect Transformance

AEDP sees the pathways of resistance and transformance as existing side by side (see Figure 3.1). State 1 has two aspects, represented by two boxes at the top of the chart to reference how a patient may enter psychotherapy. On the left is a rectangle for stress, distress, and symptoms. On the right is one for transformance. When they arrive to psychotherapy, patients often feel stuck or demoralized (as described by the left side of State 1) or possibly motivated and energized (reflecting transformance on the right side of State 1) to face the problems that have driven them to seek help. The work of the therapist is to seek to minimize the impact of defenses, from the defense of overregulated affect, which is more common to patterns of avoidance, or the defense and anxiety of underregulated affect, which is more frequent in patterns of ambivalence/resistance—as well as to reduce the inhibiting affects of shame and guilt. We aim to set the conditions to establish self-at-best, so that the patient can experience what has been hidden or felt in a dysregulated way and be met with accompaniment and care, encouraging glimmers of transformance to point the way. Aiming toward the co-creation of safety helps to mobilize the patient's openness toward the first state trans-formation and the potential for dropping down toward somatically rooted affective experience.

The first state transformation is marked by transitional affects, heralding affects, and green signal affects. Transitional affects are those in which the right brain may be ahead of the left brain, in such a way that the person feels off-kilter. Affective experience emerges with a mix of anxiety, which needs to be regulated. As the old and the new converge, settling and making room can help to soften uneasiness and begin to allow the unfolding of what may

STATE 1: Stress, Distress & Symptoms
Defenses; inhibiting affects (e.g., anxiety, shame, guilt); stress; demoralization; entrenched defenses and pathogenic self states

STATE 1: Transformance
Glimmers of resilience, health, strength; manifestations of the drive to heal; glimmers of access to embodied affective experience

Transitional Affects: Intrapsychic crisis; heralding affects, i.e., glimmers of maladaptive affective experience;
RED Signal Affects: Announcing danger of overwhelm, toxic shame, etc.

Transitional Affects: Intrapsychic crisis; heralding affects, i.e., glimmers of core affective experience
GREEN Signal Affects: Announcing openness to experience, signaling safety, readiness to shift

1st STATE TRANSFORMATION
Co-creating safety

STATE 2: Maladaptive Affective Experiences (need transforming)
"The Abyss"
The pathogenic affects (o.g., overwhelm, toxic shame, fear without solution, attachment without solution); unbearable states of traumatic aloneness (e.g., helplessness, fragmentation, brokenness; despair, "the black hole of trauma")

STATE 2: Adaptive Core Affective Experiences (are transforming)
"The Wave"
Categorical emotions; relational experience, asymmetric (attachment) or symmetric (intersubjective); coordinated relational experiences; receptive affective experiences; somatic "drop-down" states; embodied ego states and their associated emotions; authentic self-experiences; experiences of agency, will and desire; attachment strivings; the expression of core needs

2nd STATE TRANSFORMATION
The emergence of resilience

Post-Breakthrough Affects: Relief, hope, feeling stronger, lighter, etc.
Adaptive Action Tendencies

STATE 3: Transformational Experiences
"The Spiral"
The mastery affects (e.g., pride, joy); *the mourning-the-self affects* (emotional pain); *the healing affects* associated with recognition and affirmation (gratitude, tenderness, feeling moved); *the tremulous affects* associated with the intense, new experiences; *the enlivening affects* (exuberance, enthusiasm, exploratory zest) associated with delighting in the surprise at the unbrokenness of the self; *the realization affects* (e.g., the "yes!" and "wow" affects, the "click" of recognition) associated with new understanding

3rd STATE TRANSFORMATION
The co-engendering of secure attachment and the positive valuation of the self

Energy, Vitality, Openness, Aliveness

STATE 4: CORE STATE and The Truth Sense
"The Broad Path"
Calm, flow, ease; openness; compassion and self-compassion; sense of clarity; wisdom, generosity, kindness; the sense of things feeling "right;" the experience of "this is me;" new truth, new meaning; the emergence of a coherent and cohesive autobiographical narrative

Figure 3.1 The Phenomenology of the Four-State Transformational Process in AEDP, Including the Maladaptive Affective Experiences (i.e., the Pathogenic Affects and the Unbearable States of Traumatic Aloneness)
Adapted from Diana Fosha, 2020

be unknown and bring uncertainty. Heralding affects occur as the patient lowers their defense and glimmers of core affective experience arise. Tears appear in the eyes, body tone shifts, and breathing deepens or changes in some way. Language may become more direct and simple. Here the therapist's task is to stay and allow the furthering of these glimmers to manifest and take shape. Green signal affects are evidenced by pure openness to experience and markers of feeling safe; a willingness to slow down and become present—the emergent affective experience is visible and audible. Head nods, direct eye contact, verbal acknowledgment of readiness, hope, trust, curiosity, and signals of vitality appear. With these signals we want to deepen the experience, noticing our own breath, accompanying the patient with our resonance circuits engaged as they pass through the first state transformation to State 2.

State 2: Core Affective Experiences— Adaptive & Maladaptive

Therapeutic Activity: Facilitate Core Affective Experiences to Completion—Dyadic Affect Regulation

State 2 core affective phenomena is classically where the work of many experiential psychotherapies takes place. Once our patients shift from State 1, they find access to what has been previously unfinished and unresolved and resides in the core of their being. Therapist activities in State 2 involve working with many aspects of emotional experiences, such as *somatic "dropdown" states;* letting go of defense to be more in contact with the body and viscera; the somatically rooted experiences of *categorical emotions* (sadness, anger, joy, disgust, fear, surprise); and *embodied ego states* and their associated emotions, which refer to work with different ages and parts of self (Gleiser, 2021; Lamagna, 2011, 2021; Lamagna & Gleiser, 2007).

State 2 work also focuses on the explicit experience of the relationship between therapist and patient. Such relational experience may be asymmetric (*attachment*) or symmetric (*intersubjective*); *coordinated relational experiences,* which refer to attunement, disruption, and repair—the sync of coordination, miscoordination, and recoordination; *receptive affective experiences,* which refer to the process of taking in—receiving care, affirmation, and so on; and *authentic self experiences*: meaningful, unshielded, and important sharing. State 2 work also lends itself to explorations of the patient's experience of self, such as experiences of agency, will, and desire (Russell, 2021); attachment strivings; and the expression of core needs.

Our intention is for patients to become able to process their bodily-rooted unresolved traumatic experiences (Levine, 1997; Menakem, 2017) with our accompaniment to deepen and regulate emotion, for riding the waves of affective experience to completion. While our patients often encounter an adaptive pathway to processing core affective experience, it is not uncommon for a maladaptive pathway to appear. AEDP recognizes how *adaptive* affects are transforming, and that *maladaptive* affective experiences need to be transformed (Fosha, 2000b, 2021b; Piliero, 2021). Since we want to work through what is maladaptive, we describe maladaptive core affective experiences next, to be followed by adaptive core affective experiences.

Maladaptive core affective experiences include pathogenic affects, unbearable states of traumatic aloneness, and affects that compromise the individual's capacity to function and relate. They are deeply rooted in the body and are often the result of relational trauma and broken attachment bonds (Fosha, 2021a; Lamagna, 2021). When a child experiences adverse conditions of abuse, torture, or neglect, and they are alone with their suffering, they are missing connection with a caregiver/attachment figure to help them regulate and process difficult emotions, which leads to unbearable states of traumatic aloneness: brokenness, helplessness, hopelessness, fragmentation, fear of falling apart, despair (Fosha, 2021a), and the "black hole of trauma" (van der Kolk, & McFarlane, 1996, p. 3).

Patients experiencing these maladaptive affects have difficulty distinguishing *what happened to them* in their life, from *who they are*. Negative experiences become internalized, not as "something bad that happened" but as "I'm bad" (Piliero, 2021). Here, patients are riddled with self-doubt, self-recrimination, and self-hatred. Pathogenic affects are dark and difficult places, mixed with toxic shame, terror, helplessness, and states of unbearable aloneness which Lamagna, referencing Ferenczi, aptly refers to as "traumatic aloneness" (2021, p. 293). We can ascertain that historically, such pathogenic states originated in the child who experienced hefty amounts of the negative poles of experience that Ainsworth categorized on her caregiving interactions scales. Their primary caregiver might have been more interfering than cooperative with their ongoing behavior, more ignoring and neglecting than physically and psychologically available, or more rejecting or downright abusive rather than accepting of their needs as an infant and toddler (see the Maternal Caregiving and Interaction Scales in Chapter 1).

Here our work needs to attend to our patients with the utmost care and responsiveness, to attune to their experience in the moment, their readiness, and window of tolerance. We aim to undo aloneness and help them to allow us to be with them where they are. With one foot close enough to join, match, and witness, we need our other foot on the rim, outside enough to maintain perspective. We help the patient to differentiate past from present, to distinguish who they are from what was done to them or what was not done for them. By offering a hand across the barriers of self-blame and self-neglect, we reach for them, so that together we can hold, grieve, and complete whatever needs to happen for self-righting to emerge.

It is so important for the patient to feel that their suffering is validated and understood, and that what they have suffered is known (Schwartz, 1997). Understanding paves the way for them to let go, for the edges to loosen their grip so the self can expand. Our aim is to transform how the states of pathogenic affects are held, so that they are no longer trapped inside unbearable aloneness, to allow us to be together to face and process to completion whatever comes next on our patient's healing journey (Lamagna, 2021).

Adaptive core affective experiences occur when the psychotherapist and patient are regulated enough and connected enough with each other. In these states, our aim is to attune, resonate, and empathize with patients, for them to feel our presence, helping them to be with their emotional experience, coordinating lapses or disruption that may occur, tracking authenticity and receptivity along the way. State 2 work involving ego-state work utilizes portrayal work; often to recruit the adult self and related neural networks to access and connect with younger parts of self that need healing and helping. With the capacity to take in our presence, patients may be invited to explore and expand their receptive affective capacity. Processing a wave of emotional or relational core affective experience to completion, often a corrective emotional experience, gives rise to the second state transformation.

The second state transformation is marked by postbreakthrough affects (e.g., relief, feeling stronger, feeling lighter, and adaptive action tendencies). Each categorical emotion holds within itself the seed of adaptive action, which gives rise to the inner knowing of what is needed for each patient to act on their own behalf. Here, AEDP brings a major contribution to the field of psychotherapy. It is said that it is not enough for a patient to process and complete emotional experience or to have an experience of change. They must know they have had such an experience (Fosha, 2000b, 2021a). With this knowing comes the possibility of knowing that change is possible. To do this, the therapist engages metatherapeutic processing, or metaprocessing, the experiences of change that bring about further rounds of transformation, which give rise to the State 3 transformational affects.

State 3: Transformational Experiences

Therapeutic Activity: Metaprocess Experiences of Change and Transformation

Transformational affects emerge after metaprocessing experiences of change and completion. These include the *mastery affects, mourning the self, healing affects, realization affects, tremulous affects,* and *enlivening affects* (Fosha, 2000a, 2021a). Each of these transformational affects brings new experiential understandings that directly impact and expand the capacity of how the self of the patient comes to know their self. These transformational affects carve out and expand the patient's interior spaces of being. The mastery affects, the sense of "I did it!", generates pride and strengthens and lengthens the spine: confidence and agency come online. Mourning the self, through grief and being with emotional pain, deepens compassion for understanding what the self has endured through time. The healing affects, feeling moved and feeling gratitude, makes the heart tender through shared experience, deepening connection to self and other. Realization affects appear in the wake of clicks of recognition, enhanced self-understanding, the "wow" of wonder, and amazement at the changes taking place. The awareness of being seen and known stretches the perimeters of being, often bringing an upsurge of energy-enriching emotions. The tremulous affects shake loose constrictions, appearing at the edge of fear and excitement, and are distinct from anxiety as the settling of them expands the dwelling place for spirit, heart, and soul. The enlivening affects come in the wake of awareness of the unbrokenness of the self, bringing exuberance, enthusiasm, and exploratory zest, which fill and fuel the body, heart, and mind with freshness to approach life anew.

The third state transformation is marked by energy, vitality, openness, and aliveness. By staying with, deepening, and metaprocessing the experiences that arise in the wake of transformational affects, the patient's awareness of their changes continues to expand. Greater self-possession comes online, deepening the capacity to construct and restore secure attachment, while positively valuing the self.

State 4: Core State

Therapeutic Activity: Witness and Foster Reflection and Integration of Transformation Into Self

Core state is as it sounds: an arrival to a core experience of knowing self. This state is marked by *declarative knowing*, the *truth sense*, and *things feeling right*. Much self-reflection and putting pieces together happens in core state. Patients often find they are able to step back, review the patterns in their lives from a wider lens that sees how the transmission of trauma is passed intergenerationally, and how the experiences of parents and grandparents and the times they were living in has a great influence on what develops and comes to life in families. They might realize how the convergence of significant events, losses, and challenges, alongside one's unique temperament, disposition, and myriads of countless experiences, all play a part in becoming self.

In core state, the essence of self and essential knowing fall into place. Here, trust in self, capable of differentiating, stepping away from patterns, and choiceful living emerges and takes root. Beingness has room to breathe, to flex, to ripen, to become the fruit, the flower, the core self. Patients come into a calm, compassionate understanding of self and other. Self-expression is original, metaphoric, and particular. There is a core self-knowing "This is me." There is an expanded capacity to put in place and weave together life experiences, to construct their coherent and cohesive autobiographical narrative: a hallmark of earned secure attachment.

AEDP's Three Representational Schemas

To help our patients process unresolved material, it is helpful to recognize glimmers of genuine affective experience (Fosha, 2000b) and the protective patterns and strategies by which patients keep emotional and relational experiences out of awareness. In addition to the four-state map, which helps to guide clinicians about the patient's overall state, AEDP utilizes three representational schemas: the *triangle of experience* (TOE), the *self–other–emotion triangle* (SOE), and the *triangle of relational comparisons* (TORC) to depict the functioning of our internal and relational dynamics and to structure treatment (Fosha, 2000b; Frederick, 2009; Pando-Mars, 2021). They are used to organize information in a highly schematized fashion, to orient psychotherapists and help us choose how to intervene on a moment-to-moment basis. Additionally, the TOE and the SOE triangle have two versions that depict the constructs of self-at-best and self-at-worst.

The Triangle of Experience

The TOE is a schema that helps us to trace how patients move toward or away from emotional and relational experience (see also Hendel, 2018). It provides a way to map defenses, anxiety, and/or core affective experience that appear moment-to-moment in the therapeutic process (see Figure 3.2). The dynamic shifts between these aspects of internal experience display our patient's affect regulation strategy. The way a child has been responded to during affectively charged moments becomes wired into the developing child's nervous system (discussed in Chapter 2). When they are unable to rely on another for care and protection (i.e., when caregivers are unavailable to help or are actually harmful), the self uses defenses instead to protect against what is feared. Consequently, when a person becomes activated, and uses defenses to manage the arousal instead of allowing themselves to experience their underlying affect, this process becomes their affect regulation strategy.

AEDP's State 1 is represented at the top of the triangle: defenses on the upper-left corner of the triangle, and anxiety and inhibiting affects on the upper-right corner of the triangle. At the bottom of the triangle is State 2, core affective experience. To facilitate therapeutic work, we want to help our patients move toward their core affective experiences. To establish safety, we engage as a reliable other, present, available, and willing to help. Identifying where our patient's experience maps on the TOE orients us as to what kind of help is needed.

During a psychotherapy session a patient might sense an emotion, which we map at the bottom of the triangle. Since for so many of our patients, emotions and/or experiences of relatedness were not given space and support, their nervous systems react with inhibiting affects of anxiety and/or shame. The nervous system holds the body memory of an aversive reaction to experience. Anxiety appears in the mind as thought patterns, such as rumination, preoccupation, and/or distortion. Some of the ways anxiety shows up in the body are shallow breathing, fidgeting, darting eyes, and nervousness. The mixture of anxiety and defense may appear in the emotional field as dysregulation, mood fluctuations, or emotionality (emotion that is not

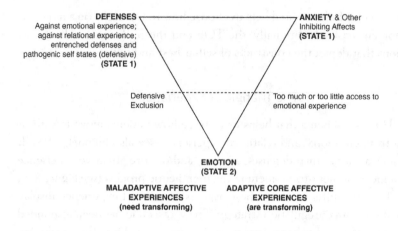

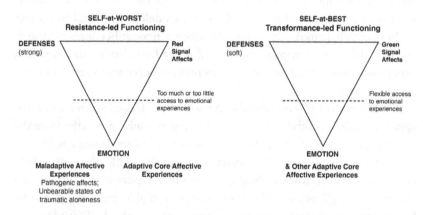

Figure 3.2 Two Versions of the Triangle of Experience:
The Self-at-Worst and the Self-at-Best
Fosha, 2020

core emotion). Anxiety can bring deactivating strategies in those who have avoidant patterns and hyperactivating strategies in those with ambivalent patterns. When anxiety is prevalent, the therapist must attend to dyadic and self-regulation (which is discussed in the AEDP maxims section of this chapter: Maxim 3: Stay With It and Stay With Me—Dyadic Regulation).

When patients are unaware of their affective signals, defensive exclusion is at play. Defenses can be anything used to exclude awareness of emotional, relational, or vulnerable experience. They can be classic like intellectual-ization, dismissiveness, withdrawal, and so on, or tactical like vagueness, changing the topic, or indirect speech. Defenses are employed to manage what is too difficult or too overwhelming to navigate alone. Emotions can be defensive, feeling sad instead of angry, or vice versa. Blocking awareness and shutting down experience protects the integrity of the self or protects the relationship with others.

The aim of using the TOE is to help therapists to track moment-to-moment how the patient's experience is unfolding. Additionally, there are the self-at-worst and the self-at-best versions of the TOE (see Figure 3.2). The self-at-worst triangle depicts resistance-led functioning, which is driven by dread or threat. Defenses are more embedded; anxiety is a "red" signal, and other inhibiting affects like shame and fear of loss of love need attention and care to be regulated, normalized, and worked through. The self-at-best version of the TOE depicts transformance-led functioning and is driven by safety and hope. Defenses are soft and more flexible, anxiety is a "green" signal, such that there is more willingness to engage with openness to experience. Each of the insecure attachment patterns are mapped out on the self-at-worst TOE in their designated intervention chapters.

As therapists track what we notice in the patient, having the TOE in mind can help us to identify and assist our patients to become aware of shifts in their experience (Hendel, 2018). Our aim is to help patients let go of defenses while being available to help them with the anxiety that stirs when approaching a previously warded-off affective experience. We aim to build a strong therapeutic relationship where the patient can feel accompanied and helped to bear and process emotion to completion. We continue our discussion of how the therapist meets each patient and helps to establish the conditions of safety by introducing the SOE triangle, including both self-at-best and self-at-worst versions of it.

The TOE is embedded at the bottom of the SOE triangle.

The Self–Other–Emotion Triangle; Two Versions of the Self–Other–Emotion Triangle, The Self-at-Best, and The Self-at-Worst Triangles

First mentioned in Chapter 1, the SOE triangle (see Figure 3.3) is a representation of the internal working model, depicting the relational matrix between what originally represents the self (child), the other (attachment figure), and emotion. The individual's internalized representation of their

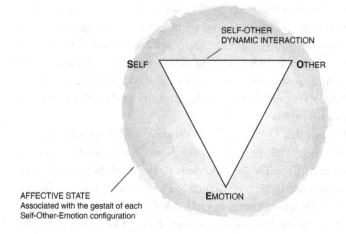

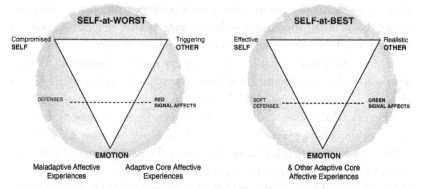

Figure 3.3 The Self–Other–Emotion Triangle; Two Versions of the Self–Other–Emotion Triangle, The Self-at-Best, and The Self-at-Worst Triangles
Fosha, 2020

own sense of self is on the upper-left corner of the triangle. The individual's internalized representation of the other is on the upper-right corner of the triangle, and how emotion is processed is represented at the bottom corner of the triangle. How the attachment figure relates to the emotions of the child affects the child's relationship to their own emotion, to themselves, and how they perceive the other. In the self-at-worst version of the SOE triangle, the self is compromised and the other is perceived as triggering with regard to handling their emotions. The self has difficulty either accessing or regulating their emotion. In the self-at-best version of the SOE triangle, the self is effective, able to regulate and manage their emotions and perceive the other realistically, even if the other is in a compromised state. The self has access to emotion and regulated expression of emotion.

AEDP psychotherapists actively and explicitly engage with the relationship between therapist and client to establish a stabilizing, collaborative, helpful alliance to foster the emergence of the patient's self-at-best. In the section on AEDP maxims, we discuss the therapist stance about setting the conditions for this secure base in our work with patients in Maxim 1, Establish Safety and Undo Aloneness. Additionally, we address how to work from this position in Maxim 8, Working With the Self-at-Worst From Under the Aegis of the Self-at-Best.

The Triangle of Relational Comparisons

AEDP's third representational schema, the triangle of relational comparisons (TORC), depicts significant relationships across time and allows us to compare them to one another: those that are repetitive and engender insecurity and those that are corrective, new, and healing (see Figure 3.4). Both the TOE and the SOE triangle are embedded in each of the three corners of the TORC. The upper-right corner depicts how the patient perceives the relationship with the therapist; the upper-left corner depicts the patient's experience of current relationships; and the bottom corner depicts the patient's experience of past relationships, usually their family of origin. This representational schema allows us to see the dynamic roots of a patient's suffering and notice what is playing out in their current relationships and then what happens between us: the therapist and patient.

The therapeutic relational corner often functions as the fulcrum that initiates the process of transformation. Through a positive relational experience our patients can find corrective or security-inducing experiences from the beginning of our work together. The current relationship corner depicts how the patient struggles or suffers in present relationships, which is often a stimulus for seeking therapy. The past relationship corner at the bottom represents suffering or wounding that occurred with historical figures. While patients may have a general understanding that their relationships from the past affect them in the present, they are often disconnected from how their expectancies, aka internal working models,

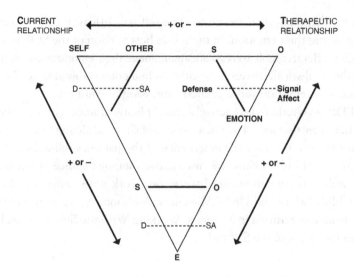

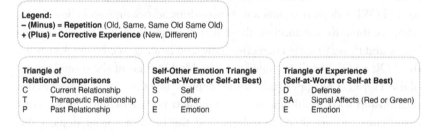

Figure 3.4 The Triangle of Relational Comparisons
Fosha, 2020

which developed in early relationships play a significant role in how they experience current relationships.

When the therapist is facilitating *working with the self-at-worst from under the aegis of the self-at-best,* and the patient is having a new experience of emotion or relatedness, the upper-right corner is lit with transformance forces. Changes springing from this therapeutic corner have ripples that potentiate changes in the other corners of the TORC, which may be the reprocessing of relationships in current time and/or bringing healing to previously unresolved trauma from past relationships. A surprising but not unusual phenomena that often occurs with patients in treatment is that once they have a new and positive experience of a therapist, they often remember a special person who had been there for them: a grandparent, neighbor, or other attachment figure. A previously held idea that "no one was ever there for me" gives way not only to a new experience in present time but a *remembering* that brings refreshing support from the past.

AEDP Maxims

With these maps and schemas in the background, we now introduce AEDP maxims, which capture the ethos of AEDP's theory and practice. While they are not all inclusive, we have chosen to discuss these adages of AEDP for their relevance to this project of tailoring treatment to attachment patterns. We refer to them as maxims, inspired by how Main et al. (2008) used Grice's maxims in their analysis of the narratives recorded by the AAI.

Maxim 1: Establish Safety and Undo
Aloneness (Fosha, 2000b, 2021b)

Being inside the patient's world as an other and the patient feeling and knowing it. In the presence of such a presence the patient's world unfolds. This presence—equal parts knowing and wanting to know, being there and wanting to be there—makes it possible for people to talk to someone about parts of themselves that are painful and hidden, frightened and frightening, dangerous and disorganizing. . . . (Fosha, 2000b, p. 29)

Establishing safety and *undoing aloneness* (Fosha, 2000b) are guiding principles of AEDP. The above quote stirs a felt sense of the quality of presence that can evoke safety and a sense of what might inspire someone to be willing to risk opening into what has been shielded and protected. It heralds some of the skillful means that are cultivated in the therapist practicing AEDP, as we directly engage the immense potential to become a collaborative, healing partnership, offering holding and encouragement to support the emergence of transformance and exploration.

The AEDP therapist stance is attachment based and draws from attachment theory (Bowlby, 1988). It informs how we as therapists step into an asymmetrical relationship as an older, wiser other, with motives to protect and to care, willing to meet our patient's distress and suffering with empathy, to help regulate affect (Fosha, 2003, 2009a, 2021a; Lipton & Fosha,

2011; Pando-Mars, 2011) and to support and encourage opportunities for stretching beyond defenses. The picture here is of two human beings, one in distress, the other leaned over in a helping stance. It doesn't matter if the dyad is composed of an infant and an adult, or two adults. By definition, the one feeling the distress is the vulnerable one and the one offering the help and succor is the one *perceived* as the attachment figure, the one, in this situation, perceived as older and wiser. It is why age doesn't matter and a therapist who is chronologically younger can be an attachment figure for someone who is chronologically older than them. It is why Bowlby (1979), ever wise, actually defined the attachment figure as someone "conceived as stronger and/or wiser" (p. 155), and yet through the years, AEDP usage has shifted the description of the attachment figure as someone *perceived as older and wiser* by the more vulnerable member of the dyad who is in need. We are wired with our own caregiving behavioral system to respond to the more vulnerable member of the dyad—in this case, the patient seeking help for their distress— whose attachment system may be activated and whose signals of distress or unmet needs may be calling. In essence, the attachment strand holds the position "I am here *for* you."

We also draw from intersubjective studies (Beebe & Lachman, 1998, 2014; Stern, 1985, 2010; Tronick, 2009), offering ourselves in a symmetrical relationship with motives for companionship and pleasure (Fosha, 2009a, 2021a). The image here is that of a child and an adult playing side by side, absorbed in a common task. In the moment of absorption, the fact that one is a baby and the other is a grown-up is lost in the commonality of the absorption in the common task, be it the building of a sandcastle or watching raindrops on a window. We delight in what is essential about our patients; eschewing neutrality, we allow our pleasure to be seen. We also allow ourselves to feel moved and to show when we feel touched, including tears that arise in resonance or response to our patients. We are judicious in our self-disclosures, intending our sharing in service of our patient's healing. Here, the essence of the intersubjective strand is "I see you. I am here *with* you." We seek to explore the impact of our transparency with our patients, with specific interventions to inquire into the patient's experiences with us. From a level playing field we recognize the honor of meeting human to human. Cultural humility comes in here, with intention to recognize power and privilege with awareness of our social identities and positions that we hold. How to be respectful and accountable, and truly helpful, is an ongoing practice in establishing a culture of shared safety and humanity.

Maxim 2: Healing From the Get-Go

AEDP sets the stage for our patients to function optimally from the start (Kranz, 2021). We draw from the research in attachment theory that recognizes that our patterns of attachment change across relationships. Mary Main (1995) has said attachment is not a trait. It is not personality. It is our response to conditions that are established between caregiver and child that repeat over time, establishing patterns. Change the conditions, and the pattern changes.

Therefore, in AEDP we maximize the potential to establish conditions for safety. As described in the first maxim, we aim to help our patients feel accompanied from the get-go. We offer help for dyadic regulation; we want to help our patients' nervous systems perceive safety so that they can feel calm and supported to make use of the process of psychotherapy. We foster safety to facilitate exploration.

By inviting our patients to have an experience, a new experience, a good experience, we aim for them to have a corrective emotional and relational experience (Alexander & French, 1946). AEDP leans into our wired-in dispositions for growth and self-righting. The AEDP therapist is a transformance detective. We are on the lookout for glimmers of health and strivings for the better so that we can help our patients to harness these glimmers, to follow their transformance, and make room for a positive, new experience. In the company of an attuned, responsive therapist, many patients have such an experience in a first session of AEDP: one that evokes a release of emotion, a revised self-understanding, and an experience of hope. For this we acknowledge the possibility for *healing from the get-go* (Kranz, 2021), and we have empirical evidence to back up that claim (DiCorcia et al., 2023).

Maxim 3: Stay With It and Stay With Me—Dyadic Regulation

When AEDP therapists are being with patients in each of the four states, our intention of establishing safety and undoing aloneness carries throughout our activities. The motto "Stay with it and stay with me" (Fosha, 2017b, p. 277), implies that we intend to accompany our patients no matter what shows up. Although previously they may have been alone with unbearable emotions or experiences, this time we want them to make use of our intention to stay with them as they approach what arises, so that they can be with what is emerging and feel the safe base of our holding environment to support their exploration. This applies from the first session onward, throughout the therapy, all the way through to, and including termination (Harrison, 2020).

At times we need to *up regulate*. When our patients use deactivating strategies or other strategies of detachment, we may want to amplify, deepen, or elongate the emotional experience, to help our patients find the correct amount of activation to allow access to their emotion. With other patients or on other occasions, we need to *down regulate*. When the emotional experience becomes too intense, or our patients are using hyperactivating strategies, we may need to step in to help them build the capacity to navigate what is arising. Learning to identify signals of our patients' emotion regulation strategies helps us to recognize how to intervene when they are either feeling flat with too little access or arousal, or when they feel overwhelmed with too much arousal in their nervous system. Another way to conceive of this *staying with it and staying with me* is "The emotional, psychobiological lending of a hand."

Maxim 4: "The Unit of Intervention Is Not the Therapist's Comment But the Therapist's Comment and the Patient's Response to It" (Fosha, 2000b, p. 214)

The therapist's efforts to establish safety and undo aloneness are only as effective as the patient's reception of our intentions and interventions. Being affectively attuned is our effort to be with our patients so that they feel seen and heard, felt, and known. What is crucial about this fourth maxim is the recognition that as well as offering a comment, the intervention is complete only when we include the patient's response to our comment.

Moment-to-moment tracking is essential. When we make a comment, we pay attention to what happens next. For example, we reflect the feeling of deep sorrow in responding to a patient's remembering the loss of their beloved grandmother. When we express empathy, we want to notice how our expression lands with the patient. Do they make eye contact with us, registering our presence? Do they move into a fuller expression of grief? Maybe tears fall, perhaps they choke back a sob and shake their head. Whatever happens is important to track. Whether the patient responds verbally and says, "Yes, I still miss her so much," or along with the shake of their head says, "No, I just can't go there right now," each response guides the therapist's next action. It informs us about what the patient needs, whether it be affect regulation, deepening the processing of an emotional expression, or attending to the patient's shift away from affective experience toward a defensive shutting down. Truly any of these responses is natural and the relational and experiential work in AEDP is to meet the patient where they are, to be with what emerges, and to be ready to coordinate step-by-step with whatever arises in each moment (Hanakawa, 2021).

Maxim 5: Check for the Patient's Receptive Affective Capacity

AEDP pays close attention to how our way of being is received. Do our patients feel helped, seen, felt, cared about, and/or understood by us? How our patients experience us may indicate what needs attention. Another touchstone by which AEDP clinicians explore the relationship between therapist and client explicitly and experientially is to monitor our patient's *receptive affective capacity*. As Fosha (2000b) has said many times, in many ways, "it is not enough that empathy and care, love or help be given: to work their potent magic, they must be taken in. For empathy to count, the patient must *receive* [emphasis added] and experience that empathy" (pp. 151–152). How do we know whether our patient is feeling seen, feeling felt, feeling understood, feeling helped, feeling known, and receiving our care? We cannot assume that because we feel moved by our patient that they are seeing the tenderness in our eyes or are taking in the kindness of our voice. The work of psychotherapy is to check for the patient's receptive affective capacity, and we do this by asking, "What do you see in my eyes?" and "How do you experience me in this moment?"

Sometimes psychotherapists who are training in AEDP find these questions challenging. They feel as if they are asking the patient to evaluate them or to provide reassurance. It is not uncommon for a patient's early pass at one of these questions to tell the therapist, "You're doing fine," and then turn to another topic. But this is where the AEDP therapist steps forward early in treatment to assess for the patient's receptive affective capacity and their willingness to engage at this interpersonal level. We want to know how they are perceiving us and what they are getting. If they see care in our eyes, are they able to take it in and notice how it affects them? Not all patients can, and if not, we want to know. Many patients in treatment don't realize how the protective mechanisms they've developed prevent them not only from getting hurt but from registering what is good. These adaptive shields also interfere with recognizing their worthiness or realizing the positive impact they have on others.

Leigh McCullough Vaillant (1997) has said, if our patients cannot "take in" [*or receive or resonate to*] what we or others offer them, no revision of their pathological inner representations is possible and little character change can occur. This gives credence to the importance of learning about our patient's receptivity. For when our patients can reveal their surprise when seeing our care, then we have an opportunity to juxtapose what is an expectation arising from the historical past with what is happening freshly between us, in the interactive field of our present-day relationship. For example, when my patient was crying with her head down and eyes closed. When she looked up, she was surprised to see me still looking at her. She had expected to see me turned away or spaced out. That I stayed present with her when her eyes were closed and downcast and was there to greet her when she came back was corrective.

As seen in the face-to-face interaction studies of Beebe et al. (2016), expectations that developed between caregiver and child often appear between therapist and patient. The potential of the therapeutic relationship is to provide an attuned response to our patients, which they most surely deserve to receive and benefit from. These corrective relational experiences can update the nervous system and engage the mechanisms of neuroplasticity. In the subsequent session with the above-mentioned patient, we saw evidence of change. The next time she had her eyes down and closed while feeling an emotion, she anticipated that when she looked up, she would see my eyes present with her.

Many of our patients with attachment trauma have restrictions that block their receptive affective capacity. In the chapters in which we explore interventions and treatment with insecure patterns of attachment we see how this plays out among those who struggle with patterns of avoidance and what may be different in those who are grappling with patterns of ambivalence. They might show up differently from what you'd expect.

Some patients will turn down receiving my caring because they assume the care is given because of the fee they are paying for my services. But as I have often replied,

> What you pay for is my time and expertise, and maybe even for this question. What you see in my eyes comes from my heart—and my heart is not on payroll. When you see care in my eyes it comes from my genuine response to you, and you are most welcome to feel into what happens inside when you know that this care is for you.

Maxim 6: Make the Implicit Explicit. Make the Explicit Experiential. Make the Experiential Relational.

Much of what enters the intersubjective space between therapist and patient is nonverbal or para-verbal. Nonverbal behaviors appear in facial expressions, gaze direction, eye contact, body movements, posture, and so forth. Para-verbal behaviors come across in voice tone, expressive utterances like "mmm" and "ooh," audible breathing, sighs, harumphs, and so on. . . . Often when a person is speaking, they are not aware of how these portions of their communication are coming across. Merriam-Webster's dictionary defines *implicit* as "capable of being understood from something else though unexpressed." Allan Schore (1994, 2003, 2019a, 2019b) speaks about implicit memory as what is encoded in the right hemisphere of the brain in the first 2 years of life, the time when many of our earliest expectancies are forming our internal working models.

In AEDP, *making the implicit explicit* refers to the therapist's attempt to bring awareness to unconscious communications from our patients. It can also refer to the therapist's bringing awareness to what may be an unconscious communication from us, perhaps by stating our intention or naming a feeling we may have in response to the patient. Implicit communication may reveal the patient's patterning around affect and defensive exclusion. When either the therapist or the patient brings clarification to an aspect of their behavior, we view this as making the implicit explicit.

Some unconscious communications might be related to internal working models—for example, a patient is sharing something meaningful with the therapist and begins to smile or laugh while they are speaking. The therapist might ask the patient, "Did you notice that you laughed while sharing what sounded quite painful?" The intention is to highlight defensive behavior to heighten the patient's awareness so they can make a choice to understand its purpose. When making the laugh explicit, the patient might discover that the laughter is covering up sadness.

Following this further brings us to the second part of the adage, *make the explicit experiential.* If sadness is underneath the laughter, we want to encourage our patient to be with the sadness. To make it experiential, the therapist would say something like "Can you give the sadness some room?" "Feel into the sadness . . . where do you notice it in your body?" In this way the patient can have the experience of letting go of the defensive laughter that kept their emotion at bay, and instead is invited to be with the emotion.

Experiencing their emotion directly can heal the disconnection that was held in place with defensive exclusion and bring connection within the self.

When a psychotherapist makes our responses or intentions explicit, and selectively shares the impact the client has on us through judicious self-disclosure, empathy, or psycho-ed, these aspects of making the implicit explicit bring awareness to the therapeutic relationship. Making our intentions overt to the patient is another form of being transparent, in service of being collaborative. Sometimes sharing psycho-ed is a form of sharing power with the patient, holding information together about the purpose of a particular intervention. It is important to follow up to learn how our comments land with our patients. In the case of revealing my care, I make the explicit experiential by asking, "What is it like for you to feel my caring for you right now?" This bridges to the third portion of the maxim about making the experiential relational.

Make the experiential relational harkens back to the larger factor of relatedness and helping our patients not only feel but also *know* that they are not alone as they face their struggles. When the above patient experienced the sadness that was underneath her laughter, the therapist makes the experiential relational by inquiring how the patient feels about experiencing emotion in their presence. We might ask, "How is it for you to have your sadness with me?" And again, what they say will determine where we go next. Nodding and acknowledging feeling okay might allow for a deepening exploration of the affective experience. A response such as "not good, I'm uncomfortable," might indicate a need for anxiety regulation or exploration. "What's uncomfortable?" might lead to an expectation of judgment or fear of losing control. Some patients have a fear that once they start crying, they will never stop (they always do).

Often, our patients use defenses to cover up the emotion that wasn't acceptable to one of their attachment figures. Many internal working models exclude awareness of emotional expression. Earlier in this chapter, we presented a representational schema of the internal working model, the SOE triangle, which depicts the relational matrix within which emotion occurs and the role of the other in helping a person to be with their emotion. Inquiring about a person's experience of having emotion with their psychotherapist provides an opportunity for us to check in about the level of safety the patient may be feeling in this moment. The safer the patient feels, the more freely they will be able to experience their emotion. Our work as AEDP therapists is to keep an eye on these dimensions of experiential processing to facilitate the patient's capacity for genuine emotional expression and ability to make optimal use of our relational presence and attuned assistance.

In AEDP we have many different intervention pathways to uncover how what is unresolved from our patient's history interferes with present-moment experiencing: to uncouple expectancies based on past attachment figures from present-moment healing experiences with the therapist (Piliero, 2021). We are continually aiming toward having new, corrective emotional and relational experiences. This maxim about making the implicit explicit, the explicit experiential, and then the experiential relational moves the process of psychotherapy forward, from the get-go and throughout AEDP treatment.

Maxim 7: The Patient Feels Safe and the Therapist Brave

The level of engagement required for a therapist to be so actively involved with the exploration of the patient–therapist relationship is a huge commitment. It requires courage to bring attention to ourselves, in service of helping our patients make use of our presence and discover how they feel in our presence. We may need to find steadiness in the face of turbulence, stepping forward when our instincts want to pull away. Our own internal working models may be challenged. And yet, this is what it means to be brave. Fosha (2000b) encourages

> Establishing the trust needed for deep affect work requires that the therapist's sense of self be engaged. . . . The patient cannot be expected to rapidly open up to a therapist who remains hidden and shielded. The emotional atmosphere should be one in which *the patient feels safe and the therapist brave* [emphasis added]. The patient's sense of safety within the therapeutic relationship is enhanced in part by the therapist's risk taking. (p. 213)

The permission to bring ourselves into the present moment with patients and have the model guiding our interventions toward what it takes to build an authentic connection is an opportunity to stretch ourselves and cultivate such bravery. Given that many of the patients we address have suffered unbearable aloneness in the face of overwhelming emotion, moving to accompany them while they open to affective experience and then processing this experience can be frightening and even disorganizing. The more therapists have explored and processed our own emotional and relational life, the more equilibrium we can offer patients by our felt sense of trusting the process.

Our unwavering interest and helping patients to be with their emotions, to accompany them in dark and unknown places and witness their courage and determination, can provide them with life-changing experiences of self and other. Stepping into these places requires that the therapist is engaged and proactive, willing to be authentic and true. Such a presence may bring vulnerability on the part of the therapist (Lipton, 2021). This adage holds the wisdom that both partners in this dyad are taking risks. The trust that is needed for this encounter acknowledges that when the therapist engages fully and bravely, patients are more apt to feel safe, and free to explore.

Maxim 8: Working With the Self-at-Worst From Under the Aegis of the Self-at-Best

This maxim of working with the self-at-worst from under the aegis of the self-at-best is exactly as it sounds. However, a reminder that self-at-best and self-at-worst are constructs that denote experience-near characteristics of behavior and in no way are they meant to be judgmental. As we discuss throughout this book, how a child is responded to during affectively charged moments is at the crux of what becomes internalized and leads to secure and insecure attachment. The AAI shows that the parent's state of mind directly correlates with the infant's pattern of attachment. Main et al. (1985) reconceptualized how individual differences appear in a person's internal working model, specifically that a person's attention, behavior, and memory change across states of mind (see Chapter 1). It is this flexibility that serves the process of working with the self-at-worst from under the aegis of the self-at-best.

Fosha (2000b, 2021a) has described how different relational dynamics give rise to different psychic organizations of behavior and identified a way to describe this with the constructs of self-at-best and self-at-worst. Self-at-best comes to the fore when safety prevails and is hope driven; forces of transformation and an openness to experience are in ascendance. Self-at-worst is stress induced and driven by dread; forces of resistance and constriction are more prevalent. To set the conditions for self-at-best to come online, each of the earlier maxims is at play, especially Maxim 1, Establish Safety and Undo Aloneness.

Case example. Consider the patient who masks their sadness with laughter. At times when their affect is clearly incongruent with what they are saying, we might feel the pain underneath the laughter and identify the laughter as a defense being used to disguise emotion. The defensive strategy is a habituated reaction (at the top of the TOE). Earlier in life, when this patient grew to anticipate their emotion being scoffed at, they learned to hide it (which we can map on the SOE triangle).

Let's look at this interaction from the perspective of working with the self-at-worst from under the aegis of the self-at-best. The therapist resonates with the patient's underlying pain, recognizes out-of-place laughter as a defense, and with a spirit of acceptance asks the patient to notice their affective experience. Or more explicitly, the therapist invites the patient to make room for their tears, countering the dreaded expectation of rejection of emotion. With the therapist's guidance and supportive resonance, the patient will often drop the defense and allow what is stirring to emerge.

Thus, they shift out of their self-at-worst version of their affect regulation strategy, which we can map onto the TOE. When the patient shifts their loyalty away from defense, and away from resistant-led functioning, to allow their emotion in the presence and resonance with the therapist, they are shifting to transformance-led functioning. Engaging their self-at-best, they are open to following their signals of emotion. We can also map this interaction onto the self-at-best version of the SOE triangle, as in this state they have access to genuine emotion while being open to connection with the other, a security-building experience that potentiates a rewiring of old internal working models.

Moment by moment the therapist is attuning and considering how to situate ourselves in the relational context with our patient, ready to help shift the focus of attention away from dread and avoidance, toward openness to what is occurring in the present moment, which can lead to a new, healing experience with self and other. Mapping these interactions onto both the TOE and the SOE triangle helps the psychotherapist organize and schematize what is taking place in treatment. Self-at-best is a hope-driven organization; transformation on the rise brings more access to emotion and memory, and new ways of perceiving and reflecting. It is not uncommon to hear a patient say, "I've never thought I would share this with anyone, but somehow I want to tell you. . . ." or "This is so strange, but now I can see. . . ." Self-at-best is an ideal state from which to explore the friction of unresolved material that is chafing to be discovered.

Maxim 9: "Existing in the Heart and Mind of the Other" (Fosha, 2000b)

The roots of security and resilience are to be found in the sense of being understood by and having the sense of existing in the *heart and mind* [emphasis added] of a loving, caring, attuned and self-possessed other, an other with a heart and mind of her own. (Fosha, 2003, p. 228)

We all have a biological need to be understood (Fonagy et al., 1995, pp. 268–269). By being accurately perceived and responded to in a time of distress, a child learns that distress is temporary and can be met with what is needed to bring soothing and relief. During attuned interactions, a parent accurately mirrors a child's affective state by showing a marked expression, speaking in a slightly higher voice, or cooing when they reflect a feeling back to a child. Fonagy describes that markedness is "signaling to the infant that the affect the caregiver is expressing is not her own but the child's" (Fonagy et al., 2002, p. 17). Having their state seen and known brings the child accompaniment and a sense of existing in the mind of another. This grows their self-reflective function; receiving attunement, one can attune to themselves. The capacity to attune develops an understanding of self and other. Bowlby addressed how this development of attachment progresses with his identification of the *goal-corrected partnership*. Each person understanding what is in their own mind and capable of holding what is in the other's mind at the same time is essential for connection, communication, and collaboration. Fosha broadens existing in the mind of another when she calls for *existing in the heart and mind of the other*, recognizing the importance of "feeling felt" (Siegel, 2007). Feeling understood and feeling held in loving care goes a long way toward undoing aloneness.

Existing in the heart and mind of the other summarizes the essence of AEDP's factor of relationship. We aim to be with our patients with the fullness of an engaged heart and mind, "being open to, accepting, and connecting with whatever is coming our way from our client" (Lipton, 2021, pp. 151–152) and for them to have an experience of being seen and understood. The initial quote in Maxim 1 begins with "Being inside the patient's world as an other and the patient feeling and knowing it. In the presence of such a presence the patient's world unfolds. . . ." The invocation is to our self-at-best, capable of holding what is in our own heart and mind, while holding what emerges with our patient. It evokes how to be a *self-possessed other:*

having the capacity to know ourselves, and for the other to know themselves, while being together. Like in a goal-corrected partnership, this comes from having a differentiated sense of self, the capacity to be with a patient without merging or being overcome; offering the resonance of right-brain to right-brain affective accompaniment, while our left brain is available for reflection on emotional experience, the patient's and our own. When we see and feel with our patients with the clarity of an engaged heart and an understanding mind, our patients can sense that they are real to us. They begin to trust their core being and knowing, perhaps in ways that never felt real before but now has the sense of feeling true and right.

Maxim 10: Going "Beyond Mirroring" to Helping

A key description of the AEDP therapist in action is the willingness to go *beyond mirroring*, and help (Fosha, 2000b, 2021a). From the get-go we are looking for glimmers of transformance in our patients to help them recognize their own strengths and capacities they are bringing to the process of psychotherapy. We engage relationally with the intention that they can feel our willingness and capability to help them. Beyond reflecting what we see to our patients, we look for how to help them get the most out of psychotherapy. And when they are engaging in fruitful ways we affirm and encourage them, so they come to recognize the pathways to transformation.

When patients avoid affective experiences, we aim to see what else is happening. Are defenses or anxiety lurking? Are patients aware of their anxiety and what might be needed to feel more calm or able to bear the emergence of emotion? If they have used defenses to avoid vulnerability, we may need to help them recognize how their defenses serve them yet also block them, and what other options might be available. When shame is surging, we might normalize what is arising or find ways of meeting them judiciously by sharing a corresponding experience.

In later sections of this book, we address ways to help our patients whose protective strategies interfere with a naturally unfolding exploration of their experiences. We have found that patients demonstrating distinctive patterns of attachment need different forms of help, and we continue to develop how to help in the chapters devoted specifically to intervening with each pattern of insecure attachment. When we can offer help with sensitivity and responsiveness to how each patient presents while understanding the dynamics involved in how each pattern has formed, our attunement has more durability. We can meet our patients in places where they may not even be aware of what they need. Defenses and anxiety are often the result of growing up without a helpful, trustworthy caregiver at crucial times. So going beyond mirroring to helping is a specific and necessary aspect of healing attachment-level wounding.

Maxim 11: Explore, Don't Explain (Lipton & Fosha, 2011): Experience, Experience, Experience

Working in an experiential model can be difficult when our patients are in State 1, especially since the bidirectional aspects of attachment relationships move in both directions, and dyadic resonance is enhanced by mirror neurons (Rizzolatti et al., 1996)! In her 2009 dissertation, Elizabeth Schoettle found that AEDP therapists are subject to matching our patients' experiences across the four states. In State 1, when our patients might be intellectualizing or stuck in entrenched patterns, therapists are subject to falling back upon our own defensive processes (Lipton, 2021). When we find our own intellectual defenses rising, the maxim *explore, don't explain*,[2] is useful to have at the ready.

Holding some awareness on our own experience while tracking our patients allows us the possibility of making a choice. Instead of meeting our patient's intellect with our intellect, or their defensive gesture with a defense of our own, we can intervene with the adage "explore, don't explain." In place of an intellectual discourse or an attempt to explain the patient's behavior, consider asking an exploratory question about the patient's experience rather than the content of what the patient is saying:

> Are you aware that when I asked you to notice the tone in your voice, how your right hand flicked out and away? Without changing anything, with acceptance and curiosity, would you be willing to make the gesture again, and notice what your hand might be saying?

This brings us to another aspect of working experientially and following affective experience. Many of our patients are unfamiliar with connecting to their visceral experience of their emotional life. To ask them to notice what is happening inside, or what are they feeling now, may put them face to face with the unknown, and may evoke blankness rather than access. We can help their exploration by tracking our patients across the Seven

Channels of Experience (Hanakawa, 2021; Mars, 2011). The Seven Channels are sensation, energy, emotion, movement, auditory, visual, and imaginal. When access to emotion isn't available, we may notice another channel that is open. Pausing and attending to gestures or movement, fluctuations in energy, and notable tension, are signals we can reflect to our patients, offering an entry point through which to explore their experience.

When we ask our patients to notice the tears (emotion channel) in their eyes, to sense the movement of their hand swiping out in front of them (movement channel), and to tune into the tone in their voice (auditory channel), we are using our observations to reflect their experience back to them. Mindell & Mindell (2002) suggest that the most powerful interventions address signals from the body that are already trying to happen. When we help our patients connect to an experience that is taking place in the present moment, we help them to explore, not explain.

Maxim 12: Turbocharge Neuroplasticity—
Metaprocess, Metaprocess, Metaprocess

Metatherapeutic processing is a way of making the positive experiences of healing, the therapeutic experiences, the focus of our joint dyadic therapeutic attention . . . so as to *turbocharge neuroplasticity* [emphasis added]. (Fosha, 2013b, p. 38)

State 2 work in AEDP is the processing of affective experience to completion. Yet, resolving trauma often entails more than the release of incomplete emotions or the repair of broken trust. Trauma gets into the fibers of how we grow and come to know ourselves (Menakem, 2017). Self-identity can become constrained by the impact and memory of trauma. Hebb (1944) is known for saying "What fires together wires together." Our brain develops pathways of merging experiences so that what happens to us often becomes intertwined with how we see ourselves in the world, in relationship with self and other. One of AEDP's most salient contributions is the continuation of therapeutic processing after the completion of previously unresolved emotional and relational experiences, after corrective experiences. In AEDP we recognize postbreakthrough affects that follow such completions. We highlight and draw attention to the activation of adaptive action tendencies of categorical emotions, relief that follows the unburdening of pain and suffering, and a lightness of being as the weight carried for so long is lifted.

Here, AEDP engages another round of processing, referred to as metatherapeutic processing, in which we inquire into the experience of change itself. When the self has processed what was previously unbearable and discovers a hitherto unimaginable relief from suffering, a rich terrain is open for discovery. When emotion releases, energy that has been trapped by mental and physical patterns becomes freed and the experience of self expands. We pay attention to the moment-to-moment changes: the rising up of the spine, openness in the chest, tears of grief for all that was lost, or gentle tears that are moved by tender awakening that stirs the soul. By leaning into these shifts and metaprocessing their somatic experience, we come to find new realizations and new experiences that profoundly impact the patient's relationship to their self, and the self then transforms.

By lingering and savoring these manifestations of change, we provide an opportunity for the body to shift and readjust to the new, expanded state. Staying and focusing on each shift provides opportunity for neural connections to grow and take hold, which has the greatest impact for integration of what is new into the core of one's being (Yeung, 2021). It is this *staying with the positive new* that turbocharges neuroplasticity and maximizes our potential for healing.

Maxim 13: Privilege the Positive

Your brain is like Velcro for negative experiences but Teflon for positive ones. (Hanson, 2013, p. 27)

As well as helping our patients to resolve their suffering, AEDP is actively engaged with helping our patients to recognize what is unbroken and essential. We have markers to identify what is going well and we affirm our patients along the way whenever possible. We notice and celebrate acts of courage and determination. We welcome the shy smile and the tentative comment toward something new. We lean into glimmers of transformance to support their emergence, honor their guidance, and help our patients to find aspects of themselves they can expand and trust.

Historically many psychotherapy models have focused on what gets in the patient's way of actualizing themselves and accomplishing the changes they want to make. AEDP takes the opportunity to highlight what is working, what is adaptive, and what is emergent. We see defensive strategies as the person's best effort at adaptation and protection, and in this light, we can align with defensive postures rather than challenge them. We can build collaboration and cooperation to recognize innate protective drives toward survival en route to health and wholeness. We help our patients to feel how positive affects accompany experiences of change for the better (Notsu et al., 2022). For example, amid facing previously avoided experience, something feels right, and relief can fuel the recognition that our work is on track.

Here, AEDP's emphasis is on supporting what is going right, what is true, and what is changing. So often when making a change a person will say, "I never do this," in an unconscious loyalty to old patterns. We encourage staying with "what you are doing now" and metaprocessing the new experience to broaden and build awareness and connection to what is emerging (Frederickson, 2001; Frederickson & Joiner, 2018). State 3 in AEDP is loaded with transformational affects, which are positive affective experiences that arise during metaprocessing change and give rise to core self and integration.

We also track vitality affects as markers of attunement (Stern, 1985) and being in sync with our patients, as well as marking moments of change with positive vitality affects as somatic/affective markers of moments of change for the better (Fosha, 2021a). When our process is unfolding, the sense of time tends to vanish. When discourse flows between therapist and patient, we might arrive at the end of a session startled and wonder "Where did the time go?" Likely we are both experiencing an enhanced state of vitality, an uplifting feeling, perhaps surges of energy, and a sense of aliveness.

Another aspect of following the positive involves transforming the energy draining—the vehement emotions—into ones that are energy enriching (Craig, 2002, 2009). If we don't recognize the valence between these emotions, it is possible to consider that processing emotions to completion means following any emotional expression. So AEDP places value on differentiating the adaptive and maladaptive categories of emotion and directly supports experiences that move in an upward direction, seeing the life-giving eros that such positivity brings.

Maxim 14: True Self—True Other

The True Self is—the position from which comes the spontaneous gesture—the personal idea—the experience of aliveness—the experience of existing. Only the True Self can be creative and only the True Self can feel real. . . . The True Self comes from the aliveness of the body tissues and the working of body-functions, including the heart's action and breathing. (Winnicott, 1965/1960, p. 148)

To have a transformational outcome in psychotherapy, we aim from the beginning to set treatment on a true course. Mobilizing the therapeutic process is much like catching the wind in our sails, making corrections when sails are luffing, and momentum is lagging. Winnicott's description of the true self is an inspiration for psychotherapists as we orient our patients to get on a path toward healing by connecting with what is genuine and authentic in themselves. Holding our tiller to what lies under defenses or is obscured by anxiety, we steer patients toward what is alive in their bodies, what shows up through spontaneous gestures, their heartbeat, and their breathing. AEDP therapists are trained to express how our patients exist in our hearts and minds.

True Other

In tandem, Fosha (2000a,b; 2005) coined the term "true other" as a counterpart to Winnicott's "true self." It is a term that aims to capture the experience patients have when they feel someone as responding to them in just the right way at just the right time. Fosha described that the true other appears in moments when one person responds to another in such a way that provides exactly what is needed, even if the need was not known to the person prior to that moment. "This phenomenon refers to an essential responsiveness, a deep way of being known and understood, seen or helped, which is meaningful, attuned, appreciative and enlivening" (Fosha, 2000b, p. 170). Such responsiveness, one person to another in just the right way, at just the right time, is experienced in that moment as true. Here, when we "get" our patient in a key moment, we shed light on an aspect of them that once recognized can be seen by the self. Being seen is a core attachment need that may or may not have been deeply met by attachment figures in our patients' lives. Sometimes when our patients expect invisibility, being met brings an awakening, as the awareness of being seen touches a core longing to be understood. Vitality emerges. Fosha calls these moments peak relational moments—known to be true.

Throughout the course of AEDP treatment, we are helping our patients to come into the right relationship with themselves, to admit feelings that arise toward significant others, events, and circumstances that have shaped who they are and what they have come to expect. This journey propels them to connect to their core self, their innate knowing that guides their becoming. When we have the grace of responding to the needs and somatic expressions of our patients as a "true other," we support their recognition of their true self.

Psychotherapists occupy a powerful position to generate new, corrective experiences by making space for what exists beneath the surface, facilitating the emergence of authenticity. Here, when therapists accept and invite awareness of emotions and aspects of our patients' experiences that were previously inaccessible, we help them to connect with what is real, in service of coming to terms with what had been unresolved.

Fosha (2000b) describes the depth of this potential when she says

> A deep transformation occurs within the self as a result of being with a "true other"; of being seen, loved, understood, empathized with, affirmed; of being able to do that which hitherto had been too frightening; of being in touch with aspects of emotional experience that previously were feared to be beyond bearing. . . . As a result of the transformation . . . one is closer to the true self, the self one has always known oneself to be. (p. 171)

There is an organismic intelligence in what allows us to respond to our patients in a way that leads them to experience us—in those moments—as being a true other. Being with our patients in just the right way to serve the patients' becoming, requires our capacity to *see* and *be* in the present moment. It takes being accessible for genuine relating and authentic expression. In the presence of our willingness to be real, we offer our patients the felt sense of resonating with what is real in themselves. Thereby, we help them to ride a current that is recognizable, yields vitality, and comes to awareness as truth.

PART II

———

NORTH STAR

4

Inspiration: A Portrait of Secure Attachment

He was so nurtured, so calm. I knew he had been loved.
He was confident. He had the skills to survive,
otherwise he surely would have died in Calcutta.
— SAROO'S ADOPTED MOM, *LION,* 2016

I'M CAPTIVATED BY THE MOVIE *LION.*

In 2016 I saw *Lion,* which moved me and has stayed with me ever since. Based on a true story, the main character, a 5-year-old boy named Saroo, falls asleep on a train, and ends up 1,000 miles from home, hopelessly lost. All the while, he maintains an unfaltering connection to his family and sense of place, which stay with him, guide him, and even help him to find his way back, 25 years later.

Lion is a true story of love and separation and a remarkable tale of attachment security. This story shows what's possible when raised in the loving gaze of his mother's eyes, how Saroo displays astounding stability and core knowing from such an early age.

I bring this story here because it clearly portrays how Saroo's brain developed optimally, and that his neurobiological core self was online. Saroo was clever and flexible in how he coped with adversity. He survived loss and was able to attach and love again. When secure attachment is internalized, mechanisms in the brain serve survival at the highest level.

We can help our patients to draw on naturally occurring mechanisms in their brains when we help them through their own journeys to heal insecure attachment.

To draw these parallels, I share some of Saroo's encounters.

Saroo's Journey

While waiting for his older brother, 5-year-old Saroo wanders into a stalled, empty train and falls asleep. When he wakes up, the train is moving, and he discovers he's alone. He bangs on the windows, alarmed, as any child—or adult—might be. He shouts at people in passing train stations, calling for help. He calls to girls sitting in the fields, pounding on the windows to get their attention, as the train speeds through the countryside of India. Another night comes and Saroo sleeps.

When the train finally stops at a station in Calcutta, Saroo squeezes through the crowds, through the noise. He climbs up onto a pillar, so he can see. He calls for his beloved mother and brother as loud as he can, as if they could hear him, imagining they will come running.

Unfortunately, his family is at least 1,000 miles away.

But that doesn't stop Saroo from seeking to find his way back, though it takes him 25 years.

At the train station in Calcutta, Saroo goes to the ticket counter and tries to say the name of his village: "Ginestlay." But the ticket master doesn't understand. Saroo repeats the name as best he can, again and again, without result, until he is finally pushed aside.

Undeterred, Saroo explores to find his way. In the station tunnels, he sees a group of children. He holds eye contact with one boy. The boy unfolds a piece of cardboard and motions Saroo over. He joins them, and curls up on the mat to sleep. He wakes as a group of patrolmen are grabbing kids. Saroo sees the danger and runs.

Saroo lives on the streets of Calcutta for 2 months. One night he is lying under a bridge, wearily moving little stones from one place to another. The scene shifts to show him listening to his mother's soothing voice, saying, "What a good boy!" He remembers visiting his mother while she is working at a rock quarry. He is helping her carry heavy rocks from one pile to another, until they sit together, and his mother shares a juicy mango with him. Under the bridge in Calcutta, we see through Saroo's mind's eye just how his mother beams at him, repeating and repeating, "What a good boy!"

Saroo replays memories of his older brother, with his cheerful, hopping gait, who turns and smiles at Saroo, cajoling him to skip across the train tracks together.

Through another engaging encounter that begins with eye contact with an older boy in a restaurant, Saroo is brought to a police station. The officers try to help him locate his home, and his mother. But Saroo cannot make them understand his name, nor the name of his village, and he only knows his mother as "mum."

From early in the story, Saroo acts, and engages others, clear signs of his self-confidence. We see how his mother lives in him, and his longing to get back to her fuels him with courage and determination.

These deeply internalized images and messages of Saroo's mother and his brother are the building blocks of representations that make our internal working models and are essential to the formation of attachment bonds with self and others. The way we see ourselves in someone else's eyes becomes the way through which we come to know ourselves. Experiences of being accompanied and nourished develop circuits in our brains that pair having a need and having that need met. Even though Saroo is lost and out of reach of his mother's arms, he can soothe himself with pictures of being with her and being fed by her. She lives inside him, and he carries her with him, and with this he maintains a sense of his own worthiness and deserving to be held and loved: pure signs of his secure attachment.

Saroo ends up in an orphanage.

Saroo holds on to the certainty that he is missed. When an Australian couple wants to adopt him, a childcare worker shows Saroo their pictures. She assures Saroo that every-thing possible has been done to find his mother. She tells him that his picture was posted throughout Calcutta, but no one appeared for him.

Accepting this, Saroo travels on a plane to meet his adoptive parents.

Saroo enters his new life, and he attaches to his new parents and thrives under their love. He grows up playing cricket and running on green grass. Saroo goes to college and falls in love. But he never forgets his first home nor his mother and brother. One evening at a dinner party with international students, he encounters a traditional Indian dessert, called "jalebi."

This stirs Saroo's memory of an experience with his older brother. They are walking through the markets, where Saroo sees and craves to taste this delicious Indian treat. This scene catalyzes his deep longing for home. The quest to find his childhood place becomes the single driving focus of his life.

Through a deep, obsessive determination to find his way back, Saroo uses Google Earth to search for familiar places. He mentally replays precise pictures, again and again, of the fields surrounding his village, recalling how he ran through narrow, stone-walled streets to get home. After an exhausting search, he locates the terrain and identifies the grassy lands he used to play in.

He travels to India, back to his village. When he arrives, he runs by body memory through the alleyways to the door of his childhood dwelling. Soon many people of the village are walking up the dirt road, surrounding a woman who is dressed in a pink sari. She is his mother, walking to him. She had never moved from this village in the hope that one day Saroo would return.

So even though Saroo was lost at 5 years old, mispronounced his own name and only knew how to refer to his mother as "mum," he was securely attached, and maintained connection to his home. From the early moments of realizing he was lost, he displayed a deep sense of confidence and faith that he would be found. Throughout his journey, he was full of zest. He showed a playful and heartfelt capacity to engage with the people and life he met, dealt with circumstances optimally, whether adverse/challenging or fortunate, all of this evidence shows that his sense of self was intact and his bonds with his loved ones were internalized within him.

The movie *Lion* is an amazing illustration of how secure attachment functions as the most profound life insurance that exists on this planet. Saroo's survival seems miraculous, given what clearly is a harrowing experience of separation and loss, and unimaginable adversity. And yet, with close examination, one can see how Saroo's internalization of his mother's and brother's profuse love and care stabilize him and orient his smart heart with deft emotional dexterity. Despite all odds, he successfully navigates dangerous circumstances. Instead of being haunted by the loss of his cherished mother and admired older brother, he is accompanied by the presence of their love, which stays constant within him. We see an SOE configuration where the self is represented as worthy; the other is represented as loving and accepting; the self–other interaction is experienced and represented as nurturing, positive, and reliable; and emotions can be processed and their adaptive action tendencies made use of. This is an illustration of secure attachment and how it underlies resilience in the face of potential trauma.

While an incredible depiction of secure attachment, this beautiful story also provides a parable for its corollary. When needs for safety and trust are not met within their primary relationships but instead are ignored or untended, a person suffers from hurt, deprivation, and loss. These experiences become represented internally as insecure attachment and form the basis for appraisals of self as unworthy and expectancies that others would not respond to favorably with care nor understanding.

To help our patients heal insecure attachment from the injuries of relational trauma, it is essential to understand how secure attachment works. We are biologically wired to care and be cared for: It is this wiring that deeply influences what happens in both secure and insecure attachment. In order to heal what has gone wrong, we must engage neural networks in the brain that can set things right.

Healing insecure attachment is nothing short of restoring nature at its best. The mechanisms of secure attachment reside deeply in our brains, despite circumstances, and under the right conditions can be activated and set healing and transformation in motion.

PART III

TRANSLATIONAL TOOLS

PART III

TRANSLATIONAL TOOLS

5

The Three Grids for Tailoring Treatment to Attachment Patterns: Their Development

*Attachment does not develop willy-nilly according to
some inner, genetic, regulating mechanism, but rather is
influenced by conditions in the baby's environment.*
—(AINSWORTH, 1967, P. 387)

PATTERNS OF ATTACHMENT REVEAL EARLY EXPERIENCES WITH OUR CARE-givers that are wired into our brains, bodies, and nervous systems. When children have received enough holding and responsive care, they develop into resilient beings with a secure foundation, able to cope with challenging situations while simultaneously being able to be in touch with their thoughts and feelings. Secure children have a self-representation as having value, being worthy of care, as such are confident to reach out for care, which Cassidy (2001) sees as a "key ability for intimacy" (p. 122). Someone with a secure sense of self moves through life and relationships with a mind and heart of their own and with the capacity to understand the mind and heart of another. When this is not the case, and instead, a child's needs for responsive care and tender holding are repeatedly unmet, they grow needing to manage their feelings of distress and angst with defenses (i.e., self-protective strategies). The defenses become in loco parentis (Fosha, 2000). These conditions give rise to patterns of insecure attachment and subsequent problems with trust and connection with self and other. How our patients arrive to psychotherapy, struggling with repetitive personal and interpersonal issues, is primed by these patterns. The strategies that were once adaptively developed to navigate the treacherous terrains with their caregivers have become installed in intrapsychic mechanisms (i.e., defensive shields). Initially designed to protect them from relational wounding and help with emotion regulation, they now interfere with both relating and self-regulation. The reliance on defense mechanisms poses challenges to developing the kinds of relationships all beings truly want and need.

The good news is that our understanding of these attachment patterns—how they came to be, how they are operationally defined, of what they are constituted—can serve as an entryway into treating the relational trauma that needs to be healed to transform relationships with self and others. Our relationships and experiences leave a neural imprint. How we've been treated leads to expectations of how we will be treated, and our nervous systems hold the memory and the promise of what we can anticipate in relationships and from the world around us.[1]

How then do we tailor treatment to heal the relational wounding, multilayered trauma, and the developmental fallout that underlies each pattern of attachment? AEDP's comprehensive theory is a robust match for this endeavor. Its *explicit relational approach* can help establish the conditions to set a secure base for psychotherapy; its method of *experiential exploration* can lead to the discovery and processing of unresolved emotions; and its *transformational focus* can galvanize the mechanisms of positive neuroplasticity, all which combine for the most stable and integrated transformational outcomes (Iwakabe et al., 2020, 2022; Iwakabe & Conceição, 2016).

With many patients, AEDP treatment inspires and activates hope, and the movement to heal and transform flows indeed, from the get-go. With others, the psychotherapist's encouragement to explore emotional or relational experience sets off alarms and internal signals of distress that are more recalcitrant and less easily melted or bypassed. The invitation to be seen or cared for can be baffling to patients who, instead, become activated at the level of attachment wounding. With them, the work can lack a sense of flow and connection. Patients who have more entrenched patterns may be wary of giving up their protective strategies and may have difficulty trusting the process of psychotherapy. Tailoring treatment and intervening with specificity to their patterns of attachment provides reassuring safety and direction and can help the treatment gain traction.

With so much going on and with so much occurring at so many different levels, Pando-Mars developed the grids, the focus of this chapter, to study the distinct elements of each configuration of attachment, and what is different across the patterns in how they form. It was important to organize all of this information systematically and coherently. The grids provide orientation about our patients' early experiences with their attachment figures, and the impact of these relationships on many different realms of our patients' subsequent adaptations. When we clinicians are informed and clued in to the deeper nature of what we are seeing in our patients, we can then tailor our interventions with precision and understanding.

There are three grids, one for secure attachment, one for insecure attachment, and one for interventions specific to attachment patterns. Grid 1, The Configuration of the Secure Attachment Pattern, defines and describes the optimal elements of the secure attachment pattern; these can function as something of a North Star (i.e., we know what we are aiming for when dealing with and treating the other attachment patterns); Grid 2, The Configurations of Insecure Attachment Patterns: Avoidant, Ambivalent/Resistant, and Disorganized, describes elements of insecure and disorganized attachment in terms of early caregiving, attachment system activation, typical defenses, characteristic fears, and the like. Finally, Grid 3, Clinical Markers & Interventions to Treat Patterns of Avoidant, Ambivalent/Resistant, and Disorganized Attachment, specifies how therapists can respond to these patterns, and matches intervention strategies and goals to the corresponding elements of each configuration in Grid 2.

Developing the Grids for Patterns of Attachment

Recognizing what is manifesting with our patients and understanding the origins of what is right before our eyes informs clinical decision making and helps us steer treatment toward what is needed for each patient, in light of how they developed. This project started in response to questions posed to me in 2012, when I was teaching attachment in an AEDP essential skills course: "But what do you do with patients who have different attachment styles?" This question, and others that followed, launched me to engage this exploration in my own clinical work. Intrigued to inquire phenomenologically, I made a template to record what I noticed occurring with my patients. I drew lines across and down on a piece of paper, creating the initial sketch of the grids, and jotted down notes to capture the distinctive features of my observations with different patients. Some of the initial features I recorded were responses to arousal of the attachment system, nervous system regulation, defenses, characteristic fears, emotion processing, and self–other relational patterning. The configuration of each pattern and how to intervene came together in the design of three grids, which I introduced in my first paper on this topic: "Tailoring AEDP Interventions to Attachment Style" (Pando-Mars, 2016).

In writing this book, I shifted away from using *attachment styles*, and have embraced Bowlby and Ainsworth's original way to identify these classifications as *patterns of attachment*. As a clinician I find patterns of attachment more user-friendly, for two reasons. First, it has bothered me that I might refer to someone I am working with as "the avoidant patient" or as "X, who is an avoidant woman," as shorthand for "the patient with a dismissive state of mind with respect to attachment," because the latter, while correct, was too cumbersome to say. Knowing and understanding how these patterns of attachment develop as adaptations and self-protective strategies, it feels both shortsighted to label the whole person by their attachment style, as well as one-dimensional, not seeing more deeply into the human being who developed while doing their best to navigate the thick and thin of family relationships and affectional bonds. And the truth is, our way of being in relationship and our attachment behavior changes across relationships. As I surveyed the research and the way different theoreticians address attachment, I realized that for my purposes, the term "attachment patterns" is the best way to describe these specific attachment configurations. The original classifications of whether a child was considered secure or insecure was made with respect to their relationship with the person with whom they were being observed. Attachment patterns develop in light of repeated experiences in relationship to an attachment figure, which seems more to the heart of the work of psychotherapy. Such specificity is crucial to healing attachment-level wounding.

In contradistinction, the term "attachment style" comes from the adult attachment literature, and refers to a manner of being and behaving, which gives an impression of an individual trait rather than a relational process with characteristic behavioral accompaniments. Attachment style is most often used to describe how a person's attachment behavior is expressed in adult romantic relationships. The use of attachment style extends from attachment theory and parallels early attachment behavior. And yet, so often attachment style refers to the assigning of types. People often seek to understand "What is my attachment style?" and search for adult self-questionnaires available on the internet. These surveys ask about behaviors in close relationships, which are tallied to reach a score. This score determines your style. The questionnaires assessed by self-report leave room for error based on how a person might rate their own behavior based on their preferences.

In the early attachment research, while collecting data for her dissertation, Mary Ainsworth (1978/2015) described that she was unsatisfied by the nature of paper-and-pencil questionnaires to gather information that would be compiled for research. She felt that an individual's defensive strategies could alter their perception; they might select their response based on how they wish to be seen. Her studies to determine patterns were based on observation and interview, which is much more closely related to our clinical activities in psychotherapy.

The word *pattern* connotes a combination of distinctive elements that repeat. In relationships, our patterns are influenced by the sequences of interactions between self and other. Most people who come into psychotherapy notice that they have certain patterns, which they repeat in themselves and with others. As psychotherapists, we interact and engage with patients, experiencing and learning how their patterns show up in our relationship. We explore our patient's implicit and explicit behaviors and look for markers of secure attachment. As well we hold that insecure patterns develop as defensive and regulatory strategies that are adaptive in nature, initially to protect the attachment relationship. We trace what influenced the patient to develop their patterns and we engage to uncover what attachment needs and emotions may be hidden underneath insecure patterns of behavior. Therefore, I find it more accurate to describe that psychotherapy treats *patterns of attachment* behavior rather than attachment styles.

Last, some studies in adult attachment indicate that attachment styles may be expressed and evoked differently in various types of close relationships—for example, with work colleagues and friendships. Therefore, bottom line, regardless of our terminology (i.e., whether referring to attachment styles or attachment patterns), the most salient convergence is that our attachment behaviors can change, and do, across relationships depending on the nature of the relationship (Ainsworth et al., 1978; Marvin et al., 2002). This is of great benefit to psychotherapists, confirming the correctness of learning how to set the conditions for building a secure base to give psychotherapy the strongest potential to be of help (Fosha, 2000b, 2021a, 2021b, 2003).

Why the Grids Were Originally Called Self-at-Best & Self-at-Worst Configurations of Attachment

Everyone has different characteristic patterns of behaving and engaging depending on their experience of the environment (i.e., on whether the environment they're in makes them feel safe or, alternately, stressed or threatened). Self-at-best and self-at-worst are AEDP constructs that also describe patterns: They describe how human beings manifest behavior that characterizes being at their best when they feel safe or being at their worst when feeling stressed or threatened. *Self-at-best* and *self-at-worst* are simple terms that are recognizable by their face validity, that come to the fore in safety versus threat.[2] Fosha (2000b, 2021a) has described how the self develops during affectively charged moments, which makes them vulnerable to being activated and triggered by persons and events that resemble difficulties and painful experiences from their history. Think of being with someone with whom you are having a most contentious moment. Notice how this activation feels in your body, notice what you express and how, and what you don't express. How much can you consider the other's perspective? Now shift and let yourself recall an experience of being with someone with whom you feel accepted, have access to your felt experience, and can get a clear picture of where they are coming from. It might not be too difficult to name which is self-at-best and which is self-at-worst. We all tend to understand the sense of being in our self-at-best or our self-at-worst.

The self-at-best constellation comes to the fore when safety prevails. Self-at-best is a state fueled by hope and thus there is openness to experience. Self-at-best is a state in which a person can access their emotions relatively easily and be present with their own experience while simultaneously being able to accurately perceive the experience of others. Self-at-best gives rise to feeling capable in oneself, while understanding and having a realistic view of others.

In contradistinction, the self-at-worst constellation is stress based and driven by dread. Self-at-worst is a compromised state in which a person has difficulty accessing their emotions, regulating them, and being in the present moment. They may experience heightened anxiety, defense, or dysregulated emotion that distorts their perception of self and other.

In the way that self-at-best and self-at-worst are representations of how one's self perceives the self, other, and their interaction, patterns of attachment can be viewed as examples of either self-at-best or self-at-worst configurations.

Thus, the patterns that characterize us when we feel safe and are represented in Grid 1 can be considered as the configuration of self-at-best. Insecure and disorganized attachment result when security is not to be had, and defense mechanisms and coping strategies had to be relied on. The two patterns of insecure attachment and disorganized attachment that are represented in Grid 2 can be considered as configurations of self-at-worst.

As psychotherapists, what is important for us to know is that the potential for both modes of functioning is always present in all individuals. Patterns of attachment become deeply ingrained in individuals and yet, at the same time, they are not static but are malleable and capable of adaptation *given alternate experiences* (i.e., different relational environments; Bowlby, 1973; Hoffman et al., 2006). As AEDP clinicians, we want to evoke self-at-best in our patients to set the stage for working together (Fosha, 2021a; Pando-Mars, 2021). Or as the AEDP adage goes, we want to connect with the patient's self-at-best and then together (i.e., therapist and the patient's self-at-best) work with the patient's self-at-worst. In choosing how to intervene, the therapist can pay attention to whether, at that given moment, patients are more motivated by dread and needing to move away from connection and experience (self-at-worst), or alternately, more motivated by hope and coming toward connection and experience (self-at-best).

I have found that thinking in terms of self-at-best and self-at-worst provides a shorthand way to consider where the patient is in the moment. If dread and distance are on the table, I need to focus on alleviating anxiety and building connection, with a focus on building more safety. If hope and openness to experience are online, then we can proceed with exploration and see what arrives next. To have access to and be able to process the relational trauma that underlies the development of each of the insecure attachment patterns (self-at-worst), we want to establish self-at-best in our patients to set the course toward healing and transformation. When secure attachment and self-at-best are engaged, treatment often proceeds with greater flow and ease.

Yet, when self-at-worst is online, attempts to establish self-at-best may instead challenge or even threaten the patient, especially when their nervous system is activated. Operating from self-at-worst, patients may rely more rigidly on habituated, defensive pathways of interaction, which can, in turn, challenge the therapist. Patients who have entrenched defensive strategies (most likely for very good reason) can be difficult to engage, as their defensive strategies interfere with making contact and relating effectively (Schoettle, 2009). For this reason, as well, I have been inspired to dive deeply into both the origins and the expression in different realms of these insecure patterns as thoroughly as possible. Having more orienting tools for the psychotherapist is the motivating force behind the development of these grids. The more clearly psychotherapists can identify the specific characteristics of each attachment pattern, and the more points of entry we can notice, the easier it may be to *respond to* the patient, rather than get *caught in reaction to* the patient, and be able to select an appropriate intervention.

Consider the following three examples:

Example 1. When we offer explicit relational accompaniment to a patient who shakes their head to say, "No, I don't need you, I'm needing some skills here," if we recognize that we may be tapping their avoidant patterning, and thus their being unaccustomed to leaning in to another for help, we can consider titrating our relational interventions.

Example 2. If we focus on the reaction this patient is describing, and we inquire into what it reminds them of from earlier in their life and they say, "Nothing, my childhood was not the problem—it was fine," we might—in reaction—think this person is not a good candidate for psychotherapy as they seem uninterested in reflecting on their patterns. Rather, it is more productive to recognize that they are expressing an avoidant deactivation around their attachment needs, which can give us clues about how to proceed.

Example 3. A person comes to treatment and tells one story about their problems after another, without stopping to catch their breath, much less to make room for any comment by the therapist. If we allow ourselves to feel overwhelmed and wait for them to get to the heart of the matter, we may soon find the session is over. Very likely we have been in a reaction that undermines our capacity to be helpful. However, if we are able to realize that they may not understand how to make use of therapy and need our guidance, we can identify that they may be lost in a preoccupied narrative that needs containment and our help to focus and proceed to do so.

These types of issues are addressed in Chapter 6, which describes each pattern, and are discussed in more depth in the intervention chapters (7–12). Now, we go to the grids (see below) and discuss them in detail.

Grid 1 and Grid 2: The Rows—Why These Categories Are Important

When I originally began to make the grids, I collected data in my psychotherapy office, recording behaviors and patterns I observed in my patients. I noted common therapeutic obstacles, relational attitudes, defensive strategies, and behavioral markers and listed them under each classification of attachment. I recognized that the behaviors I was tracking were often adaptations to the behaviors and attitudes of significant others in these patients' lives. Over time, I sorted the clusters of behaviors, and refined and clarified how they combined into the following key categories (see Tables 5.1 and 5.2). The rows contain each of these categories, the columns hold each of the attachment classifications, and thus evolved this set of charts I call the grids.

Grid 1, The Configuration of the Secure Attachment Pattern, identifies the characteristics of secure attachment. In AEDP, this is where we seek to begin (see Table 5.1). The more clearly we understand and have a felt sense of secure attachment, the easier it is to (a) set the conditions to develop a

TABLE 5.1 Grid 1. The Configuration of the Secure Attachment Pattern

		SECURE
1	Caregiver characteristics: state of mind with respect to attachment[1]	• Secure/autonomous
2	Caregiver characteristics: behavioral hallmarks	• Sensitivity • Attunement • Responsiveness • Capacity to repair
3	Response to the arousal of the attachment system	• Appropriate
4	Seeds of resilience	• Truth • Vitality • Capacity to love
5	Nervous system activation and affect regulation[2]	• Self-regulation • Dyadic regulation
6	Defense: characteristic defenses	• Flexible • Soft defenses • Responsive/adaptive • Transformance based
7	Anxiety: characteristic fears	• Normative
8	Pattern of affective competence[3]: how affect is handled relationally	• Feeling and dealing, while relating
9	Self–Other relational patterning	• Authentic • Differentiated • Connected • Collaborative, able to trust, ask for help • "Moving toward"[4]
10	Internal experience & external reality: in connection (à la Fonagy)[5]	• Mentalization • Fluidity between internal/external worlds • Understanding self and other

(Pando-Mars, 2016)
(Note. These are nonexhaustive lists)
Copyright © 2025 Pando-Mars

[1]C. George et al., 1985, Main et al., 1985   [4]K. Horney, 1945
[2]A. Schore, 1994, 2003, S. Tatkin, 2009   [5]P. Fonagy et al., 2002, D. Wallin, 2007/2017
[3]D. Fosha, 2000b

TABLE 5.2 Grid 2. The Configurations of Insecure Attachment Patterns:
Avoidant, Ambivalent/Resistant, and Disorganized

		AVOIDANT	AMBIVALENT/ RESISTANT	DISORGANIZED
1	Caregiver characteristics: state of mind[1] with respect to attachment	Dismissive	Preoccupied	Unresolved/ fearful
2	Caregiver characteristics: behavioral hallmarks	• Rejecting • Intrusive • Humiliating	• Inconsistent • Unreliable • Abandoning	• Frightened or frightening • Disordered
3	Response to the arousal of the attachment system	• Deactivation	• Hyperactivation[2]	• Collapse • Disorientation/ confusion
4	Seeds of resilience	• Preserves/ enables functioning and integrity	• Maintains relationship at any cost	• Survives trauma
5	Characteristic nervous system activation and affect regulation[3]	• Autoregulation • Overregulates affect • Flight	• External regulation • Underregulates affect • Fight	• Overwhelm • Fragments affect • Freeze
6	Defense: characteristic defenses vs. emotion & defenses vs. relatedness	• Wall of silence Defenses vs. relatedness: • Dismisses • Withdraws Defenses vs. emotion: • Intellectualizes • Overly detached • Avoids the past	• Wall of words Defenses vs. relatedness: • Preoccupied • Clings/protests Defenses vs. emotion: • Emotionality • Overly immersed • Predicts the future	• Incomplete expressions Defenses vs. relatedness: • Caregives/ controls • Threatens or collapses Defenses vs. emotion • Numbs • Dissociates • Displaces

7	Anxiety: characteristic fears	• Shame • Rejection	• Uncertainty • Abandonment	• Falling apart • Fright without solution[4] • Attachment without solution[5]
8	Patterns of affective competence[6] (or lack thereof): how affect is handled relationally	• Dealing, but not feeling	• Feeling—and reeling—but not dealing	• Not feeling, and not dealing
9	Self–Other relational patterning	• Self-reliant • "Moving away"[7]	• Other reliant • "Moving against"[7] • Boundary confusion	• Unable to rely on Self or Other • Unformed areas of self experience • Role reversal
10	Internal experience & external reality: disconnects (à la Fonagy)[8]	Pretend mode: Internal decoupled from external world	Psychic equivalence: Internal and external worlds are equated	• "Alien self"

(Pando-Mars, 2016)
(*Note.* These are nonexhaustive lists)
Copyright © 2025 Pando-Mars

[1]George et al., 1985, Main et al., 1985
[2]J, Cassidy & R. Kobak, 1988
[3]A. Schore, 1994, 2003, S. Tatkin, 2009
[4]E. Hesse & M. Main, 1999

[5]D. Fosha, this volume
[6]D. Fosha, 2000b
[7]K. Horney, 1945
[8]P. Fonagy et al., 2002, D. Wallin 2007/2017

secure base with our patients and (b) recognize and foster the sense of security, specifically the *self-at-best*, when it starts to manifest clinically.

Grid 2, The Configurations of Insecure Attachment Patterns: Avoidant, Ambivalent/Resistant, and Disorganized, follows the same design as Grid 1 to add a comparable view of the characteristics of insecure and disorganized attachment (see Table 5.2). It provides a side-by-side view of the salient features of each pattern to compare them with treatment considerations in mind.

And now the rows.

The following is a description of each of the rows that are used in Grid 1 and Grid 2 to depict the makeup of secure and insecure attachment, and

disorganization. These are merely sketched here in the briefest of ways—
each of these topics (i.e., each row) is expanded upon in Chapters 7–12, in
the context of delving deeply into the specific patterns of attachment and
their treatment.

Row 1. Caregiver Characteristics: State of Mind With Respect to Attachment

Here is where it all begins, which we can trace back through the generations.
The caregiver's *way of being* with their child and *how the caregiver responds to their
child* is correlated with the child's pattern of attachment. We saw this through
Mary Ainsworth's observations of mother–infant dyads in Uganda, her
records of home visits to observe mother–infant interactions in Baltimore,
and through the Strange Situation Protocol (SSP). And we saw the correlation between a parent's state of mind with respect to attachment and the
child's pattern of attachment through the Adult Attachment Interview (AAI;
George et al., 1985, Main et al., 1985). Row 1 identifies the caregiver state of
mind with respect to attachment and is at the root of the child's pattern of
attachment. To understand our patients, it is helpful to discover influences
from their early experiences with their caregivers and attachment figures.

In Grid 1, the column for secure shows the features of a secure/auton-
omous attachment or state of mind. Here we see that when a person values attachment experiences and needs, they show understanding of self
and other, and have the capacity to be both differentiated and connected.
The caregiver's valuing of attachment helps their child to develop a secure/
autonomous state of mind, and we see this secure state of mind when our
adult patients are in their self-at-best.

The insecure and disorganized patterns are shown in Grid 2. In the column for the insecure/avoidant pattern, we see that the caregiver's state of
mind is dismissive with respect to attachment relationships. They dismiss
their children's attachment needs (e.g., "Don't be such a baby") as something
that is said to a young child crying in distress. In the insecure ambivalent/
resistant pattern, the caregiver's state of mind is preoccupied with their
own attachment relationships. When preoccupied, caregivers are often
self-absorbed, and thus, inconsistently available to their children. For the
disorganized pattern, the caregiver's state of mind is unresolved/fearful—
unresolved for trauma due to failures in their attachment relationships,
under adverse conditions of physical, emotional, or sexual abuse, torture or

neglect. With a state of mind that is unresolved, caregivers are often frightened and/or frightening, which puts their children betwixt and between: unable to approach their caregiver as a safe haven because that same person is the source of their alarm. Hesse and Main (1999) called this predicament "fright without solution": The fright experienced toward a frightening caregiver means the child cannot run toward the caregiver because they are frightening, nor can they run away from them because they are attached to them. Thus the fright has no solution.

Noticing what happens verbally and nonverbally when adult patients speak about their attachment figures, we may learn about how they themselves view attachment and how their state of mind manifests.

Row 2. Caregiver Characteristics: Behavioral Hallmarks

The way the mother interacts with her infant is closely illustrated by Mary Ainsworth's mother–infant interaction scales. Caregiving qualities and behaviors associated with secure attachment are sensitivity, responsiveness, and accessibility, which are crucial to the development of security. How the caregiver treats the child gives the child a sense of worth in the eyes of their caregivers. Additionally, the sense of whether the child can rely on others to be there and accompany them in times of distress is represented in what Bowlby describes as internal working models. Caregiver behavioral hallmarks also include what Winnicott named by the way caregivers hold and handle their babies and children. Row 2 identifies the classic behavioral hallmarks of the caregiver that are associated with each pattern.

In secure attachment, the caregiver behavioral hallmarks are sensitivity, attunement, responsiveness, and the capacity to repair. These are ways the caregiver demonstrates how they see and understand their child. As psychotherapists we also—as attachment figures—aim toward being sensitive, responsive, and attuned to our patients. We do well to cultivate our capacity to notice when we are off base, so we can lean into following disruptions with repair.

Key here is the notion of the caregiver's—and in turn the therapist's—affective competence. Secure–autonomous caregivers have the ability to process painful affects without resorting to defensive strategies, and can hold a child on the roller coaster of attachment-related emotionality without feeling either overwhelmed or in need of distance themselves. Fosha (2000b) said the following regarding affective competence in the caregiver, which directly applies to psychotherapists: "Optimal affective competence in the caregiver [psychotherapist] reflects the delicate balance of dialectical engagement, without needing to sacrifice attunement to the affective state of either member of the pair" (p. 50).

We hope that using the grids, by identifying elements that shed light on the key aspects of the patient sitting in front of us, can help psychotherapists maintain our affective competence while attending, attuning to, and helping patients to be with and regulate their affective relational and emotional experiences. In doing so, we hope to help patients develop their own affective competence.

With avoidant patterning, the caregiver behavioral hallmarks are too often rejecting, intrusive, and/or humiliating. With ambivalent/resistant, caregivers tend to be unreliable, inconsistent, and/or abandoning, as well as self-absorbed. With disorganization, caregivers are often either frightened and/or frightening, in the aftermath of their own unresolved trauma. As we listen and learn about our patient's experiences in relationships, psychotherapists often discover our patients' expectancies, and what they have internalized about self and other, related to how they were treated by their caregivers.

Row 3. Response to the Arousal of the Attachment System

As we discussed earlier in Chapter 1, the arousal of the attachment system occurs when the child or individual is distressed, afraid, or hurt. Their attachment needs rise to the surface and they reach for, physically and/or through their emotional expression, their attachment figure for help, comfort, soothing, and /or regulation.

The early caregiver–child interactions become implicit memory during the first 2 years of life. These experiences are encoded in the child's nervous system and preconscious awareness. Under secure conditions (i.e., when a child's distress or discomfort is met often enough with an appropriate caregiver response), the child grows to trust that their needs will be cared for, and they also learn how to tend to themselves. Thus, when their attachment system is aroused (i.e., when they feel alarm or are in need of soothing or yearn to share something special), they feel safe in reaching for or out to their attachment figure. If the attachment figure is not available at that moment, there is a track record that makes for trust that the moment of having one's attachment need met will come as soon as possible. Furthermore, the security of knowing their attachment figure is there when needed allows those whose actions are characterized by a secure pattern the freedom to zestfully engage their exploratory system to discover the world around them.

In conditions of insecurity, when the child is insufficiently tended to in times of duress, the child's psychobiological response based on the inadequacy of how they were treated by their attachment figures in the past gives rise to either an activating or a deactivating strategy around the arousal of their attachment needs and behaviors. Those with avoidant patterns may deactivate their attachment system and become de-energized with respect to their attachment needs and yearnings. Disappearing their attachment needs and feelings helps them be able to better bear being rejected, unseen, and untended by their attachment figures. In contradistinction, those characterized by ambivalent patterns of attachment may hyperactivate, get big and demanding, protesting the lack of response in a way that draws attention. Finally, those with unresolved trauma who disorganize may collapse with no strategy to lean on, showing signals of disorientation or confusion.

Row 3 identifies the response to arousal that goes with each pattern of attachment when the attachment system becomes activated.

Row 4. Seeds of Resilience

Each pattern is a doorway to the wounding that gave rise to it, and each pattern has an adaptive essence that is a strength. With the secure pattern, there is a sense of truth, connection, and vitality. With avoidance comes self-reliance and confidence to achieve and get things done . . . the ability to function. With the ambivalent pattern, the person often has a big heart and the capacity to forgive easily, holding a priority for relational connection over self. With this comes the ability to maintain relationships. In disorganization—whatever it takes to survive trauma! Parts of self are often sequestered until a later time. However, we can heal from trauma, and then, those facets of self that were underdeveloped or are hidden can finally surface and take their seat at the table.

Row 5. Characteristic Nervous System
Activation and Affect Regulation

Row 5 refers to how the person regulates around attachment needs and emotions, and specifically, we are referring to the autonomic nervous system.

In secure functioning, a person develops the capacity to both self-regulate and trusts that they can turn to another to give and receive dyadic affect regulation, with attunement and care. They can communicate and respond to communication; their social engagement system is online (see Chapter 2, pp. 84–85).

When a child is unable to turn toward their caregivers for fear of reaction or humiliation (see Chapter 7), and instead develops an avoidant pattern, they tend to overregulate their emotions and rely on autoregulation of their affect. When their attachment needs are stimulated, their sympathetic nervous system response goes to flight, moving away from affective experience. Instead of reaching for their caregiver at a time of stress, they might look away and turn their attention to a toy, to avoid an unwanted reaction. When a child's caregiver is inconsistent, the child develops an ambivalent/resistant pattern, their affect is often underregulated, and they become overly reliant on external regulation. When their attachment needs are stimulated, the child's sympathetic nervous system goes to fight: They raise their voice in protest or cling to their caregiver, insisting on access, yet they are unable to be soothed. When the caregiver is unresolved for trauma, and they are frightened or frightening in the context of attachment (Hesse & Main, 1999), the children of these caregivers often become disorganized, which manifests as dysregulation, collapse, fragmentation around affect, and/or freeze. In addition to the flight or fight, which can be a part of dysregulation and fragmentation, their dorsal vagal immobilization response may kick in, when their nervous system goes into a state of freeze (Porges, 2021).

Row 6. Defense: Characteristic Defenses vs. Emotion and Defenses vs. Relatedness

Row 6 depicts the ways human beings engage defensive strategies when their affective responses are engaged. We see defenses as adaptive mechanisms in that they are a person's best means of coping with the emotions that are evoked by untenable conditions, such as when their caregivers are insufficiently responsive or unavailable. Bowlby (1973) named this defensive exclusion to identify how children learn to exclude awareness and experience of those emotions and attachment needs that trigger their caregivers, making them uncomfortable or anxious, and thus unable to respond to the emotions or attachment needs of their children. More specifically, children learn to exclude whatever emotions make their caregivers anxious or triggered. In

AEDP's Four-State Map of the Transformational Process, defenses are a part of State 1, under stress, distress, and symptoms on the left side, while the right side shows a place for transformance (described in detail in Chapter 3).

When security prevails in self-at-best, a person manages the emotions associated with attachment experiences with flexible and soft defenses, and their capacity to engage transformance strivings toward growth and repair is available.

When insecurity develops, the child comes to rely on excluding certain aspects of emotional and relational experience to maintain relationship with the caregivers and/or to protect the integrity of their self (Fosha, 2000b). The child's use of defensive exclusion and strategies helps the child do whatever was necessary to survive and maintain attachment with their caregivers. Row 6 identifies defenses against emotion and defenses against relationship, provides examples of how these strategies appear, and describes some of the characteristic features of defenses that arise when we are engaging with our patients in treatment.

Using the avoidant pattern, patients may not speak much about attachment and emotion. Through the AAI, Main et al. (1985) identified that not having many early memories of attachment figures nor expressing feelings and emotions is characteristic of the dismissive state of mind. In shorthand, these patterns become verbal defenses that can feel like a *wall of silence* (Pando-Mars, 2016). Relational defenses manifest through distancing and withdrawal, and emotional defenses include intellectualization, shutting down, being overly detached, and avoiding the past. (This is discussed in greater detail in Chapters 7 and 8.)

Using the ambivalent pattern, patients speak about emotion and relationships with pressure that builds from topic to topic and may reveal aspects of being overly immersed in others, rather than focused on their own experience. Through the AAI, Main et al. (1985) identified that there can be run-on sentences of associations and negative reactive expressions about attachment figures, revealing a preoccupied state of mind. Here, these verbal defenses feel like a wall of words (Pando-Mars, 2016). There is also a tendency to predict the future, what is colloquially known as "future tripping" (which we can surmise is based on an attempt to protect against what happened in the past). Relational defenses appear in the form of clinging behaviors, protesting, and being unsoothable. Emotional defenses include emotionality, a mixture of anxiety and emotion (Fosha, 2000b, pp. 158–159), as a defense against genuine emotions. Alternately, one emotion might be expressed in the place of another—for example, enacting anger instead of sadness. (This is discussed in greater detail in Chapters 9 and 10.)

With disorganization, we may notice it manifesting verbally in the person speaking in incomplete expressions and drifting off, as noted by Main et al. (2008) through the AAI. Defenses against relatedness come through behaviors of collapse, threat, caregiving, and/or control. Defenses against emotion include being numb, displacement, and/or dissociation. (This is discussed in greater detail in Chapters 11 and 12.)

Row 7. Anxiety: Characteristic Fears

Typically, a person's characteristic fears around attachment needs and emotions activate their attachment system. These fears become thematic and triggering as the person anticipates what occurred from the failures of their attachment figures, which they may even generalize to preconceived ideas of what "life" has in store for them.

In self-at best, a person tends towards normative levels of anxiety in keeping with what they are facing. In treatment we might see "green signal affects" indicating a mild to moderate degree of activation that supports openness to experience. When self-at-worst patterns are predominant, our patients' insecurity is often triggered by challenges that resemble their early life experiences and not being able to obtain the necessary responsiveness from their attachment figures. For example, in a person with an avoidant pattern, anxiety often arises in anticipation and fear of being shamed and/or rejected. In someone with an ambivalent pattern, anxiety manifests by their difficulty with uncertainty and fear of abandonment, which can be triggered by the perceived inconsistency and unreliability of significant others. With disorganization, anxiety appears when the attachment system is activated; love and being hurt by a loved one have been inextricably intertwined. When caregivers are frightened or frightening, their children are faced with irreconcilable dilemmas: you can't run away from and toward the same person at the same time, thus "fright without solution" (Hesse & Main, 1999, p. 484), and you can't feel secure with and rely on the person who is hurting you, thus "attachment without solution"[3] (Fosha, this volume; see also Chapter 11). In adulthood, fear of falling apart arises from mistrust in their own capacity to cope due to overwhelm, fragmentation, and/or disintegration.

Row 8. Patterns of Affective Competence:
How Affect Is Handled Relationally

Affective competence (Fosha, 2000b) refers to the capacity to simultaneously know, understand, and be with one's own experience of emotion, while also having the capacity to attune and be with the emotions of another person. John Bowlby (1969/1982) identified this internalized phase of secure attachment in a goal-corrected partnership (see Chapter 1), as being able to understand one's own mind and the mind of another.

Diana Fosha (2000b, 2021a) describes affective competence according to attachment and coined the following phrases to capture the essence of how each of the secure and insecure patterns navigate emotional and relational experiences. It boils down simply here, in a way that has face value, depicting the salient features of an individual's capacity to feel emotion and deal with life's challenges.

In secure attachment, "feeling and dealing, while relating" (Fosha, 2000b, p. 43) is the capacity to simultaneously be with self and to be with another, and to be with, experience, and process emotion, while simultaneously being engaged in relationship. It also speaks to the capacity to be with and process emotion on one's own without having to rely on defensive processes.

In insecure avoidant attachment, "dealing, but not feeling" (Fosha, 2000b, p. 43) is a defensive stance that favors self-regulation over dyadic regulation, and self-reliance above shared experience. Emotion is defended against, contained, and held beneath the surface. While avoidant defenses keep emotional and relational strivings at bay or even offline, functionality (i.e., dealing) at any cost is privileged. However, along with closeness, what is often sacrificed is energy and vitality for life. There is functionality but their exploratory zest is lacking.

In insecure ambivalent attachment, "feeling and reeling, but not dealing" (Fosha, 2000b, p. 43), there is a defensive focus on others and a compromised capacity to be with oneself. Emotionality (i.e., feeling and reeling, rather than emotion) is pronounced and is attention seeking rather than relieving, expressive, or informing the self. Emotionality is often driven by defenses against emotion. Relationship, or rather, *the appearance of relationship at all costs,* is privileged over autonomy and functionality, thus "not dealing." Patients with this pattern often present as "reeling" in response to relational challenges and "not dealing" effectively with the pressures of daily life.

And last, in disorganized attachment, "not feeling and not dealing while not relating" (Fosha, 2000b, p. 44), there is difficulty in being with self, difficulty in being with other, difficulty to experience emotion without being overwhelmed, and difficulty functioning when attachment needs are activated. For this reason, emotions are often dissociated, dysregulated, or somaticized, and self is fragmented. Functionality is either compromised or painfully achieved via dissociation (i.e., at the cost of feeling real or present).

Row 9. Self–Other Relational Patterning

To whom does the person reach out when in need? Or do they?

Variations in relational patterning usually follow early attachment experiences. In secure, self-at-best mode, people can connect with self and other in an authentic, differentiated, collaborative way. Along these lines, in sessions I pay attention to how patients share with me and whether there is a sense of growing collaboration. In a goal-corrected partnership, both members of the dyad having an understanding of each other's minds is a key marker of secure relational patterning. There is resilience and there is also the capacity to ask for help. Needing help is not viewed as shameful nor are problems heightened so as to get attention. Karlen Lyons-Ruth (2006) describes the strategies of collaborative communication that are at the heart of attachment security as "strategies that are truthful and sensitive to the states of mind of both parties" (p. 603). She describes how there are adjustments in early development when both partners in the relationship have different developmental capacities. The one in the older, wiser position may be helping the child to regulate their fearful arousal, which could well describe what occurs between psychotherapists with patients, helping them to organize affective experiences with positive engagement, which builds trust in relationship.

When the other is rejecting, humiliating, or intrusive, and thus unavailable to be of help, a child develops an avoidant pattern, becoming overly reliant on their own self, thus self-reliant, learning to not need others. When the other is sometimes available, yet inconsistent and unreliable (i.e., when their availability is attuned to their own needs rather than those of the child), a child develops an ambivalent or resistant pattern. They turn to the other again and again, thus, other reliant, in the unrelenting plea that the other would come through or in an angry protest at their being so unavailable at yet another moment of need. In the process, their self-development is neglected. In disorganization and unresolved trauma, the experience is that neither self nor other is reliable, and thus no one can be relied upon: This can lead to an unbearable aloneness, given the absence of anyone there that can be counted on for protection and help.

Row 10. Internal Experience and External Reality (á la Fonagy)

Fonagy (2002) observed the relationship between internal experience and external reality in different individuals, which he refers to as their *modes of experience*. In the secure attachment pattern, mentalization (previously called the reflective self-function) is present. There is fluidity between the internal and external worlds, which supports the capacity to understand oneself and another and thereby promotes the experience of being in connection to self and in connection with another.

When insecure, a person often has difficulty connecting their internal experience with what is actually happening in their external world, and such disparity can impair their reflective function. Thus, in the insecure patterns of attachment, there is often disconnection to self and disconnection between self and another.

The *pretend mode* is Fonagy's description for when the internal and external worlds are decoupled. There is a sense that what happens externally does not impact the person's internal sense of self. They maintain a sense of pretense, of false exclusions: The impact of certain information is not admitted into awareness. Defensive exclusion may play a part when the person ignores information from their senses. I have seen this more often with a patient presenting an avoidant strategy. Disconnected from the root of their experience, they orient by thinking. Living more from their ideas about the world, they have difficulty being with what is happening in the present moment. An unfortunate example is when one marital partner is signaling and demonstrating unhappiness in the marriage, and the other, operating from pretend mode, doesn't take their partner's feelings seriously because of being certain that the marriage is solid.

In *psychic equivalence*, the internal and external worlds are equated and there is a merger between how the person feels and thinks about themselves and what has happened to them: "Bad things happened, therefore I am bad." While this kind of internalization and confused boundaries are indeed characteristic of trauma, I placed psychic equivalence with the ambivalent pattern because boundary confusion is such a salient feature of ambivalent attachment. When one member of a couple doesn't show up and fails to follow through with an agreement, and their partner wonders why they don't deserve to be treated better, we see psychic equivalence at play.

The *alien self* is what happens when a person has introjected the behavior of another, and then may enact that behavior, while having a distinct reaction that feels like "this is not me." There is a disidentification with the connection between the internal and external worlds. When the original relationship between self and other is riddled with fear and unresolved trauma, a person may dissociate their terror. When triggered and unable to manage, they might find themselves acting in an abusive or harmful manner like their aggressor, without conscious realization of how they are repeating what was done to them.

In the following chapter, we introduce the configuration of each pattern of attachment and discuss what appears when our patients arrive to psychotherapy and how psychotherapists might be impacted by some of our patients' behaviors. Then we introduce Grid 3, Clinical Markers & Interventions to Treat Patterns of Avoidant, Ambivalent/Resistant, and Disorganized Attachment. We discuss the categories of interventions in Grid 3, which pertain to their companion rows in Grids 1 and 2. Much of the material in Grid 3 is elaborated in the chapters specifically designed to address each pattern of attachment (Chapters 7–12).

6

Putting the Grids to Work

Fortunately, the human psyche, like human bones, is strongly inclined to self-healing. The psychotherapist's job, like that of the orthopedic surgeon, is to provide the conditions in which self-healing can best take place.
—(BOWLBY, 1988, P. 152)

How to Use Grid 1: The Configuration of the Secure Attachment Pattern

(To refer to Grid 1, see Table 5.1 on p. 151)

Secure attachment develops when individuals experience enough safety through being cared for and understood. We have elaborated elements of caregiver responsiveness through Ainsworth's caregiving scales (see Chapter 1, p. 16). Grid 1 shows elements of the configuration of secure attachment that can inform psychotherapists as we set the conditions for secure functioning, so that as Bowlby (1988) says in the above quote, we can promote self-healing.

In AEDP we start with the intentions to establish safety and undo aloneness. In doing so, we are aiming to help patients experience their self-at-best, in which the wiring to connect can manifest, and transformance and openness to emotional and relational experiences can arise. When individuals feel safe, these tendencies naturally emerge. It is important to note that it is not only patients with histories of security in their past whose self-at-best comes forward. Because of the power of our innate genetically wired-in predisposition toward connection, patients with significant and even severe attachment trauma can bond with the therapist and make the most of what's offered, seemingly against all odds (Fosha et al., 2019; Kranz, 2021; Simpson, 2016). Through the therapeutic connection, they find the security they may never have had and are able to use it as a secure base to heal their relational trauma, initiating the work to transform their patterns of insecurity and disorganization in the other relationships in their life. It is thus important to note that the self-at-best constellation need not reflect history but can also reflect the power of relational experience to evoke experiences of safety and security "from the get-go" in AEDP. Much as Winnicott (1960) wrote that the true self lies in waiting as an ever-present potential awaiting environmental conditions to manifest, so secure attachment is a potential awaiting relational conditions to manifest.

If, per Bowlby's (1988) directive, psychotherapists aspire to provide a secure base for treatment, it behooves us to study the constellation of secure attachment behavior. This can serve us in two ways. First, since our work aims to set the conditions for the rise/emergence of safety and hope, Grid 1 will help us to identify the ways in which psychotherapists can bring ourselves into the therapeutic relationship that can help our patients to feel met and understood. It may help us recognize how we can *be with* our patients, and thus together co-create security (Fosha, 2013b). Second, we know that this constellation can help us register what *to see* in our patients, to recognize and affirm elements of secure attachment when they appear. Feeling more secure gives rise to the exploratory behavioral system and more openness to having new experiences with self and other, which is so necessary for the healing work of psychotherapy.

The following section is a general look at the constellation of secure attachment, how each aspect we discussed by way of the rows now fits together, and what this portends about the focus of psychotherapists' security-engendering activities in the therapy room. In later chapters, where we specify treatment aimed at working with patterns of insecure and disorganized attachment, we take a more granular approach to what we can do specifically to set the conditions for self-at-best to come forth while at the same time specifically addressing the patterns that comprise self-at-worst strategies.

Secure Attachment in Therapy

From Grid 1: The Configuration of the Secure Attachment Pattern

Caregiver characteristics: state of mind with respect to attachment. Secure/autonomous

Caregiver characteristics: behavioral hallmarks. Sensitivity, attunement, responsiveness, capacity to repair

Response to the arousal of the attachment system. Appropriate

Seeds of resilience. Truth, vitality, capacity to love

Nervous system activation and affect regulation. Self-regulation, dyadic regulation

Defense: characteristic defenses. Flexible, soft defenses, responsive/adaptive, transformation based

Anxiety: characteristic fears. Normative

Pattern of affective competence: how affect is handled relationally. Feeling and dealing, while relating

Self–other relational patterning. Authentic, differentiated, connected, collaborative, able to trust, ask for help, moving toward (Horney, 1945)

Internal experience and external reality: in connection. Mentalization, fluidity between internal/external worlds, understanding self and other (Fonagy et al., 2002)

When caregivers are sensitive, responsive, and appropriate in how they respond to their babies, and deliver care with tenderness and delight, their babies feel safe and secure: they soothe, feel loved, and they grow to feel worthy of being loved and cared for. The babies also experience love for their caregivers (Bowlby, 1991) and come to see them as reliable and capable. They will go to them in times of need for help, and in times of pleasure to share. They develop confidence in themselves as they discover the world around them, trusting their caregivers as a safe base who encourage them to explore and who will embrace them upon return to the safe haven of their care when they are done exploring. These qualities of secure attachment are of paramount importance to our work as psychotherapists as they guide us and inform how to aim to be with our patients.

In setting the conditions to establish a safe base for psychotherapy, psychotherapists enlist the qualities of secure patterning with consciousness and care from the start. We welcome our patients with acceptance and interest. Drawing from Ainsworth's mother–infant interaction scales (Ainsworth et al., 1978/2015; see Chapter 1), we engage with sensitivity by responding to our patients in a timely and appropriate manner. With focused attunement and resonance, we do our best to meet them however they arrive and we invite awareness of what has prompted them to come seek treatment and attention to what they want from psychotherapy. Our intentions are to witness and affirm signs of their health from the get-go, even though they come for help with things that don't feel good and/or don't work, and help them to find their transformance strivings to serve as a guide for the work ahead.

Our overall aim to establish safety and to accompany our patients provides the ballast to help them face the disturbing patterns in their life. As we engage from our self-at-best and enlist their curiosity and exploratory drives, we help our patients to assume their own self-at-best mode. From here, together we can examine the ways they were treated as a child and how this has formed into expectations about how they deserve to be treated. Having new corrective experiences from the get-go with us as therapists can provide disconfirmation of what they learned to expect from others and what they expect of themselves.[1] Herein lies the possibility to juxtapose beliefs arising from early experiences with what is happening in the here-and-now of the therapist–patient relationship (Ecker et al., 2012).

In terms of *attachment system arousal*, when the therapist and patient are paying attention to their relationship and how they are being with each other, they can make use of the social engagement system (Porges, 2003b, 2009, 2021; see Chapter 2) to bring about the safety feeling. The relational patterning of secure attachment, engaging in a differentiated, collaborative, autonomous way yet open to relating, supports the therapist's capacity to register the way our implicit and explicit expressions land with our patients and to navigate the art of disruption and repair with clear boundaries as we meet, heal, and expand the dyadic capacity for engagement (Tronick, 2003; see also Chapter 2).

With the secure self-at-best online, defenses are more often flexible and protective without being limiting and obstructive. Patients are usually capable of responding to the therapist's interventions to notice and set the defense aside (bypass) or to explore its purpose at the time to understand its role and open the door to underlying issues that required such protections in the first place. Anxiety may arise, indicating nervous system activation. Yet with the presence and availability of the therapist, the patient can draw upon the relationship for comfort and support, so that the defenses can be set aside, anxiety can be regulated, and unresolved memories and their emotions can surface. Together, we can navigate process with respect to the patient's window of tolerance: *safe but not too safe* (Bromberg, 2011). We notice the edges of emergent affective phenomena, and what level of activation is conducive to optimal awareness and being together in discovery. When patients are accompanied and held as they allow and process powerful experiences and emotions, they can be with what needs releasing as the process unfolds. We want patients to have enough energy so that vitality and emotion can arise, and enough accompaniment and regulation so that what emerges is tolerable and can be processed to completion. Completion yields subsequent relief, lightening, and an easing and release of adaptive action tendencies, steering toward potential transformations.

Establishing self-at-best with patients helps to set a foundation for exploring the circumstances and traumatic experiences that have promoted the strategies that constitute self-at-worst. Here psychotherapists' *affective competence*, our capacity to feel and deal while relating, is important to help us to clearly see what is happening, and be able to attune to our patients and meet them where they are in each moment. Additionally, characteristics of *self—other relational patterning*, such as engaging authentically, being differentiated, connected, and collaborative, all contribute to setting the conditions for the safety feeling to come online. With this relational base, patients are often more able to trust, and ask for and receive our help, with the aspect of secure functioning that is "moving toward."

Last, when an individual's *internal experience and external reality are in connection*, the capacity for mentalization can come online, where there is fluidity between the internal and the external worlds. When the therapist is connected both to their own internal experience and the external world of what is happening in the patient, we are more likely able to be in alignment with our therapeutic activities. Similarly when the patient is connected to their own internal experience and the external world of what is happening in the therapist, they are more likely to make use of their therapeutic endeavors. In a secure functioning dyad, understanding self and other is moving in both directions, which strengthens the secure base for exploration.

Yet as psychotherapists know, the kinds of relational trauma that give rise to our insecure strategies come in varying degrees, intensity, and complexity. Patients arrive to psychotherapy at varying levels of readiness and capacity to engage in treatment. What it may take for patients to be in connection is a tall order, as often as what has been thwarted and led to the development of their insecure attachment strategies. For this, we now go to Grid 2, The Configurations of Insecure Attachment Patterns: Avoidant, Ambivalent/Resistant, and Disorganized.

How to Use Grid 2, The Configurations of Insecure Attachment Patterns: Avoidant, Ambivalent/Resistant, and Disorganized

(To refer to Grid 2, see Table 5.2 on p. 152)

Grid 2 describes each configuration of insecure avoidant, insecure ambivalent/resistant, and disorganized attachment. It is designed as an orienting tool to help psychotherapists conceptualize our work with patients along the lines of their attachment patterning and is especially useful when the work with our patients seems blocked, challenging, or difficult to gain traction and we feel stuck, overwhelmed, or frustrated. With the side-by-side view of each configuration, we can see how the various elements fit into the whole picture of each pattern of attachment, and also which might be the salient features that stand out in our work with a particular patient.

Throughout my discussion, I refer to the child who was originally impacted by their caregiver, but I could also equally well say the individual, referring to the person in session with us for psychotherapy.

Grid 2, The Configurations of Insecure Attachment Patterns: Avoidant, Ambivalent/Resistant, and Disorganized, follows the same structure as Grid 1. Above, we discussed the rows in the context of the secure configuration. Here, we look at elements of the rows that make up each configuration and compare them across the columns of each insecure pattern of attachment.

Grid 2 begins with the historical relational environment between caregiver and child. Rows 1 and 2 identify the *caregiver characteristics: state of mind with respect to attachment* figures and attachment experiences, and the *caregiver characteristics: behavioral hallmarks*, which indicate how caregivers treat their children. As we proceed in the descending rows, we identify how the impact of these caregiver states of mind, their attitudes toward attachment, attachment needs and emotions, and their hallmark behaviors bring out compensatory adaptations in the children. Row 3, *response to the arousal of the attachment system*, depicts how the child's attachment system activates when treated in these different ways by their caregivers, which recurs later in life when the child, now grown up, is triggered by a behavioral reminder. The child raised with dismissing, rejecting caregiving develops deactivating strategies, in contrast to the child raised with inconsistent caregiving, who tends to develop hyper-activating strategies. The child whose caregiver was disorganized and unre-solved for trauma tends toward collapsing strategies or confusion.

Row 4 identifies the adaptive aspects of each pattern and despite their costly consequences, identifies the *seeds of resilience* contained therein. Under the avoidant column, the seeds of resilience manifest in the capacity to function in the world and the devotion to preserving the integrity of the self. Under the ambivalent column, the seeds of resilience manifest in the valuing of relationship at any cost. The seeds of resilience of disorganiza-tion reflect amazing capacities for surviving trauma.

Rows 5 and 6 identify what the child does for *characteristic nervous system activation and affect regulation,* and what *characteristic defenses* they use as an adap-tive move to manage distress (best response to bad circumstances) when they cannot rely on their unavailable and unresponsive caregivers. Row 7 names *characteristic fears* that are the basis for *anxiety.* Under the avoidant col-umn, children with that pattern have come to anticipate and fear rejection and shame. Under the ambivalent column, we note fears of abandonment. And under the disorganized column, *falling apart, fright without solution,* and *attachment without solution* are feared. How the child comes to navigate emo-tion is summarized in Row 8, *patterns of affective competence (or lack thereof;* Fosha, 2000b). Affective competence depicts each of the prominent features of the child's capacity to manage their emotions and cope with life's challenges. The child's affective competence (or lack thereof) reflects the internal-ization of their caregiver's affective competence (or lack thereof). Under the avoidant column, we see the pattern of *dealing, but not feeling.* Under the ambivalent column, we see the pattern of *feeling—and reeling—but not deal-ing.* Under the disorganized column, we see *not feeling, and not dealing.* Again, notice that the fallout of sensitive and responsive caregiving influences how each of the insecure or disorganized patterns either organizes around cen-tral coping strategies or disorganizes by the collapse of strategy when trust is fraught and external safety is hard to come by.

Row 9, *self–other relational patterning,* depicts to whom the child directs attention at times of need, or doesn't. To further elaborate the correlation between the caregiver state of mind and caregiver behavioral hallmarks, under the column for avoidant attachment, we see the child turning away from others in defensive self-reliance, in the move away from dreaded rejec-tion, humiliation, and/or shame. Under the column for ambivalent, we see how the child has become other reliant, focused on the other, clamoring for attention, yet moving against the other when protesting their absence and not being very good at actually making use of the other. With this pattern, we also find boundary confusion. Under disorganized, no one reliant is represented, as the child can neither lean on the other nor the self. Here, we also note there can be role reversal when the child adapts to their frightened parent and their own fear by behaving in a controlling manner toward the parent (Main & Cassidy, 1988; Main et al., 2005; Lyons-Ruth, 2006).

Row 10, *internal experience and external reality: disconnects* (Fonagy et al., 2002), refers to the relationship between internal experience and external reality that the child constructs and inhabits. Fonagy captures this relationship with the term *modes of experience*. Under the avoidant column, Fonagy's term *pretend mode* identifies how the internal and external worlds are decoupled. Continuing, under the ambivalent column *psychic equivalence* describes that the internal and external worlds are equated. With disorganization, the *alien self* is how Fonagy represents how aspects of abusive others are introjected and experienced as an alien other from within.

Thematic characteristics of the early caregiver–child relationships influence the development of the child's internalized representations and thereby influence the distinct patterns in their attachment behavior and affect regulation strategies. When we look at the grids vertically, down each column, we can also see the interrelatedness between different components of the same pattern. For example, in the avoidant column, in the descending rows, we see deactivation in the row describing attachment system arousal, and self-reliance in the row identifying self–other relational patterning. This can help us to consider how deactivation of arousal operates in tandem with self-reliance. If a person needs to shut down awareness of the other to feel safe, then relying on self is what remains; the result of course is that the self is alone with whatever ails them and with their integrity intact. Furthermore, while counterintuitive, it is important that this is also how those with an avoidant pattern actually maintain relatedness with the other. Not only is their self-integrity maintained but by deactivating attachment needs and being self-reliant, the individual with an avoidant pattern of attachment preserves their self-integrity; avoids the feared shame, rejection, or humiliation by the caregiver; and does not trigger the caregiver, thus being able to maintain relational connection through nonengagement.

Noticing how patients present along the lines of each configuration, psychotherapists can identify markers of the different categories. For example, we can tune into what each of our patients does to manage the evocation of their affective experience and look at the grid to pinpoint what follows in terms of an affect-regulation strategy and the kinds of defenses being used. This can help us to formulate what is going on for the patient, as well as what kinds of interventions might be most helpful. Some of our patients show characteristics of overregulating their affective experience, and others show signs of underregulation. Thus, we can distinguish whether our patients need help with up regulation or down regulation to access inner experience. We can observe how our patients are inclined to relate to others in times of distress. Do they turn toward another when in need of soothing and comfort? Are they flexible with the request? Demanding? Relentless and controlling? Or do they avoid reaching to another at all? We can notice whether patients display approach/avoid behaviors with us, and how well we can coordinate with them. Then, we can choose how to intervene relationally to help us meet our patients most appropriately.

Understanding these patterns in detail prepares us to realize how even the most challenging behavior has its adaptive origins. In therapy, when we focus our attention and care on the exploration of such patterns, we balance our *right-brain experiencing* with our *left-brain thinking* to steady ourselves along the way, yet remain sensitive and responsive. While the caregiver's patterns of insecure attachment behavior predispose their children to develop their own insecure patterns, each insecure attachment pattern holds the residue of experiences that has led the person to adopt certain defense mechanisms and behaviors to cope with the challenges of relational failure in the attachment relationship and represents a way of maintaining connection as best possible.

The caregiver's state of mind, their capacity to understand their child and/or their own self in relation to the child (i.e., the caregiver's affective competence; Fosha, 2000b; see Chapter 3), is a critical factor (Ainsworth et al., 1978/2015; Fonagy et al., 1991a, b; Main et al., 1985; Main, 2000). When attunement and delight have been part of the picture, the child's sense of self as worthy of care and the sense of the caregiver as helpful and available become internalized and manifest as a secure pattern of attachment. When a lack of responsiveness and misattunement are the repeated experiences, the child does not develop this sense of self as worthy of care, nor do they develop trust that an other will be reliable to provide care or be genuine in their delight. Through repetition, these experiences become internal representations, forming the kinds of internal working models that have a negative valence in how they perceive and what they have come to expect from self and other (i.e., unworthy self and unreliable [or absent or hostile] other).

And nevertheless, as we keep emphasizing, these represent the best strategies for maintaining connection, thus their name as attachment patterns.

Insecure & Disorganized Attachment in Psychotherapy

In the next section, I introduce each of the configurations of insecure and disorganized attachment and identify how elements of each of these attachment patterns may show up in a person who has come for psychotherapy. I also identify how aspects of each pattern might challenge psychotherapists, and then begin to address what we can do when that happens. Last, we introduce Grid 3, the final grid discussed in this chapter, which goes into detail about the therapist stance with respect to each attachment pattern and interventions that apply accordingly. The chapters that follow are devoted to working with each attachment pattern; they elaborate how to intervene, with ample clinical illustrations and discussion.

Anxious Avoidant Attachment in Psychotherapy (Insecure/Organized)

From Grid 2: The Configurations of Insecure Attachment Patterns—Avoidant, Ambivalent/Resistant, and Disorganized

Caregiver characteristics: state of mind with respect to attachment. Dismissive
Caregiver characteristics: behavioral hallmarks. Rejecting, intrusive, humiliating
Response to the arousal of the attachment system. Deactivation
Seeds of resilience. Preserves/enables functioning and integrity
Characteristic nervous system activation and affect regulation. Autoregulation, over-regulates affect, flight
Defense: characteristic defenses vs. emotion and defenses vs. relatedness. Wall of silence, dismisses, withdraws, intellectualizes, overly detached, avoids the past
Anxiety: characteristic fears. Shame, rejection
Patterns of affective competence. Dealing, but not feeling
Self—other relational patterning. Self-reliant, "moving away" (Horney, 1945)
Internal experience and external reality: disconnects. Pretend mode: internal decoupled from external world (Fonagy et al., 2002)

When caregivers are rejecting, intrusive, or humiliating in response to their child's bid for protection, soothing, and care, the child develops patterns of avoidance[2] (Ainsworth et al., 1978; Main et al., 1985). When they are repeatedly dismissed, children move away from the distress and anguish of rejection and learn to avoid relying on their caregivers. They turn off the attachment system (i.e., they deny their attachment needs and defend against the emotions associated with loss and separation): This deactivating strategy is undertaken to manage the distress and emotional pain that would otherwise occur when responsive care is not to be had and one's emotions are not responded to with empathy and understanding. In adulthood, these patients' memories of caregivers, attachment figures, and caregiving experiences are scarce as if their significance hasn't taken up residence in the person's psychic home in a meaningful way.

In the Strange Situation, the children who turned away from their attachment figures distracted themselves by focusing their attention on the environment (Ainsworth et al., 1978). Rather than moving toward a safe haven in the returning caregiver, the child moved away, protecting themselves from the lack of caregiver responsiveness. Avoidance of the attachment figure becomes a pattern and shows up in adults who come to psychotherapy as *defenses against relatedness*. Defenses against relatedness serve to shut down the need for the attachment figure in an adaptive move to preserve the integrity of the self (Fosha, 2000b). By avoiding interactions with the person who injures them (or who they perceive will injure them), they (hope to) prevent themselves from hurt. Rather than expose vulnerability, defenses against relatedness protect them from feared and expected rejection, humiliation, disappointment, loss, intrusion, and/or shame. They maintain attachment through avoiding relatedness and reliance on their attachment figures.

When the attachment system is activated and the child/adult is faced with potential overwhelm, *defenses against emotion*, such as shutting down and disconnecting, protect them from emotional pain or from feeling that they might fall apart or break down. Defenses serve to detach or distract the individual from suffering intense affects, even helplessness. Defenses against emotion shut down the connection to self, as an adaptive move to preserve the attachment bond for survival. When a caregiver is dismissive and unable to see the child, to function, the child needs to protect against the hurt of being treated with so little regard. They disconnect from their visceral sense of emotion and internal experience.

They also use *deactivating strategies* (Cassidy & Kobak, 1988) with respect to the attachment system. Turning off awareness of their body's signaling of need is the mechanism underlying auto-regulation and defensive self-reliance. Rather than being able to lean into the dyadic regulation that secure children can rely upon when needed, these avoidant children develop the adaptation of shutting down awareness of need altogether.

These protective strategies and defenses underlie how the patient who uses avoidant patterns responds to attention in the therapeutic relationship. The task of revealing oneself to a therapist can tap painful memories of not being seen and known by a caring other from a young age, which led them to find refuge, and even safety, from not needing others. It can also give rise to painful emotions associated with the experience of rejection and dismissal, as well as separation and loss. When we see folks in our offices who come to us, yet behave as if they do not need us or do not need psychotherapy, professing to prefer handling things on their own, we might consider that these are signals of avoidant attachment. When we feel not needed, when the person before us seems disengaged and, when in turn, we might feel disengaged, when we feel perhaps that what we are offering is insufficient, these might be indicators of how much of a relational void the patient grew up with, how alone, and how much they needed to endure privately.

Such patients may not trust that it is even possible to be understood. Some of the usual comments the AEDP therapist uses to inquire about safety and undo aloneness, such as "What is your sense of me?" or "How do you perceive my attention?" can escalate discomfort (arousal) and *increase* the defensive strategies in avoidant patients: They may even evoke yearning, which can be experienced as dangerous. Some patients who have been self-sufficient and relied on their own wits to get by may misinterpret the therapist's questions as strange, patronizing, or as simply not necessary. Attempts to inquire about childhood memories of parents and caregivers or the relational aspects of the therapeutic encounter can generate a reaction of blankness, confusion, or even irritation and dismissal. The therapist's well-intentioned interventions can bring about deactivating strategies as the patient shuts down their access to relational needs (Pando-Mars, 2016).

When our comments are dismissed, ignored, or fall flat, therapists may feel challenged and have a difficult time maintaining focus, even composure, and staying close to our own self-at-best. Patients with an avoidant pattern may be verbal and explicit with their dismissing words. Or they may use gestures of brushing off, and facial expressions of displeasure, disapproval, or disdain. Their nonverbal signals may or may not be obvious, and yet they can be quite disconcerting in their impact. During an involved exchange, these signals go by in a flash, and therapists might miss them. But we may feel them. We might find ourselves perturbed when dismissive actions diminish our progression toward relational or shared experience. As the patient avoids through their activities of doing, overfunctioning, and intellectualization, therapists might feel frustrated and ineffective when our efforts to engage fall flat as they meet the hardened stance of self-reliance. It can be so helpful to consider who, in fact, patients are perceiving and reacting to, and what imagined or real shame-inducing criticism or rejection they are defending against. We may need to bolster our own courage when attempting to move toward our patient using these dismissive defenses as we forge ahead with commitment to help them have a new experience of relationship.

Anxious Ambivalent/Resistant Attachment in Therapy (Insecure/Organized)

From Grid 2: The Configurations of Insecure Attachment Patterns: Avoidant, Ambivalent/Resistant, and Disorganized

Caregiver characteristics: state of mind with respect to attachment. Preoccupied
Caregiver characteristics: behavioral hallmarks. Inconsistent, unreliable, abandoning
Response to the arousal of the attachment system. Hyperactivation
Seeds of resilience. Maintains relationship at any cost
Characteristic nervous system activation and affect regulation. External regulation, underregulates affect, fight
Defense: characteristic defenses vs. emotion, and defenses vs. relatedness. Wall of words, preoccupied, clings/protests, emotionality, overly immersed, predicts the future
Anxiety: characteristic fears. Uncertainty, abandonment
Patterns of affective competence (or lack thereof): how affect is handled relationally. Feeling—and reeling—but not dealing
Self–other relational patterning. Other reliant, "moving against" (Horney, 1945), boundary confusion
Internal experience and external reality: disconnects. Psychic equivalence: internal and external worlds are equated (Fonagy et al., 2002)

When caregivers are inconsistent and unreliable in responding to their child, and incapable of providing the necessary care, the child develops ambivalent/resistant attachment, sometimes referred to as angry resistant. The caregiver's self-preoccupation prevents them from seeing the child in their own right. When the child cannot rely on their caregiver, they get caught in reactivity to the despair of not being met. Thus, the ambivalent/resistant attachment pattern stems from caregiver inconsistency, unreliability, and/or self-centeredness. One of the prominent features of the ambivalent pattern is an intense preoccupation and focus on the other for help, soothing, and care. The unfortunate circumstance of this pattern is that sometimes the caregiver has been available, and sometimes capable of response. However, "sometimes" is the operative word. The caregiver's state of mind is preoccupied and tends toward self-absorption. When the time is most convenient for them is when they are most likely to attend to their child's needs. Because their responsiveness is not contingent on the child's needs, their availability is unpredictable and thus unreliable.

In the face of unreliability, the child with ambivalent patterning becomes unable to trust that their call for help will reach the desired other and get a suitable response. Thus, they too develop *defenses against relatedness*. In anticipation that their caregivers will be unavailable or inept to provide help, the child reaches out, yet fears disappointment. Requests for help become mixed with anger and protest. It comes as no surprise that this strategy is also referred to as *angry resistant*. Even when the caregiver is responsive, and even when the mother in the Strange Situation does return, the child is often unable to receive their presence as meaningful and comforting. Since distress is often what has brought their mother's attention, they have difficulty settling for fear of losing her attention. The expectation of being disappointed again looms large and increases the child's difficulty of being soothed. Being unsoothable is telltale of the consistency of the inconsistency.

Defenses against relatedness manifest in the child's clinging behavior, keeping an eye on the caregiver for any sign of availability. The clinging is holding on for dear life, in response to the lack of reliability and fear of abandonment. Defenses against relatedness also manifest in protest. Karen Horney describes the pattern of "moving against," which describes the agitation and frustrated expressions about the pervasive lack of coordinated and attuned care. There is a characteristic turning on and on, as this becomes a *hyperactivating strategy* (Cassidy & Kobak, 1988), an unrelenting call to be met, while remonstrating all the calls that have gone unanswered. And yet not being able to be soothed or satisfied when in fact met.

Here we see a heightening of the expression of attachment need, which explains the term "hyperactivating strategy." Because it is used strategically, albeit unconsciously, the expression of need may seem inauthentic and may in and of itself evoke annoyance rather than empathy and responsiveness.

Lack of constancy leads to a deep-seated fear of being abandoned at a time of need, driving emotional intensity with anxiety-driven thoughts and anxiety-motored feelings. This gives rise to *defenses against emotion,* which manifest through emotionality, which obscures core emotion. Emotionality is a bundled mixture of emotion and anxiety (Fosha, 2000b; see the section "All That Glitters Is Not Gold," pp. 158–159) in the context of hyperacti-vating strategies with respect to attachment needs. Anxiety mounts as the expectation of disappointment threatens. Agitation builds. When emotions are defensive, anger covers sadness. Sadness waters down anger. There may be percussive anger that goes in circles or flatlines, but it doesn't move into the strength of assertive action.

Emotionality (i.e., anxiety-motored emotion) does not move in waves like adaptive emotion; it does not arc and move to completion (Fosha, 2000b, pp. 158–159). When emotionality is present, tears may leak and stream down the patient's face, with no sound. Therapists might find that we are unmoved, and even wonder or judge ourselves for lacking a more "normal" empathic response. Emotionality can evoke feeling put off instead of stirring the caregiving attachment system; we may find ourselves pulling back rather than moving close and wanting to comfort.

During psychotherapy sessions, if patients with the anxious ambiv-alent pattern are left to their own devices, topic after topic is pursued in the effort to "get it all out, first," without leaving room for the ther-apist to respond, much less for substantive work to be done. Tales abound, usually revealing unrealistic views of self and other, marked by emotionality rather than emotion. Driven by anxiety, patients express preoccupation in run-on sentences full of tangential themes and frag-mented logic. Therapists may feel overwhelmed, have difficulty focus-ing or following, or lose their grasp of the session. Thus exemplified, the ambivalent strategy, despite being so other focused, functions as a defense against relatedness. When digressions become a *wall of words,* their momentum thwarts the therapist's attempts to engage. Unaccus-tomed to being heard and fearing an inadequate response, they keep talking. Building a case about self or other displays a desperate need for attention and help, and a highly charged nervous system. The per-son operating in the ambivalent strategy is often unable to contain and consider their experience. Their reflective capacity may not be fully developed. Frequently, they have abandoned awareness of younger parts of self, lost contact with their instincts, or neglected their basic needs. Ironically, being so other focused, they have ignored themselves. Their hyperactivating strategies and their defenses against relatedness diminish their capacity for self-agency. The result is difficulties with self-care, lack of self-holding, and difficulties functioning in the adult world without becoming emotionally dysregulated.

At the extreme, in the presence of such a frantic need for attention and help, therapists may find ourselves susceptible to the contagion of unbounderied anxiety. Our nervous system may activate into fight, flight, or freeze. When this happens, we need to register our own markers of dysregulation so we can attend to grounding ourselves. By taking the lead to self-regulate, we can offer dyadic regulation to our patients, helping them to calm their anxiety.

Although there is such deep longing for help, taking in care and receiving soothing and comfort can be difficult. Expectations of caregiver inconsistency and unreliability weakens trust that true contact with another is possible. And yet, aiming for true contact is precisely what we must do. As therapists, we must find our way to step in, to help our patients slow down, and to recognize the barriers to connection they erect within themselves and with us. We offer this with tenderness yet firmness. With an anchor in ourselves we lend a hand, and we help our patients work through their fear that it will go away or not be enough, as we help them to build their capacity to receive and internalize care that has been longed for and is truly deserved.

Disorganized Attachment in Therapy

From Grid 2: The Configurations of Insecure Attachment Patterns: Avoidant, Ambivalent/Resistant, and Disorganized

Caregiver characteristics: state of mind with respect to attachment. Unresolved/fearful
Caregiver characteristics: behavioral hallmarks. Frightened or frightening, disordered
Response to the arousal of the attachment system. Collapse, disorientation/confusion
Seeds of resilience. Survives trauma
Characteristic nervous system activation and affect regulation. Overwhelm, fragments affect, freeze
Defense: characteristic defenses vs. emotion and defenses vs. relatedness. Incomplete expressions, caregives/controls, threatens or collapses, numbs, dissociates, displaces
Anxiety: characteristic fears. Falling apart, fright without solution, attachment without solution

Patterns of affective competence (or lack thereof): how affect is handled relationally. Not feeling, and not dealing

Self–other relational patterning. Unable to rely on self or other, unformed areas of self, role reversal

Internal experience and external reality: disconnects. "Alien self" (Fonagy et al., 2002)

In early childhood, disorganization was seen as a failure or collapse of strategy. When, due to their own unresolved trauma, caregivers respond to the child's attachment signals with being either frightening or frightened, the child was placed in an untenable situation. Eric Hesse and Mary Main (1999) aptly coined the term "fright without solution" to describe the predicament that occurs. They state:

> Being frightened by the parent places the attached infant in an irresolvable, disorganizing, and disorienting paradox in which impulses to approach the parent as the infant's "haven of safety" will inevitably conflict with impulses to flee from the parent as a source of alarm. Here, we argue that conditions of this kind place the infant in a situation involving *fright without solution,* [emphasis added] resulting in a collapse of behavioral and attentional strategies. (p. 484)

To fill out the description of this predicament we have added the complementary term "attachment without solution." These children cannot reliably turn to their parents for protection and care: It is quite the vicious circle when their loved ones are the ones who hurt them. When there is no safe haven to turn to, emotions are unsafe to feel and unsafe to express. Rather than feel emotions, someone raised in such unsafe conditions anticipates overwhelm, and may dissociate to detach from their nervous system activation. This disconnects them both from their attachment needs stirring on the inside and *disconnects* them from fear or confusion about what is happening on the outside, in the other. When two contradictory circuits are activated at the same time, the need for protection and the need to get away, it is as if there is a short circuit, with the result being overwhelm, disorientation, and confusion, and eventually the use of dissociation to deal with this unbearable situation. When this collapse occurs in therapy, the therapist might notice a shift in posture and a clouding over or light gone from the patient's eyes.

By adulthood, many individuals have developed recognizable patterns in response to disorganization. Patients' *defenses against emotion* may show up as disconnection, dissociation, displacement, and numbness. Alternately, patients may display threatening or controlling behavior that appears way out of proportion to the circumstance. For many patients who are disorganized, affective experiences get splintered off or fragmented. Sometimes these experiences are located in parts of the self and are despised and hated and become stored in images such as a pitiful, dirty child. Unintegrated parts can "pop out," and bring confusion or destabilization. Verbal defenses can manifest in incomplete utterings and sentences that drift off. During the therapy hour, approaching these dissociated parts can provoke cognitive disruption and loss of focus. This can be quite confusing for therapist and patient alike.

Defenses against relatedness show up as repeated difficulties not only with trusting others but also trusting self. The patient may reveal struggles with issues of power and control and appear threatening to self or other. They may shrink inside a submissive voice that sounds pathetic or get big with a domineering voice assuming control. Even when some trust has been established, the therapist's trust can become eroded when states of maladaptive affects arise and the patient slips into pathogenic shame, or unbearable aloneness. Patients can become immobilized, caught by self-attack, unable to reach for or be reached by the therapist. And actually, this is the work. These are opportunities for therapists to recognize the terrain of unresolved trauma. Here, the potential is to approach the patient's distress, disconnection, and/or confusion with awareness that this terrain is indeed precipitous, and needs caution, care, and sensitivity. Signals both of what is too much and what is not enough need attending and tending to in order to titrate processing within a window of tolerance, both relationally and emotionally.

Sometimes one part of the person convincingly steps forward; the disorganization seems to disappear while moving into a more organized strategy that appears to take charge and speak of decisive action. Here, the therapist might inadvertently support the apparent *strength* (or whatever aspect appears) of one part without realizing that this may be a nonintegrated expression, and that a counterpart might be close behind. This can be quite disconcerting for the therapist when the following week an opposing part arrives to session in a reactive mode, with no visible connection to the prior week's "progress." The therapist can be daunted by the backlash, a seeming undoing, when a different part surfaces after a piece of work that had seemed to be moving in a "positive" direction. Holding complexity, holding more than one part at the same time, and the relationship between parts, is necessary for psychotherapists aiming to bring organization to disorganization.

Therapists may also find themselves challenged in their perceived role as an older, wiser other to patients for whom early in life, the parent–child relationship is disordered and has switched upside down. When role reversal takes place, the child takes the upper hand and treats the parent in a domineering and controlling manner. In psychotherapy, when the therapist steps forward to offer support and guidance, the role-reversed patient can feel disoriented, agitated, or confused. They may struggle with the process of how to participate in psychotherapy, especially being the one to receive help. Or they may take an upper hand and engage in a controlling and provocative manner, which most likely comes from a trauma-based refusal to submit.

Establishing a collaborative stance is particularly important to building trust when there is role reversal, and with our patients facing expectancies of "fear without solution" and "attachment without solution." Working toward understanding of self and other by being reliable, holding proper boundaries, locating a calm strength, and helping to make meaning from confusion are all part of the picture that we take further in Chapter 12, "Working to Transform Patterns of Disorganized Attachment."

Grid 3. Clinical Markers & Interventions to Treat Patterns of Avoidant, Ambivalent/ Resistant, and Disorganized Attachment

The need for a patient-specific approach is important since what is helpful and regulating to one patient can be dysregulating and triggering for another. For this purpose, we have identified markers of each attachment pattern, to prepare the clinician to recognize that attunement will be based on differential interactions of the therapist with each patient. Now as we look at Grid 3: Clinical Markers & Interventions to Treat Patterns of Avoidant, Ambivalent/Resistant, and Disorganized Attachment (see Table 6.1), we begin with the *patient state of mind* and the *therapist common reactivities* and *therapist metaskills*, which are important interactive factors to be aware of while establishing the therapeutic alliance. Row 3 targets specific *goals of interventions* to help psychotherapists recognize what would be optimal transformational processes for each of the insecure and disorganized patterns of attachment. This is followed by Row 4, which suggests *desirable adaptive action to encourage in the patient*. Each succeeding row identifies therapist activities with corresponding interventions that would complement or match the different features of

TABLE 6.1 Grid 3. Clinical Markers & Interventions to Treat Patterns of Avoidant, Ambivalent/Resistant, and Disorganized Attachment

		AVOIDANT	AMBIVALENT/ RESISTANT	DISORGANIZED
1	Patient state of mind with respect to attachment	• Dismissive	• Preoccupied	• Unresolved/ fearful
2a	Therapist common reactivities	• Ineffective • Intellectualizing • Intimidated • Self-doubting	• Overwhelmed • Agitated • Overinvolved • Not impacted	• Over identifies with one part • Confused • Worried
2b	Therapist metaskills to counter caregiver behavioral hallmarks and therapist reactivities	• Acceptance • Respect • Courage • Kindness	• Focus • Firmness • Directiveness • Care	• Reliable/ Constant • Boundaried • Calm strength • Collaborative
3	Goals of interventions	• Develop connection to somatic experience • Cultivate kindness and acceptance of vulnerability • Recognize own needs/needs of others • Increase relational capacities	• Increase self-regulation and containment • Develop connection with abandoned parts of self • Build self-agency, self-efficacy, and self-worth • Recognize how one's own self impacts others	• Build internal security • Help to bear, understand, and communicate profound distress and contradictions • Work toward integration and wholeness • Make sense of experiences and build cohesive narrative
4	Desirable adaptive action to encourage in the patient	• Affirm relational adaptive action tendencies	• Affirm self adaptive action tendencies	• Affirm relational, self, and categorical emotion adaptive action tendencies
5	Nervous system and affect regulation	• Up regulate	• Down regulate	• Titrate work within window of tolerance

6	Working with defenses against relatedness	• Affirm glimmers of transformance • Ask permission • Affirm and/or amplify glimmers of attachment strivings, connection, vulnerability, empathy	• Contain tangential speech • Offer explicit help • Cultivate connection to self-experience • Affirm and/or amplify glimmers of transformance: self-regulating, self-care, self-knowing	• Cultivate safety with relatedness and emotion • Build self-compassion • Distinguish parts and their roles in surviving trauma • Empathize with dilemma(s)
	Working with defenses against emotion	• Focus into affect-laden words, sensations, imagery • Empathize with the defense • Build self-awareness and connection to self	• Distinguish emotionality from emotion • Empathize with core affect • Connect emotion with present experience	• Affirm and/or amplify glimmers of transformance: safety, links between traumatic history, current experience, and dissociated affects • Validate affective glimmers
7	Working with anxiety	• Build capacity for dyadic regulation	• Build capacity for self-regulation	• Build capacity for self & dyadic regulation
8	Building affective competence	• Feel into thoughts • Build capacity to process emotional experience	• Think about feelings • Distinguish emotionality from emotion	• Distinguish past vs present feelings • Build tolerance and capacity to process emotions and relatedness

continues

		AVOIDANT	AMBIVALENT/ RESISTANT	DISORGANIZED
9	Working with Self–Other relational patterning	• Build capacity to connect with and relate to another • Build receptive affective capacity	• Differentiate self and other • Develop capacity to internalize soothing • Build receptive affective capacity	• Build Self-to-Self & Self–Other collaboration • Build receptive affective capacity with therapist and between parts of self
10	Connecting internal experience & external reality	• Build self-reflective capacity • Understand other	• Build self-reflective capacity • Understand self	• Build self-reflective capacity • Understand self & other

(Pando-Mars, 2016)

(Note. These are nonexhaustive lists)

each pattern. In tandem with Grids 1 and 2, Grid 3 provides an overarching synthesis of how to both set conditions toward establishing a secure base for treatment, and specify the areas that need differential attention.

The closer we can match our interventions to what is specific in the way each patient presents, the closer we can be to helping them feel seen and understood. The *unit of intervention* (see Chapter 3) is not only a particular quality or comment by the therapist but the way the patient experiences the therapist's engagement. It is how the patient experiences the dyad and how the therapist experiences the dyad. The interaction is always co-created. Similarly, different therapists respond differently to the attachment patterns and to different patients exhibiting the same attachment pattern.

In this light, we begin our discussion of Grid 3 with a more thorough examination of Row 1, patient state of mind with respect to attachment; Row 2a, therapist common reactivities; and Row 2b, therapist metaskills to counter caregiver behavioral hallmarks and therapist reactivities. Given that our patient–therapist interactions are co-created, we delve into the potential ways our interactive activities can be disrupted, or on the other hand, how our relatedness can be strengthened to provide the maximal foundation for treatment.

Grid 3: The Rows

In this section, I describe what is essential about how each of the rows in Grid 3 addresses its companion row in Grids 1 and 2. These descriptions are preliminary and are elaborated with detailed case transcripts and discussions in the intervention chapters designed for each pattern of attachment (Chapters 8, 10, and 12). As mentioned, we begin with a more in-depth discussion of Row 2a, therapist common reactivities, and Row 2b, therapist metaskills, to consider the potential influence of Row 1, the patient's state of mind, and how therapists can be alert as we set about establishing our therapeutic relationship through co-created interactions. We continue looking at what has the potential to be activated in therapists and show up as therapist common reactivities and what metaskills and intentional sensitivities can be harnessed to counter the influence of caregivers' behavioral hallmarks in Chapters 8, 10, and 12 under the therapist stance as they relate to each insecure pattern of attachment and disorganized attachment.

The following Rows 3–10 in this section are presented with more brevity because they are substantially addressed in Chapters 8, 10, and 12, which are specifically oriented to intervening with avoidant and ambivalent/resistant patterns and with patterns of disorganization, with elaboration and case examples.

Row 1. Patient State of Mind With Respect to Attachment

In Grid 3, the first row identifies the *state of mind* associated with each pattern. While initially the AAI reported the caregiver state of mind and demonstrated its relationship to the child's pattern of attachment, in psychotherapy our adult patients reveal their state of mind about attachment. Row 1, then, refers to the attitudes toward attachment that arise in our patients' presentation, which may impact the psychotherapist and the relational environment between the therapist and patient. We see that the dismissive state of mind goes with the avoidant pattern. A preoccupied state of mind goes with the ambivalent/resistant pattern. Unresolved, fearful state of mind goes with disorganization. In the above description of Grid 2, I have included anxious in both categories of avoidant and ambivalent because anxiety exists in both kinds of insecure patterning, not only the ambivalent. One of my pet peeves is when the ambivalent pattern is referred to as the anxious pattern. This is my attempt to rectify this misrepresentation.

Row 2a. Therapist Common Reactivities

Row 2a, *therapist common reactivities*, identifies potential reactions that psychotherapists can find ourselves in, which may stir without our conscious awareness. For any number of reasons, sometimes we see the patient through our own narrow lens, which impedes our ability to be open to them. Interventions that often flow and generate positive responses from many patients miss the mark or seem to disturb *this* patient. We can be surprised or confused by these unexpected reactions, despite our best intentions and training to meet patients where they are and how they present themselves. We too have our moments.

Each insecure pattern can give rise to a predictable action–reaction sequence as a kind of generic reactivity becomes enacted in the dyadic experience of relating as patient and therapist. For example, when I am in reaction to my patient's defensive strategy, I can respond in kind, or in polarity (Lipton, 2021) in such a way that renders me less effective and more at the whim of the moment. For instance, in sitting with someone who is preoccupied, speaking tangentially, with one thought leading to another, I might get overwhelmed by the detail and lose my focus. When that happens, I am following my patient in kind; both of us become overstimulated without an anchor. Or when I ask a patient who tends to be dismissive how they are feeling about what they are saying, and they flick their hand away or look at me blankly, I might feel rejected or go blank myself, suddenly at a loss, unable to conceive of the next step. The fallout from these exchanges depends on how long it takes me to become aware that I am in a compromised state (i.e., I am not my self-at-best and some aspect of my self-at-worst has shown up).

During some moments, when our self-at-worst becomes activated, we may find ourselves off-kilter. This is natural and can be humbling and a reminder of the importance of doing our own psychotherapy and having a supportive collegial network for supervision and consultation. Given that psychotherapists have our own relational histories and patterns of attachment, it can be helpful to recall Winnicott's (1974) contribution of the *good-enough mother* and Tronick's (1989, 1998) and Tronick's and Gold's (2019) studies about disruption and repair: The distribution between attunement, disruption, and repair is about one third, one third, one third. In other words, the process of human interaction does not need to be in perfect harmony all the time. Relationships can benefit, and even strengthen, from disruption, when followed by repair in earnest.

In psychotherapy, repairs are precious opportunities, especially when our patient anticipates that rupture can only lead to bad outcomes. When we stay engaged, interested to understand what happened for the patient due to our lapse of attention, the disconnect, or microaggression—whatever they perceived—the healing power lies in what we do with it. How we hold ourselves and our patients steadily through the process is key. The fact is that some of our reactions to behaviors that stem from insecure patterns of attachment may be predictable. When we anticipate and recognize common challenges and characteristic ways in which we tend to react to them when we ourselves are triggered, we may find it easier to avoid taking such lapses personally and use them as opportunities for growth.

Generally, we intend to orient and meet each patient from our self-at-best, providing as much of a secure base as we can muster. We want to notice as soon as we possibly can when we have slipped into a reaction, so that we can shift to being responsive to our patient, offering repair and coordination within our dyad as soon as possible, or "promptly," as Ainsworth (1978/2015) says. We might recognize certain challenges at times, and consciously notice which metaskills (Row 2b, described next) provide more ballast to stabilize us as we find our way together. Within this secure base is the capacity to meet patients with flexible sensitivity and responsiveness, noticing what is happening and how to recognize and respond to each patient's specific needs and makeup. We aim to help our patients to be in contact with their own experience while also being in connection to us. And at times this may go differently for different therapists and different therapist–patient dyads.

One therapist may be more prone to be thrown off center by working with patients with an avoidant pattern but not by patients with an ambivalent pattern. Or vice versa. *And*, a therapist may be perfectly centered and able to hold most patients with an avoidant pattern but has great difficulty when it shows up in a particular way with a particular patient. What I am spelling out here are general tendencies and typical vulnerabilities for therapists in terms of our own patterns of attachment with great respect for the variations between us and within us, and the intersectionality that may intensify how we operate together as a dyad. There is a myriad of responses, for while there are regularities, each patient is unique, each patient–therapist dyad is unique, and each patient–therapist dyad is unique at each moment in time.

For this, metaskills can augment our skills by which we meet each attachment pattern and direct our attention in a differentiated manner.

Row 2b. Therapist Metaskills to Counter Caregiver Behavioral Hallmarks and Therapist Reactivities

Metaskills are background "feeling attitudes" that arise moment-to-moment (Mindell, 2001) that psychotherapists can summon with purpose in service of the patient's psychotherapy. Row 2b suggests specific *metaskills* to add to our toolbox to cultivate complementary attitudes in anticipation of working with specific insecure attachment patterns. These skills can be developed with conscious intention as we begin working with our patients and get a sense of what is needed with those who are exhibiting dismissive, preoccupied, or unresolved/fearful states of mind.

In her mother–infant caregiving scales, Mary Ainsworth defined sensitivity as having the components of (a) awareness of the signal, (b) an accurate interpretation of the signal, (c) an appropriate response, and (d) a prompt response (Ainsworth, 1978/2015; Ainsworth et al., 1978). Bowlby (1973) recognized how the internal working models of child and caregiver are often complementary. Bearing these in mind, we can bring conscious attention to using specific metaskills to counter our patient's expectations from the way they were treated by their caregiver that gave rise to their insecurity. Thus, consciously chosen metaskills can provide a contrast to what our patient might be expecting—that is, (a) meeting avoidance with kindness and acceptance; (b) meeting preoccupation with firmness and care; and (c) meeting disorganization with regulating, calm strength.

Additionally, we can use metaskills to counter therapist common reactivities. When we feel compromised by how an insecure state of mind can arise in our response to our patient's insecure state of mind, having metaskills in our back pocket and enough self-reflection online can help us to provide what may have been missing early in life for our patients. In the example of being overwhelmed by the patient who is displaying an ambivalent pattern and is shifting from one topic to the next, I need to consider how to slow down the process. When I recognize the need for more focus, I might call on the metaskill of being firm. In a clear, determined yet nurturing manner, I can move toward the patient, with a smile and/or with a sparkle in my eyes, and ask them to slow down for a moment. I can disclose something along the following lines: "Can we focus on your breath for a moment?" and "Will you take a breath and notice what's happening in your body as you speak?" The patient might share, "I'm so rattled, I just need to get this out." I would lean in and say, "Well, we also need to attend to your 'feeling so rattled.'

How you *feel* about all that you are sharing is so *important*, as important as what you are telling me."

Or when the patient, displaying avoidant patterning, looks at me blankly when asked a feeling question, I might soften and offer a reflection with kindness in my tone of voice: "I thought I heard a shift and slowing down as you were speaking, and I'm wondering whether something is coming up for you." Or I might share that "listening to our own experiences while talking to each other can be a beneficial aspect of therapy that we will find our way to discover how that is so for us."

I feel care as I write this, feeling the care for myself being present to such distress, and care for my patient in helping them to tune into the experience they are having while they are talking about what they wish to share. This care is bidirectional, and when I am caring for my patient here, I am caring for myself. And in caring for myself, I am helping my patient. This is how we orchestrate new experiences of self and other: dyadically we resonate with the up regulating and the down regulating. When we intervene in such a way that responds accordingly, we can help patients to notice and feel the difference. Here, a new level of collaboration can begin.

When these skills come from the heart, they engage the resonance circuits, drawing energy from the mind to the body and can connect the social engagement system in both the therapist and the patient. By cultivating metaskills we develop our capacity to respond with sensitivity in an intentional way. As such, we also refer to metaskills as intentional sensitivities.

Row 3. Goals of Interventions

What is necessary for each insecure pattern of attachment to transform their internal working models and earn secure attachment? Row 3 attempts to broadly name *goals of interventions* that are ideal outcomes of the interventions below. These are targets and growth areas categorized by what is most salient for each pattern of attachment and are discussed in detail in each of the designated chapters.

In avoidant patterning, *helping patients build connection is key*—connection to their own somatic experience, as well as connection to others. Building a tolerance for vulnerability and recognizing needs in self and other is crucial to restoring relational capacities.

With ambivalent patterning, *helping patients to build self-agency* and increasing their capacity for self-regulation while also building receptive capacity, is essential. Connection to abandoned parts of self and recognizing their own impact on others is also necessary to restoring relational capacities.

With disorganization, *building trust, a collaborative spirit, and relational process,* and then helping the patient to develop self-compassion, internal security, and the capacity to bear and communicate profound distress is very important. Building the capacity to hold contradictory parts and make sense of experiences goes a long way toward fostering integration and building relational capacity within self and with others.

Each of these goals is intended to generate a counterbalance that will help each patient not only to rework and transform their internal working models but to be able to build and restore their capacity for secure functioning. (Refer to Grid 1 for the constellation of secure attachment as our North Star for treatment.)

Row 4. Desirable Adaptive Action to Encourage in the Patient

Each insecure pattern is composed of strategies that the person developed to cope and regulate their affective experiences with self and other when they could not rely on their caregivers for care and protection. While these strategies were the best solutions for adapting in the past, they are limiting in current time. Helping our patients to increase their adaptive potential is necessary for healing. Row 4 identifies which *desirable adaptive action* is most salient for each pattern and as such is particularly helpful to encourage when demonstrated by our patients.

With someone who usually displays an avoidant pattern of self-reliance, we want to be keen to recognize markers of *adaptive relational action tendencies* (Fosha, 2000b). When they reach out to their partner, demonstrate being available to the giving or receiving of help, empathy, and/or care, we want to affirm their capacity for relational presence. When someone displays ambivalence/resistance in relationship and is other focused, we want to be on the lookout for *adaptive self-action tendencies* (Fosha, 2000b). When they turn toward a self-agentic way of operating, when they contain their urges rather than pressuring another for attention, we want to affirm and highlight their capacity to be there for their own self. When disorganized attachment manifests with the patient who could not turn toward their attachment figure, nor to their own self due to conditions of fear, we want to support glimmers of adaptive self-action and glimmers of adaptive relational action tendencies. Additionally, when we are working with disorganized attachment, we add the desirable adaptive action of helping patients process emotion to completion in a window of tolerance, thus enabling the release of the *adaptive action tendencies of categorical emotions* (Frijda, 1986).

While each of these adaptive actions are desirable across the board, we have found that leaning in with affirmation to the specific needs of each pattern builds upon each patient's capacity to cope, and helps increase their adaptive action repertoires. Affirmation is a powerful way to recognize the specific areas of growth that offset defensive strategies and give rise to new ways of being with self and other. And then, by engaging further with a round of metaprocessing we can broaden and build (Fosha & Thoma, 2020; Fredrickson, 2013; Fredrickson & Joiner, 2018) the patient's embodied awareness, to deepen realization of the changes and foster integration to strengthen the potential for healing.

Row 5. Nervous System and Affect Regulation

Each of the insecure patterns develops a strategy to regulate emotion, which changes across each pattern. In Row 5, *nervous system activation and affect regulation*, we identify what kind of focus is needed to bring equilibration. Someone prone to deactivating strategies will likely benefit from up regulation. Someone who uses hyperactivating strategies may need help to down regulate. Someone with disorganization may need help to titrate in order to shore up collapse and might benefit from a more tightly focused window of tolerance.

Carefully exploring our relational contact between therapist and patient is an important aspect of self and dyadic regulation. For example, we can notice what spatial distance from the therapist feels right to the patient in our seating arrangement. Checking into how we are perceived and to what degree the patient can experience our presence as nutritive and supportive is also part of how we set the stage to be most regulating to each individual. Trust may take time and building collaboration is very important with all of our patients. We address specific intervention pathways for regulating nervous system activation and affective experiences in the chapters about working with each of the patterns of insecure and disorganized attachment.

Row 6. Working With Defenses

Patterns of insecure attachment are defensive strategies that are adaptive mechanisms that a person utilizes to preserve the integrity of self or their relationship to a primary caregiver. These strategies involve defensive exclusion, which can include having an amnesic barrier or perceptual blocking (Bowlby, 1973; see also Chapter 1, p. 45), and often reveal aspects of early patterns of attachment that are wired into our nervous systems. When we can accept and be curious about their function, they often serve as entry points into the trauma that needs to be healed in order to transform relationships to self and others.

We identify a defense as any thought, feeling, or reaction used to distance our self or the other from our affective experience. The purpose of defenses can be to provide safety, to hide or conceal visibility, and to shut down or disrupt any emotional experience. Defenses can also be used to help a person avoid feeling weak or vulnerable, to distract and avert attention. They can also help to manage overwhelm.

Row 6, *working with defenses,* suggests specific interventions to address the characteristic relational and emotional defenses that are prominent with each insecure and disorganized pattern. It also identifies glimmers of transformance and glimmers of desirable adaptive action to affirm and support transformation of each pattern. For instance, we take notice when someone with an avoidant pattern expresses an interest in deepening their capacity for connection, or someone with a preoccupied pattern shares an experience of containing their protest or incessant behavior. We want to affirm these emergent capacities so that as Rick Hanson (2013) says, "mental states become good neural traits" (p. 16). How the therapist uses our self to engage relationally is a critical factor in helping our patients to relinquish their need for defenses to manage states of overwhelming aloneness or painful emotions.

Row 7. Working With Anxiety

Early life events with our primary attachment figures set up expectancies that give rise to our internal working models. These expectancies can trigger anxiety that manifests differently with each of the insecure patterns, and it is important for us to learn to recognize our patients' signals of anxiety as some are more subtle than others. A few examples: Anxiety can show up in the mind as preoccupation, rumination, distractibility, and losing focus, to name a few. Anxiety can appear in the body as shallow breathing, fidgeting hands and feet, and constricted movements or tension. Anxiety may show up in the emotional field as dysregulation and emotionality (emotions mixed with anxiety, which is not core emotion). We expand on how anxiety appears with each pattern in the chapters ahead.

Row 7 addresses how therapists can focus relationally to offset the expectancies derived from caregivers by offering the missing component. So, with someone accustomed to self-reliance, who may anticipate rejection, humiliation, or intrusiveness, we can offer acceptance, respect, and kindness. We may need to introduce slowly, with titration, the possibility of being together with them, to build their capacity for dyadic regulation. With someone who anticipates unreliability and abandonment, and longs for another to be there to help them, having them practice actually taking us in and making use of our presence for comfort and regulation goes a long way in the process of building their capacity for self-regulation.

In working with someone who is manifesting disorganized attachment, their anticipation of the complementary dilemmas of "fright without solution" and "attachment without solution" may prevent them from being able to make use of our presence at all when their nervous system is activated or their attachment system is aroused. Given that disorganized attachment is often the result of caregivers being frightening or frightened themselves, and thus, attachment being disordered, the term "attachment without solution" is meant to capture the predicament of having no one to rely on because the attachment-related disturbance is caused by the attachment figure. Helping patients to make use of our therapeutic presence for regulation and accompaniment is even more pronounced in treating disorganized attachment. We address this with specificity in Chapter 12, "Working to Transform Patterns of Disorganized Attachment."

Targeting which kind of regulation is most beneficial for each pattern of attachment can help psychotherapists apply our use of self and the therapeutic relationship with specificity when the patient's characteristic fears and subsequent anxiety appear. Our aim is to help our patients find balance and increase their affective competence. We focus on building capacities for flexible dyadic and self-regulation to support the emotional and relational exploration that is part of psychotherapeutic healing and growth.

Row 8. Building Affective Competence

Affective competence draws upon Fosha's (2000b) pithy conceptualizations that attribute the capacity to *feel and deal while relating* in secure patterning; to *deal and not feel* in avoidant patterning; to *feel and reel, but not deal* in ambivalent patterning; and to *not feel and not deal* in disorganization. Row 8, *building affec-tive competence*, identifies which side of the equation may be needed to build more trust and capacity to process affective experience. Someone who is shut down to emotion can benefit from feeling into thoughts. Someone who tends toward emotionality can benefit from thinking about their feelings and distinguishing between thoughts and emotions. Someone overwhelmed by emotion and relatedness can benefit from making connections between his-torical events and relationships and current-day, present-moment experience. Meaning making serves a critical function in building appropriate resources and stretching tolerance to grow the capacity for genuine expression.

For psychotherapists, our capacity to both feel and deal while relating is an expression of our affective competence to help us meet our patients with attunement and the capacity to offer help, understanding, and sup-port, while also maintaining connection to our own experience throughout the process.

Row 9. Working With Self–Other Relational Patterning

Given that each of the insecure patterns is derived in relationship to the primary caregiver's state of mind, our patients' responses to our relational interventions may be tarnished accordingly. Row 9, *working with self–other rela-tional patterning*, identifies specific relational foci to address the strategies that have become habitual means of protection. With someone using avoidant patterns and dismissive of attachment needs, we want to help them to grow their capacity to connect with and relate to another, specifically beginning with how we interact with one another. With someone using patterns of ambivalence and resistance, and who is preoccupied with needing help from the other, we want to help them build their capacity to stand with them-selves in their own agency, developing the capacity to differentiate between self and other. With someone who is unresolved for attachment-related trauma and manifests patterns of disorganization, building trust is a big part of relational work. Trust with the self grows by building connection between parts and self-to-self collaboration. Building trust with the therapist; we want to explore and increase the capacity for self–other collaboration.

While we want to grow relational capacities with respect to each pattern, there are also capacities that are important across all patterns to enhance secure relating. Checking our patients' receptive affective capacities, their reflective capacities, and being collaborative are all key relational skills.

Having both the capacity to connect with another and the self-hood that comes with differentiation is key to secure attachment.

Row 10. Connecting Internal Experience and External Reality

Connecting internal experience and external reality addresses the relationship between our internal experience and external reality, whether one is disconnected or overly immersed in either. In Row 10 we identify interventions to address the tendency inherent in each insecure attachment pattern. An individual who engages the pretend mode might be leaning into self-reliance, avoiding taking in new information. Here, psychotherapists can help them to expand their capacity to reflect on new experiences, and also to build their understanding of others by allowing an expanded perception and reception of others.

An individual prone to psychic equivalence may assume right off the bat that "something is wrong with me" rather than perceiving and assessing what is accurate within themselves. Here, psychotherapists can help patients to orient their reflections toward holding awareness of self and building self-understanding. In disorganization, when an alien self presents, psychotherapists can look for opportunities to link the origins of such alien behavior to their source. Here the intention is to develop more balanced interconnection between internal experience and external realities. In essence, with an intact self-reflective capacity, we can understand what belongs to whom and what comes from where.

While many of the goals are important across all patterns, reflective function or mentalization, as it is often called, is an especially significant area necessary across all patterns. Having the capacity to reflect on one's emotions and behavior, and also to communicate in real time, is a component of having a secure, autonomous state of mind. Self-reflection is a huge part of healing and self-understanding and a marker of having an integrated brain—essential to the experience of wholeness.

Before we close, I offer my learning as a therapist when I begin to do AEDP and engage in explicit and experiential relational work. Psychotherapists may be called to focus on our own healing to cultivate our own affective competence so we can be as available as we can be, to be able to make use of our experiences as we focus on helping our patients. We are the instruments of our work, so taking the time to tend to our own healing and fine-tuning our capacities for awareness of self and other can be a rich and satisfying component of our professional development.

Learning Through the Self of the Therapist

In the following section, I discuss how psychotherapists may need to engage in our own personal exploration as we notice what comes readily in our work and what doesn't. Our internal working models of self and other show up in the interactions between therapist and patient in psychotherapy. Our patients' attachment systems activate or deactivate when we approach relational work. Furthermore, under stress, so can ours.

In working with attachment wounding and the trauma of our patients, we have stated that being wired to care in response to the distress of someone perceived as more vulnerable than ourselves is something psychotherapists can draw upon. Our capacities to attune to another, while also attuning to ourselves, and being empathic and collaborative (i.e., our own affective competence), strengthen our effectiveness as psychotherapists. However, while these ways of being readily develop when a person grows up in a secure caregiving relationship, what happens when we don't have that secure base from the beginning and our capacity for secure connection has not had the opportunity to fully manifest?

When psychotherapists train in AEDP, the explicit relational stance of being emotionally engaged and intervening directly moves us to experience how our own internal working models come into play. When I began using AEDP, I noticed that experiential interventions flowed easily, and relational ones were more challenging. I began to suspect my own avoidant strategies were interfering. To be the kind of clinician I aspired to be, I realized another round of psychotherapy was in order. I chose a clinician because of his experiential orientation, which included attachment. Through my process, I discovered firsthand how holding an attachment frame could lead to so much healing. Or better said, being held by an attachment figure gave me new experiences that put me on a path toward healing what I had avoided feeling.

In an earlier psychotherapy, in the 1990s, I remember telling my therapist, "I feel like I don't exist." This was confusing to me at the time and sounded so dramatic. Many years later, when my then therapist was attuning to me with exquisite sensitivity, I found myself experiencing excruciating vulnerability. I remembered my comment, "I do not exist," and realized where that came from. I had felt alone at a deep level, having not been seen or accompanied emotionally at critical times in my life. I didn't know how to take anyone in to those places, nor how to receive deep empathy or care in the places I had been so alone. My excruciating feelings of vulnerability arose in response to beginning to let go and risk being seen and risk feeling with another in real time. The terror was that I would shatter or disintegrate. I was afraid of fragmenting at a visceral level. And yet, bearing the exposure of what I had kept sacrosanct allowed a new kind of existing to emerge. I could be with another for real: taking up residence in myself in a way that mattered, both to him and to me.

My personal work was essential. It led me to a much richer understanding and felt sense of just how vulnerable feeling vulnerable can be. Furthermore, the study of attachment theory to help me organize my understanding of relatedness with regard to myself and my patients has been deeply humanizing. When we use relational interventions to address and offer a healing dose of comfort and care, some of our patients will settle, and take in our offering. Others may not trust that our interest or care is genuine or feel understood. The source of their feeling may in fact be some miscoordination or disruption that occurred between us and needs exploration and repair. In the process, the patient might connect with a memory about early experiences that might reveal significant information. Or we might find that patterns that show up with us are also occurring in their current relationships. The more attuned we can be to what stirs in us, while also being attuned to what lies beneath our patients' defensive strategies, the more capable we can be to meet our patients and potentiate their having a corrective relational or emotional experience with us. By having our own affective competence as a strength, we can come closer to assisting each patient with a particular focus to help them to recognize what is true in present time and what belongs to the historical past.

In Summary

The intention of these grids is to elucidate with specificity and concrete detail what to do with whom and how to proceed therapeutically, and to aid clinicians in developing the sensitivity to attune and respond to each person. The following section, Part IV, "How to Understand the Origins of, Recognize, Work With, and Transform Insecure and Disorganized Patterns of Attachment With Specificity and Effectiveness," continues elaborating intervention strategies in tandem with the grids, maximizing their application to the clinical presentation of patients with specific interventions and goals designed to build secure patterns while treating each pattern of insecure attachment.

HOW TO TRANSFORM INSECURE AND DISORGANIZED PATTERNS OF ATTACHMENT WITH SPECIFICITY AND EFFECTIVENESS

PART IV

7

The Formation of Avoidant Attachment (Grid 2)

We are unaware that there is anything of which we needed to be unaware,
and then unaware that we needed to be unaware of needing to be unaware.
—(R. D. LAING, 1969, QUOTED IN BROMBERG, 2011, P. 31)

Avoidance & the Deactivating Strategy

Our attachment systems do not develop in a vacuum. Patterns develop in the light and shadow of experiences with our caregivers, in how they respond or don't respond to us, so much of which traces back to the caregiver's experiences with their own caregivers. Therefore, as we begin this chapter about working with patients who demonstrate characteristics of avoidant attachment, it is essential to hold that avoidance is an adaptation to the rejection and negatively toned behaviors of these patients' attachment figures. The avoidant pattern reflects a deactivating strategy—that is, a strategy that deactivates the attachment system and minimizes attachment needs and feelings to avoid rejection, intrusiveness, and humiliation so as to preserve the self. These patients developed this secondary strategy to maintain safety when their caregivers' own insecurity limited their capacity to respond in an attuned way. They have deactivated their relating, choosing to seemingly eschew it. We say "seemingly" because in fact the deactivation of relating is a strategy that allows attachment and connection, as these folks can best manage it as they seek to avoid the emotional pain associated with true relating.

In the face of dismissive caregivers who fail to provide contingently responsive care during times of need, avoidance is adaptive. Caregivers who dismiss their own and their children's attachment needs in turn seek to preserve their own states of mind, keeping the status quo with respect to their own histories (Main et al., 1985). When a child develops in relationship with a caregiver whose state of mind is dismissive, that child learns to turn off their attachment needs with deactivating strategies, denying their own needs and attachment yearnings to avoid their emotional pain in response to the caregiver's reaction or nonreaction. Over time, these needs and the emotions associated with them fade from awareness, and the avoidant pattern takes hold. Over time, this pattern also describes what they are able to recognize when they themselves become parents. Turning off their own attachment needs and related emotions diminishes their capacity to identify and attune to the attachment needs and emotions of their own children.

And so the cycle perpetuates. Attachment strategies are passed down intergenerationally, through caregivers who themselves were once children, developing in response to their experiences with *their* attachment figures. Therefore, it is crucial for psychotherapists to keep in mind that our dyadic experiences with our patients are influenced by each of their histories, and also our histories, and the relationship that is co-created, and co-created anew each session, in each moment. Patient and therapist—we each have our own attachment systems to be activated and utilized. How we make use of ourselves is as important to successful psychotherapy as the skills and interventions that we offer.

In the next section, we return to the original infant–caregiver interaction studies to peer into the exchanges between mothers and their children who develop avoidant patterning in order to understand what lies beneath the surface. We name pertinent characteristics of the dismissive state of mind from the AAI (Main et al., 1985) and identify markers of speech and behavioral patterns that are likely to appear in our patients' discourse in therapy sessions. These observations provide a way for us to picture what may have happened with the young children who have grown into the adults who show up in our offices who rely on relating through not relating (i.e., the adults who show up in our offices who rely on avoidant strategies instead of genuine relational connection).

Early Observations

When Mary Ainsworth was studying the growth of attachment in Uganda, she was struck by how each of the mother–infant relationships was different. As she studied and logged the interactions of mothers and their babies, a few remarkable characteristics stood out, upon which she based her preliminary conjectures, which she continued to refine with the Baltimore home observations. In keeping with her deep valuing of naturalistic observation, she studied mother–infant interactions in the first year of life in the familiar setting of their home, and later developed the SSP for the lab to correlate the results. Ainsworth noted that the mothers who had secure babies were sensitive and responsive, and physically and psychologically available; they also knew their babies really well. She noticed that these mothers were more responsive to her inquiries about their daily routines with their children and could speak with sensitive perceptions about their infants' behavior and preferences. She called these mothers "excellent informants."

In Uganda, Ainsworth had categorized a few of the children as non- or not-yet attached. They were younger and displayed none of the typical attachment behaviors toward their mothers, like crying when she left the room, nor following her when they began to crawl. Nor did they greet her with animation when she returned. Most notable was the lack of discriminatory behavior toward their mothers. One of the children in the study, Kulistina, was described as

> friendly towards everyone. Wherever she sat she smiled cheerfully at the person holding her and at others in the room; she did not appear to smile more fully, more readily or more frequently at her mother than at anyone else. Kulistina's indiscriminate friendliness displays what in later attachment research became known as over bright—marked by an absence of fear and related attachment system activation. (R. Marvin, personal communication, September, 15, 2023)

Ainsworth (1967) writes,

> Kulistina had become so accustomed to being left alone in her crib that she did not cry when put down and left, nor did she cry to be picked up. . . . Her mother felt too busy to hold her after feedings except in the afternoon after she finished her work. When the baby cried her mother did not pick her up unless the crying continued persistently. Kulistina was rarely taken anywhere and indeed she was rarely carried. (pp. 163–164)

The mothers of the "non- or not-yet attached" children in the Uganda study were noted to give less time, care, and attention to their babies than the mothers in the other two groups. They were more difficult to engage in conversations about their children. They preferred to talk of other things or were hard to settle into conversation as they "hopped about." Some of their descriptions of their children's behaviors did not match what Ainsworth and her fellow researcher observed.

At first, Ainsworth considered that age and development were to explain for the designation of not-yet attached, even though by observation, their mothers were less involved. However, when she studied mother–infant interactions in the Baltimore homes and followed up with more deliberate studies of separation and reunion behaviors between mothers and infants in the Strange Situation, Ainsworth began to recognize that children with such behaviors were displaying purposeful strategies of avoidance. In other words, they were defending against their attachment needs.

Baltimore Home Visits Correlated to the Strange Situation

In the Baltimore home observations, the children classified as avoidant cried more than the secure children, but not less than the ambivalent/resistant children. Both showed more separation distress than the secure children at home. In the Strange Situation, during the separation episodes, while the avoidant children did search for their mothers, they didn't cry, and they avoided their mothers during the reunion episodes. In contrast, the ambivalent/resistant children showed an intensification of distress during separations, and high activation of attachment behavior during reunions (Ainsworth et al., 1978). Two elements became clear. The behavior of avoidant babies was serving a defensive function (Ainsworth & Bell, 1972; Robertson & Bowlby, 1952), and because of the cross-referencing that was happening between the home studies and the SSP, what became increasingly apparent was that the mothers of avoidant babies were more rejecting than mothers in either of the other two groups (Ainsworth et al., 1971). Ainsworth acknowledges that deeper understanding of these initial results was furthered by Main and her students' additional analysis of data from the first sample of the longitudinal home observations (Ainsworth et al., 1978/2015, p. 134).

The infants' avoidance of the mothers during the Strange Situation directly linked to the mothers' rejection of the infants' expression of attachment behavior at home. During the home observations, the children were seen to follow their mothers from room to room, which is attachment behavior. Yet, when they were picked up, their mothers frequently put them down before the babies gave a signal of readiness to be put down, exemplifying the mothers' lack of sensitivity or accessibility to what the babies actually needed. Or the mothers simply ignored the babies' gestures to be picked up or held longer. Ainsworth noted that some mothers rejected their infants' desire for bodily contact and some of the mothers admitted to disliking or feeling averse to physical contact. Over time, between the home observations of the first quarter and the fourth quarter, these babies were stiffer in their mothers' arms and less likely to mold to her body. Although their attachment systems were activated, they tended not to be terminated (i.e., despite the fact that the babies cried and followed them, the mothers did not respond contingently), nor did they meet, satisfy, or address the signaling behavior of their babies' attachment systems. Rarely did these infants have the experience of being cuddled and soothed to the point of satisfaction, so that their attachment system would reach a state of quiescence (Ainsworth ct al., 1978/2015).

At home, the mothers of the avoidant babies appeared to be "more angry with and irritated by" their babies, although they attempted to suppress it. However, the presence of angry feelings was visible to the careful observer on the videotape records; the mothers' facial expressions seemed to lack mobility—more evidence of the suppression of their feelings. Another trait of the mothers of avoidant children is one of rigidity and compulsiveness. When the babies' demands interrupt the mothers' activities or the baby is not instantly cooperative with the mother, this is likely to bring irritation, rough handling, or other unpleasant experiences to her baby (Ainsworth et al., 1978/2015, p. 309). As well as crying more than the babies rated as secure, these babies expressed more anger at home toward their mothers than other babies. According to Bowlby (1973), anger is directly related to the thwarting of attachment behavior.

All of these factors lead to and stem from the pervasive discomfort prevalent in these dyads. In the Strange Situation, when the child classified as avoidant is introduced to the laboratory playroom, the child begins to explore and play, but shows no signs of affective response to the toys, nor distress at the mother's leave-taking. When she returns, the child does not orient to their mother nor greet her. They may stiffen when picked up by her; their expression remains affectless, and they may pull away and reach toward a toy on the floor. Main (1995) concludes that "attachment behavior is replaced by active avoidance . . . looking away, moving away, turning away, and leaning out of arms as well as persistent attention to the inanimate environment" (pp. 417–418).

Due to the unfamiliar setting and stress of the Strange Situation procedure, the stakes are higher, which increased the children's use of protective
strategies and defensive exclusion. At home, the babies identified as avoidant
were more demonstrative of their distress. One might imagine that under
the increased stress of the Strange Situation, the defenses would break down
and the babies would signal their needs more strongly, which did occur
with the ambivalent babies. However, as the case here shows, when a child
is more concerned about the potential for getting hurt, and has repeatedly
experienced their needs being rejected, they are more defensive. This is an
important factor for psychotherapists to consider, as we set about establishing
connection with our patients who show signs of avoidant attachment. How
significant it is for us to become astutely aware of the signals of these patients'
attachment needs and affective responses so that we can be attuned to them.

Mary Main (1995) determined that avoidant behavior shows inflexible attention. Specifically, she describes how it operates as an organized
adaptive strategy:

> The continual exploration of avoidant infants in the Strange Situation has
> been interpreted as an organized shift of attention or "diversionary activ-
> ity" that enables the infant to minimize responsiveness to fear-eliciting
> conditions and thus maintain the "deactivation" or repression of attach-
> ment behavior. (p. 418; see also Bowlby, 1980; Main, 1981)

Jude Cassidy (2001) writes,

> Bowlby proposed that the sight of the mother might activate the attach-
> ment system—which ordinarily leads the infant to engage in bids for
> contact and comfort—*but* [emphasis added] because the past expression
> of such bids has been met with painful rejection, the baby has learned
> to turn defensively toward play activity. (p. 125; see also Bowlby 1980;
> Ainsworth et al., 1978; Main 1981)

Cassidy (2001) goes on to discuss how the physiological studies (Spangler
& Grossmann, 1993) indicate that this play does not show signs of genuine
play, animated by zest and a manifestation of creativity:

> Whereas the heart rate of babies truly interested in play typically
> decreases, the heart rate of these babies does not decrease, suggesting

a lack of true focus on the play. Thus, it seems that these infants are not shifting attention *to* the toys, but rather *away from* [emphasis added] the mother. (p. 125; see also Spangler & Grossmann, 1993)

Furthermore, when a child seeking the proximity of their attachment figure is rejected and thus when their bids for care are turned down, they lose trust in their own selves as deserving. In free-play settings, Grossmann and Grossmann (1991) observed that mothers of avoidant infants withdraw from the infant especially when the infant seemed sad (Main, 1995, p. 418). For the children to show their feelings, they run the risk of being rejected, told verbally and/or nonverbally that their emotions are uncalled for or mis-placed, or to "stop being a baby." Or they may simply be ignored, although there is nothing simple about being ignored. Not being seen is an injury that pierces to the very heart of existence, or perhaps, more accurately, to the very heart of nonexistence.

While growing up, children adapt to such painful events by defen-sively excluding experiences that would threaten their caregivers (Bowlby, 1969/1982; see also Chapter 1). They inhibit that which they perceive would be upsetting, and in doing so, disconnect from their adaptive emotions—for example, perhaps emotions that would drive and motivate them to seek out protection and care from another. The children displaying avoidant patterns, and the adults who they become, are often described as self-reliant. Indeed, *learning that they cannot count on a satisfying response from another*, they become adept at relying on defensive strategies to shut down their needs. While this ultimately helps them to preserve their attachment relationship, these defensive maneuvers are costly to developing expressive-ness in emotional and relational life. This adaptation becomes hardwired into their nervous systems and brings about disconnection and protection from experiences they have learned to predict would ultimately leave them feeling invisible and annihilated.

These early life experiences and the adaptations they engender have a twofold impact. The person's capacity for bidirectional dyadic engagement with the self *and* the other has been disrupted. To maintain connection with their attachment figures, they turn off awareness of their own attachment needs. It is important to highlight that maintaining connection is the origin of these strategies: (a) shutting down awareness of their distress or their longing for comfort, they employ *defenses against emotions* and (b) in the face of caregivers whose states of mind are dismissive, they "shift attention away from potentially threatening conditions" (Main, 1995, p. 426). By turning their attention away from caregivers, they utilize *defenses against relatedness.* From an early age, they navigate distress with avoidance and distraction. Adapting to emotional and relational conditions where attuned attention and responsive care are rare, if not nonexistent, they develop expectancies that they are better off on their own. Not-needing becomes the self-protective norm. Yet underneath, there is a lack of trust that the self is worthy of loving care, and a lack of confidence that the other is capable and willing to provide love and care.

In fact, the adaptation of self-reliance is pseudo self-reliance.

At a young age, the self can't provide itself with what is truly needed.

Nancy Kaplan (1987) studied the responses of 6-year-olds to drawings in the Separation Anxiety Test. She asked children what a child (pictured in the drawings) would feel in response to a separation, and then what they could do. Most children responded to the separation with "feeling sad, crying or angry." However, when asked what they could do about a separation, distinct from the children who were secure, the children previously classified as avoidant responded with "I don't know," "Nothing," or "Run away." These children were unable to conceive of a strategy to help them cope with their feelings, even though they were able to name them (Main et al., 1985). When caregivers fail to respond appropriately to their children, what naturally would develop is hindered. The seeds for the child to grow self-understanding about how to be and what to do with their own feelings remain underground.

Turning off a need is not the same as resolving a need. Shutting down awareness of emotion is not managing the emotion. Ignoring emotion narrows the opening that would allow an adaptive response to emerge. Consequently, self-reliant is not the most accurate way to describe the person who uses an avoidant pattern. To rely only on one's own self falls short. When the self is turning away from people to avoid being hurt, turning off emotion to avoid being overwhelmed, and endures alone, the self is a closed system, an unsustainable ecosystem. Inevitably crimped in their capacity to live wholeheartedly, they may be missing the vibrancy of a life pulsing with emotional and relational connection, even suppressing energy-enriching experiences and the valence of positive emotions. For when emotions related to fear and anguish and despair and anger are shut down, positive emotions—those that arise with joyful experiences of creativity and accomplishment, self-agency, confidence, and the delight of relational connectedness—are also diminished.

Which is all the more reason psychotherapists must listen carefully for the stirrings of the little beings inside the adult who arrives to psychotherapy. To be available to the one who learned to not need and became silent, who was rejected and ignored—is to treasure them with attention and delight. We attend to both positive and negative affective signals that emerge within themselves or between us: therapist and patient. Help them to know they can get satisfaction from sharing with us as we build our psychotherapeutic relationship.

The Initial Presentation

For many people with avoidant patterns of attachment, attending psychotherapy is motivated by the despair and frustration of a loved one who wants more connection. They are sensing that something is amiss and interferes with the deepening of trust and stability in their relationship.

People who classify as dismissive/avoidant on the AAI (Main et al., 1985) have typically displayed a devaluing of attachment relationships, minimizing their importance—this protective strategy is often playing out in current life. In their article "The Rooting of the Mind in the Body," Fonagy and Target (2007) relate how language and gesture are meaningful in the way they appear in psychotherapy dialogue. They track how dismissiveness of attachment relationship shows up as a "barrenness of the narrative, an emptiness in relation to the mental world of the people who populate the individual's thoughts" (p. 441). The "mind of the other" is not internalized. The lack of a caring, responsive attachment figure has resulted in a person showing a minimal capacity to understand the other and/or a somewhat hollow description of the other.

Fonagy and Target (2007) go on to explain phrases in response to inquiries about childhood, such as "I don't know," "I can't remember," and "It was just normal" as demonstrating what happens to the children of dismissive parents at a metaphoric level. They see how "the experience of not being able to retrieve an idea—not being able to get a hold of the feeling or a thought from the past . . . is the gesture of dismissive thought." It is the "not needing and turning away—the very physical gesture of the avoidant infant upon reunion with the parent" (p. 441).

So it can be with someone who is sent to psychotherapy by their well-meaning but frustrated partner. Other than knowing their partners want more from them, such individuals often have difficulty in naming what they want from psychotherapy. Their issues mirror the fallout from their early attachment relationships, leaving them disconnected from internal, visceral, nonverbal experience, and limiting their capacity to relate to self and other with acceptance and understanding. I selected the above quote from R. D. Laing (1969, quoted in Bromberg, 2011) about being unaware, as it seems to epitomize the avoidant dilemma.

Psychotherapists benefit from remembering that this disconnection is an unfortunate consequence of being raised without enough acceptance, loving care, and responsiveness. And when our patients present with this pattern, helping them to orient to themselves with loving and kind acceptance is at the core of what we do.

8

Working to Transform Patterns of Avoidant Attachment (Grids 1 and 3)

Every man has his secret sorrows which the world knows not,
and often times we call a man cold when he is only sad.
—Henry Wadsworth Longfellow (1839)

Avoidance & the Deactivating Strategy

How can psychotherapists provide an affect-facilitating, relationally accompanying process with someone whose defenses are designed to maintain safety through avoidance? In this chapter we introduce how to put the grids to use, which we continue over the following chapters designed to work with each pattern of insecure and disorganized attachment. We call upon Grid 1, The Configuration of the Secure Attachment Pattern (see Chapter 5), to help us offer ways to enhance how we set conditions for building a safe haven with patients prone to avoidance in attachment relationships. In addition, Grid 1 can help us to recognize signs of secure functioning when it appears so that we can affirm these patients and help them to recognize and become familiar with the safety feeling of security, especially when they have an experience being in connection with themselves at the same time as being in connection with an Other. Also, we've added Grid 4, The Configuration of the Avoidant Attachment Pattern and Clinical Markers & Interventions, to accompany this chapter.

Grid 4 combines the configuration of the avoidant attachment pattern from Grid 2 with the specified and responsive interventions from Grid 3. Here we have a cross-reference of markers of the avoidant pattern, such as defenses and regulatory patterns and the interventions, desirable adaptive

TABLE 8.1 Grid 4. The Configuration of the Avoidant Attachment Pattern and Clinical Markers & Interventions

	CONFIGURATION OF AVOIDANT ATTACHMENT	AVOIDANT	CLINICAL MARKERS & INTERVENTIONS	AVOIDANT
1	Caregiver characteristics: state of mind with respect to attachment	• Dismissive	Patient state of mind Therapist common reactivities	• Dismissive • Ineffective • Intellectualizing • Intimidated • Self-doubting
2	Caregiver characteristics: behavioral hallmarks	• Rejecting • Intrusive • Humiliating	Therapist metaskills to counter caregiver hallmarks and therapist common reactivities	• Acceptance/ kindness • Respect • Courage
3	Response to arousal of the attachment system	• Deactivation	Desirable adaptive action	• Affirm relational adaptive action tendencies
4	Seeds of Resilience	• Preserves/ enables functioning and integrity	Goals of interventions	• Connection/ vulnerability • Recognize own and other's needs
5	Characteristic nervous system activation and affect regulation	• Autoregulation • Overregulates affect • Flight	Working with nervous system and affect regulation	• Up regulate
6	Defense: characteristic defenses against relatedness &	Defense vs. relatedness: • Wall of silence • Dismisses • Withdraws	Working with defenses against relatedness	• Affirm glimmers of transformance • Ask permission • Affirm and/or amplify glimmers of attachment strivings, connection, vulnerability, empathy

6	characteristic defenses against emotion	Defense vs. emotion: • Intellectualizes • Overly detached • Avoids the past	Working with defenses against emotion	• Focus into affect-laden words, sensations, imagery • Empathize with the defense • Build awareness and connection to self
7	Anxiety: characteristic fears	• Shame • Rejection	Working with anxiety	• Build capacity for dyadic regulation
8	Patterns of affective competence (or lack thereof)	• Dealing, but not feeling	Building affective competence	• Feel into thoughts • Build capacity to process emotional experience
9	Self–Other relational patterning	• Self-reliant • "Moving away"	Working with Self–Other relational patterning	• Build capacity to connect with and relate to another • Build receptive affective capacity
10	Internal experience & external reality: disconnects (à la Fonagy)	Pretend mode: • Internal, decoupled from external world	Connecting internal experience & external reality	• Build self-reflective capacity • Understand other

(*Pando-Mars, 2016*)

(*Note*. These are nonexhaustive lists)

action, and the goals of treatment tailored to address them. Going forward in this chapter we refer to Grid 4 (see Table 8.1) when referencing both the pattern and interventions designed to address avoidant attachment. The patient state of mind is opposite the caregiver state of mind to show how adults develop their state of mind with respect to their early experiences of attachment with their caregivers. Therapist common reactivities are listed below the patient state of mind and across from the caregiver state of mind to identify the relationship between the state of mind of the avoidant pattern and the typical reactivity that might arise in therapists. Across from the characteristic caregiver behavioral hallmarks are the therapist metaskills, which are suggested qualities for therapists to cultivate and embody to counter the caregiver hallmarks or help to solve or provide a positive direction for when we find ourselves in a reaction.

In order to prepare ourselves to treat our patients, it behooves psychotherapists to recognize that the way our patients have been treated has become internalized and often appears through their own state of mind. So someone who grew up with a dismissive parent is very likely to behave in dismissive ways with themselves and others. For psychotherapists, this means that our patients might be dismissive with us. Depending on our own attachment history, events of the day or purely out of surprise that our usually welcomed therapist stance is being rebuffed, we might find ourselves in an unintended reaction. For this, in Grid 4 we name *therapist common reactivities* (see Chapter 6, p. 188, for discussion) to highlight some of the potential reactions we might be having and to help us recognize that this is happening as soon as possible so we can recalibrate. We also have a section for *therapist metaskills* (Chapter 6, p. 190), the intentional sensitivities that we can call upon to counter expectancies related to caregiver hallmark behavior in our patients, to help us counter our own reactivity to our patients' dismissive state of mind, and to expand our capacity to set the sturdiest conditions for a successful psychotherapy outcome.

In my experience, having knowledge of these potential places of reaction to my patients has helped me to recognize sooner when I am triggered or caught up in reaction to one of my patients. While not easy to shake off, since by the nature of being triggered one's prefrontal cortex goes offline, I have discovered that it is helpful to know that these potential reactivities exist. By having a practice of attuning to myself, I am more available to register when I am feeling intimidated by the dismissive gesture of my patient. This awareness helps me be quicker to set myself right and our relationship back on course with kindness and curiosity. We provide examples and opportunities for discussion about therapist common reactivities and the importance of therapist metaskills as we proceed through this chapter.

Goals of Treatment

When working with someone who uses patterns of avoidance and has a dismissive state of mind, building their capacity to relate to self and others is a primary goal of treatment. Grid 4 highlights relational action tendencies as desired adaptive action for this pattern. Relational action tendencies include (a) being open to the giving and receiving of attention and empathy to another; (b) feeling close, moved, and tender with another; and (c) recognition of one's own needs and the needs of others (Fosha, 2000b). Healing avoidant attachment involves deep rewiring of meaningful connection with loved ones and meaningful emotional connection within oneself, deepening the capacity for seeing and being seen, and for understanding and being understood in relationship.

For therapists, one of the ways we use ourselves is lending our capacity to perceive and to reflect significant markers and signals to our patients to help them reestablish their own awareness and capacity to receive. Our recognizing and affirming signs of relational action tendencies is essential to healing patterns of avoidant attachment. Helping our patients to cultivate kindness and acceptance of vulnerability; to learn how to connect to their somatic, emotional, and relational experiences; and to recognize their own needs and the needs of others are major goals of interventions to help them increase their relational capacities. In this chapter, we reference the grids and AEDP representational schemas as we discuss how to organize our conceptualizations and orient patients to treatment. Then we present specific intervention sequences with clinical vignettes to target particular areas of avoidant attachment and show how to help patients move toward healing and transformation.

From the Get-Go

John Bowlby (1988) describes how psychotherapists can draw from attachment theory and serve as an attachment figure who provides a secure base and a secure haven for patients in psychotherapy. Mario Mikulincer (2015) has researched "secure priming" to show how people can intentionally evoke a sense of security. AEDP elaborates significant factors of the therapist stance that set the stage for a secure-functioning attachment relationship. Providing welcome and delight, a focus on transformance, healing from the get-go, and undoing aloneness are a few of the key intervention sequences to call upon. As we proceed, we look at how to apply specific attention to those who appear with avoidant attachment patterns, and we explore what ingredients would be most salient with them to establishing conditions for safety and security.

Developing positive expectancies to offset the anticipation of rejection and negativity. Given that avoidant strategies were formed in anticipation of a negative reaction from an Other, how therapists welcome and introduce the patient to psychotherapy is crucial. We want to meet our patients who enter psychotherapy with acceptance, kindness, and respect, offering new possibilities for developing positive expectancies of self and other. From the get-go, we aim to provide alternative experiences to offset the anticipation of rejection and negative response to emotion or relational contact. To heal, our patients need to make use of the therapeutic process and be open to receiving help and care. For someone with such limited experience of truly being able to lean on another, this is a tall order! We want to build a secure base that will lead to genuine exploration, discovery, and self-understanding. And we need to cultivate this with close attention to building alliance and collaboration with our patients. Our aim is to help them build their connection to self while also growing trust in relationship with an other.

Respecting the adaptive nature of protective mechanisms. When psychotherapists encounter avoidant self-reliance and deactivating strategies in our patients, it is paramount to remember that these strategies exist for the protective function that they serve. *That they exist is an indication that they were needed.* The challenge, like the quote from R. D. Laing (1969, quoted in Bromberg, 2011) about being unaware, is that disconnection begets disconnection, and the reason for such disconnection gets lost. It can be helpful for psychotherapists to respect the adaptive nature of such protective mechanisms as we initiate contact with our new patients. How they enter our space tells us something about them. How we meet them tells them something about us.

The Therapist Stance: Therapist Common Reactivities and Metaskills

With a spirit of welcome and interest, as we inquire about the patient's purpose for coming to therapy, we can also listen for how they feel about reaching out for help. Their feelings about reaching out for help may reveal expectancies related to an avoidant pattern. From these first moments we do our best to attune and show empathy as we pay attention to what happens relationally, and how the flow between us moves. In Grid 3, Clinical Markers & Interventions to Treat Patterns of Avoidant, Ambivalent/Resistant, and Disorganized Attachment, we noted a few therapists' common reactivities that may occur when engaging in an experiential and relationally oriented psychotherapy with patients who present with avoidance. In turn, we have identified specific therapist metaskills that can help psychotherapists set the stage for treatment, as well as provide a way to help us to regain our footing when these common reactivities occur.

Therapist common reactivities. Therapist common reactivities may arise as our unintended yet potential reactions to the expression of some of our patient's avoidant/dismissive behaviors. In the face of avoidance, psychotherapists may find ourselves feeling intimidated, ineffective, and self-doubting, or we may become overly intellectual. It is helpful to keep an eye on what is stirred within us, so that as soon as possible we can attend to what we need to be present. We can consciously raise our awareness to bring in certain metaskills to help us face what is happening and to find a constructive, kind, and respectful way to engage.

Therapist metaskills. Metaskills can be considered intentional sensitivities that psychotherapists can draw upon to establish a positive relational foundation for patients with insecure attachment. Therapist metaskills of acceptance/respect and kindness can counter caregiver hallmarks of rejecting, humiliating, or intrusive behaviors that give rise to avoidant attachment behaviors. The therapist metaskill of courage can be inspiring when we are finding our way to move toward patients whose dismissing gestures may stir our own attachment systems. Remembering that our patients' avoidant reactions have been forged by rejection or humiliation, having courage can help us to strengthen our presence as we aim toward providing a positive, new experience.

Much of the research on attachment-informed psychotherapy states the importance of establishing the therapeutic alliance with a secure base from the start (Bowlby, 1988; Mikulincer et al., 2012). Mikulincer discusses "a client's attachment security in therapy is associated with more positive attitudes toward therapy and more constructive therapeutic behavior, such as deeper self-disclosure and more complete inner exploration" (p. 610). Beginning with how we receive the patient, being accepting, kind, and respectful seems like the just right beginning to set the stage for building a patient's attachment security in psychotherapy. And if we falter, tending to what may be a *therapist common reactivity* seems like a necessary safety net for our own attachment security.

Of the metaskills, acceptance is key and *transformance detection* offers a phenomenal way to do just this. The very act of showing up for psychotherapy reveals transformance in motion. When a patient with avoidant tendencies opens with self-reflection or responds contingently to our questions, such relatedness harkens transformance. When we notice transformance glimmers and affirm these attributes in our patient right off the bat, we can convey our intention to support them and build a foundation in which safety and collaboration can be discovered. We emphasize our desire to see them in their wholeness from the first moments of being together.

In the next section we explore how to bring acceptance into the forefront and then continue to explore transformance detection in the following section.

Acceptance as Antidote to Rejection

Holding that our initial psychotherapy sessions are orienting us to each other and to what our dyad might need to function optimally, we can be present to meet and *accept* what shows up moment by moment. One way to show acceptance is by receiving what the patient offers in the way the patient offers it. What if the patient answers a question with a short, clipped response and a shrug of the shoulders? I can lean in and echo the clipped response and tilt my head with curiosity about what their shrug is saying to me, receiving this as a significant communication. In ordinary conversation, a friend could feel pushed away by the shrug, and the conversation might go flat. In psychotherapy, a *therapist common reactivity* might appear, for example, if I feel intimidated or self-doubtful with the patient's gesture. I might need to draw upon the metaskill of *courage* to move toward what may seem dismissive from the patient. I might need to pause and notice when I feel intimidated by a patient's word or gesture and take a breath and feel my feet on the floor.

Stepping in with courage means being willing to accept and engage with the patient's signals that appear dismissive. In our therapeutic conversation, I want to receive these signals as meaningful. They may be showing me that the patient expects not to be heard or taken seriously. They may reveal the patient's mixed feelings about being here. Such signals are an implicit communication to explore; they are significant. The more accepting I can be of the totality of the patient's response, the better. I want to be open to what the patient shares, to transmit a sense of *enoughness* to my patient. Perhaps when I move toward rather than away in the face of dismissiveness, I am modeling a new possibility. Whatever takes place is grist for the mill and we can appreciate that the process of reaching out for help might just bring about complex feelings. Being seen with this complexity can provide relief to the fear of being judged.

Meaning and understanding are constructed by moment-to-moment exchanges of information. On this psychotherapeutic journey, by receiving what my patient offers, we can make use of it to encourage what may emerge next, naturally. When early life experiences of rejection have built-in negative anticipations of not being enough, we can counter this by mirroring the substance of what is being communicated. Herein lies the transformance detection: to affirm what is forthcoming and help the individual to value their experience by showing our acceptance, interest, and appreciating what they offer. Attuning and attending to what occurs within ourselves is also important to this process. It involves being able to monitor and regulate what happens internally, and to choose what serves the intention for establishing our therapeutic container, which Winnicott (1960) refers to as the "holding environment," and Bion (1962) discusses as "containment" related to a caregiver's capacity to be with their child's emotional experience, with neither overwhelm nor rejection.

Transformance Detection

The AEDP stance of detecting transformance is vital to establishing the conditions that can evoke a sense of safety and trust, especially with someone who developed avoidant strategies. Showing kindness is a very important influence to fostering the security of attachment. Affirming patients that we see some of their most important motivating drives and actions is a way to validate them and help to provide a secure base for the work of self-exploration. When we can identify and reflect what we see as their value (i.e., when we affirm them), we help our patients to recognize and connect with knowing what truly matters to them. We want to allow the space and potential for transformance glimmers to shine bright: We want to be ready to be surprised by unexpected capacities that go counter to their attachment patterning and reveal something essential of their human spirit.

Look for qualities that demonstrate the patient's core values. From the start, looking for qualities that demonstrate the person's core values helps us to discover that which provides meaning and direction in their lives. Many people whose primary attachment strategies are avoidant are plenty capable and effective in their work and identify with accomplishment and success in the world. They are capable of dealing, less so feeling. Dealing in the world has often been rewarding and given them ways to provide for their families and loved ones. Expressing feelings at home is often mixed and can run the gamut from what goes unspoken to what erupts in explosion. Not speaking freely about their inner workings leaves their partners pressing for more connection. Often, their partners have urged them to seek out therapy to "get in touch with their feelings," conveying that something is lacking in this realm.

Affirmation. At the beginning of treatment, with such challenges in mind, I want to establish a base of support by *affirming* what I find noteworthy, which may not be what is acknowledged by their significant others. For example, when describing work, the person may light up when telling me about their resources that contribute to how they are supporting their families. While expressing the meaning this gives them, I get a sense of the depth of their relational care. Affirming this depth of care may come as a surprise to the patient, as longing for more emotional closeness is what provokes their partner's dissatisfaction, which is often at a saturation point by the time they have come to therapy. I have repeatedly noticed a discrepancy between what they report to me about what they feel on the inside, and what they express verbally at home. By encouraging conditions that help their *self-at-best* to come online, patients often locate a deeper range of affect than they can access when they are in the thick of their *self-at-worst* patterning.

In the compromised state of self-at-worst, when fear of rejection is looming, expression is inhibited. Anticipatory anxiety interferes with the patient's connection to what they know and feel on the inside. Amid describing to me how confusing and even overwhelming their partner's bids for intimacy can be, what may emerge are deep fears about the perceived threat of rejection or loss, as well as shame secondary to fears of personal inadequacy. These themes relate to their historical trauma and attachment-level wounding. Yet as we begin, we can affirm the profound care that they have not quite fully expressed verbally with their loved one. We can acknowledge and empathize with the complexity of how showing care is intertwined with fear of rejection (Frederick, 2019). Leaning into their capacity to care provides a stark, yet helpful contrast to what happens at home when they are confronted with frustration and complaint about their lack of expressing feelings. As an antidote to shame and not-enoughness, we help our patients reorient to what is true on the inside. We are establishing a larger and wider foundation for the work of psychotherapy. Being met can be productive, and yet, befuddling to the patient, at first.

By allowing space for the emergence of core experiences, we can begin to see how a great sensitivity may lie underneath a toughened exterior. When their partner's protest and distress pierce through the protective barriers, instead of gaining access to a caring response, what may be touched and activated, is hurt inside and a sense of inadequacy. Thus, the need for the hard steel of defenses. Noticing and reflecting sensitivity to their original attachment wounding back to the patient, sensing this as a transformance glimmer, creates an intrapsychic crisis and it surprises the unconscious (George et al., 1984; Main, 1995), in a good way. Prepared for being shamed and humiliated for being out of touch with feelings, our reflection that their sensitivity interferes with their positive and caring attributes belies their expectations, often melts defenses, and can contribute to a strong therapeutic alliance—from the get-go. For us to regard and recognize their strengths alongside their challenges, a larger understanding and perspective can be relieving and stimulating for the patient who has been living in the confines of their avoidant patterning.

And yet, for some patients, the AEDP therapist's affective expressiveness, empathy, and self-disclosure of connection can be disconcerting, and thereby evoke—by contrast—their attachment trauma and trigger expectancies of humiliation or rejection. Sooner or later, and usually sooner, something exceeds the narrow window of tolerance for emotional connection, and the road gets bumpy. What is in the room is the result of those avoidant and dismissive protective patterns. It is here, in many therapeutic dyads, where transformance detection can fall flat. The glimmers are either miniscule and/or we can't see them. Or if we do, our reflection of them is met with dismissal. Here, the transformance path is often overlooked when the therapist becomes stalled by a wall of silence, dismissiveness, or intellectualization. However, seeking out glimmers of motivation and health, and affirming when the patient is on track, are powerful interventions and essential to call upon, again and again, throughout treatment. Like water running over rocks, don't underestimate the power of our consistent and insistent attention to accumulate and penetrate the surface. Over time we continue to look for new openings. As poet and songwriter Leonard Cohen (1992) croons, "There is a crack in everything / That's how the light gets in . . . "

Organizing Experiential Work With AEDP Representational Schemas

The Triangle of Experience: Arousal and Affect Regulation

To help someone reorient to their felt experience and face what they have avoided their whole life, it helps to have a way to track what is happening in the present moment. As described in Chapter 3, the AEDP triangle of experience (TOE; see Figure 3.2) is a representational schema we can use to map interaction sequences, and thereby choose intervention strategies. The TOE incorporates Row 3 and Rows 5–8, of Grids 1 and 2: (a) a patient's response to attachment system arousal, (b) affect regulation, (c) defenses, (d) anxiety, and (e) affective competence (see Chapter 5, pp. 156–162). *While the grids identify the characteristics of each pattern of attachment, the TOE provides a way to structure our experiential work.* At the top two corners of the triangle are defenses and anxiety. Core affective experiences is at the bottom. Defenses are the behaviors and strategies used to move away from emotional or relational experiences. Anxiety is the activation of the nervous system, which rises with anticipations. Core affective experiences refers to three varieties of affective experiences, such as categorical emotions, self, and relational affective experiences (see Chapter 3, pp. 104–105). Categorical emotions are the self's reaction to events. Self-affective experiences are the self's reading of the self. Relational affective experiences are the self's reading of the emotional status of the relationship (Fosha, 2000b).

Earlier in this chapter, we identified one of the goals of treatment of avoidant patterning, as the release of relational adaptive action tendencies, such as being available to the giving and receiving of care and empathy with another. In the section on core affective experience, included in the avoidant TOE, we identify a few aspects of relational affective experiences that feature in this work with someone with avoidant patterning in our aim to heal the relational wounding that develops through experiences of rejection, humiliation, and disregard. Of course, relational affective experiences are also of great importance in therapeutic work with ambivalent/resistant and disorganized attachment. However, we emphasize the central importance of working on relational experiences while working with the avoidant pattern to counter the defensive self-reliance and avoidance of seeking help that is at the core of that pattern. In Chapter 10, which is working with ambivalent/

resistant attachment, we identify self-affective experiences as key to the goals of ambivalent patterning treatment. Of course, self experiences—authentic expression, development of agency, will, and desire, and the expression of attachment strivings and core needs—are integral to working with avoidant and disorganized attachment as well. However, we focus on self experiences with the ambivalent pattern because of how much the self is sacrificed in the desperate reach for the other. We say more about relational affective experiences in the section following the avoidant Self–Other–Emotion (SOE) triangle later in this chapter. By tracking our patients verbally and nonverbally on a moment-to-moment basis, we can identify whether they are going through an affective experience, anxiety, or defense, and the relationship between them. For instance, when emotion stirs, are they able to let it happen or do they become anxious or defensively shut down?

In the case of the person relying on avoidant strategies, their core experiences are often outside of awareness. Someone may come to therapy recognizing that certain patterns appear in relationships without understanding the heart of the problem. When their attachment behavioral system is aroused, the avoidant pattern uses deactivating strategies to disconnect from it and from the emotions associated with their attachment strivings. The person behaving with these patterns does not seek proximity in time of need but rather avoids the Other. They disconnect not only from the Other but from their need for the other, which would prompt such seeking. In turn, they may shut down the experience of emotion. This becomes an affect-regulation strategy. When the person is distressed and in need of tending and care, the attachment system is turned off to avoid further disappointment and injury. The use of defenses replaces reaching toward another and shuts down awareness of the experience of emotion and the longing for contact.

Closely tracking the patient's movement toward and away from affective experience is vital for psychotherapists engaging in an experiential process. By helping our patients to notice what happens in their body as they are speaking, we can help them to register signals that are markers of emotion, anxiety, or defense. Depending on what appears, we can address the process with specificity. When signals of anxiety appear, we can help our clients to discover their window of tolerance. There needs to be enough activation in the nervous system to allow unresolved material to surface. And the patient needs to be able to bear and process what is emerging. Helping clients to notice how they move among defense, anxiety, and emotion is useful for increasing their awareness of how they can regulate contact with emotion and relatedness. When our clients engage their defenses, we can help them to identify how this may be a self-protective pattern of response and to become curious about where it comes from.

A question for attachment-oriented psychotherapists to consider is "How do we engage ourselves, so that our patients don't have to resort to their defenses?" Our aim is to set the conditions to explore the dynamic unfolding process as a sensitive and responsive Other, building a collaborative alliance with respect and kindness. And help. We help patients orient to the present moment and build connection to their somatic experience. We explore what is happening that might be summoning the defense. Often expectancies may be arising in anticipation of a negative reaction from another. We can offer accompaniment and care in tolerable doses, to explore what happens between us, and notice whether any signals imply threat or concern. And we listen sincerely to note what the patient might be sensing or feeling and take the time to discern whether there has been a misattunement or disconnect that needs acknowledgment and repair. Tracking the process, we affirm our patients when they stretch beyond avoidance, and support and affirm efforts they make to let go of defense to try something new. The more we can point patients to notice how their patterns of avoidance serve to protect them through disconnection, often more motivation emerges to try new steps.

The TOE: Avoidant

Defenses against emotion. When the patient has difficulty connecting with moment-to-moment experience and instead tells stories, moves away from the inquiry about affect, appears overly detached, or disconnected from what is happening in the present moment, we are in the land of defenses against emotion. Shutting down and intellectualizing are two defenses against emotion that helped the person to manage being overwhelmed, suffering the aloneness or intense affects by disengaging from helplessness at a time of need. Defenses against emotion break the connection to self, which was an adaptive move to disconnect from what might threaten the attachment figure in order to preserve the attachment bond for big picture survival.

Defenses against relatedness. When the patient is uncomfortable with our attention, finds our efforts to validate and affirm too patronizing, or physically turns away, as was described by not looking at the mother when she

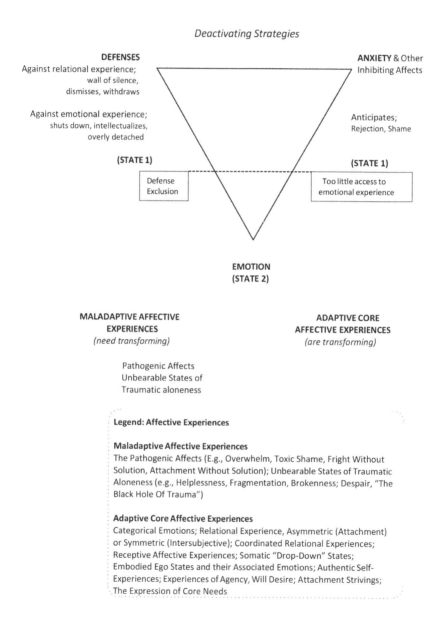

Figure 8.1 The Triangle of Experience: Avoidant
Pando-Mars, 2024, adapted from Fosha, 2020

returned in the Strange Situation, we may be in the terrain of defenses against relatedness. The patient's use of dismissiveness, gaze aversion, and withdrawal are some defenses against relatedness to ensure against exposing vulnerability and to counter the potential of being rejected. When it comes to the historical past, their verbal patterning can appear like a wall of silence, signaling the minimizing of attachment relationships as seen in the AAI. Defenses against relatedness break the connection to other, to protect from the feared and expected rejection, humiliation, disappointments, or intrusions and were an adaptative move to protect the integrity of the self.

These defenses are depicted on the upper left corner of the TOE (see Figure 8.1). Anxiety is depicted on the upper right corner. Someone who is avoiding, using a deactivating strategy, may appear to have "apparent low anxiety." This is not to say that they do not experience anxiety. The low-level display of anxiety is evidence of the deactivating strategy that occurs in response to arousal of their attachment behavioral system. Whether the triggering is based internally with activation of an emotional need or externally in response to an attachment figure, the typical avoidant response is to withdraw and conserve energy. Hence, there is difficulty for the ordinary observer to identify that the person behind these avoidant patterns may be feeling anxious. At the bottom of the TOE are maladaptive and adaptive core affective experiences. On the maladaptive side we find pathogenic affects and unbearable states of traumatic aloneness, which need transforming. While on the adaptive side, core affective emotion or relational experiences are transforming, necessary for healing and knowing the self.

Working With Defenses Against Emotion
and Disconnection From Self

The dismissive pattern also disconnects the person from their self. Not only is the connection to the other broken but so is the connection to the self. *Defenses against emotion* block awareness of what is arising in the self, in an adaptive move to manage perceived overwhelm that deflects the need for an attachment figure. When a person disavows and shuts down emotion and affective experiences, and instead turns to analyzing or trying to figure things out, the whole of their experience is incomplete. Relying on thinking and reasoning while avoiding affective experience is partial at best, which is another reason we identify the pseudo aspect of self-reliance. Operating without listening to signals that arise naturally through our bodies and being out-of-touch and disconnected from knowing what we sense and feel on a visceral and emotional level, we miss out on the adaptive action tendencies of emotions and what Panksepp (2009) refers to as "ancestral tools for living." Fosha (2000b) referred to this pattern as "dealing, but not feeling." Without the valence and enriching qualities of lived emotions, our capacity for fulfilling relationships, especially with loved ones, is often diminished.

In psychotherapy, one facet of defenses against emotion and disconnection to self is being disconnected from emotional experience when it occurs in the moment. When therapists ask open-ended questions like "How are you feeling about this?," we may be met with a blank stare or shrug of the shoulders. Reflecting specific changes, such as voice tone or posture, to the patient can orient their development of awareness. I focus my patients' attention by asking, "Do you notice how your voice became so intent as you said that?" or "I see you shifting your posture and sitting up really tall right now, are you aware of what is bringing this shift?" By sharing what I notice, I can provide a landing pad for their awareness. Sometimes signals appear from the body that provide an entry point for exploration. As is shown in the following case illustration, being specific and providing a focus can be helpful.

Case Illustration

Clinical Vignette 8A, Part 1: "Are You Aware of Your Tears?"

THERAPIST (TH): Okay (*hand on heart*). Well, let's just slow down. [**Slowing down is critical to experiential work and identifying patterns of response.**]

GAYLE (PATIENT, PT): (*tears appear*) Every time he leaves . . . (*speaking through tears appearing in her eyes*)

TH: I see emotion coming. [**Making the implicit explicit, attuning to and resonating with the bottom of the TOE.**]

PT: (*smiles*) Okay. [**In response to my comment, she slows down.**]

TH: Do you notice your tears? [**Bringing her attention to the emergence of her tears, which she missed due to her self-at-worst defensive avoidance.**]

PT: (*shakes her head side to side*) I didn't even notice them, no. [**Noticing that she didn't notice engages her self-at-best awareness.**]

TH: (*smiles warmly*) As I ask, do you notice? [**I ask this so that she can connect (admit) to becoming aware of having tears.**]

PT: Yes (*nodding*).

TH: Good for you. [**Affirmation of her opening the aperture of her awareness.**]

Intervention: notice and reflect glimmers of emotion. When I reflect "I see tears" to this patient, Gayle, I note her surprise that she is unaware of tears forming at the corners of her eyes. When I ask Gayle, "Are you aware of these tears?" and she says, "No," I then ask, "When I name them are you aware of them?" to which she says, "Yes." Taking small steps allows me to reflect what I notice, and then to check in to see whether the patient is aware of what I see. If they are not, the next intervention is to discover, if, with our help, they can tune into something that may already be happening. This allows us to hold both that the patient is unaware, and yet, once mirrored, they can become aware and pay attention to the tears that are there. Generating new connections provides a new experience that can be grounds for revising a belief like "I don't show feelings" or "Not being seen is better and safer than being seen."

The big picture. At times, patients interpret their displays of emotion as evidence of weakness, especially when they sense that their defenses are breaking down. *Being vulnerable is simply not okay and must be prevented.* As therapist I hold the big picture, seeing how fear of exposure is a foreboding that harkens back to some dreadful experiences early on, leaving the person guarding against being demeaned or disdained. Fear of overwhelm comes from being alone with unbearable, confusing, or bewildering experiences. Fear supplies the motive to shut out awareness, to shut out and keep out anything that would hurt or belittle or bring excruciating vulnerability. So, my job is to model for my patient how to befriend whatever emerges from their somatic/affective experience and relational cues. I want to be an ally in helping them notice and attend to their unfamiliar signals. I know that a lack of awareness does not mean nothing is happening. Throughout, I attempt to set conditions for relational safety, so that ultimately relational adaptive action tendencies can emerge.

Together, we can detect internal promptings and patients can learn how to allow themselves to get to know aspects of self that have been hidden, even to their own minds and hearts. I affirm the steps they take toward unfolding experience. I name what I see and hear, in a voice that conveys respect and interest so that the patient can know where I am coming from, so their neuroception picks up cues of safety as I mirror them. Bit by bit, with presence and persistence, we foster their capacity to become more self-aware and capable of shifting hard-and-fast defenses into flexible defenses that are amenable to give, so that the original emotion below wounding can surface. Once revealed, the pathway to resolving injury gets clearer.

Defenses Against Relatedness: Not-Needing Others as a Defense Against Rrrrreally Needing Others—Self-Reliance as a Defense Against Relatedness and Needs for Interpersonal Connection

The lack of connection to oneself and to one's emotional life brings challenges and difficulties in relating to, and with, another. To truly comprehend this pattern, we must explore the interweave of its origins. Originally, *defenses against relatedness* protected the person against feeling the distress, discomfort, and agonizing experiences of not having been truly seen, historically. These defenses provided escape from rejection, intrusion, humiliation, or other belittling, dehumanizing experiences. Thus, they served to ward off despair. These defenses protect the integrity of the self, by defensively excluding awareness of anything that would threaten the stability of self. Fear of falling apart is terrifying. Cutting-off awareness of an Other is a way to disconnect from needing an Other. This protection serves to avoid experiencing the very painful emotions stirred by active or passive rejection. The lack of response hurts so badly. In adult primary relationships, the defense against needing others moves in both directions, against being needed by another emotionally, as well as needing another emotionally.

Disrupted drives toward connection. Here we are up against the ruptures that occurred between the person's attachment behavioral system and the attachment caregiving system. When a child is moved by their attachment behavioral system to seek proximity in times of distress, and their attachment figure is rejecting, intrusive, or otherwise unavailable, the person's trust in innate motivational drives to seek connection are disrupted. Thus, they develop difficulties not only in receiving care, but in providing care. When the biological wiring to care and be cared for breaks down, it leaves emptiness and aloneness in its wake. This is precisely why a psychotherapy relationship that draws from attachment theory to restore safety and security is crucial to the repair of these intrinsic attachment behavioral systems.

Exploring therapeutic interactions in the present moment. In Bowlby's (1973, 1988) description of how psychotherapists can provide a secure haven for patients in psychotherapy, he specifically describes that the work of psychotherapy is to use our base so that the patient can explore how their internalized representations of their failed relationships are still operating unconsciously to predict danger and keep them safe. However, these models have become inflexible, and instead of gathering information in present time, assessing and basing choices in the here-and-now our patients become activated based on expectancies and old rules from their internal working models. To help our patients heal the deep-seated rupture between proximity and caregiving, between giving and receiving care, psychotherapists have the therapeutic task and the meaningful opportunity for repairing and restoring trust in relationship. We do this in the present moment by making sure to challenge expectancies by referencing what is happening in the here-and-now between each of us as we establish our therapeutic relationship.

And yet, the pathway toward a relationally oriented psychotherapy might be fraught. When psychotherapists ask about the experience of the relationship between ourselves and the patient, we might touch the absence of a template for accompaniment, encountering someone for whom being understood was a rarity rather than the norm. For someone with avoidant patterning, these inquiries have the potential to generate defensive intellectualization or distracting generalizations. The person might use dismissing words or gestures to push us away, really pushing away the historical source of discomfort. When therapists ask questions that patients don't have answers to, they might expect to be criticized. Subsequent feelings of inadequacy and shame might even be reminiscent of challenges in their primary relationship.

Therapist common reactivities. Dismissiveness as a defensive or protective strategy operates reflexively and automatically. When the therapist is nearing what has been experienced by the patient as dangerous territory, even the therapist's best intentions might be misperceived or simply not understood. The patient's dismissive hand gesture or turn of the head, whether subtle or strong, can have a powerful impact on the therapist. Encountering the implicit rejection in dismissiveness might understandably activate the therapist's own attachment wounds and trigger our own self-at-worst internal working model. Here, therapist common reactivities are likely to appear. When faced with dismissiveness or intellectualization, therapists can sometimes feel inadequate or doubt our effectiveness when our interventions don't land. When activated by a lack of response or dismissiveness in the patient, we might overexplain our intentions or get on a roll with psycho-ed. Inadvertently, we end up touting an intellectual lecture rather than leaning in with help and direction.

Using metaskills: being intentional with kindness and willingness to explore. When therapists can replace defensiveness with openness and mindfully regulate our own reactions, we can engage with intention. We can bring in a spirit of lightheartedness and curiosity to explore what brings about dismissiveness in the present moment, *making the implicit explicit.* We want to fortify our empathic understanding of our patient's formidable challenge. When we search under the surface and make room to hold the question "What made such defenses necessary in the first place?," we slow down our own reactions and recalibrate with a spirit of interest and willingness to explore. Slowly and carefully, moment-to-moment tracking can lead to the emergence of what has deep roots in survival. With kindness and willingness to explore we build collaborative curiosity and compassion, which can go a long way toward building understanding and bringing online both the patient's and the therapist's self-at-best. Thus, we pave the way for our patients' openness and willingness to take the small steps needed to access bottom-up experience and discovery.

Core Affective Experiences: Processing Emotion
and Relational Affective Experiences

Core affective experiences. Core affective experiences are represented at the bottom of the TOE. In addition to categorical emotions (sadness, anger, fear, disgust, surprise, and joy) an important part of core affective experiences are relational affective experiences. One aspect of helping our patients reduce their defenses against relatedness is working explicitly and directly with relational affective experiences. These include asymmetrical relational experiences (attachment) in which one person in the dyad assumes the role of "older, wiser other" who is there to care and help the "younger, more vulnerable one." Symmetrical relational (intersubjective) experiences occur as each person in the dyad enjoys the pleasure or acknowledgment of shared experience, meeting human to human. Additionally, we attend to coordinated relational experiences: coordination and miscoordination, attunement, disruption, and repair. For many of our patients, repair was not part of the picture; disruption and miscoordination were not followed by recoordination and repair. So it is especially important that psychotherapists attune to how our exchanges unfold with our patients, as our interactive sequences are fertile ground for exploration. Another significant relational affective experience is the receptive affective capacity of our patients. Are they able to take in and make use of our help, care, availability, and accompaniment? Examples of these relational affective experiences occur in the following clinical vignette:

Clinical Vignette 8B, Part 1: "Don't Be Fooled Again!"

Here is a vignette in which what starts off as a seemingly benign minimization of the significance of the therapist's care takes us into the patient's direct prohibition against daring to trust that anyone would care. "Don't believe . . . ," is quite the admonition. Slow and deliberate unpacking what is stirred in the present-moment relational experience brings this message from the depths of self-protection. It illustrates how *AEDP explicitly explores the experience of attachment in the moment-to-moment experience between therapist and patient*.

The session begins with an established patient, Beth, whom I have seen in couples therapy for over a year. While this is our first individual session, we have a fair amount of trust in our work together. During this meeting, with each of our selves-at-best online, notice how despite the fear we remain in communication while traversing self-at-worst conditioning. At the beginning of this session, Beth admitted feeling nervous, yet also acknowledged feeling safe. As the session unfolded, she encountered an early memory of being a little girl who longed to have special time with her father. Yet, simultaneously, she was terrified of doing the wrong thing that would bring him to reject her. In our session, when sadness emerged, Beth became baffled and confused. She struggled to make sense of the emotion, and subsequently that I would want to be with her.

This scene illustrates that even though we have established trust between us, when the attachment system is activated, doubt emerges. We enter here in the moment as Beth recalls how alone she was as a child, and I bring our attention into the present moment with me.

BETH (PATIENT, PT): If I had had one person, one adult who had been kind, loving . . . or somebody to just ask me who I was or what I thought about . . . [This longing is a transformance striving.]

THERAPIST (TH): Well, that's what I feel like I want to do right now. I'm really loving getting to know who you are and what you thought about. [I make a specific self-disclosure to express my sincere interest and care.] What happens when I say that? What's it like for you to know that I want to know you, what you think about, feel about? [I immediately follow by inquiring about her experience of my sharing. I want to check her receptive affective capacity to see what she can take in from me.]

PT: I think I'm not convinced anybody really wants to know who I am. It's hard for me to really believe that. [**Origins of the avoidant pattern**]

TH: Yeah . . .

PT: (*nodding*)

TH: It's hard for you to believe that I want to know you. [**Amplifying and making it explicit in the direct experience of our relationship. My tone is sincere, with kind inquiry.**]

PT: Yeah.

TH: What happens when you look at me? When I say I want to know you? [**I make the relational experiential with a here-and-now request, to see what she can perceive.**] What do you see in my eyes?

Explore what happens in the present moment between therapist and patient. As Beth expresses her mistrust, I explore what is arising in the moment, and ask her to see what she can see in my eyes. I want to engage her perception here-and-now to see what happens if she can see beyond what she expects, and if she can make use of our present-moment experience to offset her historically based expectancies that no one really cares what she thinks and feels.

PT: You're all blurry, I can't see without my glasses—that helps. (*laughs*) [**Humor is a delightful way to regulate anxiety.**]

TH: It does help . . . okay in this blurry state . . . [**I stay with her.**] What do you see through the blur? [**I meet her with laughter to bring some dyadic regulation, while also keeping the focus.**]

PT: I can see.

TH: What do you see?

PT: I don't doubt your sincerity. (*The tone of her voice deepens and drops down.*) I just don't believe that anybody really wants to know me. [**Side by side we see the glimmer of the new, with "I don't doubt your sincerity," followed by the assertion of the old "I just don't believe that anybody really wants to know me."**]

TH: You don't believe and that comes from way inside, right? And so when you see me, you don't doubt my sincerity. What does happen? [**I acknowledge her belief and encourage her to explore what is newly emerging in the here-and-now with me.**]

PT: Well, I have a whole defense: "She doesn't really want to know, that she's, well, this is part of the therapy . . . " [Although she notices her defense, she still minimizes what she can take in from me.]

TH: These are all the thoughts, but what happens with your eyes, when your eyes are seeing my eyes? [Bypassing the defense, staying with the direct relational experience.]

PT: My eyes tell me that you are truly here; truly looking at me, really want to know . . . (tense voice)

TH: And how, what's that like to . . . [Metaprocessing.]

PT: That's hard for me to trust. [Beginning to move toward the inside of self rather than staying with our present reality.]

Exploring the contrast of Beth's internal working model to our present-moment experience. Here although Beth can articulate the new experience with me, she is hesitant to let herself believe what she sees. Inside are layers of protectiveness that cover profound hurt. The fact that we have built a secure base between us allows her to have enough trust to continue exploring with me. I hold that she does see I am truly here and wanting to know, even though that's hard to trust. The next intervention is a bit of both—I acknowledge her difficulty trusting, while also asking her to notice if she can let in some of what she sees.

TH: It's hard for you to trust. (hand motioning inside) How far in can that go? [I go with the receptivity that emerges when she named "My eyes tell me you are truly here."]

PT: (sigh) I think it can go in; I think if I can just relax . . .

TH: Try out how far in that can go . . . [I make it experiential.] Try relaxing, just see how much you can take in.

PT: Yeah.

TH: Try to take in that I care about you, and I want to know you. [Sincere tone of voice: emphasis on care and want.] What happens? Let's take it slow and see what happens this time.

PT: (deep breath)

TH: That's a deep breath. [I am moment-to-moment tracking and reflecting what I see to heighten her awareness of her breath.]

PT: There's something that really is—it's like a block. It's like it doesn't just sink in. [Here she is describing what she encounters from her observing self-at-best.]

TH: Do you know where that block comes from?

PT: Um, um

TH: See if you can see . . . where that block comes from. [**I want to know if she can she make the link.**]

PT: I think it just comes from being disappointed in the past—so just like "Don't do that again!" (*Spoken in a very harsh tone with a look of warning in her eyes, and her arm makes a sharp downward gesture*)

TH: Right (*I mirror her gesture, which shows a firm marking of a boundary between self and other*) [**Affirming that I hear the message, I communicate that I am right here with her.**]

PT: DON'T do that. (*strong emphasis on "don't"*)

TH: DON'T. (*echoes the harsh tone*) [**I join her, resonating with the tone of her voice.**]

PT: DON'T let that in again.

TH: DON'T. (*repeats mirroring hand gesture—she is nodding*) That's it . . . [**Validating and amplifying her protective expression in reaction to her internal working model that expects rejection.**]

PT: Don't be stupid. Don't (*hand firmly presses her leg now*) you know? Don't believe that somebody is really interested in you. [**Defense against relatedness.**]

TH: Ohhh. (*big sigh*) How painful, right, to believe and be disappointed . . . that makes good sense—that you wouldn't let in what's here—cuz of the past disappointments. [**Explicit empathy with her need for the defense.**]

Having our secure base, with the patient's self-at-best online, provides a foundation for the emergence and exploration of harsh messages from the patient's self-at-worst. In this vivid example, Beth courageously names and speaks the harsh messages that drive her avoidant defenses. Hearing the intensity of such a prohibition brings understanding to how the patient's perception of safety can shift in an instant. And yet, having enough self-at-best online, and having the history of our experiential work together over the past year, Beth can inhabit the immensity of what lies under her relational defenses. Such an example of the way having a secure base between therapist and patient allows the exploration of scary places that usually would manifest in shutting-down and withdrawal behaviors.

PT: Yeah (*cries a bit*)

TH: Just let that through—see what that's like to recognize . . . Stay with me, what are you getting? What's happening?

PT: (*sniffs, looking down and away*) [**Avoiding eye contact.**]

TH: How do you feel right now as you are noticing this? [Checking in with her, I am also assessing her window of tolerance.]

PT: Um (*nodding*), I think a lot. It's so hard for me to go into my feelings cuz I think a lot . . . [Increased self-awareness of her defense.]

TH: Stay with me—together we can help sort this out. [I encourage her to stretch her window of tolerance, offering help from the position of older, wiser other who trusts the process we are in.]

PT: I've always been self-sufficient, didn't need anybody, developed my own thoughts. Even turned away a lot of relationships, you know, don't get too close . . . [Click of recognition . . . describes the cost of the avoidant pattern, which this process is helping her to notice. With increasing reflective capacity, she may start to reconsider her options.]

Change begins with recognizing the cost of the defense was turning away from relationships. With a new experience of exploring what is occurring in the here-and-now experience with me, Beth identifies the implicit memory that drives her relational patterning and isolation. She grows to recognize when she is thinking instead of feeling and labels this accurately as defense. As affective experience emerges and she begins to cry, she looks down and away, defending against her anticipation of rejection. Yet she does stay present to notice what is emerging, which is a signal that her trust in the process with me is growing. Her comment about not needing anybody is a reflection upon her admonition to herself, which marks another step toward self-understanding, as she identifies her pattern of self-reliance. Beth begins to identify that she has lost a lot of relationships by this turning away, naming the cost of her defensive protection, which is an important step in reorienting toward what she may want at this point in her life.

Anxiety Corner on the Avoidant TOE

In terms of anxiety, avoidantly attached patients are not typically viewed as being on the anxious side but rather more on the defensive side. And yet, as you can see in the illustration in Figure 8.1, there is clearly anxiety about getting close, especially when Beth has been close to the memory of her early longing for connection with her father. Having a lens into the anxiety underneath avoidant defenses provides more leverage for gaining traction in treatment. Those children in the Strange Situation who present as avoidant are the ones who turn away from their departing parent and play on their own without seeming to notice the leaving and return of their parent. While the child appears unaffected, and even well-adjusted, when measures of cortisol are taken, the child is revealed to be experiencing much anxiety. It is common to label insecurely attached folks as having either "avoidant" or "anxious" attachment. Those labels suggest that someone who appears avoidant is not anxious, or as anxious. Nothing could be further from the truth. What's at issue here is the way the individual copes with anxiety in relation to the attachment system.

Deactivating the attachment system turns down anxiety. I find this very significant. The anxiety corner of the TOE is also the location for inhibiting and signal affects. Considering that avoidant behavior is a move away from antici-pation of rejection by an Other, or from the felt experience of needing an Other or from the feared overwhelm of an unwanted emotion, we see inhibition in action. In response to arousal, the avoidant pattern is deacti-vating, which literally turns down or turns off awareness of emotion and/ or relational needs. When the patient in the vignette begins to show signs of emotion, she looks down and away. For her, worse than being alone with her feelings was her fear of seeing disdain on my face. She managed this anxiety by turning her head. It is vital that therapists recognize that apparent low anxiety is a signal to explore, to help regulate or titrate, and to build inroads that can scaffold the development of approach behaviors.

Markers of deactivation and apparent low anxiety. Markers of deactivation and apparent low anxiety appear in subtle and not-so-subtle forms. Some patients take a "relaxed posture," which looks like slumping into the couch or chair. Others may sit with arms folded across their chest, holding on to their elbows. Some yawn, interestingly, at the precise moment a bid for relational contact comes up. These and other behaviors may not be as they seem, at first. The patient may claim a lack of sleep to explain yawning or rubbing their eyes. It is even more important then, to notice the context in which this occurs, *tracking moment-to-moment* what is said and the patient's verbal and nonverbal response to it.

For instance, while folded arms or tightly crossed legs might appear as a "closed" body posture, what if they are markers of how the patient is holding on to their self? What if we see these gestures, from the move-ment channel, as signals of auto-regulation? What if we perceive that in this response to their nervous system gearing up, these discrete gestures are self-soothing? On a relational level this "moving away" from the other is a move toward self-reliance and an overt expression of not-needing, which was clearly articulated by my patient in the preceding example. In fact, the implicit message might indeed signal the need for a calm, regulating influence, which can cue psychotherapists to the unexpressed need for relational accompaniment. And when the therapist attempts to offer some help in the form of regulation, the patient may experience conflict. Such a place can stir a bit of crisis as patients drop down toward core experiences at the bottom of the TOE, sensing vulnerability as their avoidant strategies aren't working completely.

Develop the capacity for dyadic regulation to offset auto-regulation. So, when the defenses let go and anxiety appears in the foreground, the need for a supportive and guiding other becomes clearer. With a patient learning to let go of their pattern of avoidance, it is precisely this moment when they might recognize that help is needed. As a new terrain opens, one that brings a descent into the body, they may need help distinguishing thoughts that come to mind from the direct experience of feelings in their body. With the therapist's help, they can learn to stay with emerging sensations and feelings. Herein lies the potential for allowing the therapist to become someone to lean on and even to allow to help, to build new possibilities about collaboration and reworking negative expectancies about emotions and relatedness.

The TOE depicts the emotion regulatory patterns of patients that help us to orient our experiential work. To map out what happens relationally, we can turn to AEDP's SOE triangle, which is a representational schema of the internal working model of our patient in each moment. We can track what is occurring that harkens back to the original relationship between the caregiver (Other) and the Self. We can also track new ways of relating between the patient and the therapist or the patient and their own Self that promotes a self-at-best version of relatedness. Since the relational milieu is such an influential part of development, and the SOE triangle depicts the gestalt of relationship and emotion, I introduce the SOE triangle first before continuing to discuss the affective experience at the bottom of the TOE. For ease of using this triangle I now refer to the caregiver as the Other.[1]

The SOE Triangle (With Embedded TOE): Avoidant

How we have taken in and internally represented the experiences of our caregivers while growing up is depicted on the SOE triangle (see Figure 8.2). The SOE triangle incorporates Rows 1, 2, and 8 from Grids 1 and 2: Row 1, caregiver state of mind; Row 2, caregiver hallmarks (behavior; see Chapter 5, pp. 154–156); and Row 8, affective competence (Chapter 5, pp. 161–162). The impacts of the caregiver's state of mind and hallmark behaviors affect how the individual comes to internally represent their Self and how they internally represent the Other on the SOE triangle. Affective competence refers to how a person processes emotions, which is the individual's internalized representation of emotion on the SOE triangle. How the Other meets a person's (Self's) Emotion determines how safe or threatened the Self feels to experience their attachment needs or emotion. When an attachment longing or an emotion is met with rejection or judgment, the Self learns that "I am not safe feeling what I feel." Or the Self develops an admonition like we saw in the above case example: "Don't be stupid. Don't believe that somebody is really interested in you." When the other has a dismissive state of mind, their humiliating, rejecting, or intrusive behaviors provoke the Self to disconnect from their somatic experience. The Self shuts down their access to Emotion to protect the Self from feeling excruciating despair and/or disintegration. The Self withdraws from the Other to avoid the person who hurts them, which protects the relationship to survive, keeping the Self as intact as possible. The Self's representation of self may be "I am unlovable" or "I'm unworthy."

These repeated experiences form the person's internal working model, which is depicted on the SOE triangle. An example of the avoidant constellation of the self-at-worst version of the SOE triangle is the individual's representation of their compromised Self as avoidant/unlovable and the individual's internal representation of the triggering Other as dismissive/rejecting. The individual's representation of motion is characterized as unacceptable: blocked or detached; their affective competence is characterized by dealing, but not feeling.

One of the ways we discover what is driving the SOE template is by listening to what the patient shares as negative thoughts or beliefs (*defenses*) that disconnect them from affective experiences regarding themselves or their emotions. These thoughts often reveal expectancies derived from early and repeated experiences with the Other that have become internally

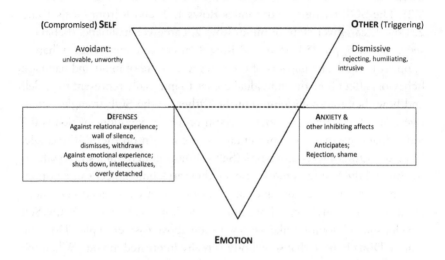

Deactivating Strategies

(Compromised) **SELF**   **OTHER** (Triggering)

Avoidant: Dismissive
unlovable, unworthy   rejecting, humiliating,
                                                                   intrusive

DEFENSES   **ANXIETY &**
Against relational experience;   other inhibiting affects
wall of silence,
dismisses, withdraws   Anticipates;
Against emotional experience;   Rejection, shame
shuts down, intellectualizes,
overly detached

EMOTION

MALADAPTIVE AFFECTIVE   ADAPTIVE CORE
EXPERIENCES   AFFECTIVE EXPERIENCES
(need transforming)   *(are transforming)*

Pathogenic Affects
Unbearable States of
Traumatic aloneness

Legend: Affective Experiences

Maladaptive Affective Experiences
The Pathogenic Affects (E.g., Overwhelm, Toxic Shame, Fright Without
Solution, Attachment Without Solution); Unbearable States of Traumatic
Aloneness (E.g., Helplessness, Fragmentation, Brokenness; Despair, "The
Black Hole Of Trauma")

Adaptive Core Affective Experiences
Categorical Emotions; Relational Experience, Asymmetric (Attachment)
or Symmetric (Intersubjective); Coordinated Relational Experiences;
Receptive Affective Experiences; Somatic "Drop-Down" States;
Embodied Ego States and their Associated Emotions; Authentic Self-
Experiences; Experiences of Agency, Will Desire; Attachment Strivings;
The Expression of Core Needs

Figure 8.2 The Self–Other–Emotion Triangle
(With Embedded Triangle of Experience): Avoidant
Pando-Mars, 2024, adapted from Fosha, 2020

represented. Expectancies contain the dismissing messages of the Other or the anticipated experiences that have laid down the tracks for internal working models to form. Some examples of self-at-worst expectancies include "I'm unlovable," "Something is wrong with me," and "I am not enough." These beliefs become the fodder to challenge in treatment, when we have enough self-at-best online, for the patient to hold this negative belief right next to what is happening in the here-and-now of the therapist–patient relationship (as evidenced by the above case illustration; Clinical Vignette 8B, Part 1).

Exploring negative beliefs can open doors to early traumatic memories. Expectancies are doorways into unresolved trauma and specific memories that need to be processed for healing to occur. The negative belief that emerges in the moment can lead to parts of us that have been hurt, holding on to painful introjects, and to the people who have been causal. Each person's internal working model shifts by relationship and even by emotion. Some emotions are safer to feel in the eyes of Others. Flexibility in our human condition arises as our perceptive survival instincts discern what saves, what soothes, and what stirs. Such flexibility is paramount to what makes psychotherapy and transformation possible. When psychotherapists can meet the patient (self) and their emotion with attunement and resonance, we help them have a new experience in the therapeutic relationship and differentiate from what occurred in their history that is represented in their self-at-worst SOE triangle. Thus, a new self-at-best constellation of the SOE triangle becomes possible, giving rise to a new internal representation of self as effective, an internal representation of the other as realistic, and emotion as able to be processed in a regulated way.

One of the goals of treatment is to shift the self-at-worst versions of the triangles, which are activated by states of dread and engage the use of defenses, to self-at-best versions of the triangles that are motivated by hope and openness to participate in emotional and relational experience. In AEDP we employ the therapist stance to explicitly provide a nutritive experience that strengthens the possibility of access to Self while being with an Other in ways that enliven and engage the relational field. When our patient has difficulty receiving our care, we can bring an exploration into the present moment between us and ask the patient how they see us. "As you look at me, what do you see in my eyes?" is an intervention that has the potential to challenge the patient's thought of being judged by focusing on what they perceive in the moment. Our aim is for the moment-to-moment

discoveries in our sessions to strengthen and fortify the therapeutic relationship to allow for authentic sharing that gets to an honest exchange
in the here-and-now These exchanges open doorways into differentiating
what is unresolved from the past, while having a new experience of the
relationship with the therapist in the present.

Discussion of Clinical Vignette 8B Through
the Lens of the SOE Triangle

As we see in the above vignette, when the therapist has built enough foundation with the patient, we may be surprised by what is revealed. Viewing
the other corner of the SOE triangle, the patient is able to perceive the
therapist's care (seeing other realistically), so in this moment the Self is
effective, which puts us in a self-at-best constellation. However, exploring
the present moment-to-moment experience between us also unearthed the
patient's harsh admonition, warning her about the threat of disappointment
(which came from the past triggering other, a self-at-worst constellation).
The patient's anticipation of rejection and humiliation gave rise to increased
anxiety. The patient's best effort to protect herself was with a relational
defense, to stand by her disbelief that someone would care or be there for
her. When this material surfaces in the experience between patient and
therapist, we are close to the moment of historical wounding, and we are
on the brink of having a new relational or emotional experience. There is a
juxtaposition: When the past and the present converge this is key to memory reconsolidation (Ecker et al., 2012). The experience of looking into my
eyes invited the patient to shift the impact of the memory on her nervous
system. Seeing and receiving my caring attention enabled her to feel calm
and juxtaposed the historical experience of rejection with a present experience of acceptance and accompaniment. As much as dread was driving the
patient's self-at-worst prohibition against opening and believing that anyone
would care, some hope emerged by experiencing our relatedness through
her self-at-best constellation, which permitted her to unburden the weight
of prohibitions and isolation to receive a new experience.

This *moment of meeting* provided the patient, Beth, with an opportunity
to recognize that the origins of her relational heartbreak had become mis-
represented internally as "something wrong with self." Misattributions are
a best strategy to avoid fresh hurt of something that happened in the past:
rejection and disappointment that brought deep sadness and then aloneness.

By giving the memory to its right place in the past, the patient can free up space to have a new experience in the present. New experiences with the therapist provide material for building new positive expectancies, in which trust can be tried and tested, thus reviving the patient's capacity for trusting self and other in relationship.

Emotion and Relatedness at the Bottom of the TOE, at the Bottom of the SOE Triangle

At the bottom of the TOE there can be maladaptive or adaptive core affective experiences. When treating avoidant strategies, the pathway to healing often involves the unveiling and addressing of relational/attachment wounds that cut to the core and then manifest in maladaptive experiences that need transforming. For instance, in working with someone who has employed avoidant strategies to survive, the lessening of defenses can give way to extreme vulnerability and fear of becoming overwhelmed by the emotion that has been so desperately and consistently warded off, sometimes for decades. Shame often encapsulates such vulnerability as the idea of being seen by another person (remember the caregiver hallmarks of those who display an avoidant pattern) brings with it an excruciating feeling of exposure that is near to, if not, totally unbearable. This is the very state that needs to be transformed for the buried trauma to be revealed.

Some individuals with an avoidant attachment strategy have experienced extreme levels of intrusiveness—for example, perhaps when the attachment figure's gaze moves beyond a loving presence into a grasping stare, eyes that penetrate too much or have a devouring nature. Another aspect of intrusiveness can be inferred from Ainsworth's Cooperation vs. Interference scale, in which the most interfering mothers don't see the baby as a separate person. There is a quality of arbitrariness to their behavior with their babies: the use of direct or forceful physical interference or the sheer number of interruptions. In the highly interfering category, caregivers seem to assume the baby is theirs, with no regard for the baby's wishes, mood, or activities (Ainsworth et al., 1978/2015). Adults who have suffered with this kind of dismissive state of mind from their caregivers, who are not seen to exist as a separate person, often have disgust as a core emotion that needs processing and integration.

Foster adaptive vulnerability in place of avoidance. In processing early traumatic memory and the related core emotions a new relationship to vulnerability is needed. Adaptive vulnerability is one that is held in relationship with another, being willing to bear visibility and even accompaniment while allowing previously avoided experience to surface. Here, we value the patient's connecting with their relational-affective experiences, specifically allowing their authentic self-expression in the presence of an Other. As patients share authentically and are received for their genuine expressions with kindness and care, the psychotherapist fosters a new experience of companionship. Growing the capacity for coordinated relational experiences with a trusted Other means identifying the experience of attunement, noticing minor and major disruptions, and working toward repair rather than shutting down. While the patient and therapist together hold the unbearable fear of exposure, their connection can contain the maladaptive affect, undoing aloneness with care and safety, thus growing the capacity to expand in the face of constriction.

The banished self was not the result of an intrinsic tarnished proof of the self's unworthiness. Undoing aloneness may generate realizations of unmet attachment longings, the remembering of specific moments in one's early history, and the processing of the emotions that have been held offline through defensive maneuvers. Herein lies the potential for corrective self, relational, and emotional experiences to bring about true adaptive action that arises in the wake of full emotional processing. Beginning with facing and transforming impoverishment in the realm of relationships with an Other brings deep relief that the banished self was not the result of some intrinsic tarnished proof of the self's unworthiness. Rather, the patient can begin to take in a new experience of being worthy in the eyes of an Other, which reverberates in the own Self's recognition of deserving that is primal and human and endowed as a birthright. First in the therapeutic relationship, as the therapist shows up as a reliable other on whom the patient can count and lean on, the patient can begin to allow contact with an Other and connection with their emotional life. Here the patient increases their capacity to feel for their own Self with care and compassion, and thereby can discover their capacity to empathize with others.

Connection to self is essential in building the capacity for relatedness with others. Helping the person who relied on an avoidant strategy to build connection first and foremost to self, starts with acceptance that there is worthy information to be found by listening to inner stirrings and receiving the attention and accompaniment of a trustworthy Other. Developing this capacity to relate to Self, building the capacity to relate to an Other, and releasing relational action tendencies are pivotal goals of treatment to heal avoidant strategies and move toward earned secure attachment. To illustrate this representation, the TOE is embedded within the SOE triangle. At the bottom of the SOE triangle the State 2 work of processing affective experiences to completion takes place, which includes both relatedness and emotion.

Befriending Vulnerability and Relatedness, Recognizing Core Values, Building Trust

Making use of the therapist provides an opportunity for the patient to be in relationship and build trust with an Other upon whom they can lean and can build a stable sense of security supporting the patient to relate to themselves or to others in new ways. Learning how to be with and receive the therapist's accompanying and caring presence and seeing themselves through kind and caring eyes can help the individual with avoidant patterning shift how they relate to attachment needs and experiences, and begin to build relational action tendencies.

The capacity for opening with another deepens: taking risks to share what isn't fully formed, being able to take in help, even ask for help, and not "going it alone." By receiving empathy, the capacity to empathize with another can grow. Some of the interventions that cultivate relational adaptive action are helping the patient to develop receptive affective capacity, allowing themselves to receive care, help, and empathy. Receiving the therapist's presence and accompaniment is needed to undo the unbearable aloneness that resides deeply inside from the impact of being rejected, dismissed, and objectified. When the patient is feeling seen and felt by the therapist, they grow their capacity to connect to themselves. To be connected to another, one must be connected to self.

Clinical Vignette 8B, Part 2: Accessing Emotion and Beginning to Identify Autobiographical Narrative

In the first section of the psychotherapy session with Beth, we saw that what lurked underneath the relational defense is huge fear of disappointment. The longing toward relating with another is wired together with a defensive warning against believing that another could truly be there. With the potential of letting in my care and interest, feelings emerge that register the pain and the loneliness of past disappointments and hurt. In Vignette 8B, as I help Beth tune into her own internal world of thought, feeling, and customary behaviors, her capacity to reflect on both her longing and dread opens. Such unfurling brings us to an adaptive action that translates into newfound curiosity with more space for understanding rather than reactivity. In this moment, revealing herself with the therapist as a collaborative other is growing,

BETH (PATIENT, PT): I try to get myself to figure out what I'm feeling. [Transformance glimmer]

THERAPIST (TH): Good! [Affirmation]

PT: I always feel like "Don't set yourself up for disappointment"; I just come back to that over and over.

TH: Right, so (*points to her head*) you learned that that is hardwired in you, right?

PT: (*nodding*)

TH: That was your motto as a kid, and something today—What if you put that right next [to each other] (*shows both hands*)? "Don't set yourself up for disappointment" and "What have we been working with today?" What do you get if you put them together? [Reflecting with a tone of collaboration and exploration, to separate the past messages from the present experience with the therapist, then metaprocessing what is seen.]

PT: (*big sigh*) That's a tough one. Because I want to believe that I can trust you, and other people, that they can give me what I need, but that's just not there (*chokes up*).

TH: You know what's there? There's feelings . . . (*gently noticing*) that still need to come out because the thing is they're getting in the way . . . of your taking this [new experience of trusting me] in . . . [I stay with her emerging emotion and lend my trust that if feelings are emerging, they deserve to be felt.]

PT: (*nodding*)

TH: Your feelings are really about all that hurt. [I am speaking gently and kindly, as the older, wiser attachment figure, who identifies her feelings with understanding and acceptance.] What's happening right now?

PT: It's a grief that makes me sad that I can't get that in my life. It makes me sad; it makes me . . . [Now she puts words to her feelings, yet she describes an expectancy based on her past.]

TH: The grief is about you *couldn't get* that in your life, you didn't get that in your life . . . from the person that you wanted it with, so this is that little girl in you who just couldn't get what you needed . . . [**Empathic elaboration, differentiating what happened in the past from her anticipation of what is possible in her life.**]

PT: (*looking down and away*)

TH: Stay with me, what are you feeling? Stay with this. [**Encouraging her to be present with me.**]

PT: You know it's hard because when I was a kid to need my dad or my mom in my family was just considered horrible; What's wrong with you? [**She registers the significant events of her early life experience that influence her prevalent attitude about her current life, now stirred by what is happening with me.**]

TH: So, come here for a second, I want to check in with you. How is it to be here with me? [**The deactivating strategy pulls at her. I see she is slipping out of the present with me and sinking into shame.**]

PT: (*stays in eye contact*)

TH: I feel like I so want to go with you to these places. [**Therapist's explicit use of self to undo aloneness and counter the old experience.**]

PT: (*gaze averts and looks around*)

TH: Because you don't have to feel alone. [**Making the implicit explicit**]

PT: I don't feel alone.

TH: Really?

PT: I really feel like you're right there with me . . . I really do. [**I must admit this feels like a surprise and a relief.**]

Sort out what happened in the past from what is happening in the present. Step-by-step, working at the edge of the window of tolerance, at the edge of what is expected and what is new, we forge ahead. As Beth began to consider that she may trust me, she feels grief about the lack of trustworthy others in her life. Anxiety emerges, revealing her internal working model that is fixed in that she looks to the future with her model of the past. My stating that this *is* what happened in her past, distinct from here-and-now raises the contrast with her parents, and marks the beginning of differentiating what happened in the past from what is happening now and is new in the present relationship with me.

Sometimes in sessions where there is a significant breakthrough, another entry point appears that we can engage with a deepened spirit of collaboration. One of these moments appeared in the next few minutes following the above exchange. Beth began speaking about how she was on her own as a child, yet she saw herself as fiercely independent. I was able to ask if we could take some accompaniment back to the little girl in her. She said yes and opened a doorway into an imaginal world that she once occupied alone.

Establishing safety: entering through the imaginal channel. Beth invites me to join her in the fields of her childhood. She imagines that I take her hand and walk alongside her through the familiar terrain she explored as a young girl. She playfully points to the big rabbits that are leaping through the tall grasses, and I respond as if talking to a 5-year old: "The jackrabbits are hopping." I narrate in a sweet voice. I feel as if I am leaning down to the level of a child, with tenderness and care. We are constructing a more trusting relationship by meeting in this imaginal world, a place that was safe back then, and seems like a transitional space we can occupy together now. I am deeply moved to be allowed inside her precious world as a trusted companion, and naturally offer company and witnessing that had been sorely missing. In this realm, I can see that sharing an imaginal space feels safer than sharing emotions. Emotions had been ridiculed and a source of unsafety as child, where her imaginal channel was an escape and a place of refuge. To join her in her safe place was an important meeting ground for deepening trust in our work together.

Getting to the Roots of Attachment Trauma: The Triangle of Relational Comparisons

(See Chapter 3, Figure 3.4, p. 114)

Bringing nutritive experiences to the little ones inside our adult patients is one corrective element of healing: opening new possibilities, shifting old expectations. Making connections between wounding from the patient's past historical relationships and the challenges they find in current relationships is key to healing repetitive patterns that arise from attachment trauma. The triangle of relational comparisons (TORC) is the AEDP representational schema that helps psychotherapists to map out both what is repetitive and what is corrective in the patient's journey. The TOE and the

SOE triangle are embedded in each corner of the TORC. The upper left corner holds the current relationship(s). The upper right corner holds the therapeutic relationship, and the bottom corner holds past relationships. (See Chapter 3, pp. 113–115, for a fuller explanation.)

Entering the dark and troubling waters of relationships and being with previously avoided emotions with a trusted psychotherapist helps patients to awaken hidden potentials. Our patients surprise themselves when these new potentials help to clarify what was puzzling and worrisome. They come to realize how to make use of their emotions, and how to share them. They can generalize new experiences of valuing emotional expression, inspiring new levels of communication in significant relationships, which opens possibilities for true exchange. When our patients shift avoidant patterns and *learn to express their feelings*—indeed, we are filling in for developmental lapses and restoring access to their core self.

In the following section I continue with the psychotherapy session of Vignette 8A, in which I am working with Gayle's *defenses against emotion*, stemming from avoidant patterns that impact her marriage. Her presenting issue was difficulty being close with her husband. She described avoidant patterns of relating, discomfort with affection, and heightened sensitivity at times of his planned departures.

Gayle has come to treatment to explore this pattern that seems to contradict the love she has for her husband. I believe her wish to address these conflicts is demonstrative of her care. This session begins with Gayle talking about her reaction to her husband going out of town, claiming "I really don't care." Engaging her with a kind and receptive presence, I intervene right away. I counter her relational defense with what I sense is her transformance striving. I say that I believe she does care.

Tracing the unfolding process with the patient on the TOE and the SOE triangle helps to organize the multiple layers of process, while also guiding a clear course of clinical action. Via the TOE, we map out how the patient moves away from emotion (defense) or feeling anxious. On the TORC, in the corner of therapeutic relationship, I occupy the place of other, one who is helpful and facilitating, rather than oblivious to Gayle's experience as were her attachment figures. With my attention, the patient learns to identify for herself when she is avoiding feelings by going into her thoughts. When she is feeling anxious, we slow down to tune into what is stirred. My engagement replaces the need for her defenses. I consistently affirm each of her steps toward emotion and ask her to repeat affect-laden words to feel into them with intention. *Feeling into thoughts* is an intervention from Grid 3, Row 7: this helps our patients with avoidant patterning to become more aware of their emotions to develop affective competence.

Our collaboration allows us to explore what happens in the current dynamic with Gayle's husband, represented on the upper left corner of the TORC. The way I am with her, as her therapist, is represented on the upper right corner. I encourage Gayle to face what is stirring, and unresolved from her historical past, which is represented at the bottom of the TORC. Once she has a new experience of feeling the unfelt emotion from earlier in her life, she starts to put the pieces together, and at the end of the session there is a shift in how she can imagine relating with her husband.

Note that the experiences represented at the top of the TOE (i.e., defenses and anxiety) are State 1 phenomena in the Four-State Map of the Transformational Process (see Chapter 2 on AEDP, for a full description) and experiences represented at the bottom of the TOE (i.e., emotions and other core affective phenomena) are State 2 phenomena. State 3 and State 4 phenomena are only represented in the Four-State Map of the Transformational Process and thus were not part of the three representational schemas discussed above.

Clinical Vignette 8A, Part 2: "I Don't Care" Heralds the Emergence of "I Would Be Devastated"

GAYLE (PATIENT, PT): I really don't care—but implicit in your partner going out of town . . . if he's just going to have fun . . . I don't really care. [**State 1: defenses in operation**]

THERAPIST (TH): But you do care. [**Pressuring with empathy by leaning into what is really at the bottom of the TOE. I am a welcoming other inviting her genuine feeling, which is a self-at-best version of other on the SOE triangle.**]

PT: I shell up. I get really defensive I suppose. [**She demonstrates self-reflection by naming her defense.**] I don't think intellectually that he's abandoning me, but I have this whole process that I go through intellectually where I get mad at him.

TH: Let's just take a minute and be . . . and feel into what you're saying . . . [**Asking her to "feel into her thoughts" builds connection to the underlying experience.**]

PT: (*nodding*)

TH: "Every time he leaves [**I repeat her words, to amplify the pattern**] I get mad" (*hand down on core*) and I see . . . sadness.

PT: I want to be able to say to him, I could, but I can't, that I'm not mad. I just feel like he's abandoning me, but that sounds so ridiculous.

TH: Can we slow down . . . when you say, "I feel like he's abandoning me . . ." What's the feeling? [**The patient projected her feeling as what he is doing, and she leaves the present moment with me.**] Can you just say the feeling if you don't put the words to it? Before you even say it, feel. Let's just be with the feeling more. [**I refocus her on the experience under her thoughts by inviting her back into what she is feeling.**]

PT: I feel tight, hot. I get short with my kids. [**She responds with sensation at first, then gets distracted by thinking about a pattern with her kids.**]

TH: Slow down. Feeling tight and hot right now? [I repeat the sensations she names to redirect her attention to what is happening in her body right now.]

PT: (*nodding*)

TH: Sounds like anxiety. [**I label the experience for her, which maps on to the TOE.**]

PT: Mm-hmm.

TH: Sounds like a reaction to the feeling . . . So, can you just see if you could let yourself be with the tightness, be with the heat? [**I want her to tune into the anxiety . . . so that both of us can be present, which is a new way of being with herself, and is also a new relational experience.**]

PT: (*she breathes and stays in contact with me*) [**Together, we regulate the anxiety.**]

TH: See if you can go back just a little bit and see if we can touch into that emotion that's nearby. [**Guiding her attention to what was occurring right before the anxiety kicked in.**]

PT: It's hard because I just think I am so used to it. [**She reflects the fixed patterning.**] I just can't even pinpoint how it is . . . that I feel.

TH: Mm-hmm.

Distinguish thoughts from body-based feelings to get to the core affect. During the next few minutes we move toward and away from the core affective experience. I help the patient distinguish thoughts from feelings and how to understand her process by mapping it on the TOE. When I realize she has shed some tears, I wonder if she experiences a felt shift that she can identify and leverage to build some trust that she can tolerate emotion.

TH: How do you feel as you have these tears? [**Metaprocess the new experience.**] Can you feel what it's like in your body to let yourself have some tears?

PT: (*settles in and breathes*)

TH: It's good to breathe too. [Affirm]

PT: It feels like a release a little bit . . . it feels like I'm calming . . . [This is a postbreakthrough affect, marking a shift that happens after she let herself experience some emotion.]

TH: So, tune into that. Let yourself just feel calming. Feel release. Just notice.

Experience each shift to gain traction. Before going for more—I invite the patient to experience the shift that occurred, which helps her to perceive the shift and strengthens her awareness of what is happening in her body, not just her thoughts. Change gets traction. Staying with the shift allows a natural deepening to unfold.

TH: Be with that. What's that like for you?

PT: (*quiet*)

TH: What do you notice?

PT: I just feel sad. [And now she simply acknowledges the experience of emotion.]

TH: Okay. Let's just give that a lot of room. Give yourself room to feel sad. It takes a lot so I just appreciate your willingness. [Stay, deepen, affirm— explicitly guiding her to be with what is unfolding.]

To surrender to *just feeling sad* is a big step for this patient, to arrive at the simple truth of her emotional experience. We landed here by the careful moment-to-moment tracking of the emergence of Gayle's affective experience and my pointing out her moving away by thinking and trying to figure things out. By first helping her to notice her tears, and then identifying the pattern by mapping out her anxiety and defense on the TOE, she became capable to drop down into her felt sense of feeling sad.

In the following segment, I continue to offer my presence as an accompanying Other, resonating with her experience while also leaning into affective moments. I narrate the process at times to reflect what is happening to help her to stay with the new space she is giving herself that allows old emotions to surface. I select affect-laden words that I ask her to repeat to attune to what is emerging. Having her repeat significant words helps to intensify her connection to self.

State 2 Work

Over the next minute the client shares more about what happens with her husband and gets to an important realization, which I have her repeat.

TH: Okay, slow down. Just let yourself very slowly say, "I'm scared for him to leave." [**Repeat affect-laden words to amplify.**]
PT: I'm scared for him to leave.

Repeat affect-laden words. Having Gayle repeat this brings up intense feeling and then defense as she moves toward and away from the experience. We stay with the emergent process over a few minutes, holding the focus.

TH: You're scared for him to leave. [**Staying very close, repeating her words.**]
PT: *(shrugs left shoulder)* It brings back old feelings, I think.
TH: Okay *(nodding)*, good for you . . . just good for you, good for you. *(deep exhale)* [**Again, there is a dropping down through another layer and I affirm her awareness and repeat her words to emphasize their importance.**]
TH: "I'm scared for him to leave." [**Reflecting her words, validating that they point to the underlying material.**] His leaving brings back old feelings . . . mm-hmm . . . that's a lot to say out loud.
PT: It feels like it is. [**She agrees that this step is significant.**]
TH: I think so too. Good for you. [**Affirmation**]
PT: Thank you. *(nodding with a very sweet and tender look into my eyes)*

Affirm each movement toward emotion. We are beginning to approach old feelings that come from a state that occurred when she was young. Notice how often I affirm each movement toward emotion. While this is attuned to her, which we know by her receptivity to my acknowledging her, it is important that psychotherapists titrate such affirmation with each patient to what serves each dyad.

As we deepen into State 2 core affective experiences, anxiety and defense rise, as the avoidant patterning kicks in. But with me, Gayle doesn't have to rely on her defenses to protect herself from anxiety about what feels so big and overwhelming. I step in quickly to regulate her anxiety about being alone and use affirmations to steady her growing awareness. We approach the previously warded-off experience. By staying with what emerges, collecting the pieces of what she knows, and being with them together, we gain more access to what she doesn't know. When she uses the word "devastated" to describe what she imagines she would feel if her husband left, I recognize this affect-laden word is probably a link to historical material. Here we can map the process on to the TORC, for the opportunity to recognize and link past and current experiences.

State 2 Phenomena: Emergence of Core Affect— Linking Current Experience to Its Historical Past

TH: What kind of vulnerability do you feel when he goes out of town? [**We explore her anxiety to regulate it, which reemerges as we get closer to historical material.**]

PT: I don't know . . . I know I would be devastated [**powerful affect-laden word**] if he didn't come back. And maybe . . . clearly, it's some subconscious level. [**Emergent realization**] I don't actually think he's not going to come back but on some level I think while he's gone I'm vulnerable. What if he didn't come back? [**New felt sense**] I've never thought about this, but he is the only man, after my dad, who I've ever loved this much. And my dad left . . . and if my husband leaves too that would be . . . (*wiping eyes*) [**Click of recognition . . . she makes the association between fear that emerges when her husband leaves to the moment when her father did leave.**]

TH: Ooh . . . just let yourself . . . [**Empathy**]

PT: I don't think he's going to, though . . . [**Bargaining: transitional affect**]

TH: Right . . . just to feel.

PT: But that's the fear. [**Realization of the old**]

TH: That's the fear. (*she is nodding*) [**Validation**] What if he leaves like Dad left . . . so this fear sounds like it's like Dad leaving . . . [**Linking the current experience with the past historical trauma: TORC.**]

PT: I think it is . . . (*wiping tears—head tilting*)

TH: Okay . . . oh (*gentle soothing tone of voice*) it's so important that we let yourself really feel this . . . [**Client breathes**] That would account for some really old feeling that didn't get comforted . . . so courageous. [**Affirming: linking a current experience with a past fear.**]

PT: Thank you. (*blows nose*)

TH: What vulnerability. [**Affirming that she is allowing herself to experience her emotion and the truth of her experience.**]

PT: (*nodding*)

TH: And that really happened.

PT: That did happen.

TH: So, what you are afraid of with your husband did happen when your dad left . . . [Names the overlay of historical material on current life experience.]

Link the current life experience to the past historical event. This is huge . . . the emergent realization that Gayle's current affective response with her husband fits what she feared, which actually did occur with her father in her past.

Metaprocessing New Awareness Leads to State 3 Transformational Affects

PT: Ooh . . . *(takes a deep breath)*

TH: Take your time, let yourself be with yourself here . . . [Following her breath, her lead]

PT: Thank you. [State 3 expression of feeling moved and expressing gratitude for the realization.]

TH: What do you feel as you say this? What's happening? [Metaprocessing the shift]

PT: That's an epiphany for me . . . it's probably so obvious . . . but I just never felt it . . . I never believed it.

TH: Feeling it makes all the difference . . . [Affirming what she did]

Undo unbearable aloneness. Gayle had disconnected from the memory of being alone with unbearable experience. Making this connection put the past in perspective. She experienced the deep realization that comes from body-based core emotion, which led her into State 3 transformational affects: mastery, feeling moved, and realization.

Stay with transformational experience to promote integration. In the next segment, I help Gayle saturate into her experience of knowing, which guides her realization about what plays out with her husband that stems from the historical traumatic departure of her dad. Staying with transformational experience harnesses neuroplasticity and promotes integration.

TH: So just feel yourself feeling what you know . . . let yourself feel it, see it . . . [Repeat to amplify and deepen.]

PT: Yeah . . . I am scared of that.

TH: Say it fully.

PT: I am scared that my husband would leave like my dad did . . . (*stays with the feeling*)

TH: Yeah . . . yeah . . . [**Affective resonance**]

PT: (*breathes, wipes eyes*)

TH: Yeah.

PT: So, what do I do with that? The fear doesn't go away, right? [**She is asking for my help.**]

TH: Come here though . . . Let's make room for the little girl whose dad left, and let her not be so alone with that right now . . . Can we somehow let her come in and really feel our care and desire to be with how devastating that is?

PT: Devastating . . . yeah . . .

TH: Yeah, can you see her, see yourself at that age? [**Initiating a portrayal**]

PT: I see a little girl who's very sad . . . and trying to be brave.

TH: Yeah . . . yeah . . . Can we be with her in some way and say you don't have to be brave right now?

PT: (*looks up*)

TH: And actually, really let yourself feel so sad . . . and you don't have to be alone with it . . . That's the thing because that little one had to be alone.

PT: Yeah. Definitely . . .

TH: So that's part of what you're up against right now . . .

PT: (*sweet smile*)

During the next few minutes, Gayle discovers what she would want to hear from her husband, which seems just right for her younger self, to bring comfort and care that had been sorely lacking.

State 2 Transformational Work: Connecting Self-to-Self Changes the SOE Triangle Configuration From Self-at-Worst to Self-at-Best

TH: Can you picture that? Letting someone say that to her? Can you see if she can receive that? "I have compassion for you and I'm so sorry that this happened to you . . ." Give her a minute with this and take your time . . . [**State 2: intrarelational work with the intervention of a mini portrayal to bring a corrective experience to the younger self.**] What's that like?

PT: I haven't done that before . . . say something to her and she acknowledges that she hears me. Before it's just me telling her things, but that's really nice . . . [From self-at-worst being talked at, to self-at-best being seen and heard: This is a corrective emotional and relational experience.]

TH: What's nice? [Metaprocess the new experience.]

PT: To connect . . . to have her . . . she just looked up at me and smiled . . . [Self-to-self connection; emotional transformation.]

TH: Ooh . . . Can you just drink in that looking up at you and smile?

Connect adult self with younger self. Here as Gayle connects with her younger self and her underlying attachment needs, she opens further. In the self-at-best configuration of the SOE triangle, through using her imaginal channel via the portrayal, she *sees* her younger self and her younger self responds *as seen.* This moment of meeting marks the moment of transformation: What was disconnected and "left behind" is now real and brought into connection, further transforming the past–current link on the TORC.

State 3: Transformational Affects

TH: That contact feels *so* necessary . . . [More affirmative reflection. Stay with, deepen, and honor this new corrective experience.]

PT: It does . . .

TH: Just feels precious to me . . . [State 3 healing affects: feeling moved]

PT: It does . . . thank you very much. [State 3: gratitude]

TH: You're welcome. What are you feeling thankful for right now? [Deepen and elaborate.]

PT: I feel tremendous gratitude that you're helping to guide me through this stuff. [Elaborating State 3: feeling gratitude] This is a tremendous piece of it . . . I think that if I have any issues in my marriage, this is the root of it. [State 4: core state declarative truth sense emerges]

TH: Yup. I love that you can know and say that—think of how far you've come in today's session. [Making explicit and celebrating the bigness of the change.]

PT: I know, it has!

TH: There's avoiding the vulnerability and now being able to acknowledge the connection between the fear of him going away . . .

PT: Or even just being intimate and letting my guard down. [More self-understanding. State 4: core state and open to seeing the other realistically and understanding herself better.]

TH: Um, yeah . . .

PT: I am prepared for him to leave, and I have done all the things for myself to prepare for when it happens. Like I believe it's a given that he is going to leave . . . [State 4: declarative; the truth sense. **She is speaking about the repetitive experience in her marriage from a new, expanded place of self-understanding, and from here she can recognize what is in her heart and truly is hers to navigate.**]

TH: So, let me just ask you: What do you want to say to your husband right now? [**I return to a concern she had raised earlier, to revisit this from the platform of the new place.**]

PT: That I'm sorry. I feel like I do this to him and then he leaves in a bad place feeling guilty and upset—like I'm taking something from him. [**Core state: As she reflects, she shifts from the SOE triangle representation of self-at-worst—compromised self—and now can perceive her husband from her SOE triangle representation of self-at-best—realistic other.**]

TH: Do you want to tell him what you're sorry for? [**Going for the specific learning.**]

PT: Not being able to articulate my feelings. [**The stage is set for effective action on behalf of herself—and shows here the potential corrective relational experience between her and her husband.**]

Summary. In this case illustration, I am focusing on helping this patient, Gayle, to move through the avoidant patterning that developed by way of her caregiver's ignoring and thus rejecting signals of her affective experience. Her adaptation to this way of relating by her parents created problems and strife in her marriage. The moment of meeting that occurs between her adult self and her younger self ignites the transformation of her internal working model. In the shock and devastation of her parent's divorce, her experience of being alone and unseen was encapsulated in her psyche and remained unprocessed through her adaptive avoidant strategy and defensive exclusion. When her adult self sees and offers compassion to her younger self, she gives her exactly the care and attention that is needed. By the look her younger self returns to the adult self, we know she receives it. The imaginal scene that occurred through the use of a portrayal is profoundly corrective, transforming her internal representations of self from "I am alone. No one sees me" into "I am seen, precious, and understood." The part of her that held her pain had been isolated and out of focus. When the older, wiser self shows up with just the right message, the younger self is grateful and welcoming of connection. In how Gayle reconnects with her adult self, we see how the younger self is untarnished. This exemplifies how under the right conditions, what is warded off in self-protection is available for awakening and integration. With a changed internal representation of Self, the internal representation of Other changes. The patient now sees her husband as someone with whom she wants to reveal her true experience, for greater mutual understanding and connection.

Healing Avoidant Attachment

Applying this vignette to the overall picture of healing avoidant attachment shows that what is broken is not the self but connection to the self. What went wrong when the individual was alone, suffering without recognition and attunement, can be repaired by the step-by-step, explicit exploration of the experience of connection to self in relationship with another. To heal the wounding that gives rise to avoidant patterning, we help patients restore their capacity to be in relationship with self and other. Establishing a capacity to tolerate vulnerability, their own and another's, enhances both the giving and receiving of responsive care. Through having corrective emotional and relational experiences, and exploring the changes through metatherapeutic processing, patients can transform their internalized representation of the self and their internalized representation of the other. By doing so, relational adaptive action comes to the fore.

Here are some of the main intervention pathways we showed in this chapter:

- Develop positive expectancies to offset the anticipation of rejection and negativity
- Affirm qualities that demonstrate the patient's core values
- Explore what happens in the present moment between therapist and patient
- Be on the lookout for therapist reactivities like feeling intimidated and intellectualizing
- Notice opportunities to use therapist metaskills of kindness and acceptance
- Develop the capacity for dyadic regulation to offset auto-regulation
- Focus into affect-laden words
- Feel into thoughts

- Affirm glimmers of attachment strivings, connections, vulnerability, and empathy
- Build the capacity to connect with and relate to another
- Build receptive affective capacity
- Develop a connection to somatic experience
- Recognize own needs and the needs of others

9

The Formation of Ambivalent/ Resistant Attachment (Grid 2)

I want you, nothing else but you.
—ANONYMOUS

Ambivalence/Resistance & the Hyperactivating Strategy

Ambivalent/resistant attachment is the inverse of avoidant attachment— opposite sides of the same coin of insecurity. As we continue to explore what happens when insecurity prevails in its many forms, it's important to remember that the origin of each strategy often goes back through generations, and yet, patterns can change according to the conditions of each current relationship. Ambivalence arises out of the conflict between wanting and not wanting. Resistance is the behavioral conflict between wanting and pushing away. Ambivalence and resistance grow when our attachment behavior (e.g., reaching for, crying, expressing need) fails to attract the consistent and reliable attention and response of our caregivers. The ambivalent/resistant pattern in children is correlated with inconsistent caregivers who have a preoccupied state of mind (Main et al., 1985) and are often excessively focused on their own needs and their own attachment figures (which can include both of their parents or their current primary partners), to the detriment of their children.

A child's attachment behavioral system is designed to attract the caregiver, who, in best-case scenarios, draws upon their innate, reciprocal caregiving behavioral system to provide the necessary comfort and care. However, in the pattern of ambivalent/resistant attachment, the caregiver's behavior is inconsistent, resulting from states of mind that are preoccupied and/or overwhelmed. These caregivers are available at times when *they can manage,* and at times when they are interested in caregiving, rather than in consistent response to their infant's signaling their need. When reaching out doesn't get the necessary or desired response, infants adjust accordingly—in this case, developing the adaptive strategy of keeping a close eye on their caregivers. Since they are not reliably monitoring the infant's signals, the infant monitors their caregiver's availability, so if they need them, the infant might be close enough to have access to them at those moments of unexpected availability (Cassidy, 2001; Main & Solomon, 1986). In this pattern the child is more focused on the caregiver than the caregiver is focused on the child.

Bretherton (2005) described the ambivalent/resistant pattern as the infant taking on more than their share of the burden of maintaining the connection. Attempting to reach a caregiver who is sometimes loving and responsive and sometimes not, children often rely on hyperactivating strategies: they exaggerate their distress, heighten their reaching, and in general they keep their attachment system on high alert. The farther away, distracted, and preoccupied the caregiver is, the more dysregulated and "needy"[1] the child may become, urgently seeking to get the caregiver's attention, clinging to the hope of getting help and love, protesting the absence of response and care.

The response of the attachment figure is based on *their* capacity to attend, rather than sensitivity to what the infant needs *at the time* the infant is in need. With a mind saturated by preoccupied thoughts and worries, caregivers are often self-absorbed and not easily accessible. Thus, infants have difficulty getting their caregivers' attention and lose trust that they can attract the care they need. When the caregiver does turn toward them, the infants are hard to settle and have difficulty receiving soothing and comfort. It may be that the arms that finally reach for them are less than adequate or are ill timed or the infant's capacity to receive is tainted, as repeated disappointment and the risk of losing their attachment figure's attention is so great.

To understand how these patterns develop, we turn to the early studies of caregiver–infant interactions. Since the individuals in treatment with us are adults, the patterns we are working with tend to have been in place for at least two decades and usually more. To get a close picture of characteristic experiences that influence how an ambivalent/resistant pattern of attachment forms, we look at some of the depictions of babies and their mothers from the early research. Learning what to see in our patients and how to imagine what they experienced when they were infants and young children can be informed by the impressions shaped by these studies.

Early Observations

In Mary Ainsworth's (1967) early observations of babies in Uganda, she categorized what we now understand as ambivalent/resistant attachment as insecure attachment, in contrast to the babies who exhibited secure attachment and distinct from those babies she initially thought were nonattached (who we now call avoidant). With her earliest criteria as frequency of crying, Ainsworth noted that the "insecure" babies were fussier than the secure babies. Many of these children's mothers were troubled and anxious themselves. When meeting to discuss their child-rearing practices, the mothers of the "insecure" babies were often more interested in having someone to talk to for themselves rather than talking about their babies.

In contrast, some of the mothers of secure babies were anxious, yet their anxiety was often directly related to their children. They were motivated to become involved in the Uganda study to learn how to care for their child (Ainsworth, 1967). Demonstrating Fosha's (2000b) description of the secure pattern, these mothers of secure babies were feeling and dealing, while relating. They dealt with their anxiety about child-rearing by taking advantage of Ainsworth's study. The secure mothers were often seen delighting in their child and enjoying the opportunity to talk about their child. Ainsworth repeatedly observed that the onset of attachment corresponded with the children taking initiative to connect with their mothers. The secure children used their mothers as a base from which to explore and sought her as a haven of safety when they were alarmed.

In the cases of babies she saw as insecure (i.e., ambivalent/resistant), Ainsworth (1967) noted how the mothers had difficulty soothing them. She observed that "there seemed to be a vicious spiral in which the babies' fussy demands exasperated the mother, who then overtly or covertly rejected the baby, who then in turn responded to the rejection by anxiety and by increasing his demands" (p. 392). She describes the crying and restlessness of one of these babies, Suliamani:

> He sat on his mother's lap sometimes fussing, sometimes merely vocalizing. Finally, he began to cry in earnest. The cry turned into a tempery scream. His mother tried to soothe him, talking to him, and rocking him. There was a perfunctory quality to her soothing, and before long she slung him over her back and rocked him there. This treatment did not quiet him, however, so finally she gave him the breast—he immediately stopped crying and began to suckle.

It appeared even by 25 weeks, that a tense and insecure relationship has grown up between them. His mother had no confidence in being able to soothe him and was made anxious by his fussing. She did not offer him the breast every time he cried, and yet she could find no other reliable method of quieting him (pp. 219–220).

In the Uganda study, Ainsworth observed how the child's security could change, for better or worse, depending on the conditions of the home, familial relationships, and life circumstances (Ainsworth, 1967; Hesse & Main, 1999). In the case of Suliamani, when the senior wife went away and his mother was much less stressed, he appeared more secure. Even in the early observations, Ainsworth tracked how attachment status changes not only by relationship but by how each relationship is affected circumstantially according to environmental conditions.

Baltimore Home Visits Correlated to the Strange Situation Procedure

In the Baltimore home observations, Ainsworth studied caregiver–infant interactions to investigate the different characteristics of the mother's caregiving behaviors and how this influenced the baby's development of secure and insecure attachment. Babies exhibiting patterns of resistance/ambivalence were seen to show more separation distress at home and in the Strange Situation. At home the babies seen as ambivalent/resistant were noted to cry more frequently than the secure babies. The secure babies' cries were noticeably clearer and more varied, and they showed more subtle forms of nonverbal communication than the other babies (Ainsworth et al., 1978, p. 125).

Mothers[2] of the ambivalent/resistant babies were observed to be less responsive to crying and other signals the babies made to express their needs. Although not rejecting like the group of mothers of the avoidant babies, nor as compulsive or lacking in emotional expression, these mothers were often lacking the fine sense of timing in responding to their babies that was exhibited by mothers of secure infants. They were seen as less comfortable holding their babies; adding to the picture that their experience of close bodily contact was not as consistently positive and pleasurable as the contact experienced by the secure infants and mothers (Ainsworth et al., 1978). In fact, one of Ainsworth's (1967) findings was that the mother's enjoyment of holding her baby and nursing her baby was central to the development of security.

Consequently, the babies classified as ambivalent/resistant lacked confidence and ease with their mother's accessibility and holding. For instance, they would protest if their mother's pickup was ill timed (i.e., if she did not pick them up when they wanted to be picked up or were put down when they wanted to be held or if she played with them when they wanted to be picked up). Related to these misattuned interactions, these babies became frustrated, showed angry ambivalence manifesting in clinging behavior— yet slowness at being soothed. They also were less likely to use their mothers as a secure base from which to explore, which points to how these babies' initiative to learn about their surroundings was often underdeveloped. That's why Fosha (2000b) dubbed this style "feeling and reeling" (i.e., these babies became frustrated, showed angry ambivalence manifesting in clinging behaviors), "but not dealing" (i.e., these babies' initiative to learn about their surroundings was often underdeveloped).

The mothers' inconsistent responsiveness resulted in their babies having more anxiety in their attachment with her. They protested angrily when what they wanted wasn't met. Some of them grew passive. Ainsworth et al. (1978/2015) noted the discrepancy between what the babies wanted and what they expected to receive and keenly surmised that their anxiety was based on fearing that "they will not get enough of what they want—in contrast to the avoidant baby who fears what they want" (p. 128). When the mother's responsiveness to their baby is badly timed or insufficient, the babies come to distrust the mother's availability and reliability.

In the Baltimore home observations, the mother–infant dyadic interactions were the focus of the study. In the Strange Situation, the infant was the primary focus of observation about how they responded to the stress of separation followed by reunion. Not surprisingly, the ambivalent/resistant babies were distressed upon the mother's departure and did not settle when she returned. When she picked them up, they sometimes squirmed uncomfortably in her lap, resisting being held. Furthermore, when they were put down, they continued to fuss and cling. If the mother pointed the child toward toys, they did not engage. Main (2000) pronounced that distress appears meaningless when, from the outset of the Strange Situation, the child is distressed and continues to be so throughout the separation and reunion scenarios. Sometimes the separation episodes had to be cut short; yet again, even with the mother's return, the infant did not calm easily.

Similar to the insecure avoidant infant, Main saw the ambivalent/resistant strategy as organized inflexible attention; the infant was focused on only one aspect of the environment to cope with the stress of the Strange Situation. In contrast to the avoidant infant, the ambivalent/resistant infant maintained focus on their attachment figure to the exclusion of exploring their surroundings (Main, 2000). Yet, despite their mother's return and attempt to comfort them, they were unable to make use of her as a safe haven. The child's resistance to settling with their mother was demonstrative of how they expected not to be satisfied or expected that they would not have enough of what they wanted. Here, we can see how the deep-seated dynamic of unrest turns into the self experience of feeling unsoothable, which often follows the ambivalent/resistant child into adulthood, where they continue to look outside of themselves for relief, yet are not hopeful that relief can be had.

With the ambivalent/resistant pattern, an inability to turn toward the self stems from the inability to rely on the other. When the caregiver's inconsistency and unreliability are the norm, the lack of a sensitive response generates a pattern of not knowing how to listen and tend to the self's own signals. Without timely and attuned care, the infant's need goes untended, and the signaling behavior itself loses meaning. Unfortunately, this gap between signal and response hinders the development of communication between the caregiver and child, like that which develops in a secure infant with a sensitive and responsive caregiver. As Bowlby allegedly said, "What cannot be communicated to the mother (caregiver) cannot be communicated to the self." Ainsworth noted that secure babies and their caregivers enjoy subtle levels of back-and-forth communication. Caregiver attunement helps the infant to develop the capacity for refining verbal and nonverbal signaling, so that natural call-and-response patterns develop to the mutual satisfaction of both caregiver and infant.

With the ambivalent/resistant pattern, the infant may resort to screaming for attention ("reeling"). When they do break through to the caregiver, the distressed call has often obscured the discrete signal, or the caregiver's preoccupation or overwhelm clouds their ability to accurately perceive and interpret the meaning of the infant's signal. For example, the caregiver misreads the baby's fussy bids for attention as a sign of fatigue and puts them to bed or quashes the baby's protest rather than recognizing something was missed (Ainsworth et al., 1978/2015). Thus the child is frustrated. For the infant, having these kinds of repeated, unfulfilled experiences develops expectancies that they are incapable of attracting a satisfying response—they lose out on the development of trusting themselves and trusting their innate signaling to draw the help that they need.

When unable to obtain the consistent, appropriate response from their caregiver, reaching for the other becomes *needing* the other desperately (i.e., nondiscriminatingly, which is another shift away from the awareness of what is specifically needed). The desperation for the caregiver's attention is so fraught with the child's anticipation of not receiving a response that reaching for the other becomes reeling, and overrides what may have begun as the child's needing soothing for a momentary discomfort. Unfortunately, what is internalized are feelings of unworthiness and inadequacy. Thus, the pattern takes root. When inconsistency and unreliability are the norm, the lack of optimal response generates a pattern in the baby of both giving up on listening to the self's own signals while also not trusting the other to provide a suitable response.

Herein lies boundary confusion. Just as self-reliance in the avoidant pattern has a pseudo quality, there is a similarity in how the self, who is preoccupied with the other, is pseudo relational (i.e., not truly relational). The caregiver who is entrenched in their own preoccupation is impermeable to the needs of their child. The child may be hollering for their caregiver's attention. Instead of reflecting the child's feelings and relating to what is happening from the child's perspective, the caregiver, self-absorbed, anxious, and/or overwhelmed, imposes their own experience of the situation. For example, they might feel frustrated that the baby's clamoring for attention is happening when they, the caregiver, are already having a really hard day. Instead of reaching tenderly for their child and sensing what is needed, they may pick them up abruptly and bounce them on their knee, with pseudo joy barely masking what is an urgent plea to calm down.

Inadvertently, the caregiver is communicating their distress and lack of ability to be sensitive to the child's needs. Unable to attune to what the child needs and provide the appropriate response, the caregiver instead transmits their turmoil rather than contact or reassurance. Thus, they add their own anxiousness to their child's discomfort. Unfortunately, the child becomes overly immersed in the caregiver's experience and internalizes the static of the caregiver's state of mind. Unable to have their need met contingently may well lead to boundary confusion, and subsequent difficulties in self-understanding.

Fonagy and Target (1997) conceptualize that "if secure attachment is the outcome of successful containment, insecure attachment may be seen as the infant's identification with the caregiver's defensive behavior" (p. 686). They refer to the following passage from Crittenden to describe the insecure ambivalent pattern.

> The preoccupied (E) caregiver may represent the infant's state with amplification and insufficient marking or complicated by responses to the parent's ambivalent preoccupation with her own experience, so much so that the symbolic potential of the exchange is lost . . . the infant internalizes the caregiver's attitude and "this dyssynchrony" becomes the content of the experience of the self. (Crittenden, 1994, p. 89)

The preoccupation and anxiety that originates in the parent's state of mind has now been transferred to the child. Rather than receiving reflection and an appropriate response, the child's experience becomes subsumed in the parent's experience, and the parent's chaotic helplessness becomes the child's as well.

When a child has the experience of being met by their caregiver with a sensitive and appropriate response, the child grows to feel confident that they can influence what happens to them. They also grow a trust in themselves to ask for what they need, and trust that the other, their caregiver, is available for the provision of that specific care and comfort. Instead, in the case of the ambivalent/resistant attachment pattern, the caregiver's preoccupation and overwhelm interfere with the child's being able to predict whether their wants and needs will be met. Thus, the natural growth of self-awareness, self-confidence, and self-agency is thwarted by the child's lack of being able to effectively influence what happens to them.

Clinical Example of the Preoccupied State of Mind

Next, we hear from a psychotherapy patient I have seen over many years. Initially, the patient presented with an ambivalent pattern of attachment, high anxiety, and marital dissatisfaction that centered around her longing for her husband to be different: more communicative, more expressive, more sensitive to her needs. In the following vignette from a late treatment session, the patient explores her experience in relationship to her mother's preoccupied state of mind. She notices her current self-awareness, compared to when she was a child. The patient recognizes that she herself has changed. I am choosing this slice of reflection for two reasons. First, because the patient clearly describes the preoccupied state of mind of her mother. And second, because it shows how the child is caught between feeling criticized on the one hand, and on the other, is trying to figure out how to please and help her mother. This dilemma illustrates how boundaries get confused between child and mother and how the child can become immersed in the mother's state of mind, and becomes preoccupied with her at the expense of connecting with their own self experience.

Clinical Vignette 9A: "Seeing the Truth of How She Really Is"

The patient, Sandy, is intrigued to remember that as a child, despite the experience of feeling criticized and judged, she longed to please her mother. The desire to please is one of the traits identified in the AAI discourse of preoccupied speakers. We enter this segment as the patient feels sadness related to the lack of being seen and acknowledged. However, instead of feeling sad from the helpless perspective of her younger self not receiving her mother's attention, Sandy feels sad acceptance to recognize how her mother is unable to give an attuned, empathic response. [AEDP State 3: mourning the self. In her self-at-best, effective self, Sandy sees the other, her mother, realistically.]

SANDY (PATIENT, PT): When I see her and she looks at me, I don't know, Karen, like you know people . . . she looks you over . . .

THERAPIST (TH): (*nodding*) Wow, and what's that like? What happens inside you when she looks you over? How about "she looks me over"? [**Inviting patient to explore her experience and shift from the general "you" to her own sense of "me."**]

PT: It's different now, I'm aware of it and I think it feels . . . or I know it feels . . . [**Her shift from "I think it feels" to "I know it feels" shows growing confidence in her self-awareness. She is able to tune into feeling for herself.**]

TH: Hmm.

PT: Like I can see myself at different times in my life feeling differently. Like I can see myself when I was younger feeling really sad about it (*right hand on heart as left reaches out, gesturing*), feeling not accepted, trying to fix myself, if I could get the right outfit on, if I could lose weight or have the right job—something that she could talk about me in a way that's good—or if I could help her more and if I could just listen to her longer

and longer and longer and figure it out for her . . . [here we see the experience of her younger self caught in the pattern of wanting to please her
mother, wanting to listen and wanting to help her . . . and not focusing on
her own experience] and then like now maybe I feel like it's different. Like
I was really aware, she's looking me over, but I didn't feel so confused.
I feel more and more like this is (pause), maybe, I don't know, I feel like
I spent less time thinking about it in a way . . . [Distinguishing that now
she is less caught up in thinking about her mother's view, which leads to
less confusion.]

As Sandy is now capable of exploring her inner experience, she notices
how she felt when she was younger and received this kind of evaluative
look. Her younger self tried to figure out what she needed to do, or be, to
find acceptance in her mother's eyes, whether it was fixing something about
herself or being available to help her mother. In the repetition of "longer
and longer and longer," I hear the circular dialogue and the feeling of being
trapped. I respond by reflecting the patient and elaborating her current
experience by recognizing that Sandy's lack of taking her mother's view
of herself was related to her increased awareness of her own experience
instead of preoccupation with her mother.

TH: You were less looking at yourself through her eyes and trying to get
   it right. It was like you stayed in yourself. [Reflecting and affirming her
   realization of what's changed.]
PT: Oh, oh (looking up) yeah . . .
TH: Cuz looking at yourself through her eyes wasn't an accurate reflection of you . . . didn't give you something, it more took you into her
   view . . . and then you tried to please that. [This is an example of how the
   child becomes overly immersed in the mother's experience.]
PT: Right . . . I think I felt being more set, firm . . . like I felt more, like I
   know the word "grounded" is a common thing, but I think I felt more like
   (arms moving down her sides close to her body), just like I wasn't penetrable or as
   easily permeable. [A somatic shift in her experience of self.]
TH: You stayed in yourself. Your boundaries were less porous to her. [Val-
   idating, emphasizing what the patient is realizing. Together we are co-
   constructing the narrative.]
PT: Yeah, yeah, and like she kept asking me, "come over to my house, come
   over to my house . . . I want you to spend time with me alone." And I

know what that means. That means like come over so I can have this conversation with you like I've had for 20 years. And I said no.

TH: Wow.

PT: Like I said it wasn't going to work and I said to her "let's enjoy our time here at Cathy's—my sister"—because she starts getting me in the corner and she starts talking to me like "I don't know what to do, I don't know what to do with the house, I don't want to live in the country." (*hands now circling and coming together in front of her*) "Help me decide what to do with my life. None of my kids want me," and she starts kind of crying . . . I was like, "Let's enjoy being together right now." You know? [**Rather than joining her mother's preoccupied worries and reeling about the future, the patient set a boundary by saying no, and repeated her invitation to enjoy being together in the present moment.**]

TH: Mm-hmm.

Here, instead of being caught in the *longer and longer* conversations, the patient was aware of her mother's pattern and knew the boundary she wanted to set and how to express herself clearly and kindly. The description of her mother's speaking shows preoccupied discourse; she is reeling as she moves from one topic to the next, with a helpless passivity trying to enlist her daughter's attention and help. We can see how the patient recognized the difference between how she feels now and the spinning she felt as a child, when she was caught up and preoccupied with her mother's view of her. In current time, the patient was able to name her boundary and respond to her mother with clear, caring redirection. Simply stated. No protest.

The above vignette shows that Sandy was "feeling and dealing, while relating." She has differentiated and is aware of her own personhood. The gold of this session was the patient's exploring how she coped in a fresh and autonomous way, in this current, yet ages-old exchange with her mother. Highlighting and exploring such moments of newfound growth and clarity is one of the ways AEDP therapy leans into transformation and promotes our patients' transformational process.

To complete this chapter, we describe how patients with this pattern arrive to psychotherapy. Additionally, we introduce markers of the preoccupied state of mind as identified through the AAI (Main et al., 1985) and elaborated by Fonagy and Target (2007) about what is noteworthy in the patient's patterns of discourse.

The Initial Presentation

Many individuals who have patterns of ambivalent/resistant attachment are motivated to seek out psychotherapy by problems in their primary relationships. The struggle is often about finding the "right" relationship or feeling satisfied in the relationship they're in. Their partners are described as elusive, rejecting, inadequate, not fully available, closed, or walled off, making them difficult to reach or the patient not feeling special. Excessive focus on the other, sensing something is "off" with the other, and the distress this causes provides clues to the patient's earlier attachment-related trauma. One presenting issue is the sense of "I am often choosing the unavailable person, who comes on strong and then seems to vanish. What am I doing wrong?" Another complaint is "I can't seem to live with them, yet I can't live without them." While real problems may exist in the relationship, working them out is riddled with clinging and protest, desperation about not having the love or attention of this most flawed other and a helplessness to bring about the necessary changes.

Here we see the patient's excessive focus on the other. Additionally, and even more to the heart of the presenting issue, is the patient's lack of focus on—and developed awareness about—their own internal experience. When an individual comes to treatment, another significant aspect of their presentation is the fallout we described earlier in how through repeated experiences of the caregiver's misattunement and/or inconsistency, the child lost trust in their capacity to affect their environment—their caregiver—to get what they need. The cost here is that the patient lacks self-awareness, and self-confidence, resulting from their continued turning toward the other instead of tuning into themselves. Often, they have difficulty with self-acceptance.

Other clues about their pattern of attachment comes through their speech, which can be pressured, driven by the hope "If I can hurry up and 'get it all out,' I will feel relieved." Some words come easily, too easily, and feel more like a wall of words. In this case, the words lead me away from connection to the patient, rather than toward greater connection. I can even get lost by the associative links, bold hints of self-deprecation, aggravation, confusion, and/or complaints about the ways others behave. Identifying these themes as indicative of the patient's state of mind from the outset, or as early as possible, can be organizing and evoke compassion for psychotherapists.

As we've been addressing throughout this chapter, it is helpful to understand that our patients who come into treatment with the ambivalent/resistant pattern of attachment were once infants who grew up with a parent whose state of mind was preoccupied. To describe this state of mind, we turn to the adults who classify as preoccupied on the AAI (i.e., who have a preoccupied state of mind regarding attachment). Their AAI interviews reveal an excessive, confused preoccupation with their attachment figures that tends toward passivity, anger, or dependency. Though they are adults, their comments are rife with complaints about their parent yet are often followed by their struggles to please them. Some speakers flip into their parent's voice as they address themselves during the interview. The discourse contains lengthy descriptions that are associative, entangled, and/or confusing (Main et al., 2008). Many infants who developed an ambivalent/resistant pattern of attachment grow into adults who exhibit a preoccupied state of mind. So the descriptions here are fitting for psychotherapists to recognize in our adult patients. My term "wall of words" describes the preoccupied narrative, which can feel more like a barrier than an access point to communication.

Fonagy & Target (2007) describe how preoccupation shows up in patients' gestural discourse in psychotherapy with run-on, entangled, or unfinished sentences. They describe that the expressed gesture is "one of needing to hold on, yet not being satisfied." Losing track of the question and rambling on to irrelevant topics is a mental gesture that expresses a feeling of being lost or perhaps the very act of losing. . . . "Sorry I lost my thread" or "What was that question again?" (p. 442). When these phrases come from the patient in psychotherapy sessions, they are illustrating some of the challenges of preoccupation. When the therapist feels lost, such lostness can be a marker of our need to step in and find an orientation with the patient. Fonagy and Target identify discourse that contains a tangled web of complaint, where there is both struggling and pushing away. Yet, despite pushing away, the patient is not letting go, preventing the possibility of separation (Fonagy & Target, 2007). This description is quite apropos for a patient whose presenting problem is serious discontent in a relationship; the patient may complain about their partner's behavior and express concern about relational incompatibility. Still yet, they have tremendous difficulty seeing a way *out* of the relationship or a way *through* to resolving conflict in the relationship.

When sitting with a patient who is presenting a preoccupied state of mind, I look for signs of the infant who did their best to adapt and developed patterns of ambivalence and/or resistance. Here, we have a clear window through which to see that how the child was treated is how they have come to treat themselves and others. I want to hold what is tangled in the light of the desire to understand how these patterns came to make sense in the first place. Sometimes I try to imagine the little one inside, wondering about their experience, imagining the turmoil of needing attention and not being tended in a timely or appropriate way. With the ambivalent/resistant pattern, we are often facing the person's expectancies that they will not be heard and attended, and the hyperactivating strategies they developed to try to reach their preoccupied caregivers, which have followed them into adulthood.

10
Working to Transform Patterns of Ambivalent/Resistant Attachment (Grids 1 and 3)

The more she learns about the nature of the creature she is caring
for the easier and more satisfying she will find it. . . .
—(BOWLBY 1953/1965, P. 20)

Ambivalence/Resistance & the Hyperactivating Strategy

As psychotherapists, our way of being with our patients is just as important as the interventions we choose, and the interventions we choose are determined by our understanding of what people need. In this chapter, we continue to apply the grids to treatment planning and intervening with our patients who present with an ambivalent/resistant pattern of attachment. These patients' insecure attachment has compromised their trust that they can get enough of what they need in attachment relationships. We refer to Grid 1, The Configuration of the Secure Attachment Pattern (see Chapter 5), to identify secure ways of being that can help us to set conditions to establish a secure base for treatment. Additionally, Grid 1 helps us recognize and affirm characteristics of secure functioning, especially with regard to building affective competence and self-agency when they arise with these patients. Also, we've added Grid 5, The Configuration of the Ambivalent/Resistant Attachment Pattern and Clinical Markers & Interventions, to accompany this chapter.

Grid 5 combines markers of 10 aspects of the ambivalent/resistant attachment patterns from Grid 2, such as characteristic fears: anxiety and characteristic defenses, arousal of the attachment system, self–other

TABLE 10.1 Grid 5. The Configuration of the Ambivalent/Resistant Attachment Pattern and Clinical Markers & Interventions

	CONFIGURATION OF AMBIVALENT/ RESISTANT ATTACHMENT	AMBIVALENT/ RESISTANT	CLINICAL MARKERS AND INTERVENTIONS	AMBIVALENT/ RESISTANT
1	Caregiver characteristics: state of mind with respect to attachment	• Preoccupied	Patient state of mind Therapist common reactivities	• Preoccupied • Overwhelmed • Agitated • Overinvolved • Not impacted
2	Caregiver characteristics: behavioral hallmarks	• Inconsistent • Unreliable • Abandoning	Therapist metaskills to counter caregiver hallmarks and therapist common reactivities	• Focus • Firmness/ directiveness • Care
3	Response to arousal of the attachment system	• Hyperactivation	Desirable adaptive action	• Affirm self-adaptive action tendencies
4	Seeds of resilience	• Maintains relationships at any cost	Goals of interventions	• Containment/self-regulation • Connect with abandoned parts of self • Self-agency/self-worth
5	Characteristic nervous system activation and affect regulation	• External regulation • Underregulates affect • Fight	Working with nervous system and affect regulation	• Down regulate

6	Defense: Characteristic defenses against relatedness	Defense vs. relatedness: • Wall of words • Preoccupied • Clings/protests	Working with defenses against relatedness	• Contain tangential speech • Offer explicit help • Cultivate connection to self experience • Affirm or amplify glimmers of self-regulating, self-care, self-knowing
	&			
	characteristic defenses against emotion	Defense vs. emotion: • Emotionality • Overly immersed • Predicts the future	Working with defenses against emotion	• Distinguish emotionality from emotion • Empathize with core affect • Connect emotion with present experience
7	Anxiety: characteristic fears	• Abandonment • Uncertainty	Working with anxiety	• Build capacity for self-regulation
8	Patterns of affective competence (or lack thereof)	• Feeling—and reeling—but not dealing	Building affective competence	• Think about feelings • Distinguish emotionality from emotion
9	Self–Other relational patterning	• Other-reliant • "Moving against" • Boundary confusion	Working with Self–Other relational patterning	• Differentiate self and other • Develop capacity to internalize soothing • Build receptive affective capacity
10	Internal experience & external reality: disconnects (à la Fonagy)	• Psychic equivalence: • Internal and external worlds are equated	Connecting internal experience & external reality	• Build self-reflective capacity • Understand self

(Pando-Mars, 2016)

(*Note.* These are nonexhaustive lists)

relational patterning, and so on, with their corresponding interventions, desirable adaptive action tendencies, and goals of interventions from Grid 3 to help tailor our treatment and interventions accordingly. In order for our psychotherapy to be effective, our way of being with our patients must foster the co-creating of new, positive experiences that help them grow confident and competent with us as an attachment figure, so that together we can establish a reliable secure base for experiential exploration.

To prepare for engaging with patients who arrive with the ambivalent/resistant pattern and a preoccupied state of mind, Grid 5 also includes both potential therapist common reactivities and also the requisite metaskills, which are discussed throughout this chapter. We acknowledge that although our nervous systems are wired to connect and to care, we all have our patterns, and, in some moments, despite our sincere wanting to help, we as psychotherapists can find ourselves in an unintended reaction to our patients. In this chapter's section on the therapist stance, we have identified therapist common reactivities that may occur and how to work with them (see also Chapter 6, pp. 188–189). To counter the potential disruption of therapist reactivities, as well to provide intentional holding and sensitivity that can give a therapeutic contrast to inconsistency and unreliability (the inconsistency and unreliability of the original attachment figures), we have pinpointed several therapist metaskills (see Chapter 6, pp. 190–192).

In my experience, being aware of therapist common reactivities and also of the necessary metaskills allows me to catch myself earlier when I go off track with my patient. Having specific suggestions to recognize and deal with the anxiety contagion prevalent with ambivalence/resistance helps me to self-right (i.e., self-correct) more quickly. Using our left-brain reflection on what is happening is a helpful coping skill both overall for managing anxiety and also specifically for treating ambivalent/resistant attachment. In contrast, when working with someone with an avoidant attachment, using our right brains to resonate with our patients' underlying affect can help them to connect with themselves and with us. Our intention here is to begin with the premise that our therapeutic container comprises two human beings, and how we meet and what we do with our meeting is as important as the skills and interventions that we subsequently provide.

Goals of Treatment

When working with someone who has an ambivalent/resistant pattern of attachment and a preoccupied state of mind, building their capacity for self-care is a central aim of treatment. Grid 3 highlights *self*-action tendencies as desirable adaptive actions for this pattern. Self-action tendencies are (a) becoming aware of one's own needs, (b) learning how to express them, and (c) being willing to stand up for oneself (Fosha, 2000). I would also add to adaptive self-action tendencies (d) the patient's learning to distinguish between their wants and their needs, and (e) how to tend to their unmet childhood needs. Healing involves a deep restoring of the capacity to listen inside and to care for and trust oneself, which ultimately improves relationships with significant others. For therapists, recognizing and affirming markers of self-action tendencies is vital for healing patterns of ambivalent/resistant attachment.

Helping our patients to increase self-regulation and containment and to connect with abandoned parts of the self that got lost in the fray builds their self-agency, self-efficacy, and self-worth. Eileen Russell (2021) has recognized the importance of the *agentic self* in healing from disrupted developmental processes. She defines agency as having a felt sense of mattering and being able to affect what happens, which is an essential component of healing ambivalent/resistant patterning. Also included in goals of interventions is recognizing how the patient impacts others. This awareness grows from differentiating between self and other, thoughts from feelings, and past from present.

As I've been working with this chapter, I noticed that my notes and parts of the first draft were repetitive, sprawling, and tangential. I could see evidence of activation, difficulty focusing, and getting lost in the words. Viewing my writing has been both fascinating and humbling; in these pages about working with the pattern of ambivalent attachment, I witnessed elements of how the ambivalent discourse appears in the AAI! Of course, it makes sense that to engage with the topic of ambivalent attachment, and the clinical experiences that follow, my writing would reflect some ambivalence/resistance and activation. I share this in the spirit of transparency and encourage psychotherapists to pay attention to ourselves in the process of being with our patients. After all, our attachment systems are hardwired in us, at the ready to be activated; they are giving us clues all the time. Putting these clues to use, by recognizing our own signals, is a key part of regulation—which is crucial in working through hyperactivating strategies with our patients.

In the next section, we proceed to setting the stage for treatment, followed by referencing the grids and some of the AEDP triangle schemas to orient and organize what we do. Then, in the following sections, we continue to discuss intervention sequences. We also share clinical vignettes that illustrate working with specific aspects of ambivalent/resistant attachment and show progression toward healing and transformation.

From the Get-Go

When our patients present with hyperactivating strategies, the intensity can be activating for psychotherapists, and we need to work on slowing down and anxiety regulation in ourselves, alongside our patients. Here, similar to the patients with avoidance who use deactivating strategies, addressing attachment needs of being seen and responded to in patients with hyperactivating strategies is necessary. As we discussed in the previous chapter, the avoidant pattern requires up regulating and building awareness. Connection to self is essential for patients to grow beyond the shutdown and what R. D. Laing (1969, quoted in Bromberg, 2011, p. 31) refers to as "unawareness" that follows the dismissing minds of their early caregivers. In contrast, when working with the hyperactivating strategies of the ambivalent/resistant pattern we focus on down regulating and containment to help patients slow down and begin to deal with the separation distress/fears of abandonment and uncertainty that are so prevalent with this pattern.

Communicating readiness to help. From the get-go, psychotherapists must situate ourselves so that we are available to help. In addition to an appropriate response, another necessary aspect of sensitivity that Ainsworth et al. (1978/2015) defined in the caregiving scales, is promptness of response. A major hallmark of inconsistent caregiving is the timing of the caregiver's response—more based on what suits them or what they are capable of in the moment, rather than based on the timing of what the infant needs when the infant needs it. AEDP Maxim 10, Going "Beyond Mirroring" to Helping (Fosha, 2000b), is central to working with ambivalent/resistant patterning: it involves being aware of what the patient needs in the moment and being available to help them in the moment. In the beginning of treatment, encouraging the patient to slow down, take a breath, and listen inside, helps them connect with how they are feeling.

Communicating to the patient what we are seeing. Second, from the get-go, finding a way to communicate what we are seeing to the patient is particularly helpful. In doing so, they can experience being seen. By reflecting what we hear, we help them feel heard. As shown in the vignette in the preceding chapter, even in later stages of treatment, reflecting the patient's words and gestures, and picking up the themes of their dialogue, provides holding and being together. And in AEDP, we privilege doing so in an affirmative fashion, heightening either the adaptive nature of patients' responses or empathy and compassion for the difficulties they are facing. Showing the patient that they are not alone, but rather, they are being seen and being heard, can substantiate for them that there is an attachment figure present and available. When this happens from the get-go and over time, we help the patient to have an experience of a consistent and reliable other, who they can predict will be seeking to understand them and helping them to understand themselves.

Helping our patients by engaging with focused levels of attention and care requires that the therapist take an active therapeutic stance.

The Therapist Stance: Therapist Common Reactivities and Metaskills

In AEDP, the therapist stance is not neutral; we do not stay hidden without expression when we meet our patients. As Fosha (2017b) said, we do not do attachment-focused therapy with a still face: therapist's affect is an important part of the therapeutic field. And here, working with our patients who present with an ambivalent resistant pattern of attachment, this is all the more central. We welcome them with openness and interest, conveying our availability and willingness to help. From our first moments of meeting the patient, we are considering how to set conditions for co-establishing safety and building a secure base for our work together. We listen to what the patients want that propel them to seek treatment, and we notice how we feel moved by them and their quest for feeling loved and known, and we let our response be knowable. How they enter the process of psychotherapy tells us something about them; how we engage tells them something about us.

Growing up with a preoccupied caregiver gave our patients a pervasive fear of not getting enough proper attention and a contingent, timely response. So when they arrive to psychotherapy they may need our help and direction to learn how to make use of our relational engagement. The consequence of the parenting they received often manifests in difficulty

understanding their own signals of distress, what they mean, how to communicate them, and even less how to use those signals of distress to inform
the kind of care that they need. The hope for connection and help is often
shielded by anticipations of being missed and mistreated, and a negative
appraisal of self. From the start, an active therapist stance is crucial to provide accompaniment and guidance to counter those expectancies and help
to set the course of the session in the right direction.

As we begin to engage, we might hear how the patient is driven by
anxiety, falls back on a hyperactivating strategy (i.e., exaggerated complaints, self-reports of clinging behaviors, excessive focus on a partner's
intentions and motivations) and little or no focus on their own internal life.
Or they speak in a preoccupied and unclear manner. When this happens,
it is important for us to pay attention to how we respond. Here is where
therapist metaskills and therapist common reactivity come into the picture
(Chapter 6, pp. 188–192). When the distress related to ambivalent/resistant
patterning arises, psychotherapists might need to check in with ourselves
"Are we feeling able to stay present and facilitative with our patients?" or
"Are we feeling thwarted?" Sometimes when our patients speak intensely
and describe dramatic displays of clinging and protest behavior, we may
be subject to a blind spot, caught up in a reaction of feeling overwhelmed
or agitated. Our own nervous system might activate; getting triggered, we
might find ourselves off center. Or when our patient is speaking breath-
lessly, shifting from one association to the next, we may see issues mounting
before us, and yet, overwhelmed by the avalanche of problems, have difficulty choosing an entry point.

Therapist common reactivities. We have identified that with an ambivalent/resis-
tant presentation, these *therapist common reactivities* may occur: feeling overwhelmed, agitated, not impacted by the patient. If we find ourselves caught
in one of these compromised states, our awareness of these reactions can
alert us to pay attention to what is happening. As soon as possible, we
need to regulate and ground ourselves, and then we have the option to
consciously draw upon a suitable metaskill to help us orient to what is
needed to help the patient. The patient is showing up the only way they
know, but we have options—and by gathering our focus and calming our
own nervous system, we can set ourselves on track to meet our patient and
provide structure to help them to establish connection with themselves
and with us.

Therapist metaskills. If we do find that we are challenged, we can hopefully quiet our self-critical voices by remembering that we all are susceptible to potential reactions that might arise in a flash and set us back. The important element here is not the setback but rather our return. As soon as possible, we engage our willingness to explore what is happening and how we can help our patients to let us help them. Having selected *metaskills* can remind us of what may be needed to counter the above common reactivities; being focused, firm, directive, and caring can help us to intervene with intentional sensitivities to promote the right action. Moving closer to a patient with big energy may seem contradictory, and yet by leaning in with care and direction we can say, "There is so much here, and I want to hear you, and if we can take a moment to take a breath together, I trust we can find our way." To connect directly like this can be containing and settling to both the patient's and therapist's nervous systems.

Case Example

The following vignette is from the first moments of an initial psychotherapy session with a new patient, Megan, which illustrates taking an active therapist stance, which I could see was necessary in response to the patient's presentation. Right off the bat, she shares with me her recent experience from a first session with another potential new therapist she consulted. I hear the patient describe a version of her wishing to "get it all out," and yet, she left that earlier session feeling dysregulated, overwhelmed, and just plain bad. I take her cue about what she needs: immediately, explicitly, I stepped in to say that I did not want her to have a repeat of that experience. It became clear that rather than "needing to get it all out" while the therapist "listens," what she really needed was a structure for our session. More precisely, she needed me, her attachment-oriented therapist, to set some structure so that she would not flounder, left to her own devices.

We enter at the first moment our session begins (on Zoom).

Vignette 10A, Part 1: "Exactly What I Don't Want You to Do!"

THERAPIST (TH): Here we are *(warmly smiling, bright eyes)* [I'm acknowledging the shift from talking on the phone to seeing each other over Zoom.] and I'd love for you to just start . . . however it feels important for you to begin. [She had told me she had much experience in therapy, so I open with a spacious invitation.]

MEGAN (PATIENT, PT): I don't really have a clear or a great idea about that [hinting she may need help]. I, I did a first session with a therapist recently and was like, well, I better just, like, vomit out all the bad stuff about my family, too. Like, I gave some background and ended up, like, really destabilized and fucked up after that . . . [I hear how she was activated in the session yet wasn't tracked for anxiety regulation and what she was managing or not managing. Plus "vomit" makes it clear that that is not the way to go.]

TH: Exactly what I don't want you to do! [I step in immediately, engaging an active therapist stance.]

PT: So, I'm not going to do that, but I'm not . . . (trails off, leans head back, eyes get wide, closes her mouth) [indicating she heard me but doesn't know what to do].

TH: [Metaskills of being directive and caring are at the ready.] How about if I give you how I would like to suggest you start? [Asking permission to offer help and guidance and to let her know how I will conduct the session.]

PT: (immediately fast nods) Yes, please. Thank you. [She is grateful for not being left to her own devices.]

TH: Okay (eyes look up), I think there's a few things that are really important. One is connecting with something that you want (hand touches heart, then palm opens) from being here today, over the long haul. Today is really important because today is about how we work together and, do we want to go forward? So, I think sometimes it's nice to start with "What do I want (hand touches heart) from being here?"

PT: Mm-hmm.

TH: And as I start to talk about that, notice what occurs . . . the important thing (hands connect, fingers interlace) is to really notice what happens as you speak, what happens in your body, and what starts to emerge feeling wise (hands open and continue to move in gesture) because that's how we'll get a sense of how you stay in your window of tolerance. [Introducing the somatic focus and the importance of connection to self, I'm reflecting the need to keep an eye out for regulation.]

PT: (nodding, eyes widen) Mm-hmm.

TH: You know, and from time to time, I'll probably check in and just ask, "How are you feeling with yourself?" and "How are you feeling with me?" (hands motion back and forth between us) How does that sound? [Metaprocessing how the structure and outline for beginning the session lands with her.]

PT: (*nods, smiles*) That sounds very doable. Yes. [**Direct and coordinated response; helps patient feel competent.**]

TH: Okay. (*cheek rests on left palm, eyes looking at patient*)

PT: Okay. (*eyes closed*) So, um, I think I mentioned to you when we spoke a couple of days ago that my main goals right now really have to do with, like, self-image and self-worth. [**I am impressed with how she drops into her clarity and motivation.**]

TH: Mm-hmm. (*brings hand down, nods*) [**affirming para-verbals**]

PT: And with (*eyes look up*) being able to trust my own judgment or feeling that my judgment is like that, it matters and that it is worth trusting (*eyes look sideways*) and also, you know, being able to have a more complex view of myself that's not like really black and white or dichotomous or extreme. (*raises eyebrows*) I'm trying to frame that in positive terms, but I don't, I literally don't know what I'm looking for on that front. So, I don't have the right language for like what the nondichotomous thing would be . . . [**The description is broadening and sounds diffuse so I step in to refocus.**]

Therapist takes an active therapeutic stance. In the first minute of our session, the patient revealed a huge red flag: how dysregulated she became in her prior session. She thought she needed to provide the potential therapist with a whole lot of negative background, and I was instantly struck by my conviction that a first session is an opportunity for the patient and therapist to learn how to work together (as opposed to gathering history). Holding an attachment-based frame, I embodied the position of the older, wiser other, who aimed to help her have a different and good experience. I recognized the need for safety and was moved to help her and offered structure and direction; it was important that she listen to herself while sharing with me. I communicated how we will monitor the need for regulation by registering and being with the experience as it unfolds. Also, I was explicit that I would check in with her about how she is feeling with herself and with me, both as preparation and reassurance that she does not have to figure this out alone.

From the earliest moments, we are appraising each other relationally, and my taking an active stance is an important intervention for guiding us to develop a safe base for our work together. Additionally, the gestures and nonverbal expressions marked in parentheses are signals that show coherence between what I'm saying and offering. Our nonverbal language communicates how we respond and coordinate with each other, which contributes to how the session unfolds.

TH: Maybe trusting in myself. What would that be like? You know, I guess I just want to offer you the sense that you can take it really slow here. [**Bringing focus to slowing down so we can tend to the experiential aspect of the process.**]

PT: (*eyes engaged, smiles, throat visibly tightens*)

TH: And even though we're talking about what you want and that sounds lofty and could be big, it could also be like, maybe I'd like to see if "I could stay connected to myself during this session today." [**I model using "I messages" to entrain the patient's focus on herself.**]

Slowing down to help patient connect with herself. As I'm listening to what Megan wants regarding self-trust, I shape a goal for this session about going slow and helping her connect with herself, working together to help her be able to learn how to pace herself, to regulate when needed, and to learn about her window of tolerance. I take the lead as empathically as I can and offer her the focus that has crystallized in my mind for establishing safety in our session. I am firm about not wanting to repeat her last experience of destabilization, helplessness, and feeling bad about herself.

PT: (*nodding, eyes open, brighten*) Okay.

TH: You know, what would that take? [**Asking for her agency and involvement**]

PT: Effort. (*smiling, squinting eyes*) Thought? Yes.

TH: Presence?

PT: Yes. (*eyes close*)

TH: (*head drops down, gesture of apology*) I mean, I don't mean to dismiss what you say, but . . . [**I have a moment of concern that I have overstepped and want to offer repair if needed.**]

PT: Nope, I appreciate it. (*laughing*)

While I feel clear about suggesting that Megan could work on staying connected to herself and see what that brings, there is also a part of me witnessing myself, aware that the patient's experience may or may not receive my good intention.

Checking in with the patient. Interventions that explicitly ask the patient how our comments land and affect them are an integral part of healing attachment wounding and a key aspect of AEDP attachment work. In my case, I was indirect in saying, "I don't mean to dismiss what you say." Fortunately, the patient gets my meaning, which she acknowledges by appreciating my stepping in: a positive signal that she understands my intention and is feeling understood by me. If the exchange had gone differently, I would have responded in kind and taken the steps to recoordinate and repair. However, our work continued to unfold, and we proceeded with our goals as established. We return to this session later in the chapter.

What This Vignette Shows About Working With Ambivalent/Resistant Attachment

When the therapist steps in and helps. In the ambivalent/resistant pattern of attachment, the patient's experience of distress is often generalized, and trusting their own self for clues about what is truly needed is foreign or fraught. As we see in the above scenario, the patient had a negative experience of becoming overwhelmed by her attempt to disclose her family background and the pain and difficulty that followed when she was left too much on her own. She knew her residual experience was not therapeutic and she didn't want a repeat. Yet, on her own, she did not know how to proceed. She didn't ask for guidance because it didn't occur to her that she could ask for help, and that if she asked, it would be given. And that if it was given, that it could be helpful.

Megan needed help to navigate the thin line between revealing history and being in the present moment where healing can happen, when new and corrective relational and emotional experience can begin to transfer into new learning, new neural pathways, and a new sense of self-trust and self-agency. Currently, the patient's self remains a bit of a mystery to her; entangled with introjects and misleading beliefs. What she needs is diffuse and at an early stage of her being able to both recognize it and articulate it. And yet, as I am engaging with an active therapist stance, with a specific intention to set conditions to establish safety and undo aloneness, we can see she has a positive response. Megan engages with her self-at-best. She is cooperative and shows receptivity to my intentions and availability. She makes good use of the help I offer and allows herself to be moved, and to share herself as best she can. She works genuinely with what arises in her as she is with me. We are forming a coordinated therapeutic relationship.

When the therapist is in a common reactivity. In contrast, when or if psychotherapists become overwhelmed or activated, we may miss clues about how to be of help and may miss opportunities to take the lead. In other words, we are in an unintended reaction. Alternately, taking such an active stance can be challenging for therapists whose training emphasized listening for a while and then interpreting. Nevertheless, with patients presenting with the ambivalent/resistant pattern of attachment, this level of therapeutic engagement (i.e., being active and taking the lead) is crucial. When we are tuned in and willing to step in, we set the pace for the session, and the patient has a much better chance of being a fuller version of themselves than when they are constricted by their attachment patterning. Our session has a very different potential to unfold with *healing from the get-go!*

Organizing Experiential Work With AEDP Representational Schemas

We presented the AEDP representational schemas used to guide experiential work in Chapter 3, "The Move to Experience and Transformation" and applied them in Chapter 8, "Working to Transform Patterns of Avoidant Attachment." As we see in the above clinical example, it is imperative for psychotherapists to have a way to track (a) the patient's attachment system arousal; (b) their means of regulating affect; (c) how anxiety and (d) defense manifest, given their attachment strategy; and finally, (e) the patient's affective competence. These five categories were introduced in Grids 1 and 2, as Row 3 and Rows 5–8, which identify the constellation of secure and insecure attachment (Chapter 5, pp. 156–162). These categories are related to the AEDP TOE, upon which defenses are represented on the upper left corner, anxiety is represented on the upper right corner, and core affective experience is represented on the bottom corner.

The TOE (see Chapter 3) provides a schema upon which we can track, moment-to-moment how the patient moves toward and away from core affective experience. In treating ambivalent/resistant patterns of attachment, affect regulation needs to be front and center in the work. The AEDP TOE is pivotal to informing therapists how to recognize anxiety, what to look for as markers of the specific kinds of emotional and relational defenses that pertain to ambivalent/resistant attachment, and how we can intervene. In the following section we present the specifics pertaining to the ambivalent/resistant TOE.

The TOE: Ambivalent/Resistant

See Figure 10.1, page 292.

Turn It On and On and On . . .

The ambivalent/resistant pattern is often referred to as anxious ambivalent or even "the anxious one." Although it is inaccurate to pin anxiety to one pattern, there is truth in that high levels of anxiety are part of the picture in a person presenting with the ambivalent/resistant pattern, which fuels hyperactivating strategies. It behooves therapists to have skills geared toward recognizing and regulating anxiety in our patients, and also in ourselves. The contagion factor is real.

Anxiety. On the ambivalent/resistant TOE (see Figure 10.1), *anxiety* is represented on the upper right corner of the triangle. Anticipation of not knowing what to expect generates arousal in the individual. Their expectancies of uncertainty, separation, and/or hurt trigger anxiety and inhibiting affects, which appear in the mind as preoccupation, rumination, vacillation in self-image or self-worth, cognitive disruption, getting lost or forgetting what was just said, and tangential or run-on sentences. Anxiety appears in the body as shallow breathing, increased heart rate, tension in muscles, big or sudden movements, worried facial expressions, and somatization.

Emotionality. A very important point when it comes to the ambivalent/resistant pattern has to do with emotionality, which is often confused with genuine emotion (much like for the avoidant pattern, defensive self-reliance is mistaken for genuine self-reliance; see the Fosha, 2000b, section entitled "All That Glitters Is Not Gold," and later in this chapter, p. 300, for a detailed discussion of this point). Anxiety and defense combine in the emotional field as emotionality, which is the mixture of anxiety and emotion that is not core emotion, and that does not subside in relief. Emotions that don't arc in waves that crest and fall, and aren't sourced in the body, are not core emotions. Arousal can often lead to emotional dysregulation and/or hyperactivating behaviors. It explains the characterization of this style as "feeling and reeling."

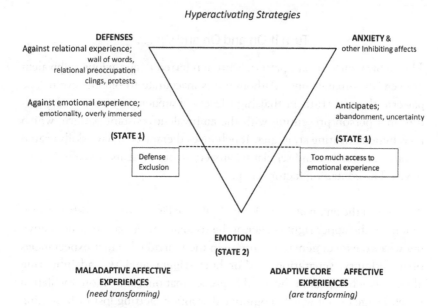

Hyperactivating Strategies

DEFENSES
Against relational experience;
wall of words,
relational preoccupation
clings, protests

ANXIETY &
other Inhibiting affects

Against emotional experience;
emotionality, overly immersed

Anticipates;
abandonment, uncertainty

(STATE 1)

(STATE 1)

Defense
Exclusion

Too much access to
emotional experience

EMOTION
(STATE 2)

MALADAPTIVE AFFECTIVE
EXPERIENCES
(need transforming)

ADAPTIVE CORE   AFFECTIVE
EXPERIENCES
(are transforming)

Pathogenic Affects
Unbearable States of
Traumatic aloneness

Legend: Affective Experiences

Maladaptive Affective Experiences
The Pathogenic Affects (E.g., Overwhelm, Toxic Shame, Fright Without
Solution, Attachment Without Solution); Unbearable States of Traumatic
Aloneness (E.g., Helplessness, Fragmentation, Brokenness; Despair, "The
Black Hole Of Trauma")

Adaptive Core Affective Experiences
Categorical Emotions; Relational Experience, Asymmetric (Attachment)
or Symmetric (Intersubjective); Coordinated Relational Experiences;
Receptive Affective Experiences; Somatic "Drop-Down" States;
Embodied Ego States and their Associated Emotions; Authentic Self-
Experiences; Experiences of Agency, Will Desire; Attachment Strivings;
The Expression of Core Needs

Figure 10.1 The Triangle of Experience: Ambivalent/Resistant
Pando-Mars, 2024, adapted from Fosha, 2020

Defenses against emotion. Defenses are represented on the upper left corner of the ambivalent/resistant TOE. Emotionality is a defense against (genuine) emotion: It is driven by anxiety-motored thoughts that intensify worry, agitation, or distress. The person is overly immersed in the emotional experiences of others, which further contributes to boundary confusion. This applies to bundled affects and defensive emotions as well. For example, *bundled affects*, a mixture of anger and sadness, or *defensive emotions*, such as anger in place of sadness, or anger that is watered down with weepy tears, are defenses against emotion seen in the ambivalent/resistant pattern. Speech patterns that include voluminous details, tangential thinking, and walls of words also act as a defense against emotion as they distract the person away from connection to bodily rooted emotional experience.

Defenses against relatedness. Relational preoccupation, the pseudo relationality we discussed earlier (see Chapter 9), is a defense against relatedness. Just as defensive self-reliance is not genuine self-reliance, and emotionality is not core emotion, relational preoccupation is not genuine relatedness. When there is excessive focus on the other, connection to oneself is often excluded. Clinging and protest are also aspects of preoccupation. Verbally, when topic after topic is expressed, tangential, and hard to follow, connection and true engagement is difficult. A mounting wall of words is a defense against relatedness, keeping people out rather than letting them in. When the person is distressed, seeks comfort, yet is unable to allow themselves to be soothed by another, this ambivalence reflects defenses against relatedness.

Core affective experience. At the bottom of the ambivalent/resistant TOE is core affective experience, which can be categorical emotions, relational affective experiences, and self-affective experiences. Core affective experience may be maladaptive or adaptive. On the bottom left are maladaptive core affective experiences, such as pathogenic affects and unbearable states of traumatic aloneness (see Chapter 3, pp. 105–106). Though these are bodily rooted, they are not intrinsically transforming and instead, they need to be transformed: they need our relational accompaniment to counter the relational wounding that gave rise to these states. Thus, we have the imperative to work through defenses against relatedness; the patient must be able to receive our relational connection to heal the deep aloneness and/ or shame that stems from attachment trauma (Chapter 3, pp. 119–120), that addresses working with receptive affective experience). On the bottom right are adaptive core affective experiences (Chapter 3, p. 106). In the presence and regulated accompaniment of another, bodily rooted core affective experiences are transforming.

In Chapter 8, working with avoidant attachment, we discussed relational affective experiences, which are key to the explicit and experiential relational work we engage to treat attachment trauma. Additionally, and often key in the treatment of ambivalent attachment, are the self-affective experiences, the self's perception, reception, and expression of the self, which we discuss below in the section about working with core affective experience. We also focus on helping our patients to experience their genuine core emotions and facilitate their experiential completion. We aim to foster the springing forth of the adaptive action tendencies rooted in each emotion. In addition to being with and processing emotion, we engage the use of portrayals. Portrayals are an experiential technique using real or imagined scenes to access, heighten, or deepen the completion of core affective experience. The patient is invited to have a reparative, longed for, or avoided experience in their imagination, which can foster healing and corrective emotional or relational experiences.

In the next section, we present interventions and practices for working with anxiety and affect regulation, including the next section of the case vignette we began above. From there, we return to a discussion about defenses against emotion and defenses against relatedness. We explore some specific issues that arise and some intervention sequences for how to work with them. After that, we discuss interventions for working with emotion/core affective experience, maladaptive and adaptive, as it pertains to the pattern of ambivalent/resistant attachment. Throughout each of these sections, we mention potential *therapist common reactivities* and the conscious use of *therapist metaskills*, since keeping an eye out for these can sharpen the implements in our tool kits.

Working With Anxiety: Dyadic Regulation and Self-Regulation

Slow down: use voice, tone, pace, and prosody to entrain the right brain. Slowing down is key to regulating anxiety. How we help our patients to slow down begins with ourselves, finding a comfortable grounded posture and way of being that offers containment, yet readiness to act. The way we use our voices, *slow down and low down* (Prenn, 2011), our voice tone, pace, and prosody, communicates our presence and can convey calm to an activated patient, entraining their right brain with our right brain. It is important to be sensitive to how the patient arrives and to see and be with them where they are, so even if they are operating at high energy, they initially feel matched and thus, they feel seen. From there, working to help them to settle can be a co-constructed process.

A potential *therapist common reactivity* can arise with a patient who is reeling (i.e., expending high levels of energy), when the therapist, in an effort to maintain a calm presence, falls back on an avoidant strategy. Instead of self-regulating, the therapist is deactivating. Tips to notice this might be that the therapist is less engaged, less explicitly containing, less attuned, and thereby less empathic to the efforts the patient is making to express their distress. Such a blind spot can happen to any of us. Perhaps, without realizing it, we go through the motions, following the patient in an effort to catch up. Our rationalization can be something like "Let me let them tell their story. They need to do that," when actually it is we who have disconnected.

Help the client make use of your presence and care. When patients present with anxiety, either by their naming it directly or through manifesting distress or agitation somatically and/or in their manner, dyadic regulation is essential. We can offer regulation verbally or nonverbally, explicitly, or implicitly. AEDP Maxim 3, Stay With It and Stay With Me (Fosha, 2017b), suggests our intention to accompany patients with whatever experience is arising. We want to help them to manage what has been overwhelming while helping to titrate their experience, regulate their anxiety, and keep the process feeling safe. Only when patients feel safe enough and regulated enough, can they drop into risking being with their genuine feelings, and only then are they able to process emotion to completion. When the above patient revealed her negative family history, to the point of feeling destabilized, her experience indicated dysregulation. As an attachment figure, we step in to help the vulnerable one who may not be aware of their limits. We track markers of anxiety to ensure that while our patient may be working at the edge, they have not exceeded the upper edge of *their* window of tolerance. We hold a steady presence to stabilize our container, and we are available to help them explore, when needed, how to recalibrate and regroup.

If the patient's speech is moving fast and changing topics, psychotherapists can step in actively, with kindness and care, and offer containment to the patient by reflecting, summarizing, or empathizing with them.

Sometimes saying, "I really want to hear you. Would it be all right to take a breath here and notice what is already on the table and where we might want to focus?" I want to help my patient find greater calm as we shape their capacity to respond to what is driving their activation.

Down regulate: help the patient learn how to reduce anxiety. To actively teach patients to recognize their own signals of anxiety is empowering. Then, giving them grounding, self-regulating skills and/or breathing practices helps them learn how to tend to their activation. The more they can regulate anxiety, the more capable they will feel to allow glimmers of core affective experiences to emerge, which we can accompany and help them to process. When focusing a patient on anxiety regulation, we are helping to redirect their attention to self-care, so as to be less at the mercy of the other that they yearn for but cannot let in.

In the following vignette, we return to the first session with Megan, the patient featured above in Vignette 10A, Part 1. From the start I bring dyadic regulation into our equation by being active and collaborative. As promised, I check in with her after some sharing and exploration. I ask about her experience to learn how activated she is, how she shows it, and how well she can manage with my help. When Megan has an experience of regulating her anxiety with my accompaniment, some core affective experience emerges in the form of a younger aspect of self and awareness of her pain.

Vignette 10A, Part 2: "Slow Down . . . Notice How You Feel in Your Body Right Now as You Tell Me . . ."

We have just spent a few minutes with Megan telling me about the painful beliefs she holds about herself and their origins in her family. I ask how she is feeling in the moment, wanting to check in to be sure we are tracking her activation together and paying attention to how she feels as she is speaking.

TH: Slow down for a second, because that's a share about your family that you just brought out. I just want you to notice how you feel in your body right now as you tell me about that.
PT: Tense (*shakes her head side to side*), worked up.
TH: Okay, so can we, like—let's just deal with that tense and worked up. So, before we add any more on to it, let's just find how to be with tense (*places hand on heart*) and what tense and worked up needs. [**Showing the**

patient how we check in along the way as she is disclosing, so we can intervene if needed to regulate each sharing, each impact of anxiety: modeling tending to the self from the start.]

PT: Okay.

TH: Where do you feel the tension?

PT: My heart rate's up and my side muscles are tensing (*hands come up, clenched*), which is something that they often do (*voice rises, hesitantly*).

TH: Okay. So, what about taking your hands and just placing them on your heart? [This self-compassion practice, called soothing touch, comes to mind as she mentions her heart.]

PT: Okay (*eyes look up*).

TH: Have you ever done this kind of soothing touch?

PT: Uh-uh (*places both hands on her heart, shakes her head no, stays in eye contact with me*).

TH: So, this is a really common practice. We put our hand on our heart to calm the nervous system. The ventral vagal nerve connects to the heart. And the people doing research on compassion talk about this as soothing touch[1] (*patient's eyes brighten and she nods*). Okay, so we can think of this as soothing touch. Whatever feels right to your heart (*patient presses her fingertips into her heart area*) [Patient's nonverbals are clearly coordinating with therapist's guidance], you want to just let the heart rate know, you know (*therapist pauses, leaning in with gentle rocking*) something kind, like what would be something kind you could say to yourself about sharing this with me?

In retrospect, I now wish I could have broken that into two interventions— with a pause in between to metaprocess the impact of the felt sense of Megan's hand on her heart. Yet given all of the negative self-beliefs that were circulating, communicating kindness to her heart was on my mind. I felt kind, tender; my body gently rocking, and wondered if she might resonate with giving a kind message to herself. And she did.

PT: (*looking up, breathes*) I mean, I guess just like "that was hard for child you." (*she frowns, eyes darken*) I don't know.

TH: Yes. Perfect. Perfect. [Affirming her self-compassion, which I also see as transformance.] So maybe the little one in you is even nearby. How old? Let's just pick an age. [The fact that her response goes to providing an empathic corrective message to her younger self moves me, and I want to follow her direction and see where we can go.]

PT: Eight. [She names an age right away.]

TH: Okay. How about if you just let yourself say to your 8-year-old self, "that was really hard." [Offering a portrayal—a way to bring her kind message to her younger self using her imagination.]

PT: (looking up, eyes shift a little, she's breathing) [She appears to be deeply engaging internally.]

TH: That was . . . hard. (I continue as if talking now to the child, still rocking, hand on my heart) And you're really okay. Just as you are. Right now . . .

PT: (eye squeeze closed for a moment as she smiles)

TH: That's the message I want you to know . . . (pause) How's that to hear me say? (speaking gently, with kindness) Was it too fast? [Metaprocessing how my comment lands, through her, to her younger self.]

PT: It's nice. I appreciate the impulse behind it. [Her response lets me know she is taking kindness in, and now I'm wondering what she perceived as the impulse behind it . . .]

TH: Can you say something like that to yourself? Can you take that? Either I can say it again or you can take that into that little 8-year-old.

PT: (nodding, sits up taller and rolls her shoulders back)

TH: Yeah. Good for you . . . right? Then you start to notice the tightness wants to roll . . . let it happen, you know, see what those tight muscles, what they need. [Affirming and reflecting how I see her engaging and seeming to listen to herself. I track her shoulders rolling and inquire as to what they might be communicating.]

Moment-to-moment tracking. As Megan straightened her spine, I detected a shift. Though the intention was anxiety regulation, and indeed that was accomplished, that spontaneously led to a piece of deep work: a piece of experiential work to acknowledge her younger self with empathy, maybe compassion. I find that when patients who present with ambivalent/resistant patterns are accompanied and able to regulate anxiety, and they can stop reeling, often an aspect of core affective experience emerges. Following the patient's lead and bringing tending to this younger self was an affirmation of our working alliance. As a dyad we were establishing enough safety and stability to open to this deeper level of work. When Megan begins to roll her shoulders, I wonder if she needs a pause, perhaps she is nearing the edge of her window of tolerance for taking in something new. By slowing down and being with her movement we give the body space for digestion and expression.

PT: Yeah. (*sits up and moves shoulders forward and back*)

TH: See if you can give yourself a little more space just to be here just as you are. [**Inviting her to bring her awareness to the present-moment experience. Here, like Mindell and Mindell (2002) said, the most powerful intervention is to focus on something that is already happening.**]

PT: (*nodding, exhales*) Okay.

TH: Okay. What's okay? (*smiling*) [**Staying with her word and exploring what she means.**]

PT: That's. I'm feeling a little better. A little less, like on edge, I guess. [**Her feeling relief after this process indicates receptivity to our tuning in and regulating together.**]

TH: So, how's that? That you can feel a little less on edge right now? [**meta-processsing the shift**]

PT: It's good. I'm, like, trying to figure out what to take from that [**self-reflective question**]. But maybe that's, like, later . . .

TH: I'm not going to make it hard for you—what to take from here is when you feel some activation, we want to tend to it right away. And when possible [**to see**], whether you can connect to where that's coming from.

Responding directly to the patient's question. I hear Megan pose genuine self-reflection and choose to respond directly. Since we are in a first session, my being explicit about the intention to regulate and be with her experience affirms the steps we have taken. We are doing what we set out to do. Here, we implement what Fosha (2000a) describes as the purpose of metaprocesssing: that is, that it is not enough for the patient to have a new experience; they need to know that they have had it. For Megan, to have an experience of regulating tension and anxiety with a new therapist is a contrast to her recent experience. She questions what to do with the new experience—I want to help her understand the lay of the land—and add a bit of psycho-education. When anxiety presents, first we regulate, and then we have an opportunity to listen for what stirs from underneath. She identified a younger self, who was directly involved in what she had been talking about. Her capacity to make the connection, offer empathy to her younger self, and reach a sense of relief was important for us, as a therapist–patient dyad who are learning how to work together.

We return later in this chapter to the last clip of this session to depict how emotional experience comes to the fore when anxiety becomes manageable.

In the following sections, we explore defenses that make up the ambivalent/resistant pattern. We present specific pathways of interventions, and how therapist common reactivities and metaskills may come into play.

Working With Defenses Against Emotion: Emotionality as a Defense Against Emotion

All that glitters is not gold: Emotionality as a defense vs. emotion: feeling and reeling but not dealing. (Fosha, 2000b, pp. 158–159)

Distinguish emotionality from core emotion. Patients who struggle with patterns of ambivalent/resistant attachment often experience emotion with a mixture of anxiety, which is emotionality. Emotion activates the need for regulated contact, and the absence of regulated and regulating contact early on becomes embedded in the patient's nervous system, which mobilizes in excess as hyperactivation. When some patients begin to engage in psychotherapy, the process can simultaneously trigger the fear of needing help and worries that nothing can help, or alternately, the fear that there will never be enough of what they need or want. These fears, and similar worries from their personal life, can instigate the onset of emotion driven by anxious thoughts. The intensity of anxiety-motored thinking is characterized by negative appraisals of self or others, catastrophic scenarios, and tangential and fragmented themes, which are often more generalized than specific. This mixture generates emotionality rather than emotion. Emotionality does not move in waves that arc and complete, the way adaptive core emotion does. Rather, emotionality tends to be draining, cyclical, unrelenting. Core emotion arises from the body, it surges and moves outward, and brings vitality and adaptive action. Emotionality is a *defense against emotion* that takes our patients away from core emotion rather than allowing it to flow and move toward completion and the release of adaptive action on behalf of the self.

Therapist common reactivities. When the patient's emotional expression contains a mixture of tears, protest, and/or anxious thoughts, we are in the terrain of emotionality. The therapist may notice feeling unmoved and even turned off by the patient's expression. Such a reaction is an indication that we are in the presence of defensive emotion (i.e., emotionality) rather than genuine emotion or core emotion. Core emotion has the quality of drawing one in, where emotionality has the quality of something feeling off and agitating. We identify a therapist common reactivity here, because sometimes our feeling like *pulling away* rather than *moving toward* can lead therapists to doubt ourselves, wondering about our own capacity for empathy. Yet, it is a signal that psychotherapists must notice and pay attention to. "How is it that my patient's experience isn't affecting me and stirring my sense of caring and wanting to be helpful?" Questioning our experience of not feeling impacted by the patient is important, and as soon as we become aware, we can look more closely at what is occurring between us and within our patient. Perhaps their tears are leaking rather than flowing. Or their emotions are flatlining or static rather than moving. Our lack of feeling impacted might be a signal that we are caught in an eddy with our patient, circling around and around, reeling with them. Here our work is to recognize the emotionality so we can get our bearings and become centered ourselves so as to be able to help our patient to connect to their genuine emotion and core affective experience.

Discern among thinking, feeling, and empathizing with core affect. When anxiety-motored thoughts are driving emotionality, a big issue involves the confusion between thoughts and feelings. Many individuals do not know the difference between them. For instance, the thought, "he is going to leave me" triggers attachment anxiety, and yet this is not a body-based emotional experience but an activating thought that is threatening. Patients build these thoughts into worrisome predictions about the future (i.e., catastrophizing), leaving themselves churning and feeling helpless. The therapist might find themselves exhausted and confused or checked out. Thinking takes the patient's attention into their head and into the stories that spin round and around. These stories are a defense against emotion as they keep the patient overly focused on the content of their complaints and thus obscure what might be stirring in their body.

It is important for us as therapists to learn the difference between thought-driven, anxiety-motored emotion and visceral, bodily based emotion. And once we know it, teach it to our patients. Many patients believe they are sharing feelings when they say, "I feel that they . . . don't love me anymore, is going to fire me, is going to leave me." Just because a sentence starts with "I feel," doesn't make it a feeling. When we hear content behind the words "I feel," we may need to help our patients to notice when they say, "I feel that . . . ," that they end up in a thought stream. Therapists must identify the specificity of feeling words versus thinking words and help patients to become discerning. With some patients it can be helpful to name the categorical emotions of sadness, anger, fear, joy, disgust, and surprise. Some appreciate having a list that gives examples of mild, moderate, and intense feeling words and they use it to learn to identify the emotional currents of their body-based experience. From here, we focus on the somatic edge of core affect and help the patient to identify and stay with what is happening in their body. We help them to notice what crests and falls, surges and wanes, arises and dissipates. No matter how small or large the wave of affect, we want to help our patient learn to recognize how affect moves, so then together we can be with these affective experiences. As we feel emotion together in our present therapeutic relationship, relevant historical memories can surface and we can link the current trigger with its early life disturbance or trauma.

Bottomless emotionality vs. productive core emotion. I once had a patient describe that after a fight with her boyfriend, she cried "all night long" and became very ill. She was convinced that nearing her emotions in our session was undesirable. And yet, as we explored her experience, it became evident that the way she spoke to herself through the night led her into a hyperactivated state with no release. As she relayed what happened, she took lots of short inhales, and her eyes, still puffy, filled with tears without spilling over into any kind of letting go. As she and I spoke together, we approached the injury between she and her boyfriend with a keen eye to her direct experience of hurt and anguish. With my support and encouragement, she was able to cry with full breath and a sense of movement through her core. This release became a vivid example of the difference between time-limited productive emotion and unrelenting, endless, bottomless emotionality (a defense against productive core emotion). Productive emotion moves in waves that arc and flow to some experience of completion, whereas unrelenting emotionality is exactly that, unrelenting and with no end.

Bundled emotions. Sometimes there can be more than one emotion in the mix of the patient's experience. When the patient is protesting the absence of their historic caregiver, or current loved one, they might feel both angry and sad. They are easily triggered by the unreliability or lack of follow-through of loved ones, whether it be by what happened with their parent while they were growing up or what just happened with their partner yesterday. Bundled emotions refer to the co-arising of more than one emotion and may occur as the patient describes a complex set of feelings that are part of their attachment wounding. While they are longing for the parent who has been so hard to reach, they are also angry and protesting the absence of this parent's response—their emotions appear as a bundle. First, it is helpful to ask the patient to slow down and make room to notice the emotions in their body and begin to name them one at a time.

Defensive affects. Second, we can ask the patient to feel into the emotion and together we notice what emotion is strongest. Here, it might be that the patient is actually feeling angry and then shifts to sadness. The shift to sadness may be serving as a defense against anger and can be understood as watering down their anger. Or anger may be covering up longing that brings more vulnerability and reminders of times when they were alone and untended. By bringing attention to what is happening we can help patients to discern what emotion is coming from the core and learn to recognize when emotion is serving as a defense.

Working With Defense Against Relatedness: Relational Preoccupation as a Defense Against Relatedness

Similar to emotionality as a defense against emotion, the person being other focused reflects a defense that moves against relatedness and closeness, not a manifestation of them. When the patient's attention is focused on the other, to what the other is doing or not doing, they are often erecting a wall of complaint or a justification about something they wanted that was not forthcoming. Such emphasis about the other is the terrain of relational preoccupation, and often coincides with hyperactivation of their attachment system. Yet as they maintain their inner eyes and ears on the other, the patient is not noticing what is happening within themselves. Invariably what is absent is the patient's attunement to their own self experience. And ironically, their preoccupation with the other may obscure them from seeing and understanding what is actually happening with the other, which blocks their capacity for relatedness.

Here is where the fallout described in the descriptions of the early caregiver–infant interactions comes into view. Having developed a keen focus on the other, the patient is remiss to notice and respond to their own signals. Thus, relational preoccupation is actually a defense against awareness of what is stirred from within. Seeking attention from the other circumvents their being present and available to their own self. Additionally, their overactive complaint and protest is more likely to drive the other away rather than draw them close.

Differentiate between self and other. To begin here, it is important to help the patient differentiate between Self and Other. When the boundary between Self and Other is confused, often the care the patient is longing for from the other is sorely needed from themselves. An important intervention is to present opportunities for our patients to learn to distinguish what's happening inside, in their own body-based experience, from their predictions and reactions about what's happening with another person. We must help them to reel in their attention, to focus inwardly and develop interest in self-discovery. We help them learn to identify what in their experience may be triggered. For someone with an ambivalent pattern of attachment, reminders of inconsistency and unreliability are especially activating and typically set off expectancies that formed their internal working models. These expectancies often hold themes of self as unworthy and incapable and the other as inconsistent and unreliable. Helping patients to differentiate between self and other is a way to steer them toward what is wounded and unresolved in themselves and in need of tending. I do so with compassion, helping them to realize that hyperactivating to get the attention of the other arises out of a best adaptive strategy they developed as a child, related to their primary attachment relationship.

Lean into self experience and what stirs from within. Boundary confusion is part of the composite of the preoccupied state of mind. What is missing is often a sense of what belongs to whom. When the patient is outwardly focused on the other, they are actually avoiding their internal experience—and is unavailable to recognize the difference between stimulus and response. We can help them to identify the behavior of the other as the stimulus, and to see that their affective response belongs to them. When they identify what arises as their own, they are closer to being able to connect to the genuine feelings that may be triggered and unresolved from earlier in life. It prompts the question, whose responsibility is it to tend to the child within an adult, whose caregivers were unreliable and left them unsure whether their needs would be heard and tended to?

In the preoccupied state of mind, the tendency to predict and project what is to come in the future, perseverations about others' perceptions and intentions, is driven by fear and anxiety. Usually, these future predictions are based on events that happened in the past, and anxiety regulation and getting connected to what is occurring in the present moment is essential for treatment.

Working With Emotion and Core Affective Experience

At the bottom of the TOE is core affective experience, which includes categorical emotions, and relational and self-affective experiences. Specific work with the experience of attachment in the here and now of the therapist–patient relationship is crucial for undoing aloneness and attending to the patient's expectancies related to their early attachment wounding. As well, how we are explicit within our attachment relationship is part of dyadic regulation and one of the ways we help our patients to manage anxiety. Once we have regulated anxiety and built a coordinate therapeutic relationship, we can help our patients approach signals of genuine emotion and self-affective experiences that are part of what emerges at the bottom of the TOE and work with AEDP State 2.

Here, while working with patients who have patterns of ambivalent/ resistant attachment it is helpful to identify self-affective experiences. Self-affective experiences can be encapsulated by an enlarged description of authentic self experience: having a felt sense of authenticity—the experience of feeling "real"; the experience of vulnerability; emergent experiences of will, agency, and desire; and emergent experiences of feeling lovable and worthy (Russell, 2021). Such self experiences and expression grow in our patients as we help them to learn to both, take in our care and turn their attention inward, to regulate anxiety, and to build their capacity for recognizing what is happening in their own experience and then processing that to completion. Learning to take their eye off of the other for soothing and for evidence of mattering, listening inside, they begin to develop their agentic self (Russell, 2021), who is capable to recognize what is happening in their own felt experience and how to tend to their own needs.

Another core affective experience is ego-state work and their related emotions. Many of our patients with unresolved attachment wounding have younger aspects of self that hold unresolved emotional experiences. Often these parts are cut off and outside of our patients' conscious awareness.

In the next clinical example, we return to a final clip from Vignette 10A. The patient and therapist, having regulated the patient's initial anxiety, are approaching the emergence of emotion after contacting a younger aspect of the patient's self. It is unsettling for Megan to feel into the magnitude of her emotion. The therapist's acknowledgment and validation turns out to be regulating and strengthening for the patient.

Vignette 10A, Part 3: "Feels Like the Sadness Will Never End"

PT: It's like if I approach the stuff at all, I just get so sad. [My comment about noticing what lies underneath the tension and fast heart rate: signals of anxiety and apprehension touched the patient and she shares what she feels.]

TH: Right. Are you feeling sad right now as you start to get there? [Being in the present moment and checking what she is aware of right now.]

PT: Yes . . . ugh. I just, like it feels like the sadness will never end. Like every time I, like, interact with this stuff, it's just like . . . (hands up in the air, a gesture of giving up) [Here, she names what is unresolved is "always" there. Our aim for the session is to regulate and help her experience safety so she and I can help her to face what ultimately needs to be processed.]

Her response is right on cue. Underneath the anxiety, in the heart of her 8-year-old self, lies sadness. And the sadness is old and overwhelming, and has probably been there a long time. She fears the sadness will never end. Here exactly is our work: to help her learn how to be with herself and me, helping her to first undo aloneness, and then feel safe enough to explore and process her feelings toward the unresolved wounding she suffered and endured, until now.

TH: Let's see what the sadness wants to bring today. And, you know, I know that many of us have a lot of sadness about stuff from childhood. And I also know that what seems endless can find its way into enoughness— enough recognition, calm enough. So I have faith that there is an end, which may not yet be in sight. [I try to normalize her fear and provide reassurance: I trust what seems like too much can find a way to be manageable. Therapist as older, wiser other, one who knows.]

PT: (nodding, wiping her eyes, one eye at a time)

TH: (looking tenderly, hand on heart) Ultimately, the goal here in some way is for you to come to terms. Right? And right now the sadness is saying, "I'm not done. This is just so deeply, disturbingly sad because my life has been so affected by this too much now." [**Empathy with the core affective experience.**]

PT: (*nodding, eyes closed, smiling, wiping tears*)

TH: Am I saying too much?

PT: No. That's exactly right. That's why I'm crying. Okay. [**Click of recognition; helps the patient make sense of her tears, which settles her; helps the therapist know that she is being received.**]

TH: I want to be here to hold this with you so it stays manageable. [**Going beyond mirroring to helping; explicit offer of undoing aloneness.**]

PT: Thank you.

Emerging core affective experience. When a patient becomes more capable of regulating anxiety, they are more likely to access core affective experience. However, sometimes the emergence of emotion leads to heightened arousal. In the above vignette, our work going back and forth to regulate anxiety, making room for experience, and establishing a coordinated therapeutic alliance created a stabilizing base of support for our work to proceed step-by-step. The therapist reflects the patient's experience by connecting the patient's sadness with her younger self and normalizes its emergence as evidence of unresolved material. The patient experiences a click of recognition, which helps her to name "this is why I'm crying." Feeling seen leads the patient to self-understanding, which furthers her sense of being okay. By approaching the emotion together that has been held inside alone and untended, alongside her recognition of where the sadness comes from, is regulating, which is a step in building her capacity to feel, bear, and process emotional pain. Next, we take one more step to make explicit the relational experience between us.

TH: I have an idea. Take a peek at me and see me. Like, how do you see me? How am I being here with you? [**Make the relational explicit.**]

PT: Attentively, calmly.

TH: Okay. Attentive and calm in the present. And what message do you get about yourself from me? [**Metaprocess the impact of my relational presence on her self experience.**]

PT: That's just that what I'm doing is acceptable. [**Building self-confidence.**]

TH: Totally. That's a great message to get. [**Affirming.**]

PT: Yes.

Our dyad is coordinating and being effective, which is establishing the conditions for the patient to experience a felt sense of security in our togetherness for the psychotherapy ahead.

Thus far, we have interpreted what has unfolded in the session in terms of the TOE. We now move to the next schema to see what revelations it has in store for us. The ambivalent Self–Other–Emotion (SOE) triangle provides a schema to depict our internal working models. Additionally, we show the self-at-best and self-at-worst versions, to help psychotherapists organize our work when self-at-worst is at play and our patient's defensive strategies need attention.

The SOE Triangle (With Embedded TOE): Ambivalent/Resistant

The SOE triangle depicts a person's internal working model: the individual's internalized representation of self, their internalized representation of other, and their internalized representation of how emotion is processed. We have discussed two versions of the SOE triangle: self-at-best and self-at-worst (Chapters 3 and 8). On the ambivalent SOE triangle (see Figure 10.2), a self-at-worst constellation, the patient's internalized representation of the triggering other is characterized by the preoccupied state of mind of their caregiver, and by their caregiver's behavioral hallmarks of inconsistency, unreliability, and being abandoning through their self-absorption. The other is represented as abandoning/unreliable. The individual's internalized representation of their compromised self is characterized by ambivalence and/or resistance. The self is represented as inadequate/unworthy. Their internalized representation of emotion is characterized by dysregulation: affective competence (or lack thereof) of feeling and reeling, but not dealing; the representation of emotion often being unmanageable.

When an individual is reminded of their *caregiver's* hallmark behaviors or state of mind, they often become activated and may engage hyperactivating strategies with a significant other, as if still trying to get their caregiver's attention. They may seek soothing yet resist receiving what is offered. They usually become dysregulated. When patients come into psychotherapy and describe a repetitive encounter with an intimate other with whom they "lost it" and an escalated, disturbing conflict ensued, we have a clue that our patient was hyperactivated and became dysregulated. While the patient may feel dismayed and embarrassed, we can hold knowing that from here

Hyperactivating Strategies

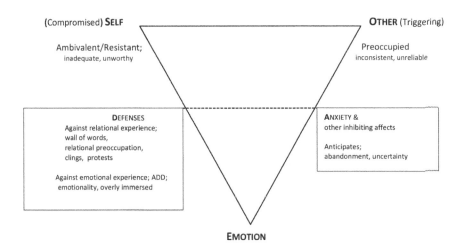

(Compromised) **SELF**

Ambivalent/Resistant;
inadequate, unworthy

OTHER (Triggering)

Preoccupied
inconsistent, unreliable

DEFENSES
Against relational experience;
wall of words,
relational preoccupation,
clings, protests

Against emotional experience; ADD;
emotionality, overly immersed

ANXIETY &
other inhibiting affects

Anticipates;
abandonment, uncertainty

EMOTION

MALADAPTIVE AFFECTIVE
EXPERIENCES
(need transforming)

ADAPTIVE CORE
AFFECTIVE EXPERIENCES
(are transforming)

Pathogenic Affects
Unbearable States of
Traumatic aloneness

Legend: Affective Experiences

Maladaptive Affective Experiences
The Pathogenic Affects (E.g., Overwhelm, Toxic Shame, Fright Without
Solution, Attachment Without Solution); Unbearable States of Traumatic
Aloneness (E.g., Helplessness, Fragmentation, Brokenness; Despair, "The
Black Hole Of Trauma")

Adaptive Core Affective Experiences
Categorical Emotions; Relational Experience, Asymmetric (Attachment)
or Symmetric (Intersubjective); Coordinated Relational Experiences;
Receptive Affective Experiences; Somatic "Drop-Down" States;
Embodied Ego States and their Associated Emotions; Authentic Self-
Experiences; Experiences of Agency, Will Desire; Attachment Strivings;
The Expression of Core Needs

Figure 10.2 The Self–Other–Emotion Triangle (With Embedded
Triangle of Experience): Ambivalent/Resistant
Pando-Mars, 2024, adapted from Diana Fosha, 2020

we may find an opening to their underlying attachment trauma, and even more, a route to corrective experience that can foster deep change.

AEDP Maxim 8, Working With the Self-at-Worst From Under the Aegis of the Self-at Best (Fosha, 2000), was illustrated by the above vignette. As therapist and patient began to develop a collaborative therapeutic relationship in our first session together, we established new grounds upon which to help the patient have an effective experience of self and a realistic experience of other. Through our coordinated efforts, we were setting conditions for Megan to generate new expectancies of self, other, and emotion, which continued throughout her treatment. A therapeutic relationship is not established at once and for all but is constantly renewed, revised, and reestablished as patients grow and what they need from us changes (Russell, 2018).

Thereby, as psychotherapists explicitly tend to how we form our dyads with patients, we help them orient to the present moment from which to face the aftermath of historical trauma, making the work of psychotherapy possible. By offering our presence, attunement, and availability to help, we pave the way for our patients to cultivate self-at-best: having an internal representation of an effective Self, the capacity for a realistic internal representation of other, and a representation of emotions as accessible and capable of being regulated enough to be processed with the company of an Other. Thus, we help them begin the process of transforming their internal working models.

For some of our patients with this pattern, who are leaning toward resistance, we may need a more targeted focus to help build our coordinated therapeutic relationship, which we address in the following section.

Building Receptive Affective Capacity

Although ambivalent/resistant patients tend to be externally focused and reliant on others, some patients actually need considerable help with learning to take in care from another and be able to use it to regulate themselves and calm their nervous system. Early experiences of abandonment or lack of consistent attention by self-absorbed caregivers have left a significant dearth of trust that anyone would want to be there for them or can provide them with enough of what they need. There can be significant doubt in the sincerity of the motivating intention behind gestures of care. In more extreme cases, stubborn bouts of angry resistance deflect such offers and exemplify defenses against relatedness and defenses against emotion, all in one.

The therapist may need to take deliberate steps to help these patients to actually make use of the therapist, even when it is hard to do so. For instance, it is important to help the patient recognize when they rebuff offers of care and help, and that such a strategy is reflexive and protective against the disappointment and fear of being missed, misunderstood, and left to be de facto alone with their distress. The therapist may need to keep reminding the patient to slow down, to listen in, and to pay attention to their experience. Besides penetrating their wall of words to help them to access their somatically based experience, we may need to help our patients learn how to recognize and make use of our presence, care, and responsiveness.

When asking a patient to slow down to emphasize that I am listening, I will say, "I hear you." When an individual expects not to be heard or seen, being explicit with this message is medicinal. Perhaps also needed is to be explicit, saying, "I am here with you." Yet here ambivalence may arise. Ambivalence is the direct result of inconsistency, so it need not be a surprise to psychotherapists when working with someone with the ambivalent/resistant pattern. The patient might respond with "You can give me what I need now, when I am in your office, but can I count on you when I really want your help, when I need you on my time frame?" For the person who is externally focused, conflict arises between receiving what is offered during a psychotherapy session and transferring that to a moment of need when they are on their own time. The delicate edge is the truth that we do meet on a schedule. Our availability is most reliable at our set place and time. The challenge, and yet the key, is for us to understand that the ambivalent dismissing of our here-and-now presence also represents their doubt in their own capacity to hold our care when we are not physically with them. The person struggling with the need for external regulation may well be lacking enough stable internal structure that can hold constancy.

Fortunately, this hails the work of AEDP Maxim 5, Check for the Patient's Receptive Affective Capacity. When the therapist provides contact and care with stability and predictability and makes a practice of checking in with the patient, we show the patient our serious intention for them to feel our presence and to begin to internalize something of how we understand them, and to notice their felt experience when they receive our care. And yet, ambivalence may show up when the therapist checks for the patient's receptive capacity. For example, when the therapist offers support and *with-ness* to undo aloneness and follows up with a relational intervention, such as "Can you feel me with you?," some patients with an ambivalent/resistant pattern might initially respond with a "maybe" or weak "yes." They might follow with an explanation like "But then I will *always* have to do this *entirely* by myself" or "That's only here, can I take you home with me?"

The dual-prong goal is to have both. I want to help patients notice what they can receive, and to notice what happens when they can't. This usually means that an early attachment strategy is activated, and something needs holding and to be known. When the therapist can meet such a place with interest and steady attention, we are overlaying a new experience of receptivity on an old experience of "something missing." When ambivalent patients receive this quality of care, and they experience it repeatedly with us, we begin to provide an experience of being reliable in contrast to the inconsistency they experienced and grew to anticipate. When we meta-process the new experience of the patient's feeling seen and helped, they can begin to realize when they feel met and soothed. Staying with the felt experience of calm or comfort, we encourage them to saturate in the new experience. Absorbing the experience helps them to register their Self's need for connection, and the felt experience of being met by the Other. I am always delighted when patients tell me how they had a conversation with me in their head during the week, or how they thought of me when they knew they needed to calm down. Bringing me to mind is clearly a transitional experience that leads to the capacity to self-regulate.

I recall one of my patients with a hyperactivating strategy who was on the edge of panic during one of the fires in Northern California. She worried about the impact of smoke inhalation. We worked together in the session to help her to regulate, by tuning into her body and being mindful of her moment-to-moment activation and focusing on what she needed to do to feel calm. At the end of the session she said, "Can I take you home in my pocket?"

A version of this question often arises from someone who externally regulates. They might feel "I can do this with you, but what about when I'm alone or you are not there or . . ." When the above patient wanted to take me home with her, I heard her need to feel my support when we were physically apart. Here, we were able to engage the power of portrayal work to enable the patient to internalize my care and presence for her to feel capable of self-regulating when needed. To enhance this integration, I invited her to see how she would do so in the imaginal play of a mini portrayal. By describing her physical experience of relaxation and pairing it with seeing me, we lit up the neural networks in the brain to connect her experience in her body with her picture of me in her mind.

THERAPIST (TH): "How do you want to do that?"

PATIENT (PT): "I'm looking at you and noticing how I feel. My body feels more still. I feel warm. My face here (*hands strokes her cheeks*), my jaw feels some warmth. My belly feels soft . . . a heaviness, some tiredness, but the heaviness is relaxation.

TH: Mm-hmm.

PT: The visual—your brown hair has a glisten to it, and the silvery bluish shawl on your back, your smile, glasses, and I can feel the warmth in your eyes. [**Filling in sensory details.**]

TH: Through the glasses. (*smiling*)

PT: Yeah, through the glasses! (*smiling*) I almost feel like when I leave, I can remember . . . I'm making it a resource, or something like a vision. [**Internalizing the experience.**]

TH: I like that you are pairing what you see to how you feel, pairing the culmination of the work we've done here today. I'm feeling connected to you and imagining that is what your process is noticing . . . "How do I transition this to myself, letting me in or taking me with you?" [**I give words to what I imagine is going on in her mind.**]

PT: Right. Connection is a good antidote or medicine for the anxiety.

TH: Awesome . . . spell that out.

PT: As I said, it could be with myself, as a scaffold, connecting with you or asking to connect in with N. [**her friend**] to help me soothe.

TH: So feel that.

PT: Yeah.

TH: Let yourself register that in your body and see how that is with you.

PT: (*deep exhale*) Thank you . . . I'll see you soon. [**Marking the end of our session.**]

The patient paired being with me with the relaxed feeling in her body and took that with her to remember during the week. Herein is the practice to cultivate building a new kind of internal representation, to consciously make a connection that she can call upon as needed, growing confidence in her capacity to self-regulate. Recalling the movie *Lion*, which was described in Chapter 4, we can see that the psychotherapeutic use of portrayals, of bringing to mind an internalized picture of the other, is making use of an instinctual mechanism that 5-year-old Saroo called upon naturally. When he was lost and alone in Calcutta, one night under a bridge Saroo brought images to mind of his beloved mother and cherished older brother. When he was missing them, he drew upon his memories of their love. Although lost from his family, he held them close in his heart. What a poignant example of self-regulation: Saroo having an internalized representation of his mother and brother to call upon when he needed soothing.

While treating patients who are healing from insecure attachment, we help them to restore a felt sense of security. We do so by applying the mechanisms of what happens naturally in secure attachment when development goes right. Like in the above example, we can reinforce healing by helping our patients practice these natural mechanisms, building their capacity to self-right when development has left some gaps.

In the case of someone who seeks comfort externally, I want to foster deepening their receptive capacity. I begin by letting the patient experience the shift that occurs through our dyadic regulation, emphasizing paying attention to signals of arousal, noticing their experience of being accompanied, undoing aloneness, finding ways to ground, and to take in soothing and care. Receiving the message "I am here with you" and can go with you, can counter the old experience of feeling left alone, unassisted to cope. Then, when the next fear arises ("But what about when I go home?"), we find ways that fit for them to call on us through their imaginal experience. The emergence of my patient's longing to take me with her shows what is possible. She can hold her new connection between her relaxed body, which we have cultivated through our work together, paired with my face and countenance—which she now knows she can call upon at any moment. This is integration: taking the effects of our work home and remembering that she is not alone, she has my help, and is discovering ways she can bring soothing and comfort online as needed.

When the Resistant Side of the Ambivalent/ Resistant Pattern Is More Pronounced

In the next section I discuss a vignette taken from a midtreatment session with a patient, Soraya, whose experiential process reflected more of the angry/resistant aspect of the ambivalent/resistant pattern. Her parents were divorced and her childhood years with her mother were difficult. Her mother was extremely self-centered and inconsistent in her caregiving. In current time, the patient was preoccupied with her boss at work and unhappy in her marriage, feeling ineffective to establish clear expectations and boundaries both at work and at home. In one of our psychotherapy sessions, we were discussing her mixed feelings about psychotherapy, and she said, "The trouble with healing is that it lets my mother off the hook."

The vignette illustrates some of the challenges of working with a patient who is struggling with resistance, and how it plays out with the therapist and within herself as she encounters the potential of connecting with a younger part of herself. Some pathogenic affects emerge, alongside the anger of angry resistance turned inward. We enter the session as Soraya reveals a memory of being alone at night at the age of 6 or 7. As her psychotherapist I aim steadily to see if we can connect with this younger self who seems stuck in the unbearable aloneness of her unresolved attachment trauma.

Vignette 10B: Reunion With Abandoned Self— Developing Self-Action Tendencies

SORAYA (PATIENT, PT): . . . going in circles over and over about the scenario. [She describes her preoccupation at work.]

THERAPIST (TH): Hmm. What about that? Where do you think that comes from in you? [**Shift to exploring.**]

PT: Well, sometimes I, I blame my mother, I just think about how I remember just even at like age 6 or 7 in my bed at night just crying myself to sleep, my mother oblivious, and me just worrying about things, just worrying, and worrying and worrying . . . [**Early preoccupation**]

TH: Ohh (*empathic tone*), can we go in and be with that little 6 year old in you and help that part of you get tended to? Because I think that's the part where you were so alone. Right? [**Active stance to offer experiential portrayal work to help her to connect with her younger self.**]

PT: (*nodding, eyes shift from looking at me to looking up, fill with tears, mouth pushes out*) [**Such a feeling response**]

TH: Mmm, seems like that part just, you know, just be with (*hand to heart*). Let's make some space, you're so available, seems that part is so available right now. [**Deep empathy**]

PT: (*closes eyes, nods*)

TH: (*nods, and head tilts to the left, exhales audibly*) Yeah, just let the feelings be here, let's be with you. (*slow quiet voice, spacious*) What are you noticing?

PT: (*wiping tears, therapist passes tissues*) Well, it's just absurd (*angry, hard tone of voice*).

The possibility of tending to herself evokes anger. At first Soraya appears moved by the possibility of tending to a younger part of herself who was so alone. Her response, nodding, tears, and eye contact show positive signals of coordination. However, when I ask what she is noticing, she moves to a defensive protest against her situation, thus revealing anger, and possibly resistance. The discrepancy between Soraya's nonverbal expression and what she says, demonstrates how the right brain can be ahead of the left brain. Right brain to right brain, she seems to be taking in my caring attention, more than her left brain, full of old preoccupied beliefs, will admit.

TH: What? What are you feeling? [**Redirect her attention from protest to affect.**]

PT: How alone I was . . . (*voice is softer*) [**Which feels more connected to her affective experience**]

TH: Yeah (*nodding, eyes close as if receiving something, then open*), yeah.

PT: Like how can that be going on, you know? [**Puzzled protest**]

As the patient is faced with feeling with herself and for herself, she also gets in touch with her disbelief and anger at the fact she was so alone, which I validate.

TH: Right. So let's try to be with that because I, you know, there's this absurd. I feel . . . how outrageous. I mean . . . [**Empathic joining and elaboration of the impact of being alone.**]

PT: (*nodding*) Right (*eyes close*). [**She acknowledges feeling seen by the therapist.**]

TH: And so that little one there, can we like really be with her, and see what we can? [**Taking the lead and focusing the patient, aiming to bring attention and care to her younger self who was so alone.**]

PT: I just feel like I'm gonna like die . . . if I think about it too much . . . [**feeling leads to reeling**] like I'm just going to crumble. [**Fearing a maladaptive affective response**]

TH: Part of what's happening, I think, is that if we don't let you think about it, then she actually gets abandoned [**Encouraging patient to think about her feelings.**]

PT: Right (*nodding more emphatically*), right. [**Coordinates with therapist**]

TH: Because then she's alone again. [**Feeling compassion for the younger part she acknowledged was so alone, therapist reaches out explicitly—taking** the lead.] So what I actually want to have happen is, you know, for us to be, like for you to let her see if she can feel me. [**Therapist checks for the receptive affective capacity of the younger self to undo aloneness and offer a psychological hand of support.**]

PT: Yeah.

TH: Because the worry is like the signal that she's there, that part of you is there.

PT: Yeah. Right.

TH: And you actually did make it through, right? [**Speaking to the adult self to acknowledge that she knows she survived into adulthood, which her younger self, who is "stuck in the past," doesn't know.**]

PT: (*exhales sharply*) Right.

TH: That younger part of you doesn't know it. I think because she's been cordoned off for survival. Right. So we kind of have to let her be seen, too. [**Being explicit about the intention to undo her aloneness and differentiate the past from the present moment.**]

PT: (*nodding*)

TH: What's that like? What's happening when I say this?

PT: Umm. Yeah, I mean, part of me just doesn't want to go back there. I mean, obviously that feels horrible to say, "Oh, I'm not going to go back there, just going to leave you on your own." [**Her ambivalence displays an inner conflict: resistance.**]

Think about feelings. When the patient, Soraya, is able to acknowledge what she feels and has a chance to put it into dialogue with me, she engages her reflective capacity, which helps her to consider what she is actually saying, and also how that might feel to her younger self. The intervention for patients with ambivalent/resistant attachment is to *think about feelings*, in contrast to asking patients with avoidant attachment to *feel into thoughts*. Soraya did not have the experience of an attachment figure who was paying attention to the impact of their behavior on her. So for her to consider the impact of her behavior on her younger self is actually groundbreaking.

TH: (*nodding, looking serious*) That's what the poor thing had to do for so long. [**Explicit empathy**]

PT: (*nodding*)

TH: Do you have an image of her? An image of that part of you? [**Bypassing the defense**]

PT: (*low voice*) Yeah . . .

TH: I wonder if we could just be with a little, you know, just try to take it step-by-step. So not like submerge you in overwhelming pain because it's too unbearable. It was so unbearable that you had to cut it off. [**Asking permission and titrating to find her window of tolerance.**]

PT: I just picture my room and I just picture a little girl sitting on the bed and I picture, but not in great detail, a little girl. Oh, and then I picture that I had a sliding glass door. [**Green signals, she is entering her imaginal channel of experience.**] And so I picture that being open and these white billowy drapes (*eyes get large*) that I didn't have, um, just blowing in and out [**transformance**] and back and forth. Um, almost like an abandoned home, you know. [**Specificity and the more vivid the scene enhances portrayal work.**]

TH: Mm-hmm, yeah . . .

PT: Like, no one's there (*blows her nose*) to close the . . . it's windy and no one's closing . . . (*trails off*)

TH: Yeah (*eyes furrowing, head leaning in*), oh (*caring tone*).

PT: Like, just abandoned, like, just abandoned.

TH: Yeah. [**These para-verbal utterances communicate therapist "withness" and presence offering comfort with soothing tones of voice.**]

PT: Even though I'm sitting on a bed, the carpet's still there and all the furniture's still there.

TH: But it really kind of gives that feeling of no one's there and this little girl is all alone. I wonder if you can put yourself in the picture as an adult, if you can go to her. [**Reunion/rescue portrayal**]

PT: I can. (*voice tone gets high, wipes tear from eye*) But then I just feel I'm not good enough. [**Her feeling unworthy comes to light.**]

When the adult self feels unworthy to go to the younger self. This may have been too big of a step for the patient, which can happen when the sense of insecurity and lack of self-confidence is strong and the patient is stuck in a self-at-worst self experience of not being enough. We could shift our exploration and focus on unblending, which is a technique for separating out two parts of the self that is used by Schwartz (1997; Schwartz & Sweezy, 2019) in internal family systems, and by Napier (1996) to help patients differentiate their present-day adult self from a younger self. Proceeding with unblending, I would help Soraya lean into what she has grown and developed as her adult self who is capable at work and responsible for her two small children.

I could have her see her younger self and notice how she feels about her, to establish what indeed might be a necessary next step. However, in this moment, I choose to accompany Soraya and to explore her feeling of not being good enough. I am sensing some pathogenic self-state needs accompanying and regulating.

TH: Well, now you need to take me with you so we can be with you. [**Extending myself as a relational bridge.**] What's the feeling of you're not good enough? Where does that come from? [**Exploring this self-at-worst compromised self.**]

PT: Just the feeling like I don't. I don't want to go get her. I want someone who's happier, more sure of herself . . . [**Self-doubt and insecure attitude come in, and yet she does say how she wants to feel.**]

TH: Oh, Soraya . . . (*sad voice*) ohh. [**Empathy for her experience**]

PT: (*sniffs, eyes closed, looks forlorn, looks down*) Yeah. I just feel yucky.

TH: Yeah. What's the yucky feeling? Can you just say more to me? [**Engaging with receptivity and acceptance to help patient regulate her shame.**]

PT: I just feel ashamed and yucky. [**When I hear "yucky" I think of disgust and the toxicity of unresolved trauma.**]

TH: Where does yucky feel in your body? [**Somatic exploration**]

PT: My stomach . . .

TH: Yeah. What does it feel like in there? [**Encouraging her to identify her experience.**]

PT: (*hand moves to jaw*) . . . and my jaw.

TH: In your jaw.

PT: Just anxious, actually. Just tight. [**Labeling somatic elements can be regulating.**]

TH: Tight.

PT: Tight, and butterflies.

TH: (*nodding*) So what happens when you look at me and how do you see me with you right now? [**Using my presence in an attempt to contact her and offer dyadic regulation, to be "in it together."**]

PT: Mm, yeah. I see you as gentle and kind, and that you're lucky because you don't have the yucky . . .

TH: Yeah, I'm lucky. (*quizzical tone*) What about my caring for you? (*looks concerned*) Can you feel my caring for you? [**I bypass the comparison—a relational defense—and redirect to offering care and checking her receptive affective capacity.**]

PT: *(quick nods)*

TH: Can that little girl feel my caring for you?

PT: *(nods again)* Yeah.

TH: Caring for you. Because that's been so on my mind right now. [**Making my relational care explicit.**]

PT: *(looking toward therapist and away, tearing, nodding)*

TH: I feel so tenderly toward you. I just want, want, you to be able to feel that, because you were so alone. And it was just so outrageous for so long, you're suffering from that. It wasn't your fault. It wasn't your fault. [**Platforming to let her know I really get how awful it was for her.**]

PT: Right . . .

TH: And it developed this way in your brain that there's this, like falling out sometimes.

PT: *(deep exhale)* [**Some receptivity reveals itself in this deep exhale.**] Yeah.

TH: *(head is tilted over like I'm talking to the young one inside)* And, and that's part of, you know, what I'm feeling like we need to bring in, you know, some caring in a deep way to that little one inside and to you.

PT: *(nodding)* Oh, it's funny, because, I mean, I do feel like we're . . . I just don't want to take people's shit anymore. I want to like, be able to stand up for myself. [**Glimmer of transformance—reveals her longing for self-action tendencies.**] You know?

TH: Yeah. Yeah.

PT: That's so hard.

TH: [**Meeting her in this transformance, striving to find some capable self she can draw upon to resource her.**] And yet that's kind of what you did the other day. [**Affirm her recent experience.**]

PT: *(nodding, eyes open wider)* Right.

Checking for her receptive affective capacity. While explicitly providing relational accompaniment, I helped the patient to explore her felt experience of not good enough, which was at the edge of a maladaptive self experience and needed transforming. By holding my attention and care and checking in with her experience in the present moment, Soraya nods that yes, both she and her younger self feel my care, which is such an important antidote to shame (Kaufman, 1980/1992, 1996). As we deepen into this experience, the patient has a shift and remarks how she doesn't want to take people's shit anymore, which has the potential of a corrective self experience. My sense is that she has been taking in something of my care and is feeling bolstered to recognize her choice about what she does take in. It's almost like instead of responding to receiving my care, she asserts what she doesn't want. This remark portends action on her own behalf, which mobilizes her. We processed more about her experience of differentiating her assertion from her coworker's response. And then she shifts back to the portrayal.

PT: *(nodding, face softens)* Yeah, I'm trying to picture like a whole bunch of people [she reenters the portrayal] encircling her, you know, people who are laughing and people who are happy, they're fighting in, you know, just encircling her . . .

TH: Yeah, good. [Affirming and goes right with her.]

PT: . . . and kind of lifting her up and floating, floating her out of there. [Spontaneous rescue portrayal—taking her out of the unbearable situation.]

This is a huge shift. Soraya imagines encircling her younger self with a whole bunch of happy people. How did this happen? One possibility is to see that we engaged in unblending her sense of not being enough from a time when she was assertive and acting on her own behalf. I had highlighted that her assertion may not have landed with the result she wanted, but that part wasn't her fault. This differentiation seemed to ignite her willingness to undo the aloneness of her younger self.

TH: What's that like? How is she? [Metaprocessing to see how the young one is experiencing this.]

PT: It feels like it will never be enough though. [After each step forward, another backward step appears.] And that's it, I mean I constantly need reassurance. [Said so quietly I don't pick up on this—otherwise that could have been a nice intervention—to see if we could go and provide reassurance.]

TH: Hold on for a second. [Recognizing we're taking a turn and wanting to regulate the feeling of not enough.] What's the visceral feeling of that? Let's just be with you. [Noticing the ambivalent defensive pattern of "never enough" has kicked back in.]

PT: It's just that it feels so good *(hand makes grasping gesture)*, and I can never get enough of it.

The ambivalent pattern expresses fear that they can never get enough. By keeping the interventions on asking Soraya what's happening in her body, we gain access to both what feels good, and what she fears isn't enough. This is ambivalence in action. Classic. Not able to take in the good feeling when she fears it won't be enough. In this vivid clinical moment we see what Mary Ainsworth (1978/2015) observed about the difference between the ambivalent child, who fears they will never get enough of what they want, in contrast to the avoidant child, who fears what they want. By carefully tracking what occurs moment-to-moment, we have the opportunity to explore the resistance.

TH: Mm-hmm. What stops you, what's not receiving that fully? [**Exploring the defense**] How does it become not enough?

PT: Right, I guess. I guess I feel like I need more than my due share or my fair share. [**Internal working model—belief. By exploring the defense we get to its origin.**]

TH: You certainly need more than you were ever given. [**Making explicit that indeed, this was her historical experience.**]

PT: Right. (*smiles and nods*)

TH: Right, right. So part of you doesn't even know what enough is. But my sense is that it has something to do with being reliable and constant.

PT: (*nods*) Constant. [**Repeating "constant," she is considering . . .**]

TH: You know, regular, like you can rely on it. [**Elaborating the meaning of constant.**]

PT: Yeah. Like I feel, you know, the little girl in the middle of all these arms around her and floating her up [**now she is back in the portrayal**], and her just sort of drinking it in, but yeah, just feeling like they're going to go away or just like (*voice trails off*) I don't know, I had something and I lost my train of thought. [**Ambivalent discourse of getting lost emerges on the precipice of the new experience and the old worry.**]

TH: And so that sense of on the one hand it feels so good, but then this fear that it's not going to be enough, that it's going to go away. What would you say to that little girl? What can those arms say to that little girl when she gets afraid that it's not going to be enough? [**Reentering the portrayal to see if we can pick up where she left off.**]

PT: Well, I'm stuck because I feel like, I don't know. You grow up. You can't always have all these people surrounding you, doting on you. [**Resistance kicks in—primarily out of her lack of experience of being soothed, she** is unable to give what she hasn't received—so I step in to offer help and provide a new message of comfort and reliability.]

TH: See, I want to say, "I'm always here." [Scaffolding her experience.]

PT: (eyes open, nodding and gazing at me) [A nonverbal look of openness and receptivity.]

TH: That this image of all these hands supporting you, are always available to you, whatever you need from me, whenever you need me, just close your eyes and I'll be there. We're always here for you. You just have to ask. [Suggesting internalizing the image as a resource.]

PT: I feel like it. I need to. This . . . but it's totally . . . It is the emptiness that I feel. I just imagine that people who are my age and still can call their mother and feel better after talking to their mom, that piece I'm just never going to get. [Reverts to old expectancy, and her pain, which emerges as angry resistance.]

On the heels of the new experience her wounding emerges, bundled with angry resistance. Curiously, or not really, given that we are working with a pattern of ambivalent/resistant, as we get closer to giving Soraya's younger self accompaniment and a way out of the past, she becomes helpless/hopeless about what she didn't get and how far away she feels from being able to come to resolution. Here again notice right next to the possibility of comfort brings the ambivalence/resistance to it. In the next section, some of Soraya's verbal discourse is extreme. She actually says that to not receive care and comfort at the right time in life, well, the person should not be living. I'll save the detail for each reader to discover in the transcript. Know that I see this as an important revelation of just how desperate and hopeless Soraya feels. And by staying with her, undoing her aloneness, the power of transformance does arise.

TH: Yeah. And that's something you have to come to terms with, there's a lot of grieving there, there's a sadness there . . .

PT: Right.

TH: That your mother's just never going to be the kind of mother you wish you could have, and that's very, very sad. But that has nothing to do with you. That has to do with her. [Empathy and distinguishing between what happened to her and who she is, building differentiation.]

PT: Right? But I just feel like I can't reconcile, like I don't feel like I can ever feel okay. [Pathogenic affect]

TH: This feeling—that's a fear.

PT: But I actually feel like people who don't get that should be euthanized. [Although this is shocking to hear, I continue to explore what drives her to say this.]

TH: People who don't get what?

PT: You don't get that right kind of core support because you can never get over it. [Extreme hopelessness]

TH: I so disagree with you (shake my head side to side), I disagree with you there. (softly) [Stepping in with a differentiated perspective.]

PT: I feel like I can't ever get over it. [Example of an anxious thought expressed as a fact.]

TH: Right (gently), you worry that you can't ever get over it. [I point out that this is a worry, not a fact.]

PT: I want that feeling. I want that safety. I want that assuredness. [Transformance longing] Like you get it at the right time, it's like in your account, you know (eyes look down, fingertips press into the couch). [Her longing arises, and fear is close behind.]

TH: Right—and that's part of what we're doing here. [Affirming the possibility of healing.]

PT: (looks at therapist, with worried eyes)

TH: There's this . . . your brain has these pathways of deficits of what you didn't get. [I move to psycho-education—to encourage thinking about her feelings as a way to build new possibilities.] But when I ask you if you can feel me and if you can take me in and you say, actually, yes, I feel your care and I feel your kindness, you know, that starts to build new pathways that the part of you who is so alone can actually start to register. There's another way. (kind eyes and tender voice)

Therapist takes the lead to affirm how change is not only possible but is actually happening. I am affirming all of the positive steps I see Soraya is taking. Even though she presents defensive and resistant patterns of thought, she is giving space to go to the younger self, to do a rescue portrayal (lifting her out of the abandoned place). She is doing way more than she believes she is doing. Here I am up against a potential therapist blind spot: to not get overwhelmed or agitated by Soraya's negativity but to hold my experience of the whole of the session. I know I am feeling patient. I have the metaskills of firm and caring online. Despite how she stops the forward momentum to verbalize something against herself after each step, I see how she keeps plugging away, stays engaged with me, and returns to a next step. I hold this, which is so important for psychotherapists to recognize and acknowledge "both/and." Only by holding both can we help our patients not to get stuck in the polarity of resistance.

PT: *(nods, as if receiving and absorbing)*

TH: And then I think there is grieving for one who felt so abandoned and really helping her to find *(pause, breath)* how to take people in now via these new pathways that are getting developed. [**Therapist provides guidance for next steps.**]

PT: I don't know, I'm mad, and I just don't want to—why should I have to live with this huge deficit? [**Angry resistance**]

TH: See, I think part of the dilemma is there's a fight. There's a fight about really letting yourself receive at the deepest level of caring that could heal some of that because there's a part of you that's so mad. [**I address the conflict of the angry resistance—remember her earlier comment that for her to heal would mean letting her mother off the hook.**]

PT: Right, right. [**Click of recognition**]

TH: That doesn't want to let it in all the way.

PT: Right. Which I'm seeing like, today, I was really seeing that. Seeing how it came on, I want to hang on to this, the awfulness of my past. [**Here she is owning her resistance, which shows how she is developing her self-reflective capacity.**] Is it time?

TH: It is.

PT: *(sits up)* Time of my childhood, like, yeah.

TH: Yeah. So that's really good to see. [**Affirming the possibility of being empowered by the understanding of her reflection.**]

PT: Hmm. Okay.

TH: I mean, it's painful, but I think it's important to recognize.

PT: Yeah, I think this was valuable. I think I was hoping to feel more, more resolved, more solved, more like, I'll leave here now and I won't have . . . Everybody will respect me. But . . . [**The conflict between what wasn't enough and what she got!**]

TH: Right. But I think that while I want that for you, I think that the truth of today might have—it's kind of like that slower, but faster.

PT: Yeah.

TH: More the deeper truth.

PT: Yeah. And sometimes I'm like—eh, and then I feel lighter, you know, later [**heralds State 2 transformation**], If that makes sense. It takes a while to sink in. Oops (*writing check*), I wrote Cando. [**Perhaps this is an unconscious slip—can do!**]

The Following Session 2 Weeks Later

Soraya comes in the following week with new reflections after digesting her experience.

PT: Uh, let's see. So I thought a lot about the exercise that we did last time, and I found it very comforting and I thought about it a lot (*with a musical tone in her voice*). [**Sometimes patients surprise themselves, and us, by what they do with the material of psychotherapy between sessions.**]

TH: Tell me what you thought about, what you found comforting.

PT: I just kept having this image of me and all those people kind of holding me up and kind of, leaving that house, that childhood house and that bedroom (*looking down, smiling*). Yeah. And I think it's been really helpful (*looks up at me*). [**In the time between sessions she has held on to the image, and metabolized the experience.**]

The proof is in the pudding. Despite all of the angry resistance, Soraya actually took in enough of our work together to allow herself to move toward her younger self. When she was on her own, she was effective in having a corrective self experience as she truly continued to make use of her image of leaving her childhood home. I believe that what she received from our session was related to not being alone with her fear of not being enough and receiving enough nourishment from me to counter her fears. These were crucial ingredients for her to take home with her and internalize, to cook up what was new into a corrective experience she could make sense of for herself.

TH: Great. Yeah. I'm interested in being with that comforting (*draws hands together and stretching them out*) and that helpful and unpacking that [**metaprocessing the specific benefits she named**], getting to know what's happening.

PT: I wonder if I can describe that. Like I think so much stuff has been stemming from just a core feeling of I'm not . . . And that image and that rallying of people behind me and rooting for me. Um, it's just making that shift a little bit. [**Making use of inner resources to shift her felt sense of not being enough.**]

TH: You have your hand here (*mirroring her hand on her heart*), and I wonder if you could just take another minute with that sense of your hand (*tapping my chest*). [**Exploring her somatic signals.**]

PT: Mm-hmm (*brings her hand to her heart*). It's, it's also part of the comforting thing of this is okay. "I'm okay." There were a lot of really bad circumstances. You know. [**Differentiating who she is from the circumstances of her past.**]

This is huge for Soraya to acknowledge—that she is "okay." She named that the circumstances were bad, in acknowledgment that she is not what happened to her, another self-corrective experience to dispel psychic equivalence.

TH: (*slow and drawn out*) Yeah.

PT: A lot of bad and unfortunate, you know, wasteful, in that I had just spent so much energy on them instead of being me, instead of just, you know, relishing me [**core state reflection**] and, um . . . [**The true sense arises with self-compassion and undoing of psychic equivalence.**]

TH: Yes.

PT: And participating in the world.

TH: Yes.

PT: Yeah, I don't know if I am like, like, ready. And when I went to my high school reunion, it was like, there was this whole other me, like maybe the real me [**true self**], you know? It was this whole other me [**declarative**]. But it was so the opposite of how I felt internally. Like in high school, I was worried I wasn't pretty. I felt fat. I didn't have a boyfriend when everyone had a boyfriend. But it really wasn't like many people talk about their, like traumatic teen years vis-à-vis their peers. [**Core state comparing past and present, weaving her autobiographical narrative.**]

TH: Yeah.

PT: But for me so minute—compared to the kind of misery I felt . . . so repressed by my mother—I had to spend so much time processing the insanity of existing in her reality. Yeah . . . like I was a prisoner.

TH: Right. I totally get what you're saying. And, and the way that you're speaking about it, feels like there's a sorting out of you and her that's happening. [**Affirming and harnessing that she is actively differentiating from her mother.**]

PT: Yeah. Yeah, that's a good way. I feel really removed. Yeah. From her. But not so much in a denial way but just in a like, I am not her. [**Declarative truth**]

TH: Yes, what a declaration. [**Differentiation**]

PT: Yeah.

TH: I mean that you get to know that in a very deep way right now. [**Affirmation of core self**]

Summary. In this vignette illustration we are working directly with the conflicts that drive ambivalent/resistant patterning. When the patient is faced with the potential of abandoning her younger self, she has an opportunity to investigate the ways she internalized how she was treated and how she wants to be with herself. When she began to get the attention and care she needed—she resisted and moved against the process. Her adult self felt unworthy of being enough for her younger self and also feared that there would never be enough of what she needed, right out of Ainsworth's (1978/2015) notebook about the ambivalent pattern. Yet, as we, therapist and patient, held and explored her fears, they released a bit at a time. When the patient takes her portrayal work home and sees her younger self being supported to leave the house and bedroom of her childhood behind, she feels comforted. The patient is able to have a corrective self experience, differentiating how she felt as a kid from who she is now, and free from "the insanity of living inside her mother's reality." Free from being overly immersed in her mother's state of mind, she now knows she is not her. Her internal working model is rewiring to a more effective internal representation of Self and a more realistic internal representation of her mother, as the Other, not the ideal mother she would want but no longer the one who holds her back from living life on her own terms.[2]

Healing Ambivalent/Resistant Attachment

In this chapter, a major theme of the vignettes has been patients differentiating from their caregiver's state of mind and turning their attention to self-discovery and self-action tendencies. In contrast to helping someone with avoidant strategies to develop relational-action tendencies—the capacity to connect to self and to others, and be able to receive and give care—someone with ambivalent strategies needs corrective self experiences, and the release of self-action tendencies. Cultivating a sense of self and the capacity to care for self is crucial. Connecting to the inner child who felt abandoned is key. Ambivalence to fully receiving comfort due to the fear it will leave or not be enough needs to be processed in the relationship between therapist and patient. By helping patients to both internalize their therapist's care and reliability and build a relationship with their younger aspects of self, the push–pull dynamic to love and be loved can ease with the presence of self-to-self connection (Lamagna, 2011; Lamagna & Gleiser, 2007).

Here are some of the main intervention pathways we showed in this chapter:

- Take an active therapist stance: help patients to *slow* down
- Offer explicit help; contain tangential speech
- Help client make use of your presence and care
- Develop patient's capacity to internalize soothing and self-compassion
- Distinguish between thoughts and feelings, emotionality, and adaptive core emotion
- Connect core emotions with present experience
- Check for and build receptive affective capacity
- Cultivate connection to self experience
- Affirm emergent signs of self-agency, internal guidance, and wisdom
- Identify and tend to younger parts that were abandoned by the patient, as well as caregivers
- Support and affirm differentiation between self and other, between past and present
- Amplify glimmers of transformance: containment, self-soothing, self-knowing, and internal guidance

11

The History of the Disorganization Category (Grid 2)

Isn't it ironic . . . we ignore those who adore us, adore those who ignore us, hurt those who love us, and love those who hurt us.
—ATTRIBUTED TO ELLEN HOPKINS

Disorganization: The Collapse of Strategy & the Strategy of Collapse

In contrast to being an organized pattern of attachment (as is true of both the secure and the insecure patterns—avoidant, ambivalent/resistant—we have discussed so far), disorganization is not a pattern of attachment per se but rather a disordered quality of experience that occurs when a person is lacking a coping strategy for dealing with attachment-related trauma that overwhelms.

Disorganization is related to unresolved trauma in caregivers. When caregivers have states of mind that are unresolved due to their own trauma, which can be historical or ongoing due to current conditions in their lives, they are usually frightened and/or frightening in response to their children's attachment needs. These caregivers often have difficulties being with themselves and with regulating their own affective experiences; this challenges their capacity to tend to the needs of their babies. Consequently, their infants and children cannot rely on them to be consistently available, much less sensitive and responsive.

Being unresolved for their own trauma interferes with how these caregivers interact with their infants. Often their behavior is disturbing and dysregulated. They are often out of sync, misreading the infant's signals.

Their actions are loaded with mismatches and incongruent behaviors, con-fusion being present for both the infant and caregiver. As a result, the child has difficulty trusting their caregiver, and then develops difficulties trust-ing others and subsequently with knowing and trusting themselves. Thus, disorganization reveals the breakdown of innate attachment behavior: the breaking down of trust in the attachment figure to provide protection and care, the breakdown of the caregiving behavioral system to respond with care to the attachment needs of the child, and the breaking down of self-trust in the child that they will be able to evoke the help that is needed.

By the time a child reaches the age of 6, patterns develop in response to the disorganization and confusion. Some of these children develop role reversal and other strategies of control: these are recognizable coping behaviors to deal with the disorganization in their caregivers, and their own disorganized/disordered attachment. We stand by the initial findings about disorganization as a collapse in strategy, since it points to the challenges inherent in treating disorganized attachment. At the same time, we recog-nize that by adulthood, many of our patients who present with disorgani-zation first present with strategies of control, which affects many of their patterns of behavior in relationship, and reveal the collapse of strategy only when they are unable to rely on those controlling strategies they have built. Or for some, feeling desperate, yet helpless to obtain the help they need, can drive them to collapse in a last-ditch effort to draw support. Thus, we identify not only the collapse of strategy but also the strategy of collapse.

In the preceding chapters on the formation of avoidant and ambivalent/resistant attachment, both insecure yet organized patterns of attachment, we brought in Mary Ainsworth's early findings of the Strange Situation, the Baltimore home observations, and the AAI to call attention to the origins of these patterns of attachment. We have also described the secure attach-ment pattern to show how psychotherapists can aim to set the conditions for secure relating with our patients. Now, as we begin to discuss working with patients who show signs of disorganization, looking at how the cate-gory itself came to be identified can help us organize ourselves in the com-plexities of disorganization. We begin with observations that came from Ainsworth's Strange Situation, and continue with research that developed with Mary Main, Beatrice Beebe, and Karlen Lyons-Ruth, and their many colleagues and collaborators. The final section of this chapter looks at how patients present in psychotherapy when disorganization/unresolved trauma is in the picture.

Ainsworth's Strange Situation Protocol

How children responded to the stress of separation and reunion with their parent was observed during the Strange Situation procedure. Originally Ainsworth and her colleagues (1978/2015) noted three patterns of response in the children: these became the categories of secure and insecure avoidant and insecure ambivalent/resistant attachment. However, Ainsworth et al. discovered that not all children could be fit into the three categories of secure and insecure attachment originally identified by Ainsworth, patterns referred to as the A, B, C categories of the Strange Situation Protocol (SSP).

The classification of "disorganized attachment" came from researching infants who were considered unclassifiable with respect to Ainsworth's A, B, C classifications. Ainsworth's student Silvia Bell made the first judgment of an infant's unclassifiable behavior in her doctoral dissertation. This infant was then assigned to a "best-fitting" category (Ainsworth et al., 1978/2015, p. 63; Ainsworth & Bell, 1970). Mary Main, who at the time was also one of Ainsworth's students, became fascinated with the kids who did not fit: furthermore, she was unsatisfied with classifying these fundamentally unclassifiable infants into a "forced" or "best-fitting" category. These infants became the focus of Main's dissertation research.

To picture what forms the basis for organized secure, organized insecure avoidant, organized insecure ambivalent/resistant, and disorganized/disordered attachment, we review the relationship between the four behavioral systems of attachment that Bowlby (1969/1982) identified, and the part they play in child–caregiver interactions.

The Four Behavioral Systems of Attachment

Bowlby's (1969/1982) four behavioral systems of attachment are the fear/wariness system, the attachment system, the caregiving system, and the exploratory system. Bowlby identified that the fear/wariness behavioral system in infants and children is aroused by external conditions, such as being alone, separated from an attachment figure, loud sounds, darkness, animals, strange objects or persons, or anything learned to cause pain. Due to fear, children express alarm in many forms of crying from whimpering to sudden cries for help or screaming. Optimally, these cries bring the attachment figure to the child. As a child becomes more mobile, they can seek contact with their caregiver.

The fear/wariness behavioral system is closely linked to the attachment behavioral system and both of them have the biological function of protecting the child. The attachment behavioral system is activated when the child is feeling distressed by (a) internal conditions, such as fatigue, hunger, pain, cold, and ill health; (b) conditions of the environment: if the attachment figure is absent or departing, or if the attachment figure discourages or even rejects proximity; or (c) rebuffs by other adults or children (Bowlby, 1969/1982).

Attachment behavior is biologically designed so that when the child's attachment system is aroused, their parent's reciprocal caregiving behavioral system is activated. When the child is alarmed or distressed and cries out, their attachment behavioral system calls the caregiver to the child. As children become mobile, the child moves toward their attachment figure for protection and care, thus drawing the attachment figure's attention.Caregiving stems from the parent's innate wiring to protect or care for their children. Ideally, the parent is capable to recognize what is distressing or potentially dangerous to their child, and to then provide an appropriate response. When the frightened child is met by a sensitive and responsive caregiver, physical contact, such as touch, cuddling, and holding, can quiet the child's attachment-seeking behavior. In other words, the child settles within the safe haven of their caregiver. In a secure functioning dyad, a child builds trust in the signaling that arises from their attachment behavioral system in tandem with the responsiveness of their parent's caregiving behavioral system. When their distress has been met, and they know their caregiver is available as a secure base, then fear subsides, and then their exploratory system is free to arise, which naturally occurs in securely attached pairs/dyads (Ainsworth et al., 1978/2015; Bowlby, 1969/1982).

The child's fear/wariness system, the attachment behavioral system, and their parent's caregiving behavioral system were studied in the Strange Situation research. Distinctions between secure and insecure attachment led researchers to identify outliers to the first three patterns identified by Ainsworth and colleagues (1978/2015).

The following section contrasts organized patterns of attachment with disorganization.

Early Observations: How the Category of Disorganization Came to Be

During the separation and reunion phases of the Strange Situation procedure, the relationship between each child's fear/wariness system and the attachment behavioral system was investigated. The child classified as secure expressed sadness upon separation from their caregiver and was soothed by their caregiver's presence when they returned, which exemplifies how a secure relationship functions. Once the child feels connected to the parent and calmed in themselves, they can return their attention to the environment and are free to engage and enjoy their exploratory behavioral system (Ainsworth et al., 1978/2015).

The infants classified as avoidant deactivate their attachment behavior by moving away and/or looking away from the caregiver, and instead, direct their attention to the environment. When their caregiver returns, the children steer away from seeking comfort. The children classified as ambivalent/resistant often hyperactivate their attachment behavior by directing their attention solely to the caregiver and alternate between inconsolable clinging and angry protest; even when their caregiver returns, the children are unable to settle or receive comfort.

As mentioned above, there were children whose behavior was not readily assigned to the secure or one of the insecure categories.

Main became intent on deciphering the behavior of the infants who were identified as unclassifiable, or as a last resort, assigned to a "best-fitting" category. Identifying the *difficult-to-classify* infants through the lens of conflict behavior led to what ultimately became the category of disorganized/disordered attachment. To understand how fear and threat-driven behavior underlie adult disorganization, and to distinguish between the conflict that drives the ambivalent/resistant pattern of attachment, we review the findings of the significant research that began with Bell and Main, and has continued with Beebe, Lyons-Ruth, and their colleagues.

Additionally, these early observations shed light on the varieties of experience that led Fosha (2000b) to describe disorganizing behavior as "not feeling and not dealing" (p. 44). "Not feeling" is shorthand meant to capture the difficulties a person may have perceiving, receiving, and expressing affective experiences because of numbness, dissociation, dysregulation, pathogenic affects, shame spirals, and fragmentation. "Not feeling" also includes incomplete affective experiences. The completion of core affective experiences leads to the release of adaptive action tendencies (Frijda, 1986) that are salient to healing unresolved trauma at the heart of disorganization.

During her doctoral studies, Main had been drawn to ethologist Robert Hinde's (1966) book *Animal Behavior* and his observations of animals in conflict situations. Hinde described "conflict behaviors" (pp. 396–421), which he determined were arising from the simultaneous activation of incompatible systems. Main (1973) related this to the appearance of conflict behavior in infants and studied Ainsworth's narrative records for evidence of infant conflict behavior with respect to their parents in the home. As part of her dissertation research, Main recorded conflict behavior in 21-month-old infants/toddlers and found about 10% of the infants difficult to classify according to the A, B, C categories of the Strange Situation. In the home observations of these five children, there were unusual levels of difficulty in the mother–infant interactions. Notably, at least three of the five mothers had behaved most peculiarly with their offspring. One of the most frightening examples Main reports was seeing one mother responding to her child with frightening animal-like behaviors (e.g., including the mother's bared teeth, and her growling, hissing, and snarling, all of which convey extreme threat).

Later, Main and her colleague Donna Weston (1981) reviewed low-risk Berkeley Strange Situations and found that 13% of the infants exhibited conflict behaviors in a stressful situation, discovering them to be unclassifiable: "Conflict behaviors have a disordered, purposeless or odd appearance and seem to lack an immediate explanation" (p. 935). Subsequently, Main and Judith Solomon (1990) reviewed 200 of their Bay Area, California, unclassified infants to search for specific themes in the diverse expressions of conflict behaviors. They noted how some of the children approached their parent by moving backward or they moved toward the parent and stopped midway as if in a freeze-frame. They identified displays of "conflicted, odd, or inexplicable" behaviors in some of the children.

Main and Solomon's (1990) significant finding was that those infants whose behavior in the Strange Situation was not classifiable in the A, B, or C systems, did not appear to resemble one another in any coherent, organized way. Instead, Main and Solomon recognized that what these infants shared in common were "bouts or sequences of behavior which seemed to lack a readily observable goal, intention, or explanation" (p. 122). They selected the following clusters of behaviors as indices of disorganization:

1. Sequential displays of contradictory behavior
2. Simultaneous displays of contradictory behavior
3. Undirected, misdirected, incomplete, or interrupted movements
4. Stereotypes, asymmetrical or mistimed movements, or anomalous postures
5. Freezing, stilling, slow movements or expression
6. Display of apprehension regarding the caregiver
7. Overt signs of disorientation, including confusion (pp. 134–140)

Main (1973, 1979) developed a scale for assessing "disorganized/disordered" behavior (Lyons-Ruth & Jacobvitz, 2008). The majority of infants showing conflict behaviors fit a description of "disorganized/disoriented," which led Main and Solomon (1986, 1990) to devise the fourth classification, *D*, to add to Ainsworth's categories. Indicators of disorganization include sequential or simultaneous displays of contradictory behavior patterns; undirected, incomplete, or interrupted movements or expressions; freezing, stilled, slow movements or expressions; apprehension regarding the parent; and aspects of disorganization or disorientation, including confusion (1990, pp. 134–140).

When There Is Fear: The Collapse of an Organized Strategy

Years later, Main and Hesse (1990, 1999) identified that dissociated fear was a hallmark of disorganized attachment, and that the *haven of safety was a source of alarm*. When children were frightened by their parents, this presented a dilemma they called "fright without solution" (1999, p. 484). They described this paradox as one in which "impulses to approach the parent as the infant's haven of safety will inevitably conflict with impulses to flee from the parent as a source of alarm" (Hesse & Main, 1999, p. 484). The children could neither approach their parent for comfort nor avoid their parent and turn their attention to the environment to cope. Instead, their behaviors showed an array of odd postures or movements; sudden inappropriate affect; and mixed signals of approach and avoid, such as moving backward toward their parent or freezing midway to the parent with arms up in the air or becoming still with a trance-like expression.

Fosha (personal communication, February 12, 2024), in conversation with Pando-Mars about the very phenomenon described by Hesse and Main's (1999) powerful phrase of "fright without solution," came up with the phrase "attachment without solution." In their dialogue, Fosha realized that "attachment without solution" is the paradox counterpart to "fright without solution": the attachment impulse to reach for the protection of the attachment figure so as to feel safe when the fear/wariness system gets activated cannot be exercised when the parent themselves is the source of the fear. The fright doesn't have a solution but neither does the attachment: the adaptive action of the fright is to escape from danger and the adaptive action tendency of the attachment system is to seek safety through reaching for the protection of the attachment figure. When the parent is the source of the fear, neither adaptive action tendency can be put into action: There is no solution. The result is the paralysis and freeze that Main and Solomon (1990) described in the behavior of the children for whom the D category, disorganized/disoriented, was created.

In the Strange Situation, the avoidant children used an organized strategy of deactivating their attachment system, stemming from their expectancies of rejection from their attachment figure. Relatedly, the ambivalent/resistant attachment children also displayed an organized strategy, hyperactivating their attachment system via inconsolable crying and angry protest to get the attention of their often inconsistently responsive attachment figure. Main and Hesse (1990) described what characterized the behavior for the disorganized children in the reunion phase of the Strange Situation: When their attachment figure appears, they were confronted by their expectancies of the often unpredictable frightening or frightened—and thus confusing—behavior of their parent. Their fright and confusion, or disorientation, stops them in their tracks, where they feel neither safe to approach nor safe to flee. And exploration does not even enter the picture.

Main and Hesse (1990) found "In contrast to both avoidant and ambivalent infants—who may be frightened by difficulties in obtaining caregiver responsiveness in stressful situations—the fear the D infant experiences stems from the parent as its source" (p. 180). Seeking comfort from the one who is frightening or frightened themselves or whose caregiving behavior is disordered, disrupts the child's approach and the child is subjected to the apprehension that Hesse and Main (1999) named "fright without solution" (p. 484).

In disorganization, collapse happens between the fear/wariness system and the attachment behavioral system. When the infant begins to engage their attachment system, fear of the parent arises and they become incapable to reach out to them for comfort nor use an organized strategy to protect themselves from fear (Main & Hesse, 1990). In other words, the child either detaches from their feelings of fear or they detach from their urge to seek protection in the caregiver, which is what Fosha (2000b) refers to as "not feeling and not dealing" (p. 44). In psychotherapy sessions, when we begin to engage relationally with some patients, our invitation to connect instigates the arousal of their attachment system, which can be especially alarming for those with disorganized attachment.

Daniel Siegel's (2007) conceptualization of the disorganized pattern is when longing and fear co-arise, no response is possible given that two neurological circuits cannot fire at the same time. When the ones who are supposed to protect and care for you are frightening or frightened themselves, to need and approach them is incompatible with fearing and wanting to get away from them. Consequently, it's as if one of the circuit breakers kicks off. Fright without solution occurs as the innate biological pairing between the neurological circuits of the fear/wariness behavioral system and the attachment behavioral system breaks down.

Disorganization can coincide with other patterns of attachment when attachment-related fear surfaces. "Disorganized and disoriented" behaviors reflect the person's absence of a coherent and adaptive coping strategy, which was correlated with the unresolved state of mind of the caregiver (Main et al., 1985). Disorganization occurs as the collapse of "behavioral or attentional strategies" (Hesse & Main, 1999) that happens when early attachment needs are wired with trauma. In adult patients, collapse might show up as sinking into pathogenic affects, dropping into states of unbearable aloneness, and having difficulty making use of the therapist's presence and care. The helplessness of "fright without solution" manifests in these dark places where trust in showing the need for comfort is shut down by anticipated fear of the attachment figure.

When the attachment figure is threatening, a child is faced with an irreconcilable dilemma. Unsafe to feel or express their fear, for lack of a suitable caregiving response, they anticipate overwhelm. Often, they dissociate, *disconnecting* longing from the attachment behavioral system and/or *disconnecting from* fear and overwhelm arising from the fear/wariness system (i.e., thus not feeling). In this way, dissociation dismantles the charge. Porges (2017) identified that the dorsal vagal branch of the parasympathetic nervous system promotes immobilization when the organism is facing life threat. Immobilization appears behaviorally as shutdown or collapse, which is associated with dissociation. Some children whose fear/wariness system is disengaged may become overly friendly or spaced out. Others whose attachment behavioral system is disrupted may become intimidated, intimidating, or hostile. Thus, disorganization manifests in disordered, interrupted, or disoriented behaviors. The above examples of psychotherapy patients shows how the patient's collapsing and shutdown interferes with their capacity to access relational accompaniment.

In adulthood, disorganization can be conceptualized as resulting from the fear associated with memories of traumatic events that remain unresolved. When such emotions are activated in current-day relationships, this can generate enormous amounts of anxiety and distress in anticipation of "fright without solution" (Hesse & Main, 1999).

We continue to discuss how disorganization manifests in psychotherapy patients later in this chapter in the section "The Initial Presentation." Next, we apply these conceptualizations to a particular psychotherapy patient.

A Clinical Example From a Psychotherapy Patient

Bowlby (1973) conceptualized how our attachment experiences are internalized and become internal working models of self and other, which he determined helps an individual build understanding of their place in their world, to predict the future and make suitable plans. One of the key features concerns the self's perception of the other, with respect to their role as caregiver. He poses the question, "How accessible and responsive [are] his attachment figures likely to be should he turn to them for support?" (p. 203). Here, the interplay of the fear/wariness system, the attachment behavioral system, and the caregiving behavioral system are interwoven. The following clinical vignette provides an example of how my patient Abigail's attachment behavior was thwarted, despite her courageous mobilization toward her mother for comfort. Abigail shared this memory when we were beginning her therapy and exploring her "sleepy defense" around closeness and contact with her husband and children. The "sleepy defense" is a way to describe the kicking in of a dorsal vagal response from Polyvagal Theory (Porges, 2004, 2009; see Chapter 2 for discussion).

Abigail told me her first childhood memory. She was barely a toddler. She was woken in the night by a huge thunderstorm. Having heard the expression "it's raining cats and dogs," she literally imagined that dead cats and dogs were falling on the roof, and she was terrified. When sharing this memory, Abigail repeated the word "terrified" seven times. She had gotten herself out of her crib and padded down the hall, toward her parents' bedroom, guided by her left hand on the wall. Her memory stopped there. Later in life she asked her mother what happened and if she remembered seeing her that night in the hallway. Her mother said yes. "What did you do?" Abigail asked. "I put you back in your crib," her mother replied.

I was immediately struck by Abigail's agency (Bowlby's goal-directed behavior) to get herself out of her crib in the middle of the night. The sound of cracking thunder, the dark, and her imagining dead cats and dogs landing on the roof activated her fear/wariness system. Bravely, she found her way down the dark hallway, instinctively driven by her attachment behavioral system to seek out the protection and care of her mother. Her mother's act of putting Abigail back in bed left her alone with her fear. I believe her memory stopped there because she had to dissociate from the terror that was unseen and untended, generating a significant link between activation of her nervous system and being put back to bed. Needing help and contact with others became a trigger for dissociation. That night, going back to sleep—in the wake of fear—became Abigail's "sleepy defense" for coping with fear.

Now, it is important to note that as a singular or infrequent incident, the above experience may not be noteworthy. As Tronick's (1989, 1998, 2009) research has shown, our attachment relationships do not need to be perfectly attuned 100% of the time. In fact the rule of thumb is one third/one third/one third for attunement, disruption, and repair, respectively. However, when such drives to reach out for help and care are repeatedly thwarted in the course of a person's development, as was the case for Abigail, insecure attachment and disorganization can often follow. For Abigail, her mother was prone to episodes of psychosis, which inevitably contributed to her diminished capacity to provide attuned and adequate care for her daughter at many significant developmental periods. Consequently, Abigail's internal working model related to receiving help and giving help, in particular being available for her young kids, was characterized by her sleepy defense. What Abigail could not articulate at the time, but shared with me years later, was that when her children were young, she was triggered by their attachment needs, and often dissociated to cope. Case vignettes from different portions of her treatment are introduced in Chapter 12, "Working to Transform Patterns of Disorganized Attachment."

Further Research and Observations of Mother–Infant Face-to-Face Interactions

Researchers continued to explore the origins of patterns of attachment and disorganization by studying interactions between infants and their caregivers, who for the most part continued to be mothers. Beebe and her collaborators investigated face-to-face communication between mothers and infants, with infants who were 4 months old. Their research corroborated the results of the Strange Situation procedure (Beebe & Lachman, 2014). Through a second-by-second microanalysis of videotaped mother–infant interactions, at a level imperceptible to real-time observation, researchers were able to examine the intricate dance of attunement, disruption, and repair (see Chapter 2, pp. 61–67). Beebe et al.'s (2016) picture book depicts still frames of the videotape analysis as realistic drawings that provide vivid illustrations of what happens when mothers are sensitively mirroring their infants and are affectively attuned to them, and what happens when they are not. Here, we are specifically identifying what occurs in dyads where the infant at 1 year is classified as disorganized, in contrast to secure dyads.

The following description of a secure mother–infant dyad provides examples of behaviors that engender secure attachment. After which, descriptions of what occurs in disorganizing mother–infant dyads provide examples of behaviors that unfortunately are predictors of disorganization. Then we provide another compare/contrast with an example of what occurs in the face-to-face mirroring studies with future avoidant babies.

A secure dyad. In the first picture frame, the infant is smiling and the mother is smiling back, with a big smile; this is referred to as a highly positive exchange. In the next frame, the infant pulls his arms and head back, and the mom leans in with a sober look on her face. Then the baby looks away, with a very negative look on his face. The mom has moved back: a sensitive gesture that attunes to her baby's signal. The following frame shows the baby reorienting toward the mother. He pulls his lips down, and the mother is pulling her lips down, which matches the baby's lower lip. Even though the baby's eyes are closed, the mother and baby appear to be in sync. The mom's attunement to her baby's distress and pulling back shows the coordination of their dance. In the next frame, the baby opens his eyes, and even though he does not appear to be seeing his mom's face, he reaches. The mom reaches toward him, still with a sober look on her face. Then the baby looks at his mother and opens his mouth. In frame six, their fingers touch, and they are in connection.

These pictures depict what happens in a split second, underneath conscious awareness. The baby looks away, and then returns, which demonstrates Tronick's (1998) findings that babies are capable of self-regulation, which is part of the dance of attunement, disruption, and repair constantly unfolding between infants and their caregivers. When the mother sensitively joins the distress of the infant, matches their infant's expression, and reflects understanding, the infant can return to balance and reengage with his mother. Beebe (2014) states that these moments of joining are crucial and an example of what is sadly missing in the dyads where their patterns of interaction are predictors of disorganization.

A disorganizing dyad. The depictions of a disorganizing dyad show the mismatch between the baby's expression and the mother's expression. In one frame, when the baby shows distress, the mother shows a look of surprise. In another, the baby shows distress and the mother smiles, as if trying to give the baby what she thinks will help. In another, the baby shows distress and she looks away. While she responds, her response is not in sync. Next, when the baby pulls away, the mother looms, and is too close (Beebe et al., 2016).

With compassion, Beebe is clear in saying that most of the mothers in the disorganizing dyads are unresolved for their own trauma and have a history of abuse. Usually these mothers are frightened. She conjectures that the infant's distress actually triggers the mom's unresolved trauma, and she becomes unable to match her infant. She is lacking the affective competence to be with her own experience and feel her infant's experience at the same time. Her behavior displays contradictory behaviors with her infant. Beebe describes that it's not that the mother isn't sensitive to her baby but rather her sensitivity picks up the baby's distress, which then triggers her (Beebe et al., 2016). For instance, the infant might be frantically distressed and the mother's face shows surprise or a smile. This mismatch adds to the distress and confusion of the baby, when their mother is unable to meet or find a way to shift what is disturbing to them. She may make threatening expressions or she may look at her baby with a blank look of emotional disconnection, further disorienting for the baby. When her baby becomes frantic, the mother's feeling of being incapable intensifies, which is disconcerting for the mother and may even impact how she feels toward her baby for "making her feel" so helpless. These disorganizing dyads are laden with examples of disturbing action sequences in which the lack of joining leaves both members of the dyad feeling alone, defeated, and confused. Beebe reports that these interactions can be painful to witness.

An avoidant dyad. In contrast, in the studies with mothers and babies who become avoidant, their sequences of interactions show out-of-sync behavior. The baby looks at the mother and she looks away. Or the mother looms in and comes too close and the baby leans back. At times her touch is intrusive and the baby pulls away. While these mismatches are disconcerting for the baby, there is a sense that the mother is there or not there in a way the baby may not like and then uses an avoiding strategy.

The difference in the disorganizing dyad lies in the quality of the mother's absence and/or her conflicted behavior (i.e., looking right at the baby with vacant eyes, which scares and adds to the baby's distress, leading to "fright without solution").

Another way to look these phenomena is through the lens of the mother's caregiving. As part of her assessment in her Baltimore study, Ainsworth (1978/2015) developed the Maternal Caregiving and Interaction Scales. She observed and identified specific qualities of caregiving that contribute to the effectiveness of caregiving behavior to bring about secure attachment (as discussed in Chapter 1). The first scale, caregiver Sensitivity vs. Insensitivity (Chapter 1, p. 18), is presented here to consider how Ainsworth et al.'s (1978/2015) definition of sensitivity articulates what is at play with disorganization when the caregiver's unresolved trauma interferes.

Caregiver sensitivity vs. insensitivity. Beebe's (2016) observations directly correlate to the subcategories of Ainsworth's first scale: Sensitivity vs. Insensitivity. The first condition of sensitivity is that (a) the mother needs to be aware of the signal, (b) then she must make an accurate interpretation of the signal, (c) respond appropriately to the signal, and (d) respond promptly (Ainsworth et al., 1978/2015). Beebe named that the unresolved mother is sensitive—however, she becomes activated by her baby's distress. Through the lens of Ainsworth's sensitivity scales, while the mother may be aware of the baby, she is not able to interpret her baby's signals accurately. Ainsworth determined that in addition to awareness of the signal there are two more components needed to be able to accurately interpret the signal. In addition to the mother's awareness, she must be free from distortion and capable of empathy (Ainsworth et al., 1978/2015). When the mother is unresolved from her own trauma and is triggered by her baby's attachment needs, she is not free from distortion and thereby is unable to provide empathy. Thus, she is unable to provide an appropriate response. Or do so promptly. Both Beebe and Ainsworth identify that when the baby's signals are not met with a meaningful response, the baby can lose confidence in the efficacy of their signaling to draw out what they need from the caregiver.

In psychotherapy sessions, some patients are more sensitive to moments of mismatch and misattunement than others. Through the examples of what happens in secure dyads, psychotherapists can identify markers of communication (i.e., attuning to the patient's shifts in gaze, perhaps noticing when they might be markers of self-regulation), which when responded to accurately can help build safety and help restore the patient's trust that coordination and repair can follow disconnection with reconnection. By meeting our patient's signals with sensitivity and responsiveness, we can help patients to experience their own emotional and relational signals as meaningful. In this way, psychotherapists have an organizing function: The aim of building a secure base is to help patients have an experience of being met, and if we miss, we aim for an opportunity to repair through attending to what the patient needs for reconnection and recoordination.

As we continue with research into the interactions with mothers and infants, Lyons-Ruth and her collaborators offer insight into disrupted communications that impact the development of secure and insecure patterns of attachment and disorganization.

When Communication Is Disrupted: Attachment and Intersubjectivity

Lyons-Ruth and associates (1999, 2006) researched the intersubjective dialogue between parents and children. Interested in what contributes to security of attachment, they emphasize the importance of collaborative communication, "strategies of sharing that are truthful and sensitive to the states of mind of both parties with adjustment in early development for the imbalance in developmental capacities of the two partners" (p. 604). Caregivers' capacity to understand and provide comfort when their child's fear is aroused is an important way caregivers help to build attachment security, helping their child not only in the moment but over time as well, to build trust in their intersubjective field. In contrast, they note that

> less collaborative strategies of sharing within the family . . . are more restricted or one-sided in that they privilege one person's voice over the other's (e.g., the parent's emotional needs, as in ambivalent strategies) or

certain forms of truth over other forms of truth (e.g., happy affects over sad or angry affects, as in avoidant strategies). (p. 604)

The influence of this one-sided strategy of communication is evident in patients who have trouble expressing their feeling or their needs, convinced there is no room to be heard. They believe that their voice is not important or they fear if they dare to speak of their own specific need, they will hear back a message from their parent akin to "it's my way or the highway . . ."

Expanding Main and Hesse's frame that the parent as a source of alarm leads to infant disorganization, Lyons-Ruth and her associates (2006) found that the absence of regulating caregiver responses will also lead to infant disorganization. They state, "The more general caregiving mechanism related to disorganization may be the lack of effective caregiver regulation of fearful arousal, rather than explicit fear of the caregiver herself" (p. 605). Just as we identified in Beebe et al.'s (2016) face-to-face studies, crucial to building security is the capacity of the caregiver to be with and help the baby to regulate both positive and negative affects.

When the caregiver is unpredictably helpless and frightened themselves, their children sometimes take the role of caregiver for their wounded parent. Facing a parent who has dissociated, who is staring off into space or crumbling to pieces, these parentified (and sometimes petrified) children summon a quality of caring-yet-dominating presence to help their parent regain some semblance of order. By the age of 6, some children develop controlling role-reversal strategies, taking control of the parent-child interaction (Main & Cassidy, 1988; Cassidy 1990), being either controlling-punitive or controlling-caregiving (Main et al., 2005). This too is protective, and such strategies enact "I can't need you and be scared of you at the same time, so I will punish you or control you through taking care of you in the meantime." And while we've been identifying how disorganization is the collapse of strategy, it is also true that some of these controlling and caregiving behaviors that these children adopt through role reversal continue into adulthood.

In the way that the self-reliance of the avoidant pattern can be seen as pseudo self-reliance, and the preoccupation with the ambivalent strategy can be seen as pseudo relational, what if we see the disorganized child who adopts role reversal as becoming a pseudo attachment figure to their parent? Their caregiving and controlling behaviors are more about managing the parent as a way to cope with their own otherwise unmanageable feelings evoked by the parent's frightened and disordered behavior. There is a quality of taking over rather than being with, of doing for rather than being helped, which characterizes the parentified nature of the disorganized child's behavior. As adults, they may become caregivers or become bossy and angry, both of which are controlling strategies to deal with the underlying disorganization. The problem lies in the tendency to treat relationships in a unilateral rather than mutual fashion, lacking in authentic relatedness, relating to others without the collaboration Lyons-Ruth talks about, and without the sense of mutual understanding that Bowlby referred to as a "goal-corrected partnership."

Lyons-Ruth (2006) describes that the key loss is that of the child's own subjectivity and initiative, as their own needs have been subjugated in service to their parent in absentia. Her studies describe how parental communications are disrupted, and how specific disruptions, in turn, have specific impacts on the children. Lyons-Ruth found "five broad aspects of disrupted communications are

a. Parental withdrawing responses
b. Negative–intrusive responses
c. Role-confused responses
d. Disoriented responses
e. A set of responses we termed affective communication errors, which include both the mother's giving simultaneous conflicting cues to the infant and her failures to respond to clear affective signals from the infant

The studies of these disrupted communication patterns show profiles of mother and infant interactions that fit in the disorganized spectrum" (p. 606).

The "disordered" aspect of the disorganized category refers to the caregiver's noncontingent responsiveness to their child, behavior that is not matching and even more so is disruptive. The absence of response or sense of being there but not really being there is disturbing to the child, which is what Lyons-Ruth refers to as parental withdrawing responses or disoriented responses. There is no there there for the child to lean into or push up against to establish a sense of self. As well as impacting the child to take on roles of controlling-caregiving, the controlling-punitive aspect of this pattern can also develop into threatening behaviors, acting out impulsively in threatening actions toward the self or others.

The classification of "disorganized/disordered" is a very important contribution that sheds light on some of the complex behavioral dynamics that
can occur through unresolved trauma. Studies by Egeland and Sroufe (1981)
have found that greater percentages of disorganization appear in high-risk
populations, those with impoverished circumstances, single parenting, and
intergenerational trauma.

We now turn our attention to addressing how disorganization manifests
in clinical settings with an adult population.

How Disorganization Manifests in Clinical Settings With an Adult Population: The Initial Presentation

Given how at times disorganization presents together with other patterns
of insecure attachment or even secure attachment, this section of initial presentation is designed to identify the salient features of disorganization when
they appear. Patients who initially show patterns of secure attachment or
insecure avoidant or insecure ambivalent/resistant attachment can become
disorganized when fear related to unresolved trauma is activated. So far
in this chapter we have identified how disorganization is the collapse of
strategy, and also how disorganization may reside underneath strategies of
control. In adults, sometimes dissociation can be a defensive strategy related
to disorganized attachment. We explore these distinct presentations in this
section and in more depth in Chapter 12.

One of the most challenging aspects of human relationships is when
there is a mix of conflicting needs and feelings toward loved ones. In secure
attachment, conflicts can be recognized and navigated with an autonomous
state of mind, which has the capacity for differentiation and connection.
In insecure attachment, conflicts can be unmanageable and bring about
patterns of avoidance, ambivalence, and resistance as discussed in the preceding chapters. In disorganization, conflicts arise in the context of unresolved trauma; conflicted behaviors stem from fear of the parent and the
impossible dilemma of "fright without solution." Also, when growing up
with a traumatized parent who is frightened and unresolved with respect to
trauma, conflicts can arise between caregiving the parent and the person's
developing their own sense of self and capacity to act on their own behalf.
Here, we add the dilemma of "attachment without solution." The self has
not developed a reliable protective strategy nor can they rely on the frightening or frightened attachment figure for a safe haven. Fosha (this volume)

recognized that "attachment without solution" is a complement to "fright without solution," as the person cannot rely on their attachment figure, nor can they do without them as they cannot fully rely on their own self.

Some patients show up to therapy with lives that appear chaotic; perhaps their primary relationship is on the brink of dissolution, or they are in relationship cycles of makeup and breakup. Relationships with loved ones can be burdened by the intensity of control issues that are bound tightly around unresolved trauma. Patients may be struggling with life transitions, when the aftermath of growing up with disorganized attachment left them with lapses and incomplete development. Confusion arises in individuals when their unresolved state of mind from the past intrudes upon the present moment, creating destabilization and triggering upset in the here and now. Present time can be difficult to distinguish from "trauma time" (van der Hart et al., 2010).

The way disorganization manifests clinically can vary immensely. The patient's presentation might become disoriented, confused, or challenging in their presentation. The patient's affect may not match their verbal expression. Emotional experience related to certain events is disconnected from explicit memories; implicit memory may drive reactive behavior. When speaking, the patient may jump from one story to the next, which can cascade into overwhelm and flooding for the patient. Or they fear "falling apart." Often their younger parts of self hold emotional memories— however, they tend to be fragmented, cordoned off, and/or neglected. Some patients describe being in relationships where they are being mistreated or they mistreat others. Some patients struggle with caregiving, and control issues and have great difficulty trusting others, sharing power, and developing collaborative strategies of relating.

In sessions, some patients describe episodes of out-of-control behaviors and dysregulated emotion, and yet appear calm and slightly bewildered as they try to relate what happened. They may be numb, even disconnected about what triggered them to the point of extreme behavior. Others may feel embarrassed yet confused. Some patients present as secure or organized insecure, yet become disoriented during the session when emotional material is triggered and breaks through their organized defensive strategies. This can surprise the clinician as the window of tolerance rapidly shrinks and disrupts the interactive flow of psychotherapy, marking the need to shift focus to affect regulation.

When working with patients who present with disorganized attachment and are unresolved for attachment trauma and related disorganization, fear and uncertainty may arise in relationship to self and other. The combination of "fright without solution" and "attachment without solution" can make for difficult influences when we are working explicitly with the therapeutic relationship. For instance, the patient may have no template for the perceived "older, wiser other" who is capable of being sensitive and responsive at a time of need, and subsequently they are befuddled with how to receive our attention. Or as they begin to acknowledge feeling the therapist's care and understanding, an opposite feeling of pushing away or dissociating may arise as longing and fear are experienced as contradictory, and the hope of safety is so improbable. Some of these challenges to our relational work are identified and addressed in the following chapter.

The state of mind we see in our adult patients with disorganized attachment is often unresolved, as was their caregiver's state of mind. Through studying individuals' discourse during the AAI, Main and Hesse (1990) identified that the caregiver's unresolved (for trauma)/disorganized state of mind correlates with disorganized behavior in the infant. When these "unresolved" caregivers were discussing topics of abuse or loss, there were lapses in speech or reasoning in their discourse. Main and Hesse attributed these lapses to the arousal of partially dissociated fear being activated and subsequently the narrative comes out in incomplete expressions or prolonged silence, and may not hold together in a coherent way. In some speakers, there were disturbances in space and time—for instance, speaking in the present tense about someone who has died (Main, 2000). During psychotherapy sessions, when patients are sharing significant memories or traumatic experiences, we might find that their narrative becomes less clear and less comprehensible, pointing to the emergence of unresolved fear and touching into previously dissociated affects.

Since confusion can be such a strong element of disorganization, finding ways to create structures and build meaning for the work of psychotherapy are essential. Explicit relational work is needed to provide new and corrective experiences in the present to counter what was missing or overwhelming in the past. The need for collaboration between therapist and patient is stronger than ever. Psychotherapists may need to cultivate bravery and monitor our affective competence, as we move toward helping patients in the destabilizing territory of disorganization and unresolved trauma. These themes are addressed in the following chapter, as we present ways to conceptualize what is happening and specific ways to intervene with clinical vignettes and discussion.

Working to Transform Patterns of Disorganized Attachment (Grids 1 and 3)

This was the full throttle type love that I never got figured out properly,
due to being raised in shotgun fashion what my twisted little raggedy
heart had always, always wanted. A mother. Simple as that.
—Barbara Kingsolver, Demon Copperhead

Disorganization: The Collapse of Strategy & the Strategy of Collapse

In avoidant attachment, at a deep level, basic trust in the Other has broken, while the person's Self has maintained its integrity, albeit in a somewhat devitalized fashion. In ambivalent/resistant attachment, while the person's basic trust in the Other is severely compromised, and the reliance on Self has been selectively unattended to, nevertheless we see them, sometimes against all odds, holding on to relational hope and expectancy for the Other to come through. When patients present with disorganized attachment patterns and have been raised in attachment relationships conditioned with fear, often both their trust in Other and their trust in Self has fractured. Therefore, as psychotherapists engage the central AEDP therapist stance of establishing safety and undoing aloneness with a patient who presents with disorganized attachment, we may be challenged by the patient's enacted helplessness, which makes sense if they have been raised in an environment in which attachment and fear were mixed, related to "fright without solution" and "attachment without solution."

Fosha (personal communication, February 12, 2024) came up with the phrase "attachment without solution" through conversation with

Pando-Mars about how to conceptualize what we are seeing when by adult-hood many of the "disorganized infants" have formed patterns of behavior to cope with the disorganized/disordered attachment of their caregivers and subsequently themselves. As well as "fright without solution," it became clear that "attachment without solution" was a significant factor.

While holding the tenet that disorganized attachment is the result of an infant's collapse of strategy, we also hold the empirically based knowledge (Main et al., 2005) that by the time many of these infants and children become adults, they have developed strategies and patterns of behavior, including the strategy of collapse, to cope with their underlying disorga-nization. Here, psychotherapists may need to fortify our affective compe-tence as we seek to build the conditions for a secure base and safe haven to help patients with disorganized attachment. Helping patients to make use of our relational accompaniment when their early attachment experiences have been so fraught with fear requires us to be both steady and brave in the process of helping these patients to explore previously unoccupied pathways in relationship with self and other.

To do so, in this chapter we continue to draw from the grids to help us organize our way of conceptualizing and attending to each patient's pre-sentation. We look to Grid 1, The Configurations of the Secure Attach-ment Pattern, for characteristics of secure attachment (see Chapter 5) to inform how we can orient our way of being and focus our intentions to aim for secure functioning and co-creating safety with each of our patients. Additionally, when we are working with disorganization and unresolved trauma, by identifying these patients' markers of secure functioning, even if scarce initially, we support their building trust in themselves and also help them locate resources they can draw upon throughout our work. As transformance detectives, we are on the lookout for those markers of secure functioning and make use of them when we encounter them.

In Grid 2, The Configurations of Insecure Attachment Patterns: Avoidant, Ambivalent/Resistant, and Disorganized (see Chapters 5 and 6), we see the configurations of disorganized attachment next to the columns of avoidance and ambivalence/resistance. Even when patients primarily show markers and signs of avoidant or ambivalent/resistant attachment, there may be some who become disorganized especially when stressed by the arousal of their attach-ment system, and then unresolved attachment trauma surfaces. Confusion becomes pronounced, or there is dissociation, staring off, clouding over, or the "light going out of their eyes." Or a pattern of caretaking and control as a coping strategy becomes more pronounced. To see the configuration of disorganized patterns of attachment alongside their corresponding interventions, we include Grid 6, The Configuration of the Disorganized Attachment Pattern With Clinical Markers & Interventions, to accompany this chapter.

Grid 6 identifies markers of specific elements of the disorganized configuration, such as response to attachment system arousal; nervous system activation and affect regulation; characteristic defenses, anxiety, and characteristic fears, with specific interventions; and desirable adaptive action and treatment goals tailored to address disorganized attachment (see Table 12.1).

We can look to Grid 6 to identify the therapist common reactivities that may arise when engaging in treatment with patients who present with disorganized attachment and an unresolved/frightening or frightened state of mind. Again, we acknowledge that despite psychotherapists' interest and dedication, it can happen that psychotherapists find ourselves in an unintended reaction with a patient we are deeply committed to helping. Each of us is human; each of us has an attachment history of our own; when we engage our nervous systems, right-brain to right-brain engagement through relational and experiential methods, miscoordination and recoordination is natural and inevitable. We can also see in Grid 6 the therapist metaskills we can draw upon if and when these reactivities are activated. In this chapter's section on the therapist stance, we identify *therapist common reactivities* and ways we can intervene when we find ourselves in a reactive mode (see Chapter 6, pp. 188–189). In order to provide the necessary ingredients for building a trusting therapeutic relationship, as well as to help work through one of our unintended reactions, we identify several *therapist metaskills* (see Chapter 6, pp. 190–192) that can help us to reorient and re-self-regulate.

In working with disorganization, when the patient has experienced an ongoing lack of safety and confusing mismatches with their attachment figure, one of the results can be difficulties in building coordinated relationships. Experiences of "attachment without solution" (Fosha, this volume) and "fright without solution" (Hesse & Main, 1999) are not helpful precedents for engaging with a present-day person offering relational connection and stirring attachment longings. Thus, it can be helpful for psychotherapists to anticipate the potential for miscoordination in these moments. An inadvertent disruption, or even a rupture, might occur when relational connection is offered. Listening for and holding how each patient describes what triggers them around relatedness may help us prepare for when we are in these moments. In addition, learning which therapist common reactivities

TABLE 12.1 Grid 6. The Configuration of the Disorganized Attachment Pattern With Clinical Markers & Interventions

	CONFIGURATION OF DISORGANIZED ATTACHMENT	DISORGANIZED	CLINICAL MARKERS & INTERVENTIONS	DISORGANIZED
1	Caregiver characteristics: state of mind with respect to attachment	• Unresolved/fearful	Patient state of mind Therapist common reactivities	• Unresolved/fearful • Overidentifies with one part • Confused • Worried
2	Caregiver characteristics: behavioral hallmarks	• Frightened or frightening • Disordered	Therapist metaskills to counter caregiver hallmarks and therapist common reactivities	• Reliable/constant • Calm strength • Boundaried • Collaborative
3	Response to arousal of the attachment system	• Collapse • Disorientation/confusion	Desirable adaptive action	• Affirm relational, self, categorical emotion adaptive action tendencies
4	Seeds of resilience	• Survives trauma	Goals of interventions	• Internal security • Bear and understand profound distress • Wholeness
5	Characteristic nervous system activation and affect regulation	• Overwhelm • Fragments affect • Freeze	Working with nervous system and affect regulation	• Titrate work within window of tolerance
6	Defense: characteristic defenses against relatedness &	Defenses vs. relatedness: • Incomplete expressions • Caregives/controls • Threatens or collapses	Working with defenses against relatedness	• Cultivate safety with relatedness and emotion • Build self-compassion • Distinguish parts and their roles in surviving trauma

6	characteristic defenses against emotion	Defense vs. emotion: • Numbs • Dissociates • Displaces	Working with defenses against emotion	• Affirm and/or amplify glimmers of safety, links between traumatic history, current experience, and dissociated affects • Empathize with dilemmas • Validate affective glimmers
7	Anxiety: characteristic fears	• Fright without solution • Falling apart • Attachment without solution	Working with anxiety	• Build capacity for self and dyadic regulation
8	Patterns of affective competence (or lack thereof)	• Not feeling, and not dealing	Building affective competence	• Distinguish past vs. present feelings • Build tolerance and capacity to process emotions and relatedness
9	Self–Other relational patterning	• Unable to rely on self or other • Unformed areas of self • Role reversal	Working with Self–Other relational patterning	• Build Self-to-Self and Self–Other collaboration • Build receptive affective capacity with therapist and between parts of self
10	Internal experience & external reality: disconnects (à la Fonagy)	• "Alien self"	Connecting internal experience & external reality	• Build self-reflective capacity • Understand self and other

(Pando-Mars, 2016)
(Note. These are nonexhaustive lists)

may arise with disorganization and which therapist metaskills might serve as a ballast to assist us in this endeavor is useful. When we find ourselves off balance, we want to be able to catch ourselves as soon as possible to reco-ordinate with the patient, and when necessary, to make a repair.

Many patients who are struggling with unresolved trauma have deep pockets of unbearable, unwilled, and unwanted traumatic aloneness (Fosha, 2000b, 2021a; Lamagna, 2021) Thus, they do not expect or have much experience with repair. To the contrary! When we can show up, even some-what faltering, and we meet patients with calm strength, repeatedly, over time, we have the potential to alleviate the suffering of disruption and the scary anticipation of being terribly alone, with no one to rely on, with the isolation that comes from being mistreated and misunderstood. Our efforts to stay in connection and do what it takes to seek repair can go a long way toward reducing unbearable aloneness and building trust in the process of working together. Whether reducing the patient's experience of being alone with us, or being isolated from parts of themselves, repair is a deeply important avenue of healing. We address the factor of unbearable traumatic aloneness throughout this chapter.

Goals of Treatment

When working with a patient who manifests disorganized attachment pat-terns, and whose state of mind is unresolved/fearful, building their capacity to trust Self and Other is a primary goal of treatment. Grid 3 identifies all of the categories: self, relational, and categorical emotion action tendencies as *desirable adaptive action* for bringing healing to disorganized attachment (see Chapter 6, pp. 192–193). The reason for recognizing and affirming self and relational action tendencies is that with this level of disrupted and dis-ordered attachment, the patient is usually in need of building their capacity to be with self and parts of self, while also building their capacity to be in relationship with another.

It is not uncommon for these patients to be bewildered about what hap-pened to them. This is especially true in cases of deep neglect when what went wrong were not *errors of commission*, but rather *errors of omission*: what was absent (Fosha, 2000b, 2003, 2021a). Such deep failures of the attach-ment relationship to provide regulating and reliable protection and care leave gaps in how individuals develop their capacity for self-trust and self-understanding. Therefore, we aim to help patients to recognize markers of adaptive self-action tendencies by encouraging them to listen inside to recognize what they need and find ways to express their need to care for themselves. We also listen for fractals of self experience (Fosha, 2013a) that arise in small bits, to allow them into awareness as parts of the patient's self emerge, as resources or that enlarge their capacity to bring access to formerly dissociated affects and memories.

We also support patients to recognize markers of adaptive relational action tendencies, helping them learn to recognize when they are able to interact with another in a collaborative way that allows both accessibility and boundaries in relatedness. In a disorganized state the patient may vacillate between seeking safety with the other and rejecting the other's response of contact and care. It is helpful to hold the possibility for *both/and* as opposed to *either/or* (Pando-Mars, 2016), since in disorganization these circuits of moving toward another and feeling safe may be at odds. Treatment needs to proceed slowly and with care to enable splintered-off selves to coexist, while building a large enough window of tolerance so that eventually it becomes a window of opportunity for corrective emotional, relational, and self experiences. Through adaptive self-action tendencies and relational accompaniment, patients with disorganized attachment have the potential to build their capacity to recognize what is safe and trustworthy in themselves and in others.

Additionally, when patients lack a full picture of what happened to them, they may have dissociated aspects of their experiences. They might have memories of hostile, abusive, or neglectful caregivers, minus their own related emotional experiences. They might have strong emotions, become dysregulated easily, or have upwellings of emotion that seem out of proportion to what is occurring in their current life, yet they lack a clear understanding that makes sense to them of why that might be. Here, another goal of treatment is to help these patients locate evidence of their historical trauma or build connection between dissociated areas of their experiences. Often, patients may sense an emotion without understanding what they are feeling, or why. Yet as we make room for their emotion, a memory or realization might emerge that gives them a piece of their puzzle and moves them closer to constructing a coherent and cohesive autobiographical narrative, which as we know is a key aspect of attachment security (Main, 1991). We seek to help them make sense of their reactions with understanding, compassion, and concrete interventions for processing heretofore unprocessable experiences and building their capacity to move forward in their lives.

Categorical emotions have adaptive action tendencies (Frijda, 1986), which are also named as desirable adaptive action for disorganized attachment. Healing what is unresolved by its very nature means to resolve (i.e., complete what was previously incomplete and unresolvable). Many of our patients who experienced unwilled and unwanted aloneness in the face of unbearable emotion need not only our relational accompaniment to undo their aloneness but our relational attunement and skillful attention, as well as our highly specific interventions to help them face, feel, and process what was profoundly distressing in the past. In the wake of processing emotion to completion, the adaptive action of emotions is released. Tendencies exist within each emotion for expressing behavior and a readiness to achieve a kind of adaptive, evolutionarily wired in end result (Frijda, 1986). Helping these patients to experience, bear, and process their emotion offers opportunities for not only processing emotion but also for completing incomplete actions, releasing the emotions' adaptive action tendencies, and thus strengthening their underdeveloped capacities and thus developing their resilience (Russell, 2015). These are all corrective emotional experiences.

Here is an example of how the action tendency of anger can become available to a patient in psychotherapy. When a child was unprotected during attacking and aggressive behavior of a caregiver or loved one, and was frightened, their behavior of dissociating by dropping into a dorsal vagal or a freeze response was how they navigated their fear or the onslaught of further attacks. This is how the action of inaction becomes a coping strategy, indispensable to short-term survival, devastating to long-term functioning. In a therapeutic relationship, we help the patient to experience the original fear (with our accompaniment, working to stay within their window of tolerance), which may then allow anger to surface. Core anger fuels the energy of self-determination and helps the patient find the words to speak up on their own behalf; or perhaps to stop the attack or find a recourse, as an organismic response. Helping patients through what may have been frozen in "trauma time" and helping them process their anger to completion enables them to discover that assertion and self-protection exist and can emerge from within them when these adaptive action tendencies are activated. When the conditions are right for expression, an individual can thaw what was frozen and liberate their capacity to stand up on their own behalf and reorient their potential for navigating through life with their protective sensors online and at the ready.

From the Get-Go

The infant does not need to acquire first-hand all the knowledge and experiences necessary to survival. Instead, the infant needs to develop the skills for sharing affective evaluations and intentional states with others. This allows the infant to participate in the cultural learning processes of human society. (Lyons-Ruth, 2006, p. 597)

Lyons-Ruth says it so clearly in the above quote. Survival is not based on acquiring firsthand all that one needs to survive. Those are the innate capacities wired into us, available from birth on. We can change the word "survival" into healing for our patients in psychotherapy. What is truly needed for healing is understanding self and other, in keeping with Bowlby's (1969/1982, 1973) *goal-corrected partnership*, Fonagy's (1995) *existing in the mind of another*, and Fosha's (2000b) addition of *existing in the heart and mind of another*. Lyons-Ruth identifies the way this happens is by developing skills, which is having the practice of sharing affective evaluations and understanding the intentions of self and other. Helping patients to share affective states and perceive intentional states with another is central in the work of healing attachment trauma; its importance is heightened when working with disorganization. This applies both to relationships with others and relationships between the self and parts, for when a part of self has been cut off for survival, making contact and bringing each part to the table is essential.

Under conditions of maltreatment, an individual does not develop their self-reflective function along a singular progressive pathway (Fonagy & Target, 1997). Rather, they evolve along varied pathways, influenced and molded by many dynamic interactions. According to Fonagy (2002), fractionation describes how the reflective function can split off, which is a more accurate depiction of what happens than underdevelopment. We see aspects of fractionation in some patients with disorganized attachment—for example, when patients have a compulsive longing to be adored and yet can't tolerate the experience of being adored. For some of them, there is a revulsion toward the younger self, who was criticized and denigrated in the past. In turn, the patient has come to despise their younger part. The patient isn't able to have an integrated receptivity to love as a result of the opposing interactions that gave rise to these distinct pathways of experience. Another example of fractionation is the separation between a patient's memory and the affective states of younger parts.

As we aim to help patients build self-trust, to realize that they are worthy of being cared for and understood, we also extend this to each of the parts of self that have been fractionated and sequestered for survival. Lamagna and Gleiser (2007) specialize in work with individuals with complex trauma and write about the need for building a secure internal attachment, specifically addressing the need for intrarelational safety and trust, as well as establishing interpersonal relatedness (Gleiser, 2021; Lamagna, 2011, 2021).

Right alongside building their self-trust is our intention to help our patients with disorganized patterns of attachment build trust in an Other, first in us as their psychotherapist, who they can discover is available and capable of helping them. We aim to reestablish trust and coordination between our patient's innate attachment behavioral system and our own functioning caregiving behavioral systems. Hence, healing requires the patient to bravely undergo facing and reworking their inner representations of Self and Other. And they need to be able to recognize that we are trustworthy to help them. Fonagy's query into epistemic trust explores how this can happen.

Epistemic Trust

Fonagy elaborated his thinking about "mentalization" (the current term for self-reflective function) as attachment-based understanding of self and other. In secure attachment, when individuals understand the intentional states of mind of the other, they are better able to understand and explain the *behavior* of the other. Fonagy became interested in how adaptation to the physical environment and social knowledge were transmitted through attachment relationships. He recognized that experiences of secure attachment help an individual build the capacity not only for mentalizing but also help form *epistemic trust*, which is "trust in the authenticity and personal relevance of interpersonally transmitted information" (from Wilson & Sperber, 2012, in Fonagy & Allison, 2014, p. 372).

Epistemic trust occurs when an individual is willing to consider new knowledge from another person as generalizable and relevant to the self (Fonagy & Allison, 2014), which is what may be necessary for psychotherapists to help our patients to feel helped. Fonagy identified that people grow to understand the world around them through *communication from a trusted source*, and that the child's trust in their attachment figure is based on the attachment figure's sensitivity and ability to convey their understanding of the child to the child (Fonagy & Allison, 2014). When a patient's usual means of learning through their attachment relationships was compromised, how psychotherapists can become a trusted source is pivotal.

We need to help our patients to have a new experience, and more specifically, a new corrective experience (Fosha, 2000b). We need to be able to help them where they do not expect help is available. Epistemic trust describes the mechanisms by which psychotherapists help our patients to feel a sense of felt security. If they can have a sense of us at their side when they are used to being painfully alone, they may begin to risk starting to rely on the relational support that they never had. They might cautiously be willing to let go of old strategies that seemed like the best protections and try new ways of being. The following case example shines a light on the process through which a therapist becomes a trusted other. The therapist's use of self, affective attunement, and skilled responsiveness all combine to become a worthy other to whom even the most frightened patient can begin to turn to with a building sense of trust.

Additionally, Fonagy's study of epistemic trust brought attention to an opposing need, that of *epistemic vigilance*. Epistemic vigilance is the need for "caution and discrimination on the part of the juvenile-observational learner to prevent them from being tricked or misinformed, intentionally, or not (Sperber et al., 2010b, in Fonagy & Campbell, 2017). When a person has been mistreated, abused, or neglected, a kind of hypervigilance is often employed when the person has little faith in the trustworthiness of another. Safety isn't a given, especially when folks have been raised in conditions where they have not felt seen and understood, nor received help when needed. With this in mind, developing epistemic trust seems invaluable for psychotherapists to foster as we go about seeking to set conditions for our patients to open to new experiences in the process of psychotherapy— namely, helping our patients to feel they can trust us to be of help to them.

Case Example

Recently I saw a clinical video of an AEDP therapist working with a patient whose presenting issue was her sense that she was caught between fears of overwhelm and detachment. The therapist recognized the relationship between the two, understanding how the patient was defending herself from overwhelm by detaching from emotions. We can see this as an example of the therapist's understanding (mentalizing) about the patient. The patient also reported a considerable amount of emptiness and exhibited notable anxiety. This AEDP therapist works from a somatic orientation, helping patients to build connection to their base of being in the body. She trusts the value of emotions and their adaptive action tendencies. The therapist also holds that being overwhelmed is the experience of trauma, which is an AEDP stance toward trauma (Fosha, 2000b, 2021a), and took to heart her responsibility to not retraumatize the patient.

Working within the patient's window of tolerance. The therapist promised the patient that they would proceed slowly and approach her affective experience with her careful attention to pick up activation and tend to it. The purpose was to protect the patient from overwhelm and needing to use detachment to manage it. The therapist suggested that together they would find the patient's window of tolerance (see Chapter 2 for discussion) so that enough activation could be experienced to surface material, and yet there was enough regulation so that the patient could tolerate what was arising. When signals of anxiety appeared in the patient, the therapist was intentional to back off, to not push forward, and ease up where it seemed too loaded. When anxiety was on the rise, she would track how it was increasing, and she was flexible to shift gears and proceed with care. They focused on the patient's breathing to regulate her.

Proceeding by titrating the emerging emotion. As the work unfolded, a feeling of adaptive anger emerged. The therapist suggested that the patient see the anger as if it were on a screen, so she could observe it from a distance, and together they could explore it. Indeed, this provided a measure of titration in which the patient was able to turn down the dial of intensity, increasing her sense of control and safety alongside the therapist's close attention and accompaniment.

Therapist's sensitivity and responsiveness. I was struck by how this intervention on the therapist's part, more than 30 minutes into the session, was such an excellent example of how the therapist remembered the patient's fear and found her way to effectively help her patient when she needed help. The therapist understood the patient's presenting fear of overwhelm, and truly helped her navigate the terrain of her affective experience so that she could safely explore an emotion. Such an apt example of therapist responsiveness seemed the perfect stage for the patient to have an experience of epistemic trust. She could lean into the suggestions of an "attachment figure" and gain access to a calmer, more relaxed way of being, allowing her to explore and learn about herself with new affective competence.

Patient's experience of epistemic trust. At the end of the session the patient acknowledged how she felt protected by the therapist. The patient was aware that she didn't need to worry or take care about the boundary of the therapist, which was relieving to her. Out of this new experience, she wanted this new thing for herself: she found a new trust in the possibility of working together with another person in a way that not only did not hurt her but actually helped her. Here is evidence of her growing epistemic trust. What she gained through this experience opened her "willingness to consider new knowledge from another person as trustworthy, generalizable, and relevant to the self." Having an experience of epistemic trust begets the desire for more connection and communication, and potentiates the possibilities of developing a collaborative, effective psychotherapy treatment.

The Therapist Stance: Therapist Common
Reactivities and Therapist Metaskills

In preparing to meet a patient who may have disorganized attachment, our foundations of AEDP are an important first order. Set the conditions to establish safety and undo aloneness. Provide welcome, interest, and look for glimmers of transformance to affirm in the patient. Find some aspect of the patient to affirm, to appreciate, to delight in, to love. With an intention to notice what is going right when patients arrive to psychotherapy, we can often offset the patient's expectation of shame or even doom that "needing help has come to this!" And as pictured in the above case example, listening with an ear for how we can be of help, and addressing the patient's concern through an attentive, responsive capacity to help where help is actually needed, seeds the conditions necessary for therapy to be helpful and effective.

Disorganization may not be apparent at first. A patient might present with another primary attachment strategy or perhaps some of the control strategies that developed around disorganization. Yet, some patients may present with a quality of something missing that can be amorphous due to an emptiness of inner contact, a sense of not really knowing what happened. For these patients, something feels off in their life and they want help to understand what they might even need. Emotions may surface, yet the patient has difficulty relating what they are feeling and what it may be about. They might have difficulty trusting others, yet not understand why or even that the pos-sibility of trust can be had. Sometimes patients with disorganized attachment vacillate between longing and fear with the therapist. Liotti (1995) describes that patients with disorganized attachment may express different and incom-patible attitudes and feelings toward the therapist and/or their self, across many sessions or in rapid succession during the same session.

Therapist Common Reactivities

Here it can be helpful to recognize some therapist common reactivities that might appear in working with a patient with disorganization; they include *confusion, overidentifying with one part*, or *worry*.

Therapist becomes confused. Sometimes the therapist notices discrepancies in what the person is saying and feeling. In the AAI research, Main found while in conversation with the interviewer, the discourse of the interviewee revealed lapses in reasoning and faulty logic, which indicates disorga-nization. Alternatively, the interviewee would be drawn away from the immediate context of the interview and then return with a notable gap in continuity. There were often long silences (up to 90 seconds) as the inter-viewee was caught by extreme absorption (Main et al., 2005).

In a psychotherapy session, when a patient is approaching an area of wounding, it is not uncommon to see the pattern of faulty logic that Main observed in the AAI. When such lapses in reasoning occur, the therapist might become confused. Considering the origins of such confusion and noticing when the logic of the patient doesn't hold together might be a clue that we are in the terrain of unresolved trauma. Such discrepancies in logic might also herald the possibility of fragmentation between parts of the patient or fractionation in the patient's self-reflective function. At the beginning of the therapeutic relationship, the possibility that the patient has disorganized attachment may not be immediately apparent, and yet when we find ourselves noting discrepancies between what the patient is saying or feeling, or we find ourselves confused, this may indicate that the patient may be showing signs of dissociation or fragmentation.

Therapist overidentifying with one "part." The therapist might try to make sense of the discrepancy or faulty logic by leaning into one part of what the patient is saying. Sometimes one part of the patient convincingly steps forward, seeming to take a stand, bringing order to what had been chaotic and disorganized. Something appears to have shifted and settled. I remember a patient whose primary love relationship fluctuated between extremes. One day, she arrived at a session after she and her partner had one of their earth-shattering fights. She declared that this was the last time she was going to tolerate such emotional abuse. She looked me in the eye and said, "I really mean it." She considered leaving, and described how she would support herself living separately.

The first time this occurred, I believed she was finding her core strength and that my role was to support her courageous, self-affirming move to decide that she was in an intolerable relationship and had the right to choose to leave. I had seen signs that reverberated with her experiences of childhood abuse and appreciated her moving toward acting on her own behalf. Inadvertently, I was supporting the apparent strength of one part of her, without realizing that this was a fractionated expression, and that a counterpart might be excluded, yet nearby.

The following week, she arrived at the session and reported feeling reconnected to her partner. Her fury was out of sight, and she was clearly in a different place. She seemed disconnected to what was said the week before. I was quite thrown and disoriented. This gave me pause to realize that this apparent "undoing" was actually a different part of the patient surfacing. She was operating from an opposing drive in her that was driven by her longing for connection. I began to realize that what I had seen as an adaptive action to move away from a volatile and triggering relationship was actually a state that was not free to act, for the fact that it excluded her relational need for connection. While in hindsight this seems obvious, I was at first confused. Yet I learned how fragmentation and fractionation operates when it surfaces with the emergence of contradictory parts. This led me to the intervention of holding awareness that multiple aspects of experience reside side by side and need to be invited into the room. The need for understanding parts and ego states is necessary in working with patients with disorganization.

Feeling worried or fearful about the patient. When I find myself repeatedly concerned about a patient, I need to attend to my concern, consider if information was disclosed in our session, maybe even in an off-handed way, that I had not fully registered at the time that is now rising to my awareness. Perhaps I need to notice if there are any aspects of our interactive communications that need further addressing and containment. Has there been a miscommunication that seemed minor but the patient continues to reference it? Am I concerned that the patient may be a threat to self or to another? Do I have concern that the patient is being threatened and might be in danger? These are important considerations and sometimes our nervous system's neuroception may be signaling an alarm.

It behooves us to take care and be thorough in our considerations, to be present and focused about how we raise our concerns with patients, holding AEDP Maxim 4, The Unit of Intervention Is Not the Therapist's Comment but the Therapist's Comment and the Patient's Response to It. Our concern could be triggering for the patient. Even here, especially here, as we hold our responsibility to attend to the patient's safety, we may also be faced with the patient's feelings about our concern. Before naming it, what rises to the level of concern for us might have been outside of the patient's conscious awareness, which might impact the patient and require careful processing on a number of levels: our relationship with the patient, the patient's relationship to self and parts of self, and the patient's relationship with others.

Therapist Metaskills

A few intentional sensitivities, being *reliable, constant, boundaried, embodying calm strength,* and holding a *collaborative stance* can be helpful and stabilizing to therapists when working with someone in a disorganized state or who has disorganized attachment.

Be reliable, constant, embody calm strength. It is important to hold that the conditions of the relationship and our way of being give rise to attachment security or insecurity. So even when someone presents with huge developmental trauma, our capacity to be constant, reliable, and embody calm strength goes a long way to establish conditions for secure functioning with patients. At first, it might be that the patient feels safe enough to say how lost they feel. Some folks with disorganization may have developmental gaps, which can come across as unformed areas of experience (Fosha, 2013a). By adulthood, individuals who developed disorganization as an infant often have learned to disconnect from their unbearable affects and may use dissociation to varying degrees as a coping strategy to manage overwhelm and aloneness in times of anguish. So while they may not "know themselves," by our holding steady and offering a place to land, we can help them get to know what has been lost and out of sight to themselves.

For these patients fear of fear is often looming. They have been frightened and helpless. Some have been themselves frightening and out of control. To offer a calm presence is regulating, often "going beyond mirroring" to helping is necessary and indicated when a patient is exceeding their window of tolerance and anxiety turns to panic. When patients have cognitive disruptions and lose the capacity to focus, they may become disorientated and/or agitated. By understanding that the terrain of working with disorganization is to expand the window of tolerance within a collaborative alliance, we can approach these edges with an eye to see what is needed to assist and accompany the patient.

Case Example

Here, I present a case vignette that demonstrates the early steps of establishing the focus of individual work with a patient who is showing signs of dissociation, as the quality of fear mounts in the background. This is Abigail, from Chapter 11, whose first childhood memory was being a toddler who woke in the middle of the night to "cats and dogs raining on the roof," a memory that she brought up 2 weeks *after* the session I describe below.

I had seen Abigail for 14 sessions of couple therapy, which ended 8 months prior to this session. Her husband agreed for her to engage in individual psychotherapy with me. Abigail returned to therapy when she was feeling "stuck, trapped, and depressed." She felt confusion about her relationship with her husband, and ultimately that she had to "go it alone." She noted anger about having and expressing needs. The session that follows was our third.

Case Vignette 12A, Part 1: "I Want to Know What Happened to Me"

Abigail began with an external focus about whether her husband was the right guy for her. She was lying on the couch, and as she spoke, a quality of sleepiness and emptiness drew my attention. I asked her to sit up, which was an up-regulating intervention and initiated a deeper unfolding. This vignette begins 20 minutes into the session when I ask what is happening in her body to shift her attention away from "thinking" about her husband and toward focusing her awareness on her experience.

ABIGAIL (PATIENT, PT): Anxiety . . . heavy, dense, and dead. Scared. Almost like I'm gonna get raped, reminds of date rape, let him do what I didn't want, shut down, painful . . . not that but similar. Especially if he does anything aggressive. I get scared and close down (*her head is bent over, she is looking down*). So it's just awful . . . [**Her discourse is associative, yet turning to her own experience, something seems to emerge.**]

THERAPIST (TH): Mm-hmm. So what's it like to even say that, just to tell me, and just to kinda be here so far? [**I focus on what's happening in the present moment as she shares with me, to offer dyadic regulation.**]

PT: Not good.

TH: What's the part that's not good right now? [**Clarifying the generalized judgment**]

PT: I just feel so broken, you know, so, like so, it's not a normal response to having sex, you know (*she looks down and away, closing her eyes*).

TH: When you close your eyes, I kinda get the sense like, there's a little shame maybe? Like you're closing your eyes around this when you're saying you're broken . . . [**I name the shame explicitly and describe what I see happening in the present moment between us. My language "kinda get the sense like . . ." matches her tentativeness. This is happening right brain to right brain.**]

By my mirroring that Abigail closes her eyes when she says she feels broken, I let her know what I see and that I sense shame. However, I do not presume that I am right about *her* experience. Thus, I then ask her to notice what is her experience. My intention is to foster a collaborative alliance, to respect her capacity to register what she is feeling rather than my simply naming, or interpreting, her behavior. She drops into a deeper place by identifying more about her experience than her judgment.

PT: I feel really kind of . . . starting to feel really little. [**She speaks in clauses, describing what she feels underneath the judgment of "feeling broken."**]

TH: Mmm.

PT: Little, and I just wanna like be curled up, you know? (*she puts arms around her knees, pulls them up to her chest, and tucks her chin into her left shoulder*) . . . and be left alone. [**Her language is simple and reveals a helpless expectation of being alone.**]

TH: What are you feeling right now? Just right now? Just be with it. [**I ask her to pay attention to what's happening in the present moment and to be with it.**]

PT: I'm checking in and out a little bit. What happens a lot of times with this is, I kinda go up here . . . (*raises right hand up from in front of her torso to her* *head)* [She describes dissociating, and that it is familiar to her, which gives the impression that anxiety may be arising.]

TH: Yeah . . .

PT: And I feel my . . . almost make myself unconscious *(brushes her left hand over her head and behind).* It sounds weird, dizzy. [She describes a defensive strategy to shut down what may be overwhelming—dorsal vagal response is becoming activated.]

TH: So I want you to look, if you can, to make contact with me, because I feel like we need to work together. [AEDP Maxim 3: Stay With It and Stay With Me] And I'm afraid when your eyes are closed that you may dissociate a bit . . . that you're going away . . . [sharing what I perceive, in the effort to be collaborative]. *(I mirror her movement by putting my right hand over my head)* [I am matching her without my conscious awareness.] So let yourself see what happens if you let yourself see me and be with me. I really want to go with you. I don't want you to go too far on your own, because this is scary and it's a hard journey . . . So what happens if we make eye contact? [I invite her to explore what happens if she lets herself become aware of seeing me with her, and I self-disclose my intention to accompany her.]

Stay with it and stay with me. Here, Abigail is cooperative and my orienting her to engage her somatic awareness puts her in touch with emotional experience operating at a level below her self-judgment and shame. Yet her resources are limited, and she resorts to dissociation to avoid a state that may be familiar and unbearable if not dissociating. By moment-to-moment tracking, I check in with each step of her experience, which next brings her attention to describe how she is shutting down, which she describes as "sounding weird," judging herself, which she immediately follows with "dizzy," a body-based description of dissociation.

I invite Abigail to make contact with me. I am concerned that she is managing overwhelm with defensive dissociation. The intervention, *stay with it and stay with me,* offers explicit accompaniment, to help her to regulate her experience with me, dyadically, instead of alone. By asking her to explore making eye contact with me, I want to engage her senses and see if we can help her know if she feels she is safe enough with me.

TH: Umm . . . *(I start cooing tenderly upon seeing her face soften and become young)*

PT: *(nodding, looking at therapist, sighs noticeably)* I feel sad. [She clearly states her

emotion, which tells me that our contact is giving her support to be with
her experience and that she is accessing an emotion that seems to be within
her window of tolerance.]

TH: You feel sad. [Mirroring her words closely demonstrates that I am hearing
and being with her.]

PT: (nods)

TH: So I want you to just start with that, to let it be.

PT: (tears up, looks at therapist, takes breath in and out) [She responds, coordinating with therapist, resonating right brain to right brain, and engages her
feelings more.]

TH: (looks with concern and care, breathing in and out, seeming to be in rhythm with the
patient) Pretty deep sadness, huh? (both of us are nodding, holding eye contact)
Pretty deep pain around this stuff . . . [Affective resonance; explicit empathy conveyed by my words, voice tone, and eye contact.]

PT: I feel really alone. It feels like that little . . . (drifts off) I close my eyes
sometimes because that helps me go there, too (hunches shoulders). [Now
she shares what she knows about her experience to help me understand her,
which furthers our collaborating.]

TH: (slowly) Right . . .

PT: Really little, alone, kinda confused, like not knowing what to do and just
disassociating, you know? [Notice fragments of speech and shifting back
and forth between feeling alone and feeling with me.]

TH: Right, and that's why I want us to slow that down. Because I understand, yeah, be in touch with the little one, on her own, but I'm here,
and it's really important (fingers motion back and forth between the two of us)
that we stay connected to help, to help that little one. [Offering therapist
self to provide nurturing and comfort; dyadic regulation, while inviting
the patient to engage her own instinctive turning toward the young one
in herself.]

PT: (head drops down and gentle sobbing begins . . . breath comes in as body racks a bit,
holds, and goes out, she looks back at therapist) [Connection with self and with
therapist is engaged.]

TH: (very gently) Where are these tears coming from?

PT: (crying renews, lips tremble)

TH: Just stay with them, I'm here. [I back off as I realized I had asked a reflective question too soon and want to privilege being with her feeling first; in
saying "I am here," I offer dyadic affect regulation.]

PT: (blows out her breath) There's a lot of anger in there, too.

TH: Uh-huh . . .

PT: And the anger, I just felt so alone . . . I didn't have anyone to help me. [Connects to the source of her feeling so alone in the past. More capacity for feeling adaptive emotions is in evidence.]

TH: *So* much aloneness and the anger that you were so alone with no one to help you. [Staying with her, explicitly mirroring]

PT: (*nodding, continues crying*)

TH: Ohh . . .

To receive help stirs the realization that help was missing in the historical past. When patients have an experience of receiving help, there is often a realization of what was missing. For Abigail, her realization stirs an adaptive feeling of anger. She notes the experience of tightness in her jaw, which she describes as "killing her." First, I invite her to be with the experience of anger in her jaw—however, she shifts back to crying. Then, I return to the new experience of connection happening between us, which had given rise to her realization of how alone she felt and having no one there to help her. Here the choice point is to strengthen our alliance and our growing rapport; she does not have to be alone with her emotional experiences.

TH: Ahhhh . . . When I say I'm here and I want to be with you and help you, how does that land? Makes you realize what wasn't there, kind of stirs up anger . . . [Relational metaprocessing to register the impact of our interactions on her experience]

PT: Yeah . . . (*deep breath in and out*) [Regulating breath] There's part of me that . . . I just want to know what happened to me. [Discontinuous statement, which heralds an important aspect of her treatment.]

TH: Yeah. You want to know what happened to you . . . ooh. [I repeat her words to reflect I am hearing her.]

PT: (*nodding, starts crying some more*) [As I resonate with her, she lets go into more feeling.]

TH: Such a vulnerable place . . .

PT: (*shaking head left and right*) I don't know . . .

TH: You don't know, ohh. [I reflect that she doesn't know and add an empathic para-verbal.]

PT: (*shakes head no, pained look, takes deep breath*) I just feel young. It feels younger than my date rape and all that stuff when I was older.

TH: Uh-huh, mm-hmm. I want to know, too, and I want us to find out

together to see if we can be with you in a way that . . . [**I explicitly join her
desire to know what happened. Also, I perceive a deep quality of pervasive
aloneness, and am explicitly intervening to undo her aloneness.**]
PT: (*exhales deeply*) [**Receptive moment**]
TH: We can just follow what you feel and see where that takes us. [**Inviting
bottom-up processing of the experience.**]

Transformance glimmers bode well for our therapeutic alliance. When Abigail begins
to turn her attention to her body and what is happening internally, she
becomes overwhelmed. Once I reflect her experience and am explicit
about being in contact with her, she connects with emerging sadness. It
is amorphous, undefined, yet seems adaptive, not pathogenic. She has no
clear picture of where it is coming from other than a young, sad place.
When I offer a hand of support, she senses and feels angry about what she
didn't receive in the past. This moment heralds a deepened feeling, a body-/
emotion-based recognition of how alone she had been with no one to help
her, which arose as she was receiving help from me. These movements
between my interventions and Abigail's deepening process are glimmers of
transformance that bode well for our working together. In this early session
we are establishing safety and undoing aloneness, which is evidenced by
her dropping down into core affect and the realization that she wants to
know more about herself. She is speaking to me as an older, wiser other
who she sees is providing help—markers of growing epistemic trust.

Organizing Experiential Work With
AEDP Representational Schemas

We explained the AEDP representational schemas used to guide experiential work in Chapter 3, "The Move to Experience and Transformation," and
we applied them in Chapter 8, "Working to Transform Patterns of Avoidant
Attachment," and in Chapter 10, "Working to Transform Patterns of Ambiv-
alent/Resistant Attachment." To work with disorganization, we continue to
provide specified versions of the representational schemas for psychotherapists to track, which include five categories from Grids 1 and 2, Row 3 and
Rows 5–8: (a) patient's response to attachment system arousal, (b) nervous
system activation and affect regulation, (c) how defenses and (d) anxiety
manifest, and finally, (e) the patient's affective competence (see Chapter 5).
These categories are related to the AEDP TOE: defenses are represented on

the upper left corner, anxiety is represented on the upper right corner, and core affective experience is represented on the bottom corner.

The TOE (Chapter 3) provides a schema upon which therapists can track a patient's behavior toward and away from affective experience. In disorganization, the experiences of both affect and relatedness are complex. In the above vignette we see how the patient's experiences were shifting among partial memory, association, self-judgment/shame, dissociation, and the core emotions of sadness and anger. When I closely tracked and reflected Abigail's experience, she was able to make use of our dyadic regulation, and the somatic focus helped to organize her experience; each subsequent piece that emerged was meaningful. My providing explicit relational accompaniment was key to Abigail's accessing her sadness and touching into her experience of unbearable aloneness.

As described in Chapter 3, the TOE has two versions. The self-at-best is transformance-led functioning and is driven by safety and hope. Defenses are soft and more flexible and when anxiety arises, it is mild and has the quality of a green signal, which is marked by openness to experience. The self-at-worst version of the TOE is resistance-led functioning and is driven by dread or threat. Defenses are more inflexible, can be embedded, and include shame-based self states. In a self-at-worst state, anxiety and also shame, both conceived of inhibitory affects, have a red signal function.

It can be helpful to normalize shame and anxiety, and both need to be regulated. The above vignette with Abigail provides an example of how the therapeutic relationship offered a stabilizing function that helped her be in her self-at-best in which she was open to feel into the compromised version of herself, self-at-worst, while being in connection with the therapist. We established that she would not be alone in the present day with her feelings that were related to how alone she had been in her childhood.

Next, we describe the markers and behaviors of anxiety and defense on the TOE: disorganized.

The Triangle of Experience: Disorganized

Anxiety. Anxiety is represented on the upper right corner of the TOE (see Figure 12.1), which is activated by attachment needs of their own or another, related to the patient's anticipation of "fright without solution." It may also be related to the patient's anticipation of "attachment without solution," in which the patient may be lacking a template for an older,

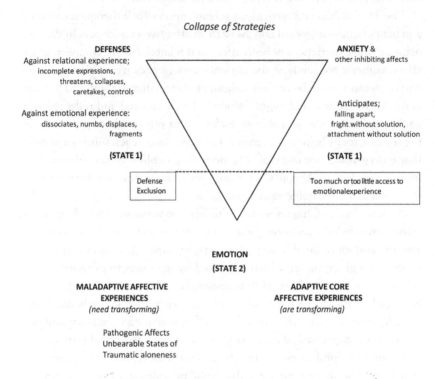

Figure 12.1 The Triangle of Experience: Disorganized
Pando-Mars, 2024, adapted from Diana Fosha, 2020

wiser other who would be available to help them. In the absence of a trust-worthy attachment figure, some individuals adopt a role with others in which they become caretaking and controlling. The anticipation of *no one reliant* (Grid 2) can give rise to anxiety about being overcome by emotion and falling apart.

By the time some of these folks are adults and arrive to therapy, they have a mixture of coping strategies to manage their anxiety, such as shutting down, dissociation, and fragmentation. When they are unable to use a defensive strategy to cope, their anticipation of fright without solution or attachment without solution may trigger a collapse in strategy, in which helplessness and intense fear of being hurt again come to the fore. This is the realm of pathogenic affects and unbearable states of traumatic alone-ness, on the maladaptive side of the bottom of the TOE, which we discuss in the section on core affective experience.

Defenses against relational experience. Verbally, when patients have difficulty fin-ishing their sentences, trail off, and stop speaking for an extended period of time and/or resume in a disconnected fashion, we are in the terrain of *incomplete expressions,* a hallmark of disorganized discourse as identified in the AAI. Therapists may find themselves confused about what is happen-ing in these inchoate, fragmented ideas that seem to be nonsequiturs. It might be that unresolved material is activated in the moment. Or that by the time many of our patients have become adults, these speech patterns have become habitual and are indicative of the fragmentation that lies below the surface.

Defenses against relational experience appear when an individual takes either a *threatening* position toward another, or a *submissive* position. *Control* takes the form of the individual's need to have their own way, to an extreme with little capacity to compromise. Excessive *caregiving* is another defense against relatedness, an outgrowth of role reversal when the individual has little expe-rience of being on the receiving end of care from an "older, wiser other." Sometimes collapse can also become a strategy, when an individual falls to pieces in a desperate plea to enlist the attention and care of another and also to altogether avoid the emotions associated with the situation at hand.

Defenses against emotional experience. Defenses are represented on the upper left corner of the TOE. In the face of threatening overwhelm, by the time many of the disorganized children reach adulthood, *dissociation* and being *numb* become defensive strategies they have mastered to protect themselves against emotional experience. During sessions, approaching these dissociated emotions can provoke a loss of focus and cognitive disruption (which might be the kind of lapse in discourse that shows up as a prolonged silence or difficulty staying on track). A shift in posture, fogging over, spacing out, or the light going out from the patient's eyes may indicate dissociation. Anxiety is often the culprit behind such dissociative defenses, the fear of being overwhelmed and alone with unbearable emotion produces a shutting down awareness of that emotion.

Fragmentation and *displacement* are also defenses against emotional experience, which are used to manage the terror, humiliation, and despair that is often a result of traumatic aloneness with the underlying and unresolved attachment trauma. Affective experiences and memory may be disconnected from each other and sequestered to protect the individual from the intrusion of these affects and memories. However, at other times the defensive barriers do break down, which is what has become referred to as "trauma time" (van der Hart et al., 2010), when a person is overtaken in current time by unresolved emotions and memories from the past. Sometimes "subparts" may suddenly pop out, when the barriers against these splintered-off affective states give way.

The TOE is embedded in the bottom of the SOE triangle, which is discussed after the following vignette. We discuss core affective experience with the SOE triangle.

Track the anxiety that precedes dissociation. In the following vignette, we return to a session with Abigail that took place 2 weeks after the first vignette. She is beginning to track her dissociation at home, and notices that she often feels sleepy with her husband and children. I explore what happens in the here-and-now between us to help her to regulate the anxiety that I believe contributes to her use of dissociation. Abigail's disorganized attachment was the result of neglect and deep deprivation, from her experience of being alone and untended for hours at a time as a child. Currently, she had a strong capacity in her work life and was able to function with an avoidant strategy, high intelligence, and good rapport with people. However, in her intimate relationships the precarious edge of unbearable aloneness at the core of her wounding was just below the surface, which she had been quite adept at keeping at bay through the use of avoidant strategies and dissociation. Until our work together.

Case Vignette 12A, Part 2: Letting in Care

We begin this vignette with an exploratory question. Since Abigail began to feel sleepy in response to our interaction that just preceded this moment, I am interested in whether she is aware of some anxiety that may have precipitated a dissociative defense.

TH: I wonder if even our contact made you a little anxious like if that's new, to have me on your side being affirmative of you or seeing the big picture. What does that feel like? [**Making the implicit explicit; exploring the experience of contact between us, platforming with empathic elaboration.**]

PT: Hmm, yeah. It's definitely something.

TH: How do you know it's something? What does it touch? [**Connect to what is happening moment-to-moment in her inner experience.**]

PT: I feel a little anxious, feel a little anxiety. [**Signal affect**]

TH: Where? [**Identify the physical experience.**]

PT: Here. (*waves her hands up and down in front of her torso*)

TH: In your core? [**I use evocative words to help her name and hopefully deepen her experience.**]

PT: Mm-hmm.

Explore anxiety. Since anxiety is rising while we are speaking about the contact between us, I turn my attention to exploring her anxiety and I ask her to give it words. It may be coming up due to implicit memory, a right-brain experience. Speaking from the anxiety may help her to regulate, by putting words to her concern. It also might help to organize her experience by potentially giving voice to her expectancies or what she may be anticipating.

TH: So if that little anxiety is going to speak, what words might be there? [**Using words brings the left brain online, which can be regulating, as well as informative.**]

PT: I'm scared like somebody might be nice to me. (*looks younger*) [**Shift into State 2, core affective phenomena: relational experience.**]

TH: You're scared cuz somebody's being nice to you? [**I shift into a small voice like talking to a child.**]

PT: (*nodding*)

TH: What's someone being nice to you going to do? [Explore the anxiety.]

PT: I don't know.

TH: You look really scared, I see it in your face. [I reflect what I see, and attune to her by speaking in a tender voice.]

PT: (nods)

TH: And sad too . . . [I name feelings as a mother reflects to a small child.]

A: (nodding)

TH: Just stay with it, just let it have some room. Is this okay? [Making space to be with her feeling, and asking permission to guard safety.]

PT: (nodding, closes eyes for a second)

TH: Is it too much? Is it okay just this much? (she responds nonverbally, shakes head left to right) What do you see on my face when I'm being nice to you? What do you see now? [Asking for her perception of my expression.]

PT: (slowly) You're being nice to me (in a small voice).

TH: How come I'm being nice to you, I wonder. Do you know why I'm being nice to you, where it comes from? [I continue deepening her perception and reception by asking her to reflect on the experience, to see if she might understand where I am coming from. I sense we are in unknown territory.]

PT: You understand me? [Click]

TH: Yeah . . .

PT: I feel like pain . . . right here and right here (points to her shoulders). [Constriction, physical defense, another part emerges]

TH: So what would the pain say if the pain was going to go into words? [Explore this part]

PT: Like all in up here . . . (points to her neck and shoulders)

TH: That just came up, so just listen to it, see if an image comes, or words. (we both have slight nods of our heads, syncing with each other) Anything come to mind?

PT: Just pain.

TH: So I just want to say . . .

PT: Tense, here and here (she brushes from the back of her neck to the front with both hands)

TH: I just want to say, when you say, "I understand" that I'm being nice to you, I'm understanding—do you feel understood? Or are you thinking I'm understanding you, which is why I'm being nice . . . [I circle back to reconnect with her experience before the pain and constriction emerged.]

We stay with the fact that I am "being nice" to Abigail, and her voice sounds like she is coming from a much younger part of herself. She looks a little bewildered and speaks hesitantly, which might reflect that she is between two parts of her experience. She tells me she feels pain in her shoulders. But then she says the following:

PT: It's like, like, you, you care . . . [She perceives me accurately, although she continues sounding hesitant. I wonder if she is unsure that she can say this in therapy or if overall, the experience is unfamiliar.]

TH: Yeah, that actually feels like what I feel. [Validating with kind, reassuring tone in my voice.]

PT: (nods) Mm-hmm.

TH: Like I care about you, and out of caring, I want to understand. And . . .

PT: Wanting to be with me and understand me, yup . . . [Now she is clear that she gets me and lets me know that she is perceiving my care.]

TH: Now, what's happening as we acknowledge that there's caring, that you can see caring and that's where that comes from? How does that feel . . . to the part that feels scared or pain? [I elaborate the experience of being with another who wants to understand her and care for her; I invite her to process the experience, with attention to the part of her that was feeing scared.]

PT: I don't know. I'm just going with it, but it just um, I had a flip to feeling really little again. [So directing my question to the part that felt scared brought her into feeling little again. This is an AEDP State 2 experience: accessing a different ego state or gaining access to a younger part of herself. As we make contact and make the relational experience explicit, she "flips" to being little.]

TH: Hmm, a flip to feeling really little again. (I mirror the same flipping gesture with my hand as she does with her hand) [Mirroring gesture—physical attunement]

PT: Back there.

TH: Right now? [I am trying to locate where this flip actually took her.]

PT: When I was in tears, felt really small again, like when I was 4 years old. [She is referring to the prior session, which was in the previous vignette, 12A.]

TH: What's it like to feel that 4-year-old? Can the 4-year-old part feel the caring, feel my caring? [Processing the experience of her younger self from her being in her self-at-best, open, and able to describe her experience. I also check for the receptive affective capacity of the younger self. This was at least two interventions—yet they land and move the process.]

PT: (*nods slowly, looking deeply into my eyes*) [**Begins to gaze at me. Signals that she is taking in the caring I offer.**]

TH: I'm glad, actually. What's happening right now?

PT: (*brushes across, referring to her shoulders*) I'm just conscious of the anxiety and my body reaction.

Here, we stayed in eye contact for an extended time. There was no defense, and Abigail's anxiety calmed way down. Earlier in the session she said that she doesn't bask in the positive. Now, we were gazing into each other's eyes, with a simple purity, right brain to right brain. Abigail named how she felt herself just being with me (*core state*). I am struck that in these moments, we were *basking* in eye contact.

Before these moments of contact, Abigail and I were exploring the activation that came up in her relationship with her spouse and her children. I noticed how we were treading in the zone of dorsal vagal shutdown. By helping Abigail to understand that her sleepy defense was meaningful and then helping her to stay present and engaged with me, a strong feeling of connection and ease arose between us, though not without tension and a constrictive aspect emerging first.

Years later, Abigail told me how being with her children when they were small was incredibly activating and difficult for her. And we recognized how she was struggling with her own unresolved state of mind after growing up with her psychotic mother who really was unable to be present and available with her.

In this session, we have a corrective relational experience through gazing—patient and therapist—perhaps infant and mother, or mother to young girl. In a place that was once incredibly stark, marked by such deep aloneness, we arrived at the fullness of pure contact. Instead of initiating fear, sleepiness, and avoidance, contact with me in the here and now brought Abigail to recognize the felt sense of care and being cared for. Our connection felt like a warm and nourishing balm to the soul.

With recognition came new awareness of more parts of herself. Abigail identified that right before our gaze, she had experienced pain in her shoulders, and realized it was coming from her critic/protector part. The protector was on the verge of swooping in to take her away. When we metaprocessed the experience of eye contact, she realized that while she was having a new experience of connection, the protector was also there, as a reminder of its vigilance and resolute way to keep her together and safe. However, she had the sense that this time the critic voice was outside of her. What was truer and more real was our contact and the simplicity of *being* together. In addition to having a new experience of relational contact, her capacity to reflect on her experience and with a sense of inner knowing and self-understanding was expanding.

The SOE Triangle (With Embedded TOE): Disorganized

The SOE triangle (see Figure 12.2) is the AEDP representational schema that depicts the relational matrix surrounding a person's internal working model: the individual's internalized representation of Self, the individual's internalized representation of Other, and the individual's internalized representation of Emotion and its processing. These representations can change according to the relationship, and whether one's environment is experienced as safe or threatening. For this, we have two versions of the SOE triangle: the self-at-best and the self-at-worst (see Chapter 3, Maxim 8, Working With the Self-at-Worst From Under the Aegis of the Self-at-Best, pp. 124–125) and Chapter 5, pp. 147–150). When psychotherapists establish conditions of safety with our patients, we help them to access their self-at-best, a hope-driven state. Being in connection with us and open to their own experience supports their capacity to work with their self-at-worst, a state driven by dread. In self-at-best, the individual's internalized representation of the Other is realistic; even if problematic, the individual is able to maintain perspective to see the there clearly. The individual's internalized representation of their Self is effective. They are able to stay connected to themselves and act appropriately to the situation.

The constellation of self-at-worst manifests when there is threat in the environment or the individual is triggered and gets thrown into "trauma time." The individual's internalized representation of the Self is compromised, while the individual's representation of the Other is triggering. We have modified the SOE triangle to each of the insecure attachment patterns: in Chapter 8 to avoidant attachment, in Chapter 10 to ambivalent/resistant attachment. Here, we describe what happens in disorganized attachment.

On the disorganized SOE triangle, a self-at-worst constellation, the individual's representation of the triggering other is characterized by the Other's unresolved/fearful state of mind, and their behavioral hallmarks of being frightened or frightening, or disordered. The experience and interaction

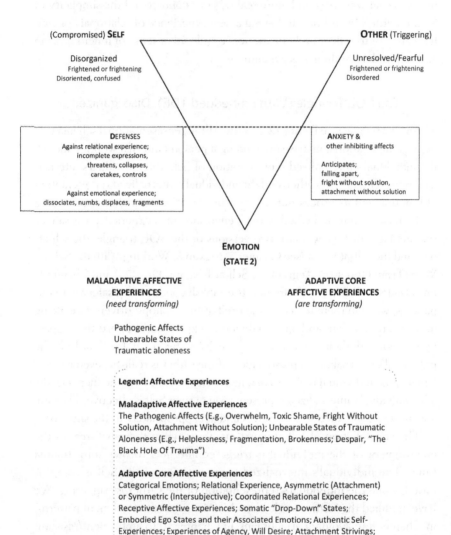

Collapse of Strategies

(Compromised) **SELF**

Disorganized
Frightened or frightening
Disoriented, confused

OTHER (Triggering)

Unresolved/Fearful
Frightened or frightening
Disordered

DEFENSES
Against relational experience;
incomplete expressions,
threatens, collapses,
caretakes, controls

Against emotional experience;
dissociates, numbs, displaces, fragments

ANXIETY &
other inhibiting affects

Anticipates;
falling apart,
fright without solution,
attachment without solution

EMOTION
(STATE 2)

MALADAPTIVE AFFECTIVE
EXPERIENCES
(need transforming)

ADAPTIVE CORE
AFFECTIVE EXPERIENCES
(are transforming)

Pathogenic Affects
Unbearable States of
Traumatic aloneness

Legend: Affective Experiences

Maladaptive Affective Experiences
The Pathogenic Affects (E.g., Overwhelm, Toxic Shame, Fright Without
Solution, Attachment Without Solution); Unbearable States of Traumatic
Aloneness (E.g., Helplessness, Fragmentation, Brokenness; Despair, "The
Black Hole Of Trauma")

Adaptive Core Affective Experiences
Categorical Emotions; Relational Experience, Asymmetric (Attachment)
or Symmetric (Intersubjective); Coordinated Relational Experiences;
Receptive Affective Experiences; Somatic "Drop-Down" States;
Embodied Ego States and their Associated Emotions; Authentic Self-
Experiences; Experiences of Agency, Will Desire; Attachment Strivings;
The Expression of Core Needs

Figure 12.2 The Self–Other–Emotion Triangle (With
Embedded Triangle of Experience): Disorganized
Adapted from Diana Fosha, 2020

between the child and their primary attachment figure is what sets the stage for the individual's internal working model. Here, the individual's internalized representation of the Other is frightened or frightening, or disordered. Consequently, the individual's representation of their compromised Self is characterized by disorganization. The Self is represented as frightened or frightening, disoriented or confused. Their internalized representation of Emotion is characterized by fear of falling apart; affective competence (or lack thereof) of not feeling and not dealing. Emotion is often represented as overwhelming.

There are multiple combinations that can occur in the representations of disorganized attachment, ways in which the individual perceives Self and Other. The caregiver's unresolved trauma impacts their capacity to function as a caregiver when they are triggered; thereby they are unable to feel and unable to deal with their own affective state, much less respond to their child. There are many permutations that arise in the internal working models of children growing up with parents who are unresolved. Some individuals' internal working models hold their own Self-representation as frightening, from seeing in response to their needs how their parent would get triggered. Or the individual's Self-representation may be disoriented and confused, when they cannot seem to communicate their needs to their parent, and subsequently they develop an internalized representation of the Other as disordered or frightening. Some of the children developed role-reversal strategies, and instead of leaning into their attachment figure, it's as if they became a pseudo-attachment figure for their parent. They may develop a Self-representation related to the role of caregiving, stepping in to control their caregivers who were rendered helpless by their own trauma-based fear. The role-reversed kid may develop an internalized representation of the Other as helpless or incapable.

In psychotherapy, when a patient is confronted with the potential of someone who could be an attachment figure responding to them with help and care, they may have difficulty in a number of different ways. They might take charge and become controlling of the therapeutic interaction. They might become anxious or fearful. Or they may feel that they are in unknown territory, confused and unfamiliar with the possibility of having someone explicitly there for them. An important part of working with disorganized attachment is for psychotherapists to aim to provide new and corrective relational experiences that set the conditions for the patients to be able to trust their perception of a trustworthy other, starting with therapists.

The need for titration. One of my patients was overwhelmed by the potential of allowing herself to feel me with her. She described feeling like "if you've been anorexic and you haven't been eating and you finally decide you're going to eat, it would be dangerous to eat an entire sandwich." She imagined that if she were to allow herself to let her guard down, she "would lose control because she is just so hungry." Another patient couldn't imagine letting in my care, and when for a moment she did find herself drawn to feeling nourished, fear showed in the whites of her eyes. The idea that I might be a caretaker threw her into a quandary. It felt overwhelming. She said, "The floor just drops out, nothing to stand on. . . ." These examples are vivid descriptions of the "black hole of trauma," when the offer of relatedness triggers intense fear, and a fear without solution at that.

Therapist common reactivity. Offering help that is sorely needed, but wasn't had, can rock the foundations for some of our patients, and can be upsetting for therapists as well when it is not received and it is even triggering. When the conundrum of "attachment without solution" is triggered in a patient, we might feel worried and want to back away from activating them further. Yet the therapist metaskills of constancy and embodying calm strength can be stabilizing for both therapist and patient. It can be helpful to recognize how important it is that the patient is communicating their experience. Our work is to stay engaged, to both respect the patient's window of tolerance and provide enough contact to meet at the edge of what is tolerable. Here, we can build safety through talking about the patient's experience through responding to their imagery or sensations to convey understanding, while also titrating the experience of relatedness.

Holding a space that both gives the patient room to feel into their experience, while having a new experience of being attuned to and listened to holds the intention of being in it together, while distinctly meeting what the patient is going through. For example, to explore with the person who fears the danger of eating an entire sandwich, to imagine taking a small bite or a sliver, and then see what happens. For the person afraid of collapsing with the offer of a hand, what might happen if we were to offer a pinky? Or if we remove the "take" from "caretaker," can they feel the therapist's care? Or if possible, to acknowledge and respect the patient's fear of collapsing and explore the experience of collapse from a distance, the way the therapist earlier in this chapter helped the patient to explore her anger as if it were on a screen. Since unbearable aloneness is such a major part of the black hole of trauma, finding our way to undo the patient's experience of aloneness in incremental steps is key: to neither move too far away and risk exacerbating their aloneness, nor move in too close and risk overwhelming our togetherness.

Working With Emotion and Core Affective Experience

At the bottom of the SOE triangle and the TOE is core affective experience, which includes categorical emotions, self-affective experiences, and relational affective experiences. Affective experiences can be maladaptive or adaptive. Maladaptive experiences include pathogenic affects and unbearable states of traumatic aloneness (see Chapter 3, pp. 105–106), which are prevalent in disorganized attachment resulting from "fright without solution" and "attachment without solution." For some, the offer of providing what was sorely missing is frightening, and the fear of collapse and overwhelm is hugely triggering, as described in the above examples. Here collaboration between therapist and patient is essential. We are also on the lookout for self-affective experiences and relational affective experiences (to help patients restore self-trust and trust in other).

In working with disorganization, we want to help the patient make links between their current life experiences that are triggering and their past unresolved traumatic experiences that are at play. By making room to attend and explore affects that may have been previously dissociated, our aim is to provide corrective emotional and relational experiences to ultimately help the patient to mobilize adaptive action on behalf of their self. We can explore specific memories through the use of *portrayal*, in which we locate and reenter a representation of a scene with the intention to provide a different outcome, one that provides a corrective experience. An outcome through which emotion can be processed, aloneness can be undone, and the patient's self-agency and efficacy can be restored.

The following vignette (which we introduced in Chapter 11) shows portrayal work with core affective experience during the third of this series of sessions with Abigail. She opened this session by asking if she ever told me her first childhood memory. She remembered waking up terrified by the pounding sounds of a heavy rainstorm. She got herself out of her crib and down the pitch-black hallway to find her parents' room, which is where her memory stopped. When as an adult she asked her mother if she remembered the big storm and what happened, her mother told her how surprised she had been to find Abigail at her bedroom door. When Abigail asked her what she did, her mother said that she put her back into her crib. We enter the following vignette about 20 minutes into the session, after three or four failed attempts to engage an experiential focus in our work. After some reflection about what was so frightening that her memory stopped, I reach out to the little one who does remember feeling afraid. Reentering this part of the memory, with the channels of experience that were available, provided the entry point we needed.

Case Vignette 12A, Part 3: The Move to "I'm Worthwhile"

TH: How can we be with that little one in you, because it feels like that was so important, and that impulse to get what you need is so valiant and courageous and right. [**I want to restore her motivational vector toward reaching out to an Other for comfort and protection.**]

PT: Uh-huh, yup. I don't remember the part of her putting me back in the crib. I only remember the part up until I got in the room and saw her, and my memory is blank after that . . . [**When her adaptive action in response to her fear was not recognized, she reverted to the oldest neurological circuit, the dorsal vagal complex, and shut down.**]

TH: So I wonder what makes that the part you don't remember. Like why do you think that would be the part you don't remember? [**Inviting mentalizing about her experience**]

PT: Because as terrifying as this whole thing was, that was probably the worst part of it. [**Recognition of being alone when she was so terrified.**]

TH: Reaching out and having someone not get you . . . [**Empathic elaboration**]

PT: Or just putting me back in the situation where I'm scared. [**She elaborates in the spirit of collaboration.**]

TH: Mm-hmm.

PT: And alone . . . ohh . . . [**Nonverbal emphasis about the impact of being alone with her fear**]

TH: So I feel like there's a little, little one in you, a little 2-year-old who's still holding this. I want us to somehow touch her or feel her or let her know that we want to do it differently. [**Setting the intention to build connection between the dissociated parts of herself.**]

PT: Yeah, I don't have a lot of feeling connection to that. It's like I'm telling it but I'm not feeling it. [**Disconnection/dissociation**]

Situating the patient properly in affective space (Panksepp, 2009). In AEDP terms, "properly" is being with another and in touch with the somatic, sensory elements of emotional experience to facilitate bottom-up processing. Abigail has difficulty finding and offering comfort to her young self. In the next segment, I ask her to tune into the channels of experience (Hanakawa, 2021; Mars, 2011), which are awake to the memory. This is similar to lighting up the neural networks in eye movement desensitization and reprocessing (EMDR; Parnell, 1999). [**We begin processing by noticing what is happening and building a platform from there.**]

PT: I remember seeing the dark, like it was dark and shadowy and I felt really little cuz the hall walls were so big. [**Visual channel of experience**]

TH: So big. [**I enter the memory with her by echoing what she says.**]

PT: And bang, bang, like huge bangs on the roof. [**Auditory channel of experience**]

TH: Oh yeah, so the hearing's really . . .

PT: I'm trying really hard with my hand; my hand is going against the wall like this, trying to find my way . . . (*shows how she was reaching to touch the wall with her fingertips*) [**Sensation channel of experience**]

TH: Yeah . . . feeling that feeling in your hand, and hearing the sounds just letting that . . . cuz those channels are awake to this memory. [**Deepening the experience**]

PT: And the pictures of the cats and dogs . . . [**Visual channel**]

TH: Pounding, falling down on the roof . . . [**Amplifying the sounds: hearing**] I'm seeing you. I'm seeing this little baby girl in the dark, young enough . . . [**I witness her to provide an experience of being seen (Adler, 2002).**]

PT: I think I might have been less than 2 because I'm holding the wall because I'm not a great walker.

TH: Ohh . . . (*tender nonverbal cooing*)

PT: I'm having trouble, like, I'm not . . . (*she stares off*)

TH: Yeah, stay. Stay here . . . maybe take in . . . see me seeing you, because you know sometimes when you go into that . . . [**I see her starting to dissociate and bring her attention to our relational contact for dyadic regulation, and make an explicit self-disclosure**] because I just want you to know that I see this little, little one in the dark and that if I'm the mom, what I imagine, is just picking you up immediately, and just picking you up, and, and I imagine like listening with you to the sounds,

like wow, "It's really loud isn't it? It's loud, ohh you must be scared
if you came here, right, you must be so scared." [**I feel compelled to
enter the scene and provide the missing help and empathy that was
needed.**]

PT: Mm-hmm.

TH: Ohh, and then maybe you would say, "cats and dogs, roof . . . oh no."
(*tone of concern*) I would say, "you hear cats and dogs on the roof, that's
a saying, it's raining, really hard raining. It's really loud." [**To give the
terrified child an accurate understanding of the phrase "it's raining cats
and dogs"**]

PT: It's like cats and dogs, like *dead* cats and dogs landing on the roof, tons of
them. [**She lets me know the picture she imagined as a child.**]

TH: "*Dead* cats and dogs" (*said with strong emphasis*), how awful, what an awful
image, yeah, yeah. What happens if I say, "It's not cats and dogs. It's just
rain, rain, rain?" That's just how we speak about it, but it's really rain.
What happens? [**Metaprocess**]

PT: I feel some relief. [**Postbreakthrough affect**]

TH: So feel that relief, where do you feel it? [**Notice the somatic aspect of
the feeling.**]

PT: I felt like "a ahh, ahh, ahh, haaaa . . . " (*nonverbal sounds of release*)

TH: Do you want to stay with me? Do you want to stay with your mom?
[**Explicit caregiving response**]

PT: (*nods*)

TH: Of course you do, I want you to stay with me.

Consciously filling in a missing element. I explicitly name my immediate, instinctive desire to reach out to the scared baby girl, to offer comfort as a mother
would to a child. I am cognizant that I am Abigail's therapist and we are in
a psychotherapy session doing portrayal work. And the imperative to step
in to offer what was clearly missing was strong. I trust I am coming from
my own affective competence, being present in myself and present with
her, making a conscious choice, attentive to what happens next. The unit
of intervention is the therapist's intervention and the patient's response to
it. (Fosha, 2000b).

PT: That's what I wanted. [**Click of recognition**]

TH: I want you to stay with me. I want you to stay with me . . . [**Affirmation,
amplifying**]

PT: (*starts shaking and sobs*) [**Core affect**]

TH: Keep breathing . . . yeah, just feel into it. [**Dyadic affect regulation; making room to feel the emotion, to let it move**]

PT: I feel like she didn't want me. [**Verbalizing her core wounding**]

TH: Ohh.

PT: I wanted her to want to take care of me. [**The reparative longing**]

TH: Of course you did. Yes . . . yeah . . . yeah . . . ahhh, yeah . . . yeah . . . [**Deep affirmation of her longing**] Just be with that, you wanted her to want to take care of you . . . of course you did. So much . . . uh-huh. You got yourself out of your crib and down the hall in the dark, holding on to the wall. Such a brave girl. Ooohhhh.

Corrective relational experience. In the above scenario, I saw the little baby girl as so valiant and brave to get herself what she needed, and in this imaginary scene we are able to have a redo. Instead of being put back in bed, the little girl is seen for what is terrifying her, and offered understanding and comfort. When the patient feels seen and cared for, she immediately realizes what she wanted and didn't receive, which was that her mother would understand what she needed and respond to her.

In the following segment we metaprocess what occurred between us. This corrective relational experience holds the potential to impact the patient's internal working model, to shift her self-representation, helping her to integrate how her self-perception is impacted by being responded to.

TH: And what about you . . . what does it tell you about you that what was evoked in me was just wanting to take care of you. What does that tell you about you? [**Relational metaprocessing**]

PT: That I'm worthwhile. (*her voice is hesitant*)

TH: Uh-huh. Is that a question or are you letting that in? Feel into it, feel into it because I think that's a really important recognition.

PT: You know, I just internalized that there was something wrong with me. [**Recognizing shame and the compromised self-representation of her disorganized internal working model**]

TH: Yeah, that needs to be dispelled, right?

PT: Yeah.

TH: Cuz you made a valiant effort to get something that you needed and you deserve to be given that comfort. Check in with me as I'm saying this, right? I just want to know if you can take that in if you're needing to shut down a little or . . . [I was seeing her close her eyes, so I checked in with her.]

PT: Say it again . . .

TH: That I see that you made this valiant effort to get what you needed and you deserve to be responded to.

PT: I feel very angry. [Underneath the shutting down and the shame is anger.]

TH: Yeah. How do you know that?

PT: I feel, I just feel angry. It's all well and good that we can sit here and talk about it. You can pretend to be my mom but it doesn't make up for what happened.

TH: Yeah.

PT: There's like this feeling of like just anger and like I have to deal with the repercussions of this so deeply in my life, you know, and it wasn't my fuckin fault. [Core affect of anger, with the adaptive action of releasing her from being at fault.]

TH: Anything else you want to say to her from this place, as you're waking up to yourself? [Inviting a mini portrayal, to express her feelings to her mother.]

PT: I really, really, really wanted to have a mom who would look at me and see me like that, and kinda smile or not smile but soften and take me in her arms and feel loved and just be taken care of. That's what I needed. [Recognition of her core needs]

TH: Yeah. What you needed and what I want to add that you totally deserve. [Affirmation]

PT: (nodding) I deserve that and should have had that.

Building the reflective capacity. In the above vignette, I asked Abigail, "What does it mean about you that what was evoked in me was wanting to care for you?" When she said, "I'm worthwhile . . ." she was identifying a shift in her internal representation of Self to one who deserved to be responded to. When a child is responded to, accurately reflected, and able to rely on their attachment figures, they feel loved and cared for; they feel known and develop the capacity to know themselves; they develop agency and security in relationships. These interactive layers of support are the building blocks of the capacity for self-reflective functioning or mentalization. When self-reflective function is fractioned by dissociation, the self is compromised. When parts of self that hold affective experience are met and tended to, knowing and self-reflection can flow between these parts of self and within the individual as a whole. The capacity to think about one's feelings and feel about one's thoughts leads to self-understanding and the ability to understand another (Fonagy & Target, 1997).

In the final moments of the above session with Abigail, I asked her about her experience of the session and our work together. Her response actually pointed to the beginnings of our developing epistemic trust and the newness of her experiences with me.

TH: How is it for you if we review where we started out with this memory and finding your way into it and getting what you got about your mom and you? [**Metaprocessing the arc of the session**]

PT: It was interesting. For a long time I felt like I wasn't getting, you know like getting into it, you know, and then it was kinda good, we kinda found the way in. [**She recalls the failed attempts to get somewhere.**]

TH: Yeah. How is it that we weren't finding our way in, and then we just kept shifting around? [**I metaprocess her experience of this aspect of our work. It's *all* grist for the mill.**]

PT: It was fine, it was good. That was good. Um, it was great. And I know I feel like we always get to it one way or the other. [**Trust emerges.**]

TH: Uh-huh. What's that like? What's that like that we always get to it one way or another? That you can say that? [**Staying with the emergent, I continue to metaprocess.**]

PT: It's good. Um, like I said, this isn't the usual experience in therapy for me. So that's really good. It feels very different. [**She articulates the corrective nature of the experience.**]

TH: I mean, it feels like that's something about us like how it is to do this with me and there's something about us that's just . . . [**Here, I receive her experience and reflect that I also see that we have a connection to work from.**]

PT: It works, yeah. I was telling Jim, I do. I feel like you're remothering me in a way I definitely. . . . You have a lot of that mom energy for me, which is really nice. So thank you. [**She names the corrective emotional/relational experience.**]

In AEDP, we engage *metaprocessing* interventions to help patients reflect on shifts in their experience, especially new and positive ones. By asking a metaprocessing question, we help the patient who is having a new and corrective experience to know they are having it, to feel what it means that they are having it, and to feel what they feel by having the new experience. Questions like "How is it that we weren't finding our way in, and then we just kept shifting around?" and "What's that like that we always get to it one way or another? That you can say that?" get patient and therapist engaged to reflect together on what they have just processed and experienced, and what has unfolded. We process their response as thoroughly as possible. Sometimes this deepens the embodied experience of the shift. Sometimes metaprocessing unleashes another round of core affect, as happened when Abigail felt angry about how her life was affected by her mom's lack of capacity to understand and respond to what she needed. And sometimes metaprocessing helps us to get a sense of how we are working together and can make the implicit explicit about our process.

Reflection fosters meaning making, which can lead a patient to increased self-awareness and increased self-understanding (i.e., Abigail's recognizing her core attachment needs). The aspect of self that is aware of having a feeling, knowing one is having the feeling, and having a sense of connection and meaning about the feeling is hugely important in psychotherapy. Reducing fractionation in the self-reflective capacity can help patients to shift out of outdated internal working models into updated self-representations— shifting from a self-at-worst (compromised) self-representation to a self-at-best (effective) self-representation. AEDP's use of metaprocessing as a key mechanism of change not only enhances integration but also helps patients to heal fractures in their reflective function.

In working with disorganized attachment, helping our patients to have new experiences of receiving care gives rise to a feeling of self-worth, promoting a new self-affective experience. To have an experience of self-worth arise out of interaction with a therapist may also feature a new relational affective experience. Having new, corrective self and relational experiences gives rise to transforming internal working models of self and other. In the following section, we present work with a patient who is beginning to understand how her experience of growing up with her mother, who was unresolved from her own trauma, was a significant influence in the patient's relational patterning. In addition to the therapist's active engagement to provide the patient with attuned care and affect regulation, the patient also realigns her own caregiving behaviors to attune to the needs of her younger self.

Working With Role Reversal

Lyons-Ruth (2006) describes the two types of controlling strategies identified in the Berkeley Longitudinal Study (Main et al., 2005). Children who grow up with caregivers who are unresolved for their own trauma may develop: (a) controlling-caregiving, in which they control the parent's attention and involvement through caring, nurturing, entertaining, and organizing the parent; or (b) controlling-punitive, in which they control the parent's attention and involvement through angry, coercive, demeaning interactions with the parent.

The final case example depicts the first strategy of controlling-caregiving, in which the patient, Sylvia, oriented to become her mother's caregiver. When a child is faced with "fright without solution" in their parent who is unresolved, confusion often arises. The child sees the parent in a freeze state or tranced out, which can evoke the caregiving system in the child, turning them away from their own needs as they become hyperaware of their parent's fragility. In the following vignette, this kind of interaction with her parent is an example of "attachment without solution," which initiated a pattern of role reversal in the patient and led to confusion in her adult primary relationship around caregiving. We enter the session when the patient is making peace with her confusion, which up to this point has made it difficult for her to establish boundaries in her current partnership. We stay with this newfound self-acceptance around the patient's confusion to establish her self-at-best as a springboard for the session.

The session progresses through an exploration that leads to the origins of Sylvia taking the role of protector and locates the child part who was overexposed to her mother's trauma and took on the role of protector. It shows the complexity of what can happen when fear goes untended. In the session, as the patient faced aspects of her previously dissociated experience, our dyadic regulation was crucial to helping her stay with what was unfolding. We engage the use of a portrayal to help the patient reorient her adult self to care for her inner child and to release the child from the role of being the mother's caregiver. The selected vignettes show the highlights of the transformative process of the session.

Case Vignette 12B: "Walking Into the Fire"—
Uncovering and Restructuring Role Reversal

State One Work—Following Transformance: Befriending
confusion leads to feeling more real.

THERAPIST (TH): Please elongate *(touches fingertips and pulls hands apart)* to really open into what you are finding in yourself. [**Detecting transformance. I invite her to deepen into the new experience**]

SYLVIA (PATIENT, PT): I see, it feels to me like seeing more clearly. I see my confusion. I don't have to get rid of my confusion anymore. I see it. It's being human. I feel the energy of it. It's like this murky, can sort of sometimes be panicked, um. And now I feel like my confusion is my friend. I don't have wisdom. [**From self-at-best she is able to have perspective and even to befriend her process that at times becomes activated and confused.**]

TH: *(rocks back and leans in)* Wow. What's that like to see? [**Metaprocessing her new way of being with her confusion.**]

PT: That's the thing. It's not trying to fix my confusion or get out of it. It's accepting it and then, um, and actually I am appreciating these glimpses of being more real. [**By accepting herself as she is, she describes a self experience with the action tendency that she is feeling more real.**]

When possible, begin the session with affirmation, which in this case was the affirmation of the patient's transformance glimmer of seeing more clearly, and then metaprocess. In this segment at the opening of the session, the patient is having a new, positive experience of confusion, which has been a problematic area in herself, and as we do in AEDP, we take a moment to metaprocess the new experience, which generates a platform of self-at-best for what follows.

The following interaction sequence developed in response to the patient's attempt to figure out what to say when she needed a boundary with her partner. My sense was that early material was triggered and preempting her from having access to her own knowing in the present moment.

Exploring the defense (difficulty of setting a boundary)
links to her historical role.

PT: It's not coming naturally to me. [**She is referring to setting a boundary.**]

TH: Right. And so that to me, it's not about me teaching you the right words and you writing them down and memorizing them. [**In a state of high anxiety, she would ask me what she could say to her partner that would help her to establish a boundary.**] It's like we have to hold the question "How come it's so hard for you to protect yourself by setting a boundary?" [**Setting the intention to explore**]

PT: Right, right, right.

TH: Right?

PT: Yeah. Yeah, I think that's true. (*she tears up and gets weepy*) I got to find that, that authentic kind of . . . I got to feel it, and I, why am I not able to connect to that? Yeah. Yeah. And I think I mentioned before there's this feeling of, I'm needing to put the other person first or I don't deserve to sort of have that protection because my role is protector. [**Identifying how she feels leads to her historical role.**]

TH: Wow, there's something here . . . like, how do we really pay attention to the origins of this pattern? Because it's a pattern and it runs really deep and it goes back a long way. [**Validation and making the implicit explicit— that her role has deep origins.**]

Linking the current-day experience with the historical past. The connection Sylvia makes is important and I am sure there is a link between her current life issue and her historical past. By naming that the pattern goes back a long way, I create space with my words, inviting the patient to slow down, and mark that her identifying her role is an entry point for experiential exploration.

PT: I'm also walking into fire, you know? And so I'm like going toward it. I'm almost sacrificing myself. (*she winces, starts crying, body shakes as she cries*) It's hard to say that. [**The patient is describing her experience when she takes on this role of being a protector.**]

TH: Let's be with you here . . . "It's hard to say it." [**Slowing down, suggesting that we face this together is dyadic regulation, and I repeat her affect-laden words.**]

PT: Yeah, you know, I'm trying to sort of kill myself or, you know . . . [**Intensity grows**]

TH: Wow.

PT: Like it was so trying to destroy myself, so it's not. [**The references are unclear, which may be a hallmark of nearing unresolved trauma.**]

TH: So it's that really wow, right, right, right, right. (*therapist leans in as patient is leaning over, sobbing*) Wow, wow, let's really be with this energy that wants to go self-destruct in order to sacrifice for someone else. **[I am following her closely and know she is describing the intensity of self-sacrifice, even if what we are talking about is not entirely clear.]**

PT: *(rocking)* Yeah, well. I was always, like, so drawn to that idea.

TH: Right. Right. Where does that come from? Well . . . **[Exploring]**

PT: My mom and, you know, she would tell me stories of her child abuse when I was way too young. **[The link: We are now talking about her trauma in the shadows of her mother's unresolved trauma.]**

TH: Oh, I see.

PT: So yeah. So I felt like I wanted to protect her . . . right? **[Role reversal]**

Recognizing the origins of role reversal. The patient is uncovering that self-sacrifice is what comes naturally to her. In response to my question "Where does this come from?" Sylvia identifies what was overwhelming for her as a child. Here, we begin to see why it was so difficult for her to set boundaries. When she was young, she was unable to engage protective action on behalf of herself. Instead, "needing to put the other person first" took precedence and was how she took on the role of being protector: the origins of her role reversal with her mother.

In the following section, I have in mind the possibility to use the AEDP intervention of portrayal work, using the patient's imagination to enter the scene and find a way to be with the younger self who until now was scared and alone and also became the protector of her mother. Know that even though I enter this piece of work with an intention, I am listening to the patient to follow the natural next steps as they arise for her. It is important that our relational alliance is coordinated and is one in which her healing is ultimately driven by what emerges from within her, albeit with my support and guidance.

State Two work: exploring the origins of role reversal leads
to the traumatic experiences of the younger self.

TH: So Sylvia, let's see that little, little, little, little one. **[Focusing her attention to the younger self, who is the holder of her distress.]**

PT: Yeah.

TH: That one of you that was so overexposed. **[Platforming by collecting the pieces of what has been named, to focus this next piece of work.]**

PT: Yeah. And so.

TH: And, had no one to protect you. . . .

PT: And I just turned it into, well, I'm the protector. Like, I remember I was around fourth grade when that started to happen, that sort of persona. And I just remember I think my mom would tell these things and I, I'm sure what I felt was so much fear. [**She reports both the role that she took on as the protector, while also acknowledging the emotion of so much fear.**] I was afraid of my great-aunt. I didn't understand why she would still come around after my mom would tell me terrible stories of physical abuse that were like torture [**which the patient named, but I am not repeating here for confidentiality; and give rise to fright without solution**].

TH: Oh my god . . .

PT: Yeah, she would tell me stories about this when I was in fourth grade. And, and then this woman would come to our house and I was so confused.

The younger self unburdens what she's been holding. The session unfolds as we turn our attention to the younger one. Then, Sylvia began to name horrible memories that her mother told her, which frightened her. Here is an example of unburdening (Schwartz, 1997), when a younger part of self that was isolated and alone begins to reveal and share their memories and affective experiences. As Sylvia speaks and shares her fear and confusion, I notice a quality of growing detachment that seems defensive. Suspecting she was at the edge of her window of tolerance, I explore what was happening with her and sense we are dealing with two neural networks that have been disconnected before now.

When I reflect her detachment, Sylvia describes that she feels sad for her younger self but can see that she is also in an analytical frame of mind. I remind her that we can approach this together, offering dyadic regulation, at which point Sylvia shifts into being more engaged with our exploration.

Building the window of tolerance by undoing aloneness. The younger self's need for a boundary emerges spontaneously.

TH: And is this okay? [**Asking permission is especially important when we are working with patients who are describing a violation in which they had no choice.**] It's not that I want you to saturate into it. Can you and I be connected, while you stay connected in your adult self who sees and

feels for . . . that little one? From your adult self who is connected here
with me, can you see what your little self needs because she's too young
to be the protector? [**I am providing both accompaniment and guidelines
to unblend her adult and younger self, in order to help the younger one
who has surfaced.**]

PT: Yeah. (*opens her eyes and makes eye contact with me*)

TH: She can't . . . nobody's watching out for her. So we need to find her and
find out what she needs. [**I sense the adult is present enough, and advocate
to reach the little one and bring her some help.**]

PT: She needs to not be told these things. You know, I think she's like "I
don't want to know this. I don't want to hear this." [**Green signal affect—
expressing what is needed.**]

Sylvia inhabits her adult self who is now standing in as a protector for her
younger self, expressing that she knows what she needs: "She needs to not
be told these things." Once the adult self names that she need not be told
these things, the younger one says twice, "I don't want to hear this." With
this response she is asserting a boundary, which emerges spontaneously
once her adult self steps in.

PT: This is abusive of my mom. You know, it's like, it's like to do that. It's like
there's a . . . Well, that's not her. Her language is like "I'm scared. I don't
want to hear this." [**The adult shifts from figuring out her mother's behavior, to listening to her younger self. Then she voices what her younger self
is saying.**]

TH: So how do you feel toward her when you hear that?

Check the intrarelational field. I am asking how her adult self feels toward her
younger self, which is an important part of intrarelational work between
parts of self. I'm checking to see if they are aware of each other, how they
feel about each other, if they can communicate and listen in both directions. These are important steps and features of building a secure internal
attachment between the adult self and the younger self.

State Two corrective relational experience: Protection shifts away from
the mother toward younger self. Portrayal work.

PT: Protective.

TH: Right. Right. What does the protective energy want to do for her?

PT: Just take care of her and let her know she doesn't have to play that role. [Clear corrective message]

TH: Okay.

PT: Yeah, like she shouldn't . . . (drifts off)

TH: So here, stay with me for a second [my response to her drift]. I'm wondering if on some level, let's see what this is like for you to imagine [checking in with her for her response]. I have this imagining of like on one level, you have your arm around your younger self and on the other, you have your other arm out in front of you (my arms show one arm wrapped around my waist and one arm pushing out the other, hand up in a stopping gesture)

PT: Yeah.

TH: Making some gesture of stop to the mother. Like, can you as the adult move that impulse to protect your little one with care and take her away, but then also see the adult in you saying or doing more along the lines of she shouldn't be told these things that you said earlier . . . to that overexposure?

PT: "Stop talking to me about this. Stop talking to me this way." [She speaks directly as if talking to her mother. And then she clarifies what is at the heart of her experience.] I could say that. I think a big part of it is some kind thought to where it's remembering . . . "You, Mom, are an adult and you are responsible for taking care of yourself. I'm not going to." [She declares a limit]

TH: Wow, that's important. [I repeat her words and tune into the tone I hear in her voice, focusing on the auditory channel.] Can you hear the tone in your voice that says, "You are the adult. You're responsible for taking care of yourself? Not this little one, right? Not her, not me as her." Feel the energy of this—it feels important. [Offering reflection to support and validate her, and encouragement to feel into her body, via the energy channel.]

PT: Yeah, it's really hard for me because it's really hard to go there. [Anxiety stirs]

TH: Okay. Can you keep your eyes open for a second? Pull me in like, let yourself, see if you can take me with you, if that helps. [Using our relationship to help her regulate, and checking to see if this makes a difference.]

Working with the edges of the window of tolerance. Notice that anxiety arises with each new step: First when she hears from the younger self and now as she speaks up on her own behalf and speaks the truth that her mother was the adult, and she asks that her mother take responsibility for herself. Dyadic regulation and being in it together is crucial, and together we have an opportunity to notice the new experience and to then reflect on it, recalibrate, and digest it. In this case by checking in and exploring the anxiety, Sylvia reveals that she is up against a prohibition of changing the role with her mother. By taking our time to talk together we are following a key element of AEDP, to alternate between experience and reflection to stabilize our work.

Boundary confusion emerges next, around who needs more protection.

State Two work: Working through boundary confusion; accessing core anger and adaptive action

PT: Right. I have to put her first before that. Yeah, I see that, as a young one, so I get all sympathetic for that young one [**meaning her mother**]. But that's not a young one. That's an adult. [**The boundaries are confused, and we see how the patient's perspective is distorted, yet is coming into view by the process of exploring what is the correct next step.**]

TH: That's an adult who's being run by her young one who's untreated. That's true. There's truth there. [**Validation**] But the fact is, she was your mother in an adult body not getting the message that she was out of order. She was untreated for her trauma. I'm so sorry. And right now, we're trying to treat you for your trauma. [**I am advocating for my patient, while also recognizing and having empathy for her mother's situation of being untreated for her abuse.**]

PT: Right? Right.

TH: We're saying this part of your mom that got taken over by her unbounded, unhealed, untreated trauma and was dosing it on to you and getting your attachment caregiving system acting on her behalf rather than her being the caregiver to you. It reversed the role. Right? So we've got to hand that back. [**I'm platforming and also being collaborative, offering psychoeducation to share how I hold what happened, so that my patient understands my motives.**]

PT: Hand it back, yeah.

TH: Feel into the yeah and find out what's ringing true for you. [**I took a stand about handing the role back and I want to find out how it is landing with the patient.**]

PT: Well, I can feel it, too. I can tap into anger, like stop-it kind of anger. Just stop it and take care of yourself. I'm very angry. Stop, stop it, stop it, stop it! [**Core emotion of anger releases an adaptive action tendency.**]

TH: Yes. Go for it.

PT: Yeah. No.

TH: What's happening right now? [**Metaprocessing**]

PT: I feel good.

TH: Okay, tell me what feels good.

PT: I'm glad I did that.

TH: Okay. Tell me what you're glad about. Stay with me with this. [**Meta-processing the new experience of speaking up and declaring a boundary on her own behalf. Stay with it and stay with me in the context of metaprocessing.**]

PT: I don't know, I want to do that more often. I'm just visualizing her and I see her and then just have this feeling it's not okay. And she's. Yeah, she's just got to stop.

TH: So good! [**Affirmation**] What are you seeing when you see her? [**Meta-processing the relational experience of speaking up to her mother to see what effect this has on the patient.**]

Metaprocessing the emotional expression on her own behalf and then following up with the channel of experience that opens. Sylvia spoke her anger and set a boundary by saying stop to her mother. There is a shift internally of feeling that the oversharing is not okay, which is an adaptive action tendency of the categorical emotion of anger. While I am listening and looking for a bodily rooted shift, I pick up that she is seeing something in her visual channel. I follow that by asking her what she is seeing when she sees her mother, which turns out to be an important inquiry.

State Three: Realization affects, leads to more corrective relational experiences.

PT: She looks very young and not knowing how to take care of me, and very confused. She's always seemed in a trance here. [**Sylvia's description of her mother sounds like the mothers in the early mother–infant interactions who were unresolved for their own trauma.**]

TH: Okay.

PT: Not really . . . there. That's how I always felt her. Not really there. She was somewhere else in there, kind of saying things. I kind of want to say, "Go away or leave me alone or don't bring this to me, just mine to fix or solve for." [**She is speaking in incomplete expressions, which might indicate that she is nearing a disorganized state in her younger self who was seeing** her mother's tranced-out expression. It might also indicate that in the face of the new she is feeling some tremulous affects.]

TH: Say that with energy. [I was hearing her slipping into more of a spacing-out state.]

PT: "So, you know, it's not mine to fix or solve for you. You don't. What is that? It's like I don't deserve this. I don't want this. I don't need this."

TH: Yes.

PT: "I am hurt by it. I am afraid. Frightened by it. Take this back and this is yours to deal with." [Assertion is a corrective message]

TH: Right! Feel that. [Repeats the patient's words] "Take this back. This is yours to deal with." What's that like? What's that like to hear yourself say? [Metaprocess this boundary setting]

PT: Yeah. "This is yours to deal with." Huh. "This is yours to deal with." I, I think this feeling comes up of how I used to not be able to . . . (she trails off) The heartbreaker that was that I, I didn't think she could . . . deal with it. So that's why I'd step in. [She articulates the plight of the role-reversed kid. Her mother's helplessness was extreme; the child felt the only option was to become the protector/caregiver.] But now it's like there's this feeling of "this is yours to deal with." I know if she actually consents to this, whether she does or doesn't, is not my job.

TH: Right. Feel that. [Affirmation and encouragement]

PT: And I feel this quality in her that no matter what, there's something else protecting her or guiding her. It's not. It's not mine. It's not mine (hand pushes away from her body and up).

TH: Okay, so let's notice what your hand wants to say. "It's not mine." That came up organically. That was pretty interesting. Something about you getting to the place that this is yours [boundary] and whether or not she does or doesn't follow. . . . The hook was, she can't, she's too weak. Right. But then there's the 9-year-old who has the strength to deal with what the adult can't do. And now you're seeing she needs help from somebody who can help her, not a 9-year-old. [Empathic elaboration]

PT: Right.

TH: Right. And then you say you've got a sense of like whether or not she does or doesn't go for help to an appropriate place. . . . "That's not my job!" Wow—right. What's it like to say that? [Metaprocess the corrective experience]

PT: Yes. Feels good because I also actually, for me, think that feels the best, it's kind of this higher-power concept, like she has her own or whatever form you want to have.

TH: Yes, like she's, she has guidance. She has her own wisdom.

PT: Yeah. Yes. Yeah that's, that's a good place to land and I am just letting go. Go feels kind of like go, go find that and go.

TH: Find your own . . .

PT: Yeah. Yeah.

Relinquishing her role as protector. The surprising element of this process was how the patient was able to recognize that she is not only not responsible for her mother but that her mother is responsible for herself and has her own capacity (even if unrealized) to reach for a higher power, or inner guidance, which was liberating. Sylvia felt her own deserving to be on her own behalf, she shifted where her true responsibility wanted to be, which allowed her to be in more current time with herself, rather than being caught in "trauma time" in the role of protector. In the last moments of the session I metaprocess with her how this is for her to consider.

State Four: Unpacking core state knowing and integration.

TH: Feel into that knowing that she has her own higher power. How does that affect you? [**Metaprocessing**]

PT: Yeah. It's a relief. I don't want that job anymore. [**Declarative—core state**]

TH: How's the 9-year-old in you feeling as she's witnessing it? She's seeing what you're doing on her behalf. [**Metaprocessing the intrarelational experience between her adult self and her younger self.**]

PT: Yeah.

TH: How's that landing with her? Check in with her, see what you can see, what you can find out. [**Making the exploration experiential, looking to discover what has shifted in the senses.**]

PT: I think she feels more settled and more safe, more just knowing that I'm putting her first and not just, you know, not my mom. I'm putting her first. [**Another affirmation and declaration**]

TH: What tells how she is in your imagery?

PT: She just seems more relaxed.

TH: Do you get a picture of her body sense? What is it? [**Deepening the new experience**]

PT: Yeah, like a body sense of just relaxation and sort of sitting under a tree or kind of being in nature and like feeling that she can relax.

TH: Okay.

PT: Feeling that she can relax and let go and doesn't need to be running things or be in charge, yeah. [**The younger one now has some action tendencies on behalf of herself, letting go of strategies of control from her role reversal.**]

TH: Let her know. Give her a sense and let her hear from the adult how you feel when you hear she is ready to relax and wants to go be in nature and just let go and be under a tree. What's that like for you to see this? [**In AEDP we stay with the new experience for another round of relational metaprocessing, which creates a spiral of transformation, in this case it deepens the channels of communication between the adult self and the younger self.**]

PT: I'm so happy she can release that burden of other people and know that she's supported and held by me, by other forces, and also other people are, too. [**She names her feeling for her younger self and for the corrective experience of relinquishing her role reversal and feeling the support that she is capable of giving to her younger self.**]

In this vignette, Sylvia began the session with a new feeling of acceptance about being confused and befriending her activation. She is in self-at-best here, as she reports openness to her experience that allows for exploration of the pattern of difficulty she has in setting boundaries. The work of setting the boundary with her mother (in her imagination through the portrayal) was challenging at times. And yet, with our dyadic regulation and my helping her to stay in her moment-to-moment experience, she could feel her reactions, and she recalled what was evoked historically with her mother. Then she could differentiate from the past and tune into her younger self and respond to what she needed. Here, from her self-at-best she was able to recognize the origin of her role reversal, while noticing and providing care and a corrective message for her younger self. From here emerged relinquishing the role of protector/caregiver. This session marked a significant shift in Sylvia's feeling less confused and helpless around her role of being protector and opened her capacity to be more responsive and caring to the stirrings from her inner experience. In this session, she accessed self and relational adaptive action, as well as the adaptive action of categorical emotion.

Healing Disorganized Attachment

Embodying the role of a trustworthy other who is constant and collaborative is a high bar for psychotherapists working with patients who manifest
the disorganized attachment pattern. And yet, to help our patients build
trust in and understanding of their own Self, alone and with an Other,
to co-create a secure base and a safe haven that can meet "fright without
solution" and "attachment without solution," our capacity for showing up
in relationship in a steady reliable fashion is crucial. It is what will allow
discovering the "solutions" to both fright and attachment. We have identified common therapist reactivities to disorganization (as identified for each
of the insecure patterns) to help us recognize the predictable ways we as
therapists might go off track, and also the specific metaskills to allow us to
get back on track. We do so to (a) normalize this part of the process and (b)
encourage therapists to reestablish coordination and collaboration.

With disorganization, we aim to help patients face the struggles of their
current life by helping them to link and process their traumatic history,
including how to be with and collaborate with parts of themselves that
have been heretofore dissociated, untended and/or unformed.. When we
are able to accompany our patients and hold their compartmentalized parts
and fragmented affects with care and compassion and reflect our patients'
strengths and resilience, we can function as our patients' prefrontal cortex, serving their mentalizing function until they are able to mentalize for
themselves. When patients can metaprocess the corrective experiences
they have with us, they may notice an increase in their felt sense of being
real, worthy, and lovable and an increased trust in their own capacity to
know what they know and feel what they feel. Thus, deepening integration,
the felt experience of self-awareness helps patients make sense of how they
have come to be who they are, building their trust in becoming who they
want to become. Holding the work with a collaborative spirit is essential in
treating disorganized attachment.

Here are some of the main intervention pathways we showed in
this chapter:

• Work within and at the edges of the patient's window of tolerance
• Proceed by titrating emotion that emerges

- Therapist's use of self, sensitivity, responsiveness, and building collaboration
- Tend to the missing attachment experiences
- Help the patient to develop epistemic trust
- Follow the channel of experience that opens
- Link the current-day experience with the historical past
- Check the intrarelational field (between parts of self)
- Unburden what the younger self has been holding
- Metaprocess the patient's emotional expression on their own behalf
- Help the patient to build resources
- Recognize and relinquish the origins of role reversal

Epilogue: Why We Love Our Patients

We are responding from our caregiving behavioral system that is wired to care.

Our patients are vulnerable, in need of being loved, and they touch our hearts. While it is natural to love them and care for them, it would be delusional to imagine that we could love them enough to fill their pores from all the years and memories of not feeling loved, or loved enough, or understood or truly known.

Our job is to provide an experience of care and safety so that the barriers to taking in love and care can melt away. Then they can take in our love and care, as well as that of others (friends, partners) so they know in their hearts they are deserving of love, and they can know in their bodies what being cared for feels like, what being helped feels like, and what this tells them about themselves.

How Do We Love Our Patients?

By tailoring treatment to the specific patterns of attachment, we aim to meet our patients where they need to be met. It is not enough that we seek to give them refuge and a safe base from which to explore. We listen to them in ways that help them listen to themselves. We track their somatic and emotional experiences, deeming each moment-to-moment fluctuation important, to help them tune into their own bodies and feel their emotions. We track our co-created relational experiences to foster their relational intelligence. We seek to care for them—and work on their being able to take in that care—in ways that help them to come to care for themselves and others. We honor their own capacity to know and to *trust that they can know* what is authentic and genuine. These are the gifts that they take with them when they close the doors to our offices, and step into their own worlds.

In this way, we help them to transform their internal working models so they can go out into their lives trusting that they can know what feels right and trust their perceptions to guide them. We want to help our patients to have access to the compass inside that holds True North for their own sense of direction and capacity, so they can flourish and participate in life in whatever form is theirs to take. Like Saroo, they can know when they are in danger, and they can run. And they can recognize when they are being cared for and tended to, and they can relax into being cared for. And in turn, they can love. And if they need to, they can find their way home.

Thus they can know when they give their love whether it is being received, and thus whether they are in a relationship that is able to build through collaboration. A relationship where both people matter, mutual sharing is possible—even if invariably at times off-balance when life presents challenges—and they know solutions lie in feeling and sharing emotions and existing with another . . . in other words, understanding and being understood.

The grids and the attachment pattern–specific interventions are ways that make it more likely that our love and care, combined with our clinical skills, can heal the wounds of past attachment hurts and rewire our patients' internal models in such a way that they know they are worthy of love. And thus, they can receive and benefit from the love we are wired to give them, when they come to us with their suffering and hopes for healing, and in healing, their capacity to give and receive love can continue to grow.

Notes

Preface

1. The preference for the term "attachment patterns" rather than "attachment styles" is explained in Chapter 5.
2. Describing the aim of AEDP relational work as "making attachment safe again" was introduced in a presentation I gave at the International Boston Trauma Conference in May 2023 (Fosha, 2023).
3. Bowlby wisely qualified his description of the attachment figure as one "perceived to be" older and wiser, with "perceived to be" as the key. If the attachment figure had to actually be wiser, we would all be doomed. And if the attachment figure had to actually be "older and wiser," the enterprise of attachment-informed therapy would be hard-pressed.
4. Bowlby (1973) wrote about attachment as "developmental pathways" open to change throughout the lifespan.
5. Hopefully it goes without saying, though in the spirit of AEDP's ethos of making the implicit explicit, we are saying it: Any self-disclosure needs to be first and foremost for the benefit of the patient!
6. This corrective emotional experience, like all corrective emotional experiences, can be amplified through metatherapeutic processing, which is discussed shortly.
7. For a more detailed account of the transformational affects (i.e., the positive emotional states that arise spontaneously in the wake of processing painful emotions of trauma and suffering), see Fosha and Thoma (2020) and Chapter 3, this volume.

Trajectory of the Book

1. As noted on the grid, this is a nonexhaustive list. These are the 10 aspects named here. Other aspects could conceivably be added.

Chapter 1

1. "True other" is a counterpart to Winnicott's "true self." Diana Fosha (2000b) describes the "true other" as one person who responds to another in just the right way, at just the right time, to provide exactly what is needed in that moment. Being a true other is an essential responsiveness that is attuned, helpful, and enlivening.
2. Ganda and Uganda are both used to locate where this early study took place.
3. Bowlby made it clear on numerous occasions that he referred to the attachment figure with the intention of acknowledging that there may be others than the child's biological mother providing mothering to the child.
4. This conceptualization of control systems theory is drawn from how Bowlby was influenced and is not representative of the advances in control systems theory over the past 50 years.

Chapter 2

1. See Stern (1985) on vitality affects.
2. See Ecker et al. (2012) on memory reconsolidation.
3. And even though initially the baby may increase their signaling to garner the mother's attuned response, when she is unable to provide this, the baby begins to lose trust not only in other but in self to elicit what is needed.

Chapter 3

1. Introduced in Chapter 1, Grice's maxims informed Main and Kaplan while they were coding transcripts of the Adult Attachment Interview (AAI).
2. The phrase "explore, don't explain" was coined by Ben Lipton (2011).

Chapter 5

1. The lifelong potential for neuroplasticity means that other experiences, such as healing ones, can also leave an imprint and thus attachment trauma can be healed (Fosha, 2019, 2021a, Frederick 2021). But that's not the thrust of this chapter.
2. Read these terms of self-at-best and self-at worst as constructs that can help provide a way to identify adaptive and maladaptive patterns in a commonsense way. Our intention is to create a recognizable fork in the road to identify self-states that are driven by hope or by dread, by feeling seen or feeling invisible, and so on. While reducing our binary lens in so many ways to respect the multidimensionality of being human—in this case, we have found self-at-best and self-at-worst to be illustrative of the concepts. We hope you can accept and learn through this lens to explore the vast terrains they are attempting to hold in view.

3. Fosha coined the phrase "attachment without solution" in conversation with Pando-Mars through their discourse to describe what behavioral systems were aroused during disorganized attachment and what appears clinically when patients arrive to psychotherapy and manifest disorganized attachment.

Chapter 6

1. See Fosha (2000b) for corrective emotional experience without repetition.
2. I want to include that the avoidant pattern has anxiety in the mix, even though it may be less visible due to the deactivating strategies.

Chapter 8

1. Throughout the clinical chapters we capitalize Self and Other, to both highlight what is happening in the moment, and also to indicate how the self or other are internally represented, which points to the corners of the SOE triangle and the focus of our work.

Chapter 9

1. We put "needy" in quotes because the only reason the child is "needy" is because their needs are not being responded to, and not out of some defect of character.
2. We use the term "mother" rather than "caregiver" here due to the fact that these early studies were observing mothers with their babies.

Chapter 10

1. Soothing touch is a self-compassion meditation practice I learned from Michael Klein, who teaches a mindful self-compassion course, founded on the evidence-based work of Kristin Neff and Christopher Germer.
2. Soraya's differentiation from her mother allowed her to engage more deeply in her psychotherapy. After this session, she was able to process some of her anger regarding her mother, shifting the angry resistance turned against herself into the expression of core anger and release of adaptive action that continued to augment her growth.

References

Adler, J. (2002). *Offering from the conscious body. The discipline of authentic movement.* Inner Traditions.

Ainsworth, M. S. (1967). *Infancy in Uganda.* The Johns Hopkins Press.

Ainsworth, M. D. S. (1983). Autobiography. In A. N. O'Connell & N. F. Russo (Eds.), *Models of achievement: Reflections of eminent women in psychology* (pp. 200–219). Columbia University Press.

Ainsworth, M. (1990). Epilogue. In M. T. Greenberg, D. Cicchetti, & E. M. Cummings (Eds.), *Attachment in the preschool years* (pp. 463–488). Chicago University Press.

Ainsworth, M. (1991). Attachments and other affectional bonds across the life cycle. In C. M. Parkes, J. Stevenson-Hinde, & P. Marris (Eds.), *Attachment across the life cycle* (pp. 33–51). Routledge.

Ainsworth, M. D., & Bell, S. M. (1970). Attachment, exploration, and separation: Illustrated by the behavior of one-year-olds in a strange situation. *Child Development, 41*(1), 49–67.

Ainsworth, M. D. S., & Bell, S. M. (1972). Mother–infant interaction and the development of competence. *Institute of Education Sciences,* 1–36.

Ainsworth, M. D. S., Bell, S. M., & Stayton, D. J. (1971). Individual differences in strange-situation behavior of one-year-olds. In H. R. Schaffer (Ed.), *The origins of human social relations* (pp. 17–57). Academic Press.

Ainsworth, M. D. S., Blehar, M. C., Waters, E., & Wall, S. (Eds.). (1978/2015). *Patterns of attachment.* Erlbaum.

Ainsworth, M. S., & Bowlby, J. (1991). An ethological approach to personality development. *American Psychologist, 46*(4), 333–341.

Ainsworth, M. D. S., & Eichberg, C. G. (1991). Effects on infant–mother attachment of mother's unresolved loss of an attachment figure or other traumatic experience. In P. Marris, J. Stevenson-Hinde, & C. Parkes (Eds.), *Attachment across the life cycle* (pp. 160–183). Routledge.

Alexander, F., & French, T. M. (1946). *Psychoanalytic therapy: Principles and application.* Ronald Press.

Beebe, B., Cohen, P., & Lachman, F. M. (2016). *The mother–infant interaction picture book: Origins of attachment.* Norton.

Beebe, B., & Lachman, F. M. (1998). Co-constructing inner and relational processes: Self and mutual regulation in infant research and adult treatment. *Psychoanalytic Psychology, 15*(4), 480–516.

Beebe, B., & Lachman, F. M. (2014). *Origins of attachment: Infant research and adult treatment.* Routledge.

Bion, W. R. (1962). *Learning from experience.* London: Heinemann

Blatz, W. (1966) *Human security: Some reflections.* Toronto: University of Toronto Press.

Bowlby, J. (1944). Forty-four juvenile thieves: their characters and home-life (II). *The International Journal of Psychoanalysis, 25,* 107–128.

Bowlby, J. (1958). The nature of the child's tie to his mother. *International Journal of Psychoanalysis, 39,* 350–373.

Bowlby, J. (1965). *Child care and the growth of love.* Penguin Books. (Original work published 1953)

Bowlby, J. (1973). *Attachment and loss: Volume II. Separation, anxiety and anger.* Basic Books.

Bowlby, J. (1979). *The making and breaking of affectional bonds.* Tavistock.

Bowlby, J. (1980). *Attachment and loss: Volume III. Loss, sadness and depression.* Basic Books.

Bowlby, J. (1982). *Attachment and loss: Volume I. Attachment.* Basic Books. (Original work published 1969)

Bowlby, J. (1988). *A secure base: Parent–child attachment and healthy human development.* Basic Books.

Bowlby, J. (1991). Postscript. In Parkes, C. M., Stevenson-Hinde, J., & Marris, P. (Eds.). *Attachment across the life cycle* (pp. 293–297). Routledge.

Bretherton, I. (1985). Attachment theory: Retrospect and prospect. *Monographs of the Society for Research in Child Development, 50*(1–2), 3–35.

Bretherton, I. (1992). The origins of attachment theory: John Bowlby and Mary Ainsworth. *Developmental Psychology, 28*(5), 759–775.

Bretherton, I. (2003). Mary Ainsworth: Insightful observer and courageous theoretician. *Portraits of Pioneers in Psychology, 5,* 317–331.

Bretherton, I. (2005). In pursuit of the internal working model construct and its relevance to attachment relationships. In K. E. Grossmann, K. Grossmann, & E. Waters (Eds.), *Attachment from infancy to adulthood: The major longitudinal studies* (pp. 13–47). Guilford Press.

Bretherton, I., & Munholland, K. A. (2008). Internal working models in attachment relationships: Elaborating a central construct in attachment theory. In J. Cassidy & P. R. Shaver (Eds.), *Handbook of attachment: Theory, research, and clinical applications* (2nd ed., pp. 102–127). Guilford Press.

Bromberg, P. (2011). *The shadow of the tsunami and the growth of the relational mind.* Routledge.

Buber, Martin. (1958). *I and Thou..* 2d ed. New York, Scribner.

Buber, M. (1965). *The knowledge of man: Selected essays.* Harper Torchbooks.

Carlile, B. (2007). *The story.* On *The Story.* Universal Music Corp. & Southern Oracle Music, LLC.

Cassidy, J. (1990). Theoretical and methodological consideration in the study of attachment and the self in young children. In M. T. Greenberg, D. Cicchetti, & E. M. Cummings (Eds.), *Attachment in the preschool years* (pp. 87–119). Chicago University Press.

Cassidy, J. (1994). Emotion regulation: Influences of attachment relationships. *Monographs of the Society for Research in Child Development, 59*(2–3), 228–249.

Cassidy, J. (2001). Truth, lies, and intimacy: An attachment perspective. *Attachment and Human Development, 3*(2), 121–155.

Cassidy, J., & Kobak, R. R. (1988). Avoidance and its relationship with other defensive processes. In J. Belsky & T. Nezworski (Eds.), *Clinical implications of attachment* (pp. 300–323). Erlbaum.

Cohen, L. (1992). *Anthem.* On *The Future.* Columbia.

Cozolino, L. (2006). *The neuroscience of human relationships: Attachment and the developing social brain.* Norton.

Craig, A. D. (2002). How do you feel? Interoception: the sense of the physiological condition of the body. *Nature reviews. Neuroscience, 3*(8), 655–666. doi:10.1038/nrn894

Craig, A. D. (2009). How do you feel—now? The anterior insula and human awareness. *Perspectives.* Macmillan (10): 59–70.

Craig, A. D. (2010). The sentient self. *Brain Structure and Function, 214,* 563–577.

Craig, A. D. (2015). *How do you feel: An interoceptive moment with your neurobiological self.* Princeton University Press.

Craik, K. J. W. (1943). *The nature of explanation.* University Press, Macmillan.

Crittenden, P. M. (1994). Emotion regulation, attachment and the development of the self. In S. Parker, R. Mitchell, & M. Boccia (Eds.), *Self-awareness in animals and humans: Developmental perspectives* (pp. 81–96). Cambridge University Press.

Crittenden, P. M. (2017). Gifts from Mary Ainsworth and John Bowlby. *Clinical Child Psychology and Psychiatry, 22*(3), 436–442. doi: 10.1177/1359104517716214

Damasio, A. R. (1994). *Descartes' error: Emotion, reason and the human brain.* Penguin Books.

Damasio, A. R. (1998). Emotion in the perspective of an integrated nervous system. *Brain Research Reviews, 26*(2–3), 83–86.

Damasio, A. R. (1999). *The feeling of what happens: Body and emotion in the making of consciousness.* Harcourt Brace.

Damasio, A. R. (2010). *Self comes to mind: Constructing the conscious brain.* Pantheon.

Damasio, A. R. (2018). *The Strange order of things: Life, feeling, and the making of cultures.* Vintage.

Darwin, C. R. (1965). *The expression of the emotions in man and animals*. Murray. (Original work published 1872)

Davidson, R. J., & Schuyler, B. S. (2015). Neuroscience of happiness. In J. F. Helliwell, R. Laryard, & J. Sachs (Eds.), *World happiness report 2015* (pp. 82–105). Sustainable Development Solutions Network. *http://unsdsn.org/wpcontent/uploads/2015/04/WHR15.pdf*

Davis, G. (2017). Lion.

DiCorcia, M., Iwakabe, S., Thoma, N. C., & Yamazaki, W. (2023). Transformational Process Scale: An initial validation and application to the first psychotherapy session. *Journal of Psychotherapy Integration, 33*(3), 248–264. https://dx.doi.org/10.1037/int0000296

Doidge, N. (2007). *The brain that changes itself: Stories of personal triumph from the frontiers of brain science*. Penguin Books.

Doidge, N. (2016). *The brain's way of healing: Remarkable discoveries and recoveries from the frontiers of neuroplasticity*. Penguin Books.

Dozier, M., & Kobak, R. R. (1992). Psychophysiology in attachment interviews: converging evidence for deactivating strategies. *Child Development, 63*(6), 1473–1480.

Ecker, B., Ticic, R., & Hulley, L. (2012). *Unlocking the emotional brain: Eliminating symptoms at their roots using memory reconsolidation*. Routledge.

Egeland, B., & Stroufe, L. A. (1981). Attachment and early maltreatment. *Child Development, 52*, 44–52.

Emde, R. N. (1988). Development terminable and interminable: I. Innate and motivational factors from infancy. *International Journal of Psychoanalysis, 69*, 23–42.

Fonagy, P., & Allison, E. (2014). The role of mentalizing and epistemic trust in the therapeutic relationship. *Psychotherapy, 51*(3), 372–380.

Fonagy, P., & Campbell, C. (2017). Mentalizing, attachment and epistemic trust: How psychotherapy can promote resilience. *Psychiatria Hungarica, 32*(3), 283–287.

Fonagy, P., Gergely, G., Jurist, E., & Target, M. (2002). *Affect regulation, mentalization and the development of the self*. Routledge.

Fonagy, P., Steele, H., & Steele, M. (1991). Maternal representations of attachment during pregnancy predict the organization of infant–mother attachment at one year of age. *Child Development, 62*(5), 891–905.

Fonagy, P., Steele, H., Steele, M., Moran, G. S., & Higgitt, A. C. (1991). The capacity for understanding mental states: The reflective self in parent and child and its significance for security of attachment. *Infant Mental Health Journal, 12*, 201–218.

Fonagy, P., Steele, M., Steele, H., Leigh, T., Kennedy, R., Mattoon, G., & Target, M. (1995). Attachment, the reflective self, and borderline states: The predictive specificity of the Adult Attachment Interview and pathological emotional development. In S. Goldberg, R. Muir, & J. Kerr (Eds.), *Attachment theory: Social developmental and clinical perspectives* (pp. 233–278). Routledge.

Fonagy, P., & Target, M. (1997). Attachment and reflective function: Their role in self-organization. *Development and Psychopathology, 9,* 679–700.

Fonagy, P., & Target, M. (2007). The rooting of the mind in the body: New links between psychoanalytic theory and psychoanalytic thought. *Journal of the American Psychoanalytic Association, 55*(2), 411–456.

Fosha, D. (2000a). Meta-therapeutic processes and the affects of transformation. *Journal of Psychotherapy Integration, 10,* 71–97.

Fosha, D. (2000b). *The transforming power of affect: A model for accelerated change.* Basic Books.

Fosha, D. (2002). The activation of affective change processes in accelerated experiential-dynamic psychotherapy (AEDP). In F. W. Kaslow & J. J. Magnavita (Eds.), *Comprehensive handbook of psychotherapy: Psychodynamic/object relations* (Vol. 1, pp. 309–343). Wiley.

Fosha, D. (2003). Dyadic regulation and experiential work with emotion and relatedness in trauma and disordered attachment. In M. F. Solomon & D. J. Siegel (Eds.), *Healing trauma: Attachment, trauma, the brain and the mind* (pp. 221–281). Norton.

Fosha, D. (2005). Emotion, true self, true other, core state: Towards a clinical theory of affective change processes. *Psychoanalytic Review, 92*(4), 513–552.

Fosha, D. (2006). Quantum transformation in trauma and treatment: Traversing the crisis of healing change. *Journal of Clinical Psychology, 62*(5), 569–583.

Fosha, D. (2008). Transformance, recognition of self by self, and effective action. In K. J. Schneider (Ed.), *Existential–integrative psychotherapy: Guideposts to the core of practice* (pp. 290–320). Routledge.

Fosha, D. (2009a). Emotion and recognition at work: Energy, vitality, pleasure, truth, desire & the emergent phenomenology of transformational experience. In D. Fosha, D. J. Siegel, & M. F. Solomon (Eds.), *The healing power of emotion: Affective neuroscience, development, and clinical practice* (pp. 172–203). Norton.

Fosha, D. (2009b). Healing attachment trauma with attachment (and then some)! In M. Kerman (Ed.), *Clinical pearls of wisdom: 21 leading therapists offer their key insights* (pp.). Norton.

Fosha, D. (2009c). Positive affects and the transformation of suffering into flourishing. In W. C. Bushell, E. L. Olivo, & N. D. Theise (Eds.), *Longevity, regeneration, and optimal health: Integrating Eastern and Western perspectives* (pp. 252–261). Annals of the New York Academy of Sciences.

Fosha, D. (2013a). A heaven in a wildflower: Self, dissociation, and treatment in the context of the neurobiological core self. *Psychoanalytic Inquiry, 33,* 496–523.

Fosha, D. (2013b). Turbocharging the affects of healing and redressing the evolutionary tilt. In D. J. Siegel & M. F. Solomon (Eds.), *Healing moments in psychotherapy* (pp. 129–168). Norton.

Fosha, D. (2017a). How to be a transformational therapist: AEDP harnesses innate healing affects to re-wire experience and accelerate transformation. In J. Loizzo,

M. Neale, & E. Wolf (Eds.), *Advances in contemplative psychotherapy: Accelerating transformation* (pp. 204–219). Norton.

Fosha, D. (2017b). Something more than "something more than interpretation": AEDP works the experiential edge of transformational experience to transform the internal working model. In S. Lord (Ed.), *Moments of meeting in psychoanalysis: Interaction and change in the therapeutic encounter* (pp.). Routledge.

Fosha, D. (Ed.). (2021a). How AEDP works. In *Undoing aloneness & the transformation of suffering into flourishing* (pp. 27–52). American Psychological Association.

Fosha, D. (Ed.). (2021b). *Undoing aloneness & the transformation of suffering into flourishing.* American Psychological Association.

Fosha, D. (Ed.). (2021c). "We are organized to be better than fine": Building the transformational theory of AEDP 2.0. In *Undoing aloneness & the transformation of suffering into flourishing* (pp. 377–400). American Psychological Association.

Fosha, D. (2023, May 20). *Making attachment safe again: Treating attachment trauma with AEDP* [Poster presentation]. Annual Boston International Trauma Conference, Boston, MA.

Fosha, D., Coleman, J. J., Iwakabe, S., Gretton, S., Nakamura, K., Nunnink, S., Joseph, A., Quirk, K. & Owen, J. (2024). The development of the Moments of Flourishing Experience Scale: A new scale to measure positive, affect based flourishing state experiences. *Counselling Psychology Quarterly.* https://doi.org/10.10 80/09515070.2024.2377167

Fosha, D., Siegel, D. J., & Solomon, M. F. (Eds.). (2009b). *The healing power of emotion: Affective neuroscience, development, and clinical practice.* Norton.

Fosha, D., & Thoma, N. (2020). Metatherapeutic processing supports the emergence of flourishing in psychotherapy. *Psychotherapy, 57*(3), 323–339.

Fosha, D., Thoma, N., & Yeung, D. (2019). Transforming emotional suffering into flourishing: Metatherapeutic processing of positive affect as a trans-theoretical vehicle for change. *Counseling Psychology Quarterly, 32*(3–4), 563–593.

Fosha, D., & Yeung, D. (2006). AEDP exemplifies the seamless integration of emotional transformation and dyadic relatedness at work. In G. Stricker & J. Gold (Eds.), *A casebook of integrative psychotherapy* (pp. 165–184). American Psychological Association.

Frederick, R. (2009). *Living like you mean it: Use the wisdom and power of your emotions to get the life you really want.* Jossey-Bass.

Frederick, R. (2019). *Loving like you mean it: Use the power of emotional mindfulness to transform your relationships.* Central Recovery Press.

Frederick, R. (2021). Neuroplasticity in action: Rewiring internal working models of attachment. In D. Fosha (Ed.), *Undoing aloneness & the transformation of suffering into flourishing* (pp. 189–216). American Psychological Association.

Fredrickson, B. L. (2001). The role of positive emotions in positive psychology: The broaden-and-build theory of positive emotions. *American Psychologist, 56*(3), 218–226.

Fredrickson, B. L. (2013). Positive emotions broaden and build. *Advances in Experimental Social Psychology, 47,* 1–53.

Frederickson, B. L., & Joiner, T. (2018). Reflections on positive emotions and upward spirals. *Perspectives on Psychological Science, 13*(2), 194–199. doi: 10.1177/1745691617692106

Frijda, N. H. (1986). *The emotions.* Cambridge University Press.

Gendlin, E. T. (1982). *Focusing.* Bantam New Age Paperbacks. (Original work published 1978)

Gendlin, E. T. (1996). *Focusing-oriented psychotherapy: A manual of the experiential method.* Guilford Press.

George, C., Main, M., & Kaplan, N. (1985). *Adult Attachment Interview* [Database record]. APA PsycTests.

Gleiser, K. (2021). Relational prisms: Navigating experiential attachment work with dissociation and multiplicity in AEDP. In D. Fosha (Ed.), *Undoing aloneness & the transformation of suffering into flourishing* (pp. 321–345). American Psychological Association.

Graham, L. (2013). *Bouncing back.* New World Library.

Greenberg, M. T., & Marvin, R. S. (1982). Reactions of preschool children to an adult stranger: A behavioral systems approach. *Child Development, 53*(2), pp. 481–490.

Grice, H. P. (1975). Logic and conversation. In P. Cole & J. Morgan (Eds.), *Syntax and semantics* (Vol. 3, pp. 41–58). Academic Press.

Grossmann, K. E., & Grossmann, K. (1991). Attachment quality as an organizer of emotional and behavioral responses in a longitudinal perspective. In C. M. Parkes, J. Stevenson-Hinde, & P. Marris (Eds.), *Attachment across the life cycle* (pp. 93–114). Tavistock/Routledge.

Hanakawa, Y. (2021). What just happened? and what is happening now? The art and science of moment-to-moment tracking in AEDP. In D. Fosha (Ed.), *Undoing aloneness & the transformation of suffering into flourishing* (pp. 107–131). American Psychological Association.

Hanson, R. (2013). *Hardwiring happiness: The new brain science of contentment, calm, and confidence.* Harmony Books.

Hanson, R., & Hanson, F. (2020). *Resilient: How to grow an unshakable core of calm, strength, and happiness.* Harmony Books.

Harrison, R. L. (2020). Termination in 16-session accelerated experiential dynamic psychotherapy (AEDP): Together in how we say goodbye. *Psychotherapy, 57*(4), 531–547. *https://doi.org/10.1037/pst0000343*

Hebb, D. O. (1944). *The organization of behavior.* Wiley.

Hendel, H. J. (2018). *It's not always depression: Working the change triangle to listen to the body, discover core emotions, and connect to your authentic self.* Penguin Random House.

Hesse, E. (1996). Discourse, memory and the Adult Attachment Interview: A note with emphasis on the emerging cannot classify category. *Infant Mental Health Journal, 17,* 4–11.

Hesse, E., & Main, M. (1999). Second-generation effects of unresolved trauma in normal treating parents: Dissociated, frightened, and threatening parental behavior. *Psychoanalytic Inquiry, 19,* 482–540.

Hesse, E., & Main, M. (2000). Disorganized infant, child, and adult attachment: Collapse in behavioral and attentional strategies. *Journal of the American Psychoanalytic Association, 48*(4), 1097–1127.

Hinde, R. A. (1966). *Animal behavior.* McGraw-Hill.

Hoffman, K., Marvin, R., Powell, B., & Cooper, G. (2006). Changing toddlers' and preschoolers' attachment. *Journal of Consulting and Clinical Psychology, 74*(6), 1017–1026.

Horney, K. (1945). Our inner conflicts: a constructive theory of neurosis. New York: Norton.

Iwakabe, S., & Conceição, N. (2016). Metatherapeutic processing as a change-based therapeutic immediacy task: Building an initial process model using a task-analytic research strategy. *Journal of Psychotherapy Integration, 26*(3), 230–247.

Iwakabe, S., Edlin, E., Fosha, D., Gretton, H., Joseph, A. J., Nakamura, K., & Thoma, N. (2022). The long-term outcome of accelerated experiential dynamic psychotherapy (AEDP): 6- and 12-month follow-up results. *Psychotherapy, 59*(3), 431–446.

Iwakabe, S., Edlin, E., Fosha, D., Gretton, H., Joseph, A. J., Nunnink, S., Nakamura, K., & Thoma, N. (2020). The effectiveness of accelerated experiential dynamic psychotherapy (AEDP) in private practice settings: A transdiagnostic study conducted within the context of a practice research network. *Psychotherapy, 57*(4), 548–561.

James, W. (1902). *The varieties of religious experience: A study in human nature.* Penguin Books.

Kaplan, N. (1987). *Individual differences in six-year-olds' thoughts about separation: Predicted from attachment to mother at age one* [Doctoral dissertation]. University of California, Berkeley.

Kaufman, G. (1980/1985/1992) *Shame: the power of caring. Third Edition.* Schenkman Books.

Kaufman, G. (1996). *The psychology of shame: Theory and treatment of shame-based syndromes* (2nd ed.). Springer.

Kingsolver, B. (2022). *Demon Copperhead.* Harper.

Kranz, K. (2021). The first session in AEDP: Harnessing transformance and cocreating a secure attachment. In D. Fosha (Ed.), *Undoing aloneness & the transformation of suffering into flourishing* (pp. 53–79). American Psychological Association.

Lamagna, J. (2011). Of the self, by the self, and for the self: An intra-relational perspective on intra-psychic attunement and psychological change. *Journal of Psychotherapy Integration, 21*(3), 280–307.

Lamagna, J. (2021). Finding healing in the broken places: Intra-relational AEDP work with traumatic aloneness. In D. Fosha (Ed.), *Undoing aloneness & the trans-*

formation of suffering into flourishing (pp. 293–319). American Psychological Association.

Lamagna, J., & Gleiser, K. (2007). Building a secure internal attachment: An intra-relational approach to ego strengthening and emotional processing with chronically traumatized clients. *Journal of Trauma and Dissociation,* 8(1), 25–52.

Lamb, M. E. (1987). Predictive implications of individual differences in attachment. *Journal of Consulting and Clinical Psychology,* 55, 817–824.

LeDoux, J. (1996). *The emotional brain: The mysterious underpinnings of emotional life.* Simon & Schuster.

Levine, P. (1997). *Waking the tiger: Healing trauma.* Berkeley, CA: North Atlantic Books.

Liotti, G. (1995). Disorganized/disoriented attachment in the psychotherapy of the dissociative disorders. In S. Goldberg, R. Muir, & J. Kerr (Eds.), *Attachment theory: Social, developmental, and clinical perspectives* (pp. 343–363). Analytic Press.

Lipton, B. (2021) A Shift in focus: Making use of therapist experience in AEDP. In D. Fosha (Ed.), *Undoing aloneness & the transformation of suffering into flourishing* (pp. 133–158). American Psychological Association.

Lipton, B., & Fosha, D. (2011). Attachment as a transformative process in AEDP: Operationalizing the intersection of attachment theory and affective neuroscience. *Journal of Psychotherapy Integration,* 21(3), 253–279.

Longfellow, H. W. (1939). *Hyperion: A romance.* New York: Samuel Coleman.

Lyons-Ruth, K. (1999). The two-person unconscious: Intersubjective dialogue, enactive relational representation and the emergence of new forms of relational organization. *Psychoanalytic Inquiry,* 19, 576–617.

Lyons-Ruth, K. (2006). The interface between attachment and intersubjectivity: Perspective from the longitudinal study of disorganized attachment. *Psychoanalytic Inquiry,* 26(4), 595–616.

Lyons-Ruth, K., Bronfman, E., & Parsons, E. (1999). Atypical attachment in infancy and early childhood among children at developmental risk: IV. Maternal frightened, frightening, or atypical behavior and disorganized infant attachment patterns. *Monographs of the Society for Research in Child Development,* 64(3), 67–96, discussion 213–220.

Lyons-Ruth, K., & Jacobvitz, D. (2008). Attachment disorganization: Genetic factors, parenting contexts, and developmental transformation from infancy to adulthood. In J. Cassidy & P. R. Shaver (Eds.), *Handbook of attachment: Theory, research, and clinical applications* (2nd ed., pp. 666–697). Guilford Press.

Main, M. (1973). *Exploration, play, and cognitive functioning as related to child–mother attachment* [Unpublished doctoral dissertation]. Johns Hopkins University.

Main, M. (1979). *Scale for disordered/disoriented infant behavior in response to the Main and Weston clown sessions* [Unpublished manuscript]. University of California, Berkeley.

Main, M. (1981). Avoidance in the service of attachment: A working paper. In: *Behavioral Development,* K. Immehnann, G. Barlow, L. Petrinovitch, & M. Main. New York: Cambridge University Press, pp. 651–693.

Main, M. (1991). Metacognitive knowledge. Metacognitive monitoring, and singular (coherent) vs. multiple (incoherent) model of attachment: Findings and
directions for future research. In C. M. Parkes, J. Stevenson-Hinde, & P. Marris
(Eds.), *Attachment across the life cycle* (pp. 127–159). Routledge.

Main, M. (1995). Recent studies in attachment: Overview with selected implications for clinical work. In S. Goldberg, R. Muir, & J. Kerr (Eds.), *Attachment theory:
Social, developmental, and clinical perspectives* (pp. 407–472). Analytic Press.

Main, M. (1999a). Epilogue. Attachment theory: Eighteen points with suggestions
for future studies. In J. Cassidy & P. R. Shaver (Eds.), *Handbook of attachment: Theory, research, and clinical applications* (pp. 845–888). Guilford Press.

Main, M. (1999b). Mary D. Salter Ainsworth: Tribute and portrait. *Psychoanalytic
Inquiry, 19*, 682–776.

Main, M. (2000). The organized categories of infant, child, and adult attachment:
Flexible vs. inflexible attention under attachment-related stress. *Journal of the
American Psychoanalytic Association, 48*, 1055–1096.

Main, M., & Cassidy, J. (1988). Categories of response to reunion with the parent
at age 6: Predictable from infant attachment classifications and stable over a
1-month period. *Developmental Psychology, 24*(3), 415–426. *https://doi.org/10.1037/
0012-1649.24.3.415*

Main, M., & Hesse, E. (1990). Parents' unresolved traumatic experiences are related
to infant disorganized attachment status: Is frightened and/or frightening parental behavior the linking mechanism? In M. T. Greenberg, D. Cicchetti, & E. M.
Cummings (Eds.), *Attachment in the preschool years: Theory, research, and intervention*
(pp. 161–182). University of Chicago Press.

Main, M., Hesse, E., & Goldwyn, R. (2008). Studying differences in language usage
in recounting attachment history: An introduction to the AAI. In H. Steele &
M. Steele (Eds.), *Clinical applications of the Adult Attachment Interview* (pp. 31–68).
Guilford Press.

Main, M., Hesse, E., & Kaplan, N. (2005). Predictability of attachment behavior
and representational processes at 1, 6, and 19 years of age: The Berkeley longitudinal study. In K. E. Grossmann, K. Grossmann, & E. Waters (Eds.), *Attachment
from infancy to adulthood: The major longitudinal studies* (pp. 245–304). Guilford Press.

Main, M., Kaplan, N., & Cassidy, J. (1985). Security in infancy, childhood, and
adulthood: A move to the level of representation. *Monographs of the Society for
Research in Child Development, 50*(1–2), 66–104.

Main, M., & Solomon, J. (1986). Discovery of an insecure-disorganized/disoriented
attachment pattern. In T. B. Brazelton & M. W. Yogman (Eds.), *Affective development in infancy* (pp. 95–124). Ablex.

Main, M., & Solomon, J. (1990). Procedures for identifying infants as disorganized/
disoriented during the Ainsworth strange situation. In M. Greenberg, D. Cicchetti, & M. Cummings (Eds.), *Attachment in the preschool years: Theory, research, and
intervention* (pp. 121–160). University of Chicago Press.

Main, M., & Weston, D. R. (1981). The quality of the toddler's relationship to mother and father: Related to conflict behavior and the readiness to establish new relationships. *Child Development, 52,* 932–940.

Mars, D. (2011). From stuckness and reactivity to the felt experience of love. *Transformance: The AEDP Journal, 1*(2).

Marvin, R., Cooper, G., Hoffman, K., & Powell, B. (2002). The circle of security project: Attachment based intervention with caregiver–preschool child dyads. *Attachment and Human Development, 4*(1), 107–124.

McCullough Vaillant, L. (1997). *Changing character: Short-term anxiety-regulating psychotherapy for restructuring defenses, affects, and attachment.* Basic Books.

Medbo, A. (2023). *From no self to core self: The process. Advanced seminar & skills training.* AEDP Institute.

Medley, B. (2021). Portrayals in work with emotion in AEDP: Processing core affective experience to completion. In D. Fosha (Ed.), *Undoing aloneness & the transformation of suffering into flourishing* (pp. 217–240). American Psychological Association.

Menakem, R. (2017). *My grandmother's hands: Racialized trauma and the pathway to mending our hearts and bodies.* Central Recovery Press.

Merriam-Webster. (n.d.). Implicit. In *Merriam-Webster.com dictionary.* Retrieved July 15, 2024 from *https://www.merriam-webster.com/dictionary/implicit*

Mikulincer, M. (2015, September). *Adult attachment research: Intrapsychic and social relational aspects.* European Association for Cognitive and Behavioral Therapies.

Mikulincer, M., Shaver, P. R., & Berant E. (2012). An attachment perspective on therapeutic processes and outcomes. *Journal of Personality, 81*(6), 606–616.

Mindell, A. (2001). *Metaskills: The spiritual art of therapy.* Lao Tse Press.

Mindell, A., & Mindell, A. (2002). *Riding the horse backwards: Process work in theory and practice.* Lao Tse Press.

Napier, N. (1996) *Recreating your self: Building self-esteem through imaging and self-hypnosis.* Norton.

Northoff, G., & Panksepp, J. (2008). The trans-species concept of self and the subcortical–cortical midline system. *Trends in Cognitive Sciences, 12*(7), 259–264.

Notsu, H., Iwakabe, S., & Thoma, N. C. (2022). Enhancing working alliance through positive emotional experience: A cross-lag analysis. *Psychotherapy Research, 33*(3), 328–341. *https://doi.org/10.1080/10503307.2022.2124893*

Pando-Mars, K. (2011). Building attachment bonds in AEDP in the wake of neglect and abandonment: Through the lens and practice of AEDP, attachment and polyvagal theory. *Transformance: The AEDP Journal, 1*(2). *www.transformancejournal.com*

Pando-Mars, K. (2016). Tailoring AEDP interventions to attachment style. *Transformance: The AEDP Journal, 4*(2). *www.transformancejournal.com*

Pando-Mars, K. (2021). Using AEDP's representational schemas to orient therapist's attunement and engagement. In D. Fosha (Ed.), *Undoing aloneness & the transformation of suffering into flourishing* (pp. 159–186). American Psychological Association.

Panksepp, J. (2009). Brain emotional systems and qualities of mental life: From animal models of affect to implications for psychotherapeutics. In D. Fosha, D. J. Siegel and M. F. Solomon, (Eds.). *The healing power of emotion: Affective neuro-science, development & clinical practice.* pp. 1–26. New York: Norton.

Panksepp, J., & Biven, L. (2012). *The archaeology of mind: Neuroevolutionary origins of human emotion.* Norton.

Panksepp, J., & Northoff, G. (2009). The trans-species core SELF: The emergence of active cultural and neuro-ecological agents through self-related process-ing within subcortical–cortical midline networks. *Consciousness and Cognition,* 18(1), 193–215.

Parnell, L. (1999). *EMDR in the treatment of adults abused as children.* Norton.

Piaget, J. (1952). *The origins of intelligence.* International Universities Press.

Piliero, S. (2021). Fierce Love: Championing the core self to transform trauma and pathogenic states. In D. Fosha (Ed.), Undoing aloneness & the transformation of suffering into flourishing (pp. 269-291). American Psychological Association.

Porges, S. W. (2003a). The polyvagal theory: Phylogenetic contributions to social behavior. *Physiology and Behavior, 79,* 503–513.

Porges, S. W. (2003b). Social engagement and attachment: A phylogenetic per-spective. *Annals of the New York Academy of Sciences, 1008,* 31–47.

Porges, S. W. (2004). Neuroception: A subconscious system for detecting threat and safety. *Zero to Three: Bulletin of the National Center for Clinical Infant Programs,* 24(5), 19–24.

Porges, S. W., Doussard-Roosevelt, J. A., & Maita, A. K. (1994). Vagal tone and the physiological regulation of emotion. Monographs of the Society for Research in Child Development, 59(2-3), 167–186, 250–283. https://doi.org/10 .2307/1166144

Porges, S. (2009). Reciprocal influences between body and brain in the perception and expression of affect: A polyvagal perspective. In D. Fosha, D. Siegel, & M. Solomon (Eds.), *The healing power of emotion: Affective neuroscience, development, and clinical practice* (pp. 27–54). Norton.

Porges, S. (2010). *Polyvagal theory: Demystifying clinical features of trauma, autism, and early development.* California Institute for Integral Studies.

Porges, S. (2017). *The pocket guide to the polyvagal theory: The transformative power of feeling.* Norton.

Powell, B., Cooper, G., Hoffman, K., & Marvin, R. (2014). *The circle of security inter-vention: Enhancing attachment in early parent–child relationships.* Guilford Press.

Prenn, N. (2009). I second that emotion! On self-disclosure and its metaprocessing. In A. Bloomgarden & R. B. Mennuti (Eds.), *Psychotherapist revealed: Therapists speak about self-disclosure in psychotherapy* (pp. 85–99). Routledge.

Prenn, N., (2010). How to set transformance into action: The AEDP Protocol *Transformance: The AEDP Journal, 1*(1). www.transformancejournal.com.

Prenn, N. (2011). Mind the gap: AEDP interventions translating attachment theory into clinical practice. *Journal of Psychotherapy Integration, 21*(3), 308–329.

Prenn, N. C. N., & Fosha, D. (2016). *Supervision essentials for accelerated experiential dynamic psychotherapy (clinical supervision essentials)*. American Psychological Association.

Prenn, N. C. N., & Levenson, H. (2025). *Deliberate practice in accelerated experiential dynamic psychotherapy*. American Psychological Association.

Rizzolatti, G., Fadiga, L., Gallese, V., & Fogassi, L. (1996). Premotor cortex, and the recognition of motor actions. *Cognitive Brain Research, 3*(2), 131–141.

Robertson, J., & Bowlby, J. (1952). Responses of young children to separation from their mothers. *Courier of the International Children's Centre, Paris, 2*, 131–140.

Roisman, G. I., Padron, E., Sroufe, L. A., & Egeland, B. (2002). Earned-secure attachment status in retrospect and prospect. *Child Development, 73*(4), 1204–1219.

Russell, E. (2015). *Restoring resilience: Discovering your clients' capacity for healing*. Norton.

Russell, E. (2018). *Building, renovating and reconstructing a secure therapeutic attachment: It's not a once and for all kind of deal*. AEDP Retreat-Style Essential Skills course. AEDP Institute. New York, New York.

Russell, E. (2021). Agency, will and desire as core affective experience: Undoing disempowerment to foster the emergence of the agentic self. In D. Fosha (Ed.), *Undoing aloneness & the transformation of suffering into flourishing* (pp. 241–265). American Psychological Association.

Russell, E., & Fosha, D. (2008). Transformational affects and core state in AEDP: The emergence and consolidation of joy, hope, gratitude and confidence in (the solid goodness) of the self. *Journal of Psychotherapy Integration, 18*(2), 167–190.

Salter, M. D. (1940). *An evaluation of adjustment based upon the concept of security*. University of Toronto Press.

Saunders, R., Jacobovitz, D., Zaccagnino, M., Beverung, L. M., & Hazen, N. (2011). Pathways to earned-security: The role of alternative support figures. *Attachment and Human Development, 13*(4), 403–420.

Schoettle, E. (2009). *A qualitative study of the therapist's experience practicing accelerated experiential dynamic psychotherapy (AEDP): An exploration of the dyadic process from the clinician's perspective* [Doctoral dissertation]. Wright Institute, Berkeley, CA.

Schore, A. N. (1994). *Affect regulation and the origin of the self: The neurobiology of emotional development*. Erlbaum.

Schore, A. N. (1996). The experience-dependent maturation of a regulatory system in the orbital prefrontal cortex and the origins of developmental psychopathology. *Development and Psychopathology, 8*, 59–87.

Schore, A. N. (2000a, March). *Attachment, the developing brain, and psychotherapy*. Seventh John Bowlby memorial lecture, London.

Schore, A. N. (2000b). Attachment and the regulation of the right brain. *Attachment and Human Development, 2*, 23–47.

Schore, A. N. (2000c). *Foreword to the reissue of attachment and loss: Volume I. Attachment by John Bowlby*. Basic Books.

Schore, A. N. (2001). Effects of a secure attachment relationship on right brain development, affect regulation, and infant mental health. *Infant Mental Health Journal*, 22(1–2), 7–66.

Schore, A. N. (2003). *Affect regulation and the repair of the self.* Norton.

Schore, A. N. (2009). Right brain affect regulation: An essential mechanism of development, trauma, dissociation, and psychotherapy. In D. Fosha, D. J. Siegel, & M. F. Solomon (Eds.), *The healing power of emotion: Affective neuroscience, development & clinical practice* (pp. 112–144). Norton.

Schore, A. N. (2012). *The science and the art of psychotherapy.* Norton.

Schore, A. N. (2019a). *Right brain psychotherapy.* Norton.

Schore, A. N. (2019b). *The development of the unconscious mind.* Norton.

Schwartz, R. C. (1997). *Internal family systems therapy.* Guilford Press.

Schwartz, R. C., & Sweezy, M. (2019). *Internal family systems therapy, second edition.* Guilford Press.

Siegel, D. (1999/2020). *The developing mind: Toward a neurobiology of interpersonal experience, third edition.* New York: Guilford.

Siegel, D. (2007). *The mindful brain.* Norton.

Siegel, D. J. (2010). *The mindful therapist.* Norton.

Siegel, D. (2012). *The developing mind: Toward a neurobiology of interpersonal experience.* Guilford Press. (Original work published 1999)

Siegel, D. (2017). *Mind: A journey to the heart of being human.* Norton.

Simpson, M. L. (2016). Feeling seen: A pathway to transformation. *International Journal of Transpersonal Studies*, 35(1), 78–91.

Solomon, J., & George, C. (2008). The measurement of attachment security and related constructs in infancy and early childhood. In J. Cassidy & P. R. Shaver (Eds.), *Handbook of attachment: Theory, research, and clinical applications* (2nd ed., pp. 383–416). Guilford Press.

Solomon, M., & Tatkin (2011). *Love and war in intimate relationships: connection, disconnection and mutual regulation in couple therapy.* Norton.

Spangler, G., & Grossmann, K. E. (1993). Biobehavioral organization in securely and insecurely attached infants. Child Development, 64(5), 1439–1450. https://doi.org/10.2307/1131544

Sroufe, L. A. (1996). *Emotional development: The organization of emotional life in the early years.* Cambridge University Press.

Sroufe, L. A. (2005). Attachment and development: A prospective, longitudinal study from birth to adulthood. *Attachment and Human Development*, 7(4), 349–367.

Sroufe, L. A., Egeland, B., Carlson, E., & Collins, W. A. (2005). Placing early attachment experiences in developmental context: The Minnesota Longitudinal Study. In K. E. Grossmann, K. Grossmann, & E. Waters (Eds.), *Attachment from infancy to adulthood: The major longitudinal studies* (pp. 48–70). Guilford Press.

Steele, H., & Steele, M. (Eds.). (2008). *Clinical applications of the Adult Attachment Interview.* Guilford Press.

Stern, D. (1985). *The interpersonal world of the infant.* Basic Books.

Stern, D. N. (2010). *Forms of vitality: Exploring dynamic experience in psychology, the arts, psychotherapy, and development.* Oxford University Press.

Tatkin, S. (2009). *Psychobiological approach to couple therapy.* Monthly training program.

Tomkins, S. S. (1962). *Affect, imagery, consciousness: Vol. 1. The positive affects.* Springer.

Tomkins, S. S. (1963). *Affect, imagery, consciousness: II. The negative affects.* Springer.

Trevarthen, C. (1979). Communication and cooperation in early infancy: A description of primary intersubjectivity. In M. Bullowa (Ed.), *Before speech: The beginning of human communication* (pp. 321–347). Cambridge University Press.

Trevarthen, C. (2001). Intrinsic motives for companionship in understanding: Their origin, development, and significance for infant mental health. *Infant Mental Health Journal, 22,* 95–131.

Trevarthen, C. (2009). The functions of emotions in infancy: The regulation and communication of rhythm, sympathy, and meaning in human development. In D. Fosha, D. J. Siegel, & M. F. Solomon (Eds.), *The healing power of emotion: Affective neuroscience, development & clinical practice* (pp. 55–85). Norton.

Tronick, E., & Gold, C. M. (2019). *The power of discord: Why the ups and downs of relationships are the secret to building intimacy, resilience and trust.* Little Brown Spark.

Tronick, E. Z. (1989). Emotions and emotional communication in infants. *American Psychologist, 44,* 112–119.

Tronick, E. Z. (1998). Dyadically expanded states of consciousness and the process of therapeutic change. *Infant Mental Health Journal, 19*(3), 290–299.

Tronick, E. Z. (2003). "Of course all relationships are unique": How co-creative processes generate unique mother–infant and patient–therapist relationships and change other relationships. *Psychoanalytic Inquiry, 23,* 473–491.

Tronick, E. Z. (2009). Multilevel meaning making and dyadic expansion of consciousness theory: The polymorphic polysemic flow of meaning. In D. Fosha, D. J. Siegel, & M. F. Solomon (Eds.), *The healing power of emotion: Affective neuroscience, development & clinical practice* (pp. 86–111). Norton.

Tunnell, G., & Osiason, J. (2021). Historical context: AEDP's place in the world of psychotherapy. In D. Fosha (Ed.). *Undoing aloneness and the transformation of suffering into flourishing: AEDP 2.0.* (pp. 83–106). American Psychological Association

van den Boom, D. (1990). Preventive intervention and the quality of mother–infant interaction and infant exploration in irritable infants. In W. Koops (Ed.), *Developmental psychology behind the dykes* (pp. 249–270). Eburon.

van der Hart, O., Nijenhuis, E. R. S., & Solomon, R. (2010). Dissociation of the personality in complex trauma-related disorders and EMDR: Theoretical considerations. *Journal of EMDR Practice and Research, 4*(2), 76–92.

van der Kolk, B. A., & McFarlane, A. C. (1996). The black hole of trauma. In B. A. van der Kolk, A. C. McFarlane, & L. Weisaeth (Eds.). *Traumatic stress: The effects of overwhelming experience on mind, body, and society* (pp. 3–23). Guilford Press.

Wachtel, P. L. (2014). When the context is in the room: Extending the relational paradigm. *Psychoanalytic Dialogues, 24*(4), 419–426.

Wallin, D. J. (2007). *Attachment in psychotherapy*. Guilford Press.

Winnicott, D. W. (1960). The theory of the parent–infant relationship. *International Journal of Psychoanalysis*, 41, 585–595.

Winnicott, D. W. (1965). Ego distortion in terms of true and false self. In *The maturational processes and the facilitating environment*. (pp. 140–152). Hogarth Press, reprinted by Karmac.

Winnicott, D. W. (1965). The theory of the parent–infant relationship. In *The maturational processes and the facilitating environment: Studies in the theory of emotional development*. (pp. 37–55). Hogarth Press, reprinted by Karmac.

Yeung, D. (2021). What went right? What happens in the brain during AEDP's metatherapeutic processing. In D. Fosha (Ed.), *Undoing aloneness & the transformation of suffering into flourishing* (pp. 349–376). American Psychological Association.

Young, J. Z. (1964). *A model of the brain*. Clarendon Press.

Index

In this index, the following abbreviations are used: chap. for chapter, *f* for figure, *n* for note, and *t* for table.

About the Authors

Karen Pando-Mars, MFT, is a psychotherapist in San Anselmo, California, and senior faculty at the AEDP® Institute. A passionate advocate for the transformational power of AEDP, she has contributed extensively to its development, including founding AEDP West and chairing the first AEDP Institute Education Committee. As adjunct faculty at Dominican University in San Rafael, California, she taught AEDP as the overarching theoretical model in the Alternative and Innovative Psychotherapies course. Her deep commitment to fostering connection and healing is enriched by attachment theory, neuroscience, and her background in somatic and experiential therapies. She teaches AEDP across the U.S. and internationally.

Diana Fosha, PhD, is founder and director of the AEDP Institute, and the developer of AEDP®, a healing-oriented, radically relational, experiential psychotherapy for healing trauma and connecting people to their vitality. Described by psychoanalyst James Grotstein as a "prizefighter of intimacy," and by David Malan as "the Winnicott of [experiential dynamic] psychotherapy," Diana Fosha is known for her powerful, personal, poetic-yet-precise writing and presentation style. Her recent work focuses on flourishing as a seamless part of AEDP's process of transforming emotional suffering. She has authored several books and numerous articles, many of which can be found at www.aedpinstitute.org.